D1127010

Modern Cell Biology

MODERN CELL BIOLOGY

SERIES EDITOR

Birgit H. Satir
Department of Anatomy and Structural Biology
Albert Einstein College of Medicine
1300 Morris Park Avenue
Bronx, New York 10461

ADVISORY BOARD

SENSORY RECEPTORS AND SIGNAL TRANSDUCTION

SENSORY RECEPTORS AND SIGNAL TRANSDUCTION

Editors

John L. Spudich
Department of Microbiology and Molecular Genetics
University of Texas Medical School
Houston, Texas

Birgit H. Satir
Department of Anatomy and Structural Biology
Albert Einstein College of Medicine
Bronx, New York

WILEY-LISS

A JOHN WILEY & SONS, INC., PUBLICATION
New York • Chichester • Brisbane • Toronto • Singapore

Address all Inquiries to the Publisher
Wiley-Liss, Inc., 605 Third Avenue, New York, NY 10158-0012

Copyright © 1991 Wiley-Liss, Inc.

Printed in United States of America

While the authors, editors, and publisher believe that drug selection and dosage and the specifications and usage of equipment and devices, as set forth in this book, are in accord with current recommendations and practice at the time of publication, they accept no legal responsibility for any errors or omissions, and make no warranty, express or implied, with respect to material contained herein. In view of ongoing research, equipment modifications, changes in governmental regulations and the constant flow of information relating to drug therapy, drug reactions and the use of equipment and devices, the reader is urged to review and evaluate the information provided in the package insert or instructions for each drug, piece of equipment or device for, among other things, any changes in the instructions or indications of dosage or usage and for added warnings and precautions.

Recognizing the importance of preserving what has been written, it is a policy of John Wiley & Sons, Inc. to have books of enduring value published in the United States printed on acid-free paper, and we exert our best efforts to that end.

Library of Congress Cataloging-in-Publication Data

Sensory receptors and signal transduction / editors, John L. Spudich,
Birgit H. Satir.
    p.   cm. — (Modern cell biology ; v. 10)
    Includes bibliographical references and index.
    ISBN 0-471-56105-3
    1. Sensory receptors. 2. Cellular signal transduction.
  I. Spudich, John Lee. II. Satir, Birgit H. III. Series.
    [DNLM: 1. Cell Communication—physiology. 2. Receptors, Sensory—
physiology. 3. Signal Transduction—physiology. W1 MO124T v. 10
/ WL 102.9 S478]
    QH573.M63   vol. 10
    [QP447]
    574.87 s—dc20
    [599.01′82]
    DNLM/DLC
  for Library of Congress   91-24289
                                               CIP

Contents

Contributors

Roberto A. Bogomolni, Department of Chemistry, University of California, Santa Cruz, CA 95035 [233]

Michael Eisenbach, Department of Membrane Research and Biophysics, The Weizmann Institute of Science, 76100 Rehovot, Israel [137]

B.A. Horwitz, Department of Biology, Technion, Haifa 32000, Israel [1]

E.D. Lipson, Department of Physics, Syracuse University, Syracuse, NY 13244-1130 [1]

Lorraine Marsh, Department of Cell Biology, Albert Einstein College of Medicine, Bronx, NY 10461 [209]

John L. Spudich, Department of Anatomy and Structural Biology and Department of Physiology and Biophysics, Albert Einstein College of Medicine, Bronx, NY 10461; present address: Department of Microbiology and Molecular Genetics, University of Texas Medical School, Houston, TX 77030 [233]

Judith Van Houten, Department of Zoology, University of Vermont, Burlington, VT 05405 [65]

The numbers in brackets are the opening page numbers of the contributors' articles.

Preface

The authors in this volume are researchers investigating the processes of (1) sensory receptor activation, i.e., the mechanism by which ligand binding by chemoreceptors or photon absorption by photoreceptors initiates a message to the cell, and (2) signal transduction, i.e., the relay of this message to modulate cell behavior. We have selected a few key examples of model systems that encompass the range of approaches being applied, rather than attempt a comprehensive review of this vast field. E.D. Lipson and B.A. Horwitz survey photosensory receptors and photosignal transduction, and Judith Van Houton covers analogous, and in some cases, homologous, chemoreceptors and ligand-activated processes. Prime examples of a prokaryotic and a eukaryotic model system with strong genetics are presented, respectively, by Michael Eisenbach[*] (bacterial chemotaxis) and Lorraine Marsh (yeast mating factor receptors). Roberto Bogomolni and I review the archaebacterial rhodopsins, incorporating progress on photoinduced molecular transformations since our 1988 review.

Major transitions occurring in sensory transduction research are evident in these reviews. First, we are poised at the onset of what promises to be an exciting period in receptor activation. This first step in sensory signaling, the conversion of the extracellular stimulus into an intracellular signal by the receptor protein, has been in the past largely a black box. Stimuli "activate" the receptor protein by inducing structural alterations that are then relayed to the first post-receptor transducing component. Molecular genetic and biophysical methods are converging to identify the structural basis of activation and relay, especially for photosensory receptors. In the next few years we can expect receptor proteins to be crystallized in active and nonactive states, providing information regarding structural differences, and to be analyzed by complementary time-resolved methods to assess stimulus-induced alterations and their functional significance.

A second transition is occurring in work on post-receptor processes, which is progressing from the identification and system level understanding of the roles of the various signal-transducing components, the main focus over the past decade, to their chemical mechanisms of signal transmission via protein/protein interaction and catalytic cascades.

John L. Spudich

*Michael Eisenbach has compiled an extensive bibliography on prokaryotic sensory reception and signal transduction that is available in electronic form as EISENBACH_BIBLIO.TXT by anonymous ftp at the following internet address: utmmg.med.uth.tmc.edu.

Sensory Receptors and Signal Transduction: 1–64
© 1991 Wiley-Liss, Inc.

Photosensory Reception and Transduction

E.D. Lipson and B.A. Horwitz

Department of Physics, Syracuse University, Syracuse, New York 13244-1130
(E.D.L.); Department of Biology, Technion, Haifa 32000, Israel (B.A.H.)

I. INTRODUCTION

Besides providing essential energy for life on earth, light provides signals and images that enable organisms to manage successfully in their environments. Animal vision constitutes the most familiar example and the most sophisticated, yet organisms ranging throughout the phylogenetic kingdoms take ample advantage of light signals and patterns to control their behavior, metabolism, and development. Many sensory systems, notably vision, exhibit the property called "adaptation," which allows them to adjust their sensitivity kinetically over many orders of magnitude of light intensity [Fein and Szuts, 1982; Galland, 1989].

The present survey of sensory receptor pigments and the associated transduction processes is guided by a remarkable, but little appreciated, point made by the late Max Delbrück in a 1976 commemorative lecture at the Carlsberg Laboratory. Delbrück chose the title "Light and Life III" for the lecture, following in the footsteps of the quantum physicist Niels Bohr, who had given lectures entitled, respectively, "Light and Life" (in 1932) and "Light and Life Revisited" (in 1962, the last year of his life). Bohr's 1932 lecture was a major influence in convincing Max Delbrück to switch from physics to biology. The special point made by Delbrück [1976] was that there is a remarkably small group of chromophores used repeatedly throughout photobiology as photochemically active photoreceptors.

The reasons for this photomolecular economy in nature are not entirely clear, but a salient argument raised by Delbrück concerns the high energy introduced into a biochemical system when a photon of visible or near-ultraviolet (UV) light is absorbed (viz., 400 nm photons introduce $\sim$70 kcal/mol). This energy, if not carefully controlled, can wreak havoc, for example by the superoxide anion, which is normally disabled by superoxide dismutase (in concert with enzymes detoxifying peroxide), or by excited singlet oxygen, which is quenched by β-carotene [Bendich and Olson, 1989; Krinsky, 1989; Spikes, 1989]. These highly toxic oxidative species must be kept limited. Evidently, one preventative way to confine their production has been to limit—during the course of evolution—the presence of those types of chromophores that are photochemically active. The problem of dealing with these toxic derivatives of molecular oxygen must have been especially severe in primordial atmospheres before the generation of the ozone layer from oxygen produced by photosynthetic organisms.

Delbrück's article featured a ''short list'' of molecules whose photochemistry is relevant for biology. The list needs some updating, in particular because the sensory rhodopsins of *Halobacterium halobium* and the multicyclic hypericin-like [Durán and Song, 1986] receptor pigments stentorin and blepharismin in ciliated protozoa [Song, 1983; Lenci and Ghetti, 1989] were unknown[1] in 1976. Moreover, the scope of Delbrück's analysis was broader than that of the present chapter; it included not only sensory transducing pigments, but also energy transducing pigments, such as chlorophyll and bacteriorhodopsin, to which we should now add halorhodopsin. Nevertheless, the main point of his essay still holds, namely, that nature has been highly conservative—one might even say stingy—in choosing the range of chromophores for photobiological functions.

The short list included the following entries: retinal pigments,[2] phytochrome, cryptochrome (blue light receptor), photoreactivating enzyme (photolyase), chlorophyll, and protochlorophyll. Delbrück noted that the list could be contracted by lumping the tetrapyrrole pigments together (chlorophyll, protochlorophyll, and phytochrome). Furthermore, it was then undiscovered that photolyases are actually flavoproteins with pterin cofactors, so they could be lumped with the cryptochrome class. The updated list has thus become shorter: retinal pigments, tetrapyrroles, cryptochromes (including flavin and pterin chromophores), and hypericin pigments. This shorter list accommodates known photoreceptor and energy transducing pigments, although the latter class is beyond the scope of this chapter.

Notably absent from the above accounting are carotenoids and heme pigments. Neither of these seems to play a significant role as receptor pigments with direct photochemistry. Carotenoids do serve as accessory pigments, as photoprotective agents, and as metabolic precursors for retinal pigments. The photophysical reason why heme and carotene pigments do not play a direct photochemical role in nature is that the quantum efficiency for internal conversion is overwhelming in these pigments, so that there is insufficient time for effective photochemistry to proceed from the excited state. Again, these serve as examples of pigments that are safe to have around (because of the rapid, innocuous quenching of the excited state) despite the general dangers associated with photoexcited molecules.

---

[1] Actually, there was already a report suggesting that the *Blepharisma* receptor pigment might be related to hypericin [Sevenants, 1965], but the confirmation and extensive characterization of the hypericin-based receptor pigments in *Blepharisma* and *Stentor* took place after Delbrück's lecture was published.

[2] In Delbrück's list, this entry was simply called ''retinal.'' However, because the other entries are chromoproteins rather than chromophores, we have modified this entry accordingly to refer to rhodopsin and related pigments that use retinal (or, more properly, *N*-retinylidene) chromophores.

Because this chapter has been organized in terms of photoreceptor pigments, it deemphasizes many systems that have been characterized mainly at the phenomenological level. The interested reader is referred to some books and review articles organized in terms of the photoresponses or organisms with notable photobehaviors [Haupt and Feinleib, 1979; Lenci and Colombetti, 1980; Senger, 1980, 1984, 1987; Colombetti et al., 1985]. Introductory coverage of general photobiological principles and methodologies is available in two recent books [Häder and Tevini, 1987; Smith, 1989].

The chromophores employed for photosensory reception are either polyenes (retinal and related molecules derived from the isoprenoid β-carotene) or multicyclic compounds like flavins, tetrapyrroles, and hypericin. As is typical for chromophores that absorb visible and near-UV light, all have conjugated double-bond systems that accommodate delocalized π electrons. The associated electronic transitions are in the right energy range for absorption of visible and UV light. For further background on these photochemical and related photophysical issues (in the framework of molecular orbital theory and the so-called Jablonski diagram, which summarizes photophysical processes), the reader is referred to the introductory chapters of a current photobiology book [Grossweiner, 1989a,b].

II. RHODOPSINS

Rhodopsin pigments, which employ retinal (vitamin A aldehyde; in the form of N-retinylidene) chromophores, serve as photoreceptors for vision in animals. In some cases, the chromophore is instead 3-dehydroretinal (vitamin A_2 aldehyde). For brevity, these chromophores are designated as A1 and A2 [Wald, 1968; Dratz, 1989]. Rhodopsins with A1 chromophores generally absorb at longer wavelengths than those with A2. The large red shift of rhodopsins relative to isolated chromophores is due partly to protonation of the Schiff base linkage between chromophore and opsin apoprotein. Further electrostatic interactions of retinal with the opsin polypeptide are responsible in large part for the variation of absorption maxima.

This rhodopsin class of pigments is evidently of ancient origin, given the occurrence of rhodopsins in prokaryotic and lower eukaryotic organisms such as *H. halobium* [Oesterhelt and Stoeckenius, 1971; Bogomolni and Spudich, 1982] and *Chlamydomonas reinhardtii* [Foster et al., 1984], respectively. Three recent books are devoted to retinal proteins [Ebrey et al., 1987; Ovchinnikov, 1987a; Hara, 1988]; among other books providing coverage of the topic are those by Schichi [1983] and Stieve [1985a]. Various chromophores found in rhodopsin pigments are shown in Figure 1 (see also Table I).

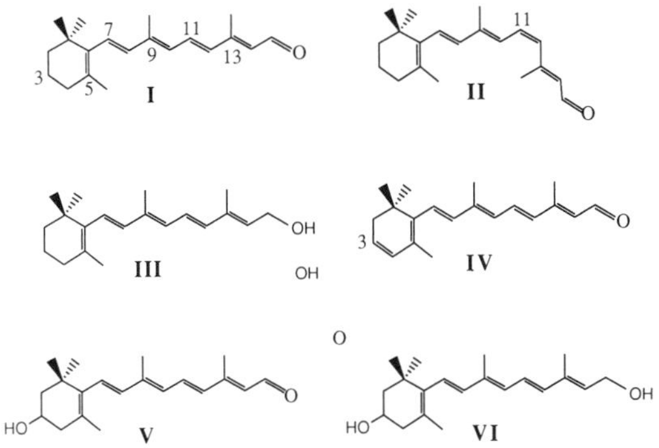

Fig. 1. Structures of several vitamin A derivatives that are important in vision. **I:** All-*trans*-retinal (vitamin A1 aldehyde). **II:** 11-*cis*-Retinal. **III:** Retinol (vitamin A1). **IV:** 3-Dehydroretinal (vitamin A2 aldehyde). **V:** 3-Hydroxyretinal. **VI:** 3-Hydroxyretinol.

A. Sensory Rhodopsins in *Halobacterium halobium*

In *H. halobium,* an extensively studied halophilic archaebacterium, four rhodopsin pigments have been discovered, all of which reside in the plasma membrane. Bacteriorhodopsin (BR) and halorhodopsin (HR) have bioenergetic functions [Stoeckenius and Bogomolni, 1982; Stoeckenius, 1985; Oesterhelt and Tittor, 1989; Lanyi, 1990]. Accordingly, they will be mentioned only briefly in this chapter, which is devoted primarily to photosensory pigments. BR is a light-driven proton pump that is abundant in the cell under conditions of low oxygen tension and is organized into crystalline arrays in purple membrane patches [Oesterhelt and Stoeckenius, 1971, 1973; Stoeckenius and Bogomolni, 1982]. The light-driven extrusion of protons from the cell generates a pH gradient across the plasma membrane that is exploited subsequently for chemiosmotic phosphorylation of ADP to ATP. Thus *H. halobium* features a primitive, distinctive form of photophosphorylation, or bona fide photosynthesis without any involvement of chlorophyll pigments; this photophosphorylation comes into play when the oxygen supply is insufficient for respiration. The related pigment HR serves a related energy transducing function, namely, as a light-driven chloride pump [Schobert and Lanyi, 1982; Bogomolni et al., 1984; Lanyi, 1984; Oesterhelt and Tittor, 1989].

The remaining two rhodopsin pigments discovered more recently in *H. halobium* have photobehavioral functions. They are sensory rhodopsin I (SR-I; also slow-cycling rhodopsin) and sensory rhodopsin II (SR-II; also P_{480} and phoborhodopsin). The discovery of the sensory pigments was facilitated by an elegant genetic approach in which mutants were isolated lacking the more abundant bioenergetic pigments BR and HR [Spudich and Spudich, 1982; Spudich, 1984].

TABLE I. Properties of Representative Sensory Pigments

Pigment	Molecular mass ($\times 10^{-3}$)	Chromophore*	Protein structure	Peak wavelength (nm)	Molar extinction coefficient ($mM^{-1} cm^{-1}$)	Quantum efficiency	Process†
Rhodopsin and related pigments							
Bovine	40	11-*cis*-Retinal	Monomer	500	40	0.67	Bleaching
Human‡							
Rod	40	11-*cis*-Retinal	Monomer	495	40		
Blue				420			
Green				530			
Red				560			
*Chlamydomonas***		Retinal		503			
H. halobium							
SR-I	24	All-*trans*-retinal	Dimer‖	587			
SR-II		All-*trans*-retinal		487			
Ec. halophila							
PYP§	13				48	0.65	
Phytochrome‖	124	Phytochromobilin	Dimer	668 (Pr)	132	0.153	Pr→Pfr
				730 (Pfr)	74	0.062	Pfr→Pr

Photolyase#	49	Pterin derivative and FADH$_2$	Monomer	380	25.9	0.75	Dimer repair
Cryptochrome(s)		Flavin		450	12		
		Pterin		357	22		
Hypericin pigment systems							
Stentor‖							
Stentorin I	~50–100	Hypericin	≥2 Subunits	610			
Stentorin II	>500	Hypericin	Molecular complex	620			
Blepharisma							
blepharismin		Hypericin		<600***			

*The retinal chromophores are, strictly speaking, N-retinylidene.
†The process for which the quantum efficiency is quoted.
‡See Nathans and Hogness [1984] and Nathans et al. [1986b] and references therein.
**Foster et al. [1984].
¶In the purified state (detergent micelles), SR-I was found to be a dimer [Schegk and Oesterhelt, 1988].
§Meyer et al. [1987].
‖Spectroscopic data from Lagarias et al. [1987].
#Sancar et al. [1984].
‖‖See Kim et al. [1990].
***See Colombetti [1990].

The polarly flagellated cells of *H. halobium* respond to light and chemical stimuli by modulating the frequency of reversals in the direction of swimming. These reversals are accomplished by alternating the sense of rotation of motors at the bases of the flagellae. *H. halobium* cells avoid regions of blue and near-UV light that could exert injurious photodynamic effects. Conversely, they are attracted to red and orange light, which is absorbed efficiently by the energy transducing pigments BR (568 nm peak) and HR (578 nm). In the absence of stimulation, the cells switch direction spontaneously in a stochastic fashion and thereby perform a three-dimensional random walk. Increases in red/orange light intensity or decreases in blue and near-UV light intensity constitute attractant light stimuli and conversely for repellent stimuli. An attractant stimulus decreases the rate of reversal of the motors (i.e., increases the interval between switches in direction), and a repellent stimulus increases the reversal rate.

Figure 2a shows the photocycles of SR-I and SR-II [Bogomolni and Spudich, 1982; Takahashi et al., 1986; Tomioka et al., 1986; Spudich and Bogomolni, 1988]. For SR-I the resting state is $SR\text{-}I_{587}$. Absorption of orange light (~587 nm) produces transient intermediates S_{610} and S_{560} that relax thermally in the submillisecond time scale to S_{373}, which has a 750 msec half-life for reversion to $SR\text{-}I_{587}$. Near-UV or blue light absorbed by the pigment in this metastable state converts it to S^b_{510} which relaxes to $SR\text{-}I_{587}$ with an 80 msec half-life. This photocycle, which was determined by flash spectroscopy applied to membrane preparations, can account for much of the phototaxis color-sensing behavior [Spudich and Bogomolni, 1984]. In particular, $SR\text{-}I_{587}$ and the intermediate S_{373} act as photoreceptors respectively for positive phototaxis (by suppression of flagellar reversal) in response to attractant stimuli and for negative phototaxis (by promotion of flagellar reversal) in response to repellent stimuli.

For SR-II, the photocycle is simpler (Fig. 2a). After absorbing repellent blue-green light, the resting form, $SR\text{-}II_{487}$, proceeds through intermediates including $S\text{-}II_{350}$ and $S\text{-}II_{530}$, completing the slow dark reaction cycle in under 1 sec. SR-II is responsible for negative phototaxis to repellent stimuli in the blue and green spectral regions. The details of these photocycles, including the genetic and spectroscopic work that led to their determination and their relationship to the photobehavior, are discussed by Bogomolni and Spudich (this volume).

SR-I and SR-II, as well as BR and HR, employ all-*trans* retinal as their chromophores. In the bacterial rhodopsin photocycles, only all-*trans*/13-*cis* isomerization has been detected. When an analog of all-*trans* retinal that is locked to prevent such isomerization was incorporated into SR-I and SR-II apoproteins in vivo, phototaxis was not restored [Yan et al., 1990]. This result indicates that the *trans*–*cis* isomerization is essential for phototaxis signal transduction in *H. halobium*, unlike the situation with *Chlamydomonas* phototaxis, where isomerization is not required (see below).

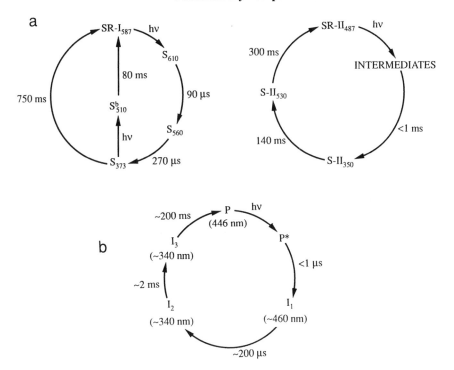

Fig. 2. Photocycles of sensory rhodopsins SR-I and SR-II from *Halobacterium halobium* (**a**) [Spudich and Bogomolni, 1988] and photoactive yellow protein (PYP at bottom) from *Ectothiorhodospira halophila* (**b**) [Meyer et al., 1987]. Light reactions are indicated by hν. Half-times are shown for thermal reactions (conditions for photoactive yellow protein (PYP) 5 mM phosphate, pH 7). Wavelengths of maximal absorption are shown as subscripts for SR-I and SR-II and in parentheses for PYP.

An open question in the photobehavior of *H. halobium* is whether the energy transducing pigments BR and HR might participate also as photoreceptors (or photosensitizers). While the properties of SR-I and SR-II seem sufficient to account for the photosensitivity for phototaxis, the power of genetic dissection [Spudich, 1984] could help to resolve this issue, as it did so well for the identification of the SR-I and SR-II. What is needed is a set of null mutants that are complementary to the existing Flx (BR⁻ HR−) mutants. If such mutants, lacking SR-I and SR-II but retaining BR and/or HR, still showed phototaxis, this would speak in favor of a direct photobehavioral role for BR and/or HR.

Retinal radiolabeling of membranes isolated from various mutants indicated apparent molecular weights of 25 kD and 23 kD, respectively, for SR-I and SR-II [Spudich et al., 1986], in the same range as for BR and HR [Bogomolni et al., 1984; Lanyi, 1984; Oesterhelt and Tittor, 1989]. Recently, SR-I has been purified [Schegk and Oesterhelt, 1988] and its gene sequence and amino acid sequence determined [Blanck et al., 1989]. Comparison of chromatographic and electrophoretic results indicates that SR-I may be a dimer, with the apparent molecular weight of each monomer being about 24,000. The DNA sequence encodes 239 amino acids in the SR-I monomer. The amino acid sequence for SR-I shows substantial homology with BR and HR, but not with animal rhodopsins.

Relatively little is known about the transduction steps in *H. halobium* between photoreception and reversal of the flagellar motors compared with the knowledge of these steps in eubacterial chemotaxis (see Eisenbach, this volume) [Stewart and Dahlquist, 1987; Berg, 1988; Stock et al., 1990] or in vertebrate vision (see below). The signals generated by SR-I and SR-II remain unknown. Unlike the energy transducing pigments BR and HR, the sensory pigments are not electrogenic, i.e., they do not generate changes in membrane potential upon excitation [Spudich and Bogomolni, 1988]. Calcium and cGMP may be involved in signaling [Schimz and Hildebrand, 1987]. Reversible carboxylmethylation of proteins has also been associated with signal transduction in phototaxis and chemotaxis in *H. halobium* [Schimz, 1981; Spudich et al., 1988, 1989; Alam et al., 1989; Hildebrand and Schimz, 1990]. In diverse eubacteria, including *Escherichia coli* and *Salmonella typhimurium*, carboxylmethylation of methyl-accepting chemotaxis proteins (MCPs), which function as receptors/transducers for chemotaxis, governs adaptation [Springer et al., 1979; Stewart and Dahlquist, 1987].

A further advance in unraveling the signal transduction chain for phototaxis in *H. halobium* is the surprising discovery that the citric acid cycle intermediate fumarate plays a role in controlling flagellar reversal [Marwan et al., 1990]. Complementation assays with wild-type extracts applied to a straight-swimming mutant provide strong evidence that fumarate functions as the so-called switch factor and that there is a binding protein for it. Only one or a few molecules per cell of fumarate are needed to restore responsiveness to the mutant.

B. Photoactive Yellow Protein From *Ectothiorhodospira halophila*

A soluble 13 kD photoactive yellow protein (PYP) has been isolated from the purple photoautotrophic bacterium *E. halophila* [Meyer et al., 1987]. Its three-dimensional structure has been determined recently at 2.4 Å atomic resolution [McRee et al., 1989]. PYP exhibits a photocycle (Fig. 2b) resembling that of the slow-cycling sensory rhodopsins in *H. halobium* and has a high photochemical quantum efficiency of 0.65 [McRee et al., 1989]. It also shows reversible photoisomerization.

The protein structure consists of two antiparallel β-sheets enclosing the chromophore. Accordingly, it belongs to a newly recognized class of proteins binding small amphipathic molecules. This structurally based class includes fatty acid–binding protein, P2 myelin protein, serum retinol–binding protein, insecticyanin, bilirubin–binding protein, and β-lactoglobulin; PYP also shares sequence homology with rat odorant-binding protein, α_1-microglobulin, apolipoprotein D, and α_1-acid glycoprotein [see references cited in McRee et al., 1989]. Among these proteins, however, PYP is unique in being photoactive.

The chromophore of PYP is not all-*trans*-retinal [Meyer et al., 1987], but could be another form of retinal. Like retinal chromophores, the PYP chromophore can be bleached by treatment with hydroxylamine [Meyer et al., 1987]. Furthermore, it appears to be bound by a Schiff base linkage to a lysine residue (Lys-111) [McRee et al., 1989]. Although PYP has not been shown to be a phototaxis receptor, a sensory function has been suggested based on the similarity of its slow photochemical cycle to the cycles of *H. halobium* sensory rhodopsins [Meyer et al., 1987]. It will be especially interesting to establish the mode of operation of this putative rhodopsin, which is soluble rather than membrane bound. In any case, these studies on PYP in *Ec. halophila* are novel and remarkable by virtue of the successful determination of the three-dimensional structure of a probable sensory receptor pigment before the associated behavior has been investigated. This represents a bold and highly promising ''back door'' approach (actually through the front door, given that this concerns a putative photoreceptor at the beginning of a photosensory transduction chain) that is unique in the field of photosensory reception.

Recently a PYP with similar spectroscopic and chromatographic properties was isolated from a purple phototrophic bacterium, *Rhodospirillum salexigens* [Meyer et al., 1990]. It differs from the *Ec. halophila* PYP in that it is denatured at low ionic strength whereas the *Ec. halophila* PYP is stable.

C. Rhodopsin in *Chlamydomonas*

The flagellated green alga *C. reinhardtii* shows phototaxis toward or away from light. The wavelength of maximal sensitivity is 503 nm [Nultsch et al., 1971; Foster and Smyth, 1980; Foster et al., 1984; Nultsch and Häder, 1988]. A prominent eyespot, or stigma, in the cell had long been implicated in phototaxis, and for many years a favored hypothesis had been that it functions by shading during the axial rotation of the cell as it swims. However, the observation of layered structure within the eyespot led to the alternative hypothesis that this structure serves instead as a quarter-wave interference reflector or optical antenna [Foster and Smyth, 1980], concentrating the reflected light at the adjacent plasma membrane where the photoreceptor molecules evidently reside [Melkonian and Robenek, 1980, 1984]. This hypothesis was supported by the further observation that the eyespots are indeed highly reflective under epiillumination [Foster and Smyth, 1980]. The transduction chain for phototaxis and related photomovement responses in *Chlamydomonas* remains to be elucidated. Calcium seems to play a key role [Nultsch, 1983], and membrane potential changes may also be involved [Nultsch and Häder, 1988]. Preliminary evidence suggests the involvement of a G protein and cGMP-phosphodiesterase–based enzyme cascade in *Chlamydomonas* analogous to that found in vertebrate photoreceptor cells [Dumler et al., 1989; and see below]. Phototaxis is a highly sensitive response in *Chlamydomonas*, and it appears that individual cells are able to detect single photons [Hegemann and Marwan, 1988], as is the case with animal photoreceptor cells (see below).

Demonstration that a rhodopsin pigment serves as photoreceptor for phototaxis was inferred by use of retinal analogs and a sensitive behavioral assay involving action spectroscopy of phototaxis [Foster et al., 1984; Smyth et al., 1988]. This work exploited a mutant unable to synthesize carotene (the C_{40} metabolic precursor of the C_{20} polyene retinal) in darkness; the mutant does, however, produce opsin apoprotein in the dark. Addition of retinal analogs in vivo typically restored phototaxis with spectral sensitivity similar to that found spectrophotometrically with the corresponding analogs bound to bovine opsin.

In a related study, it was discovered that this rhodopsin also serves as photoreceptor for light-induced synthesis of carotene and retinal [Foster et al., 1988b]. Thus *Chlamydomonas* rhodopsin autoregulates the synthesis of its own chromophore, or, stated differently, the retinal product derived from carotene serves as the chromophore for photoregulation of carotene synthesis. This is the only case known to date where a rhodopsin has been demonstrated to act as photoreceptor for light-induced carotene synthesis. In most other organisms studied for this effect, the photoreception is attributed to cryptochrome-type photoreceptors, most likely with flavin chromophores (see below).

The prevailing view in the field of vision research (see below) is that the primary photochemical event in the excitation of vertebrate rhodopsin is the isomerization of retinal from the 11-*cis* to the all-*trans* configuration [Wald, 1968] and thus implicitly that this isomerization is essential to visual excitation. This paradigm has been challenged by Foster et al. [1988a, 1989, 1990] because, in the model system *Chlamydomonas*, locked analogs and short acyclic analogs of retinal that are unable to isomerize are still highly effective for phototaxis. The *Chlamydomonas* data suggest that the rhodopsin activation may be due primarily to the change in electric dipole moment after the chromophore absorbs light. Now, either *Chlamydomonas* rhodopsin functions quite differently from vertebrate rhodopsin, or else the standard dogma may have to be reconsidered. DNA hybridization experiments [Martin et al., 1986] indicate homology between *Chlamydomonas* and bovine rhodopsin. Further evidence is provided by reconstitution experiments [Dumler et al., 1989] demonstrating that a *Chlamydomonas* rhodopsin fraction could activate bovine transducin and cGMP-phosphodiesterase (see below). As expected, a fraction from a caroteneless mutant (lacking functional rhodopsin because the retinal chromophore is not synthesized) was unable to produce such activation.

There is no dispute about the fact that the retinal chromophore in vertebrate rhodopsin isomerizes from 11-*cis* to all-*trans* immediately after photoexcitation. The issue is whether this isomerization is the principal mode for activating rhodopsin as an enzyme catalyzing the exchange of GDP for GTP in the G protein transducin (the initial amplification step in the transduction cascade in vertebrate photoreceptor cells, as detailed below). The alternative of an electronic activation mechanism, as suggested by the *Chlamydomonas* results, does not exclude that isomerization may play an essential, supporting role such as preventing reversal of a protein conformation brought about by the putative electronic mechanism [Foster et al., 1990]. The corresponding experiment, needed in vertebrate systems, is difficult, especially with sensitivity approaching that of the bioassay in *Chlamydomonas*.

The viewpoint that *Chlamydomonas* rhodopsin may be fundamentally different from vertebrate rhodopsin is argued in the current review by Birge [1990]. The case for the homology between structure and function of *Chlamydomonas* rhodopsin vis à vis bovine rhodopsin could be strengthened once the complete gene and protein sequences for *Chlamydomonas* rhodopsin have been obtained and once it has been purified and characterized spectroscopically. In the meantime, the sensitive in vivo assay by action spectroscopy provides a unique perspective on this novel receptor pigment. Moreover, the discovery that a rhodopsin governs phototaxis in an alga has implications for the evolution of rhodopsin pigments in eukaryotes, particularly in view of the recent finding that an enzyme cascade like that in vertebrate photoreceptor cells may be operating in this lower eukaryote too. From electrophysiological studies, there is evidence for rhodopsin photoreceptors in other green algae, namely, *Acetabularia* [Schilde, 1968] and *Haematococcus* [Sineshchekov et al., 1990].

D. Vertebrate Rhodopsins

The field of vision research in both vertebrate and invertebrate systems has been reviewed by Fein and Szuts [1982] and by Dratz [1989]. The rod photoreceptor cell of the vertebrate retina, in particular, is one of the best understood sensory systems with respect to the underlying processes of reception, transduction, and adaptation.

In the human retina there are $\sim 10^8$ rod cells, which provide vision under low light conditions, and $\sim 10^6$ cone cells, which operate at higher light intensity and provide color vision. The main objects of study in vertebrate vision have been the outer segments of rod cells, which are highly differentiated structures specialized for visual reception and transduction. A mammalian rod outer segment (diameter $\sim$ a few μm) consists of a compressed stack of $\sim 10^3$ disk sacs each containing $\sim 10^5$ rhodopsin molecules in their membranes; nearly all the protein in the disk membrane is rhodopsin (>90%). There are thus $\sim 10^8$ rhodopsin molecules in a rod outer segment. Rod cells are capable of detecting single photons [Hecht et al., 1942]; absorption of a photon can modulate a photocurrent by ~1 pA [Baylor et al., 1979], leading to a hyperpolarization of ~1 mV. Prodigious amplification processes must therefore occur after excitation of a rhodopsin molecule (see below).

1. Rhodopsin structure and photochemistry. Biochemical and spectroscopic analyses of rhodopsin, especially in vertebrate systems, have been amply reviewed [Crouch, 1986; Koutalos and Ebrey, 1986; Ovchinnikov, 1987a,b; Becker, 1988; DeGrip, 1988; Birge, 1990]. The amino acid sequences of visual pigments have been determined for the following vertebrate systems: bovine [Hargrave et al., 1983; Nathans and Hogness, 1983; Ovchinnikov et al., 1983], chicken [Takao et al., 1988], mouse [Baehr et al., 1988], and human [Nathans and Hogness, 1984; Nathans et al., 1986b].

For bovine (and ovine) rhodopsin, consisting of 348 amino acid residues, the N terminus is blocked by an acetyl group. Two oligosaccharide chains are attached to the opsin apoprotein at Asn-2 and Asn-15. The residue to which the retinal chromophore is bound is Lys-296. As is the case with many membrane proteins, the polypeptide chain of rhodopsin contains alternating hydrophilic and hydrophobic regions. Although there is no crystallographically determined structure of rhodopsin yet, it is well accepted from the sequence data and comparison with the diffraction-derived structure of BR that the rhodopsin polypeptide threads its way back and forth through the membrane with a total of seven transmembrane helical segments forming a basket-like structure (Fig. 3). This structure is characteristic of several receptor proteins, includ-

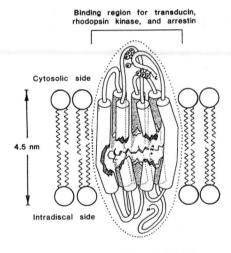

Fig. 3. Model for structure of vertebrate rhodopsin in the rod disk membrane [Dratz and Hargrave, 1983]. The 11-*cis*-retinal chromophore is shown bound to one of the bent α-helical rods of the opsin apoprotein. Phosphorylation sites in the cytoplasmic region are labeled with circles containing the letter P.

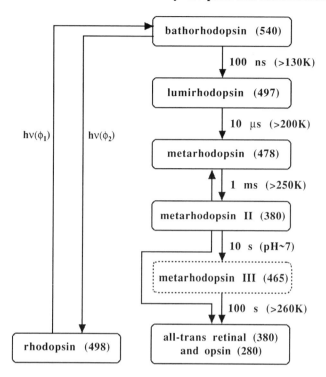

Fig. 4. Photobleaching sequence of vertebrate rhodopsin. The names of the individual species are given in the boxes along with the approximate wavelength (nm) of maximum absorption extrapolated to room temperature. The metarhodopsin III species indicated within the dotted box is tentative. Approximate time constants (extrapolated to room temperature) for formation of subsequent species are indicated to the right of the arrows connecting the boxes, along with the temperatures required for observing their formation. (After Birge [1990].)

ing the β-adrenergic receptor. Indeed, on the basis of sequence data, rhodopsin is clearly homologous with the β-adrenergic receptor and the muscarinic acetylcholine receptor [Dixon et al., 1986; Lefkowitz et al., 1986; Hall, 1987; Tsendina et al., 1988].

Various spectroscopic approaches have been applied to rhodopsin and correspondingly to BR [Birge, 1990]. Fundamental results on the photocycle (Fig. 4) have been obtained by kinetic spectrophotometry (flash photolysis) [Wald, 1968] and fluorescence spectroscopy [Doukas et al., 1985]. Two vibrational spectroscopy methods, namely, resonance Raman spectroscopy [Callender and Honig, 1977; Eyring and Mathies, 1979; Callender, 1982] and Fourier transform infrared (FTIR) spectroscopy [Brainman and Rothschild, 1988; DeGrip et al., 1988; Bagley et al., 1989], have been especially powerful in elucidating the structure of the chromophore and apoprotein of bovine rhodopsin, as well as of the more readily available BR [Mathies et al., 1987; Kitagawa and Maeda, 1989]. Resonance Raman spectroscopy, in particular, has established the state of protonation of the Schiff base linking the retinal chromophore to the opsin apoprotein, specifically to the ε-amino group of Lys-296 (see below). The large red shift of rhodopsins relative to isolated chromophore is due in part to protonation of the Schiff base linkage. The locations of counterions (from the polypeptide; probably carboxyl groups) in the vicinity of the chromophore are responsible in part for the variation of absorption maxima. Resonance Raman and other spectroscopic studies [reviewed in Birge, 1990] have revealed that the retinal chromophore is protonated in rhodopsin, bathorhodopsin, lumirhodopsin, metarhodopsin I, and metarhodopsin III, but is deprotonated in metarhodopsin II (Fig. 4). Additionally, the energy storage of the primary photochemical event, discussed above, is $\sim$32 kcal mol^{-1} [Birge, 1990].

While resonance Raman spectroscopy has provided data primarily on the chromophore, the complementary FTIR technique is able to probe the apoprotein as well. With the application of modern molecular biological techniques to rhodopsin, it has been possible to modify the apoprotein at selected amino acid residues and determine the effects of FTIR spectra as well as absorbance spectra. This approach complements the long-standing strategy of investigating the chromophore function by using retinal analogs [Crouch, 1986].

Recent studies have employed site-directed mutagenesis to examine the possible role of certain charged amino acids around the chromophore-binding site with respect to the spectral tuning of bovine rhodopsin. Candidates for the primary counterion to the protonated Schiff base at Lys-296 have included Asp-83, Glu-122, and Glu-134. Nathans [1990] measured absorbance spectra of rhodopsins modified at positions 83, 86, 122, 134, 135, and 211; these constitute the charged residues in the transmembrane segments. All spectra of single and double mutants showed little variation from the native pigment. Therefore, these residues seem not to control the spectral tuning. Sakmar et al. [1989] and Zhukovsky and Oprian [1989] have concluded that glutamic acid at position 113 serves as counterion for the retinylidene Schiff base. Substitution of other amino acid residues at position 113 led to substantial shifts in the wavelength of maximum absorbance. The shift was greatest when glutamine was used (30 nm compared with 500 nm for native rhodopsin).

2. Molecular biology of mammalian visual pigments. Recombinant DNA cloning and sequencing techniques have been applied effectively to visual pigment genes [Applebury and Hargrave, 1986; Pak and O'Tousa, 1988; Piantanida, 1988; Nathans, 1989a,b]. Molecular biology studies of mammalian visual pigment genes have contributed greatly to our understanding of the rod and cone pigments and of the nature of their alterations in disorders of color vision. In particular, this work has led at last to clear confirmation of the trichromatic theory of color vision [Young, 1802] and to an understanding of the molecular basis of human color blindness. Very recently, a form of the retinal degeneration disease retinitis pigmentosa has been attributed to a point mutation in the human rhodopsin gene [Dryja et al., 1990].

During the past decade, Nathans, Hogness, and coworkers successfully cloned the genes for the human visual pigments [Nathans, 1989b]. This work was based on the hypothesis that the genes for these visual pigments would constitute a gene family and in particular that the human rhodopsin gene could be probed by a bovine rhodopsin clone. The first step was the isolation of the bovine rhodopsin gene [Nathans and Hogness, 1983] using an oligonucleotide probe based on the amino acid sequence.

The 6.4 kb gene for bovine rhodopsin includes the following sequences homologous to opsin mRNA: a 96 bp 5'-untranslated region, a 1,044 bp region encoding the 348 residue bovine opsin, and a long (~ 1.4 kb) 3'-untranslated region. The coding region is divided into five exons and four introns. The sequence of the coding region indicates seven membrane-spanning segments (see above) based on the structure of BR [Henderson and Unwin, 1975; Henderson et al., 1986] that are characteristic of a class of membrane receptor proteins including the closely related β-adrenergic receptor and the muscarinic acetylcholine receptor (see above).

Three of the intron–exon boundaries correspond to the carboxyl ends of transmembrane segments. This arrangement of functional domains is compatible with the concept of an evolutionary function of introns' serving to permit exon shuffling [Gilbert, 1978, 1987].

Using the bovine rhodopsin gene as a hybridization probe on libraries of human genomic DNA, Nathans and Hogness [1984] next isolated the gene for human rhodopsin. The intron–exon structures of the human and bovine rhodopsin genes are similar. The apoprotein for human and bovine rhodopsin both have 348 amino acid residues. They share 93.4% homology in general and complete conservation of the three cytoplasmic loops in particular.

Having isolated the human rhodopsin gene, Nathans and coworkers [1986b] proceeded to isolate the genes for the cone pigments, now using the human rhodopsin gene as the probe. The pigments, which have yet to be purified biochemically, have been determined by psychophysics and in vivo microspectrophotometry to have the following wavelengths of maximal sensitivity: 420 nm for the blue-sensitive cone pigment, 530 nm for the green pigment, and 560 nm for the red pigment [Boynton, 1979; Mollon and Sharpe, 1983]. It was determined that red-green color blindness is due to alterations—arising from unequal recombination and/or gene conversion—in the genes coding the red and green cone pigments [Nathans et al., 1986a]; that the red and green pigment genes reside on the X chromosome, as expected (in view of the well-known sex linkage of red-green visual abnormalities); that the blue pigment gene is on chromosome 7; and that the rhodopsin gene is on chromosome 3. The human rhodopsin and cone pigment genes clearly constitute a gene family. The ancestral gene diverged at an early stage of evolution to produce the precursors of the rhodopsin and blue pigment genes as well as a third gene that was duplicated more recently to yield the red and green pigment genes.

The amino acid sequences for the cone pigments show 41% ± 1% identity with rhodopsin. The apoproteins for the red and green pigments show 96% identity to each other, but only 43% with respect to the blue pigment. Among the individuals studied with normal color vision, there were variable numbers of green pigment genes arranged in tandem with a single red pigment. The copy number of green pigment genes evidently varies as a result of unequal crossing-over in the intergenic region.

Whereas red-green color blindness is quite common among the male population (~8%), another form of color blindness, namely, blue cone monochromacy, is a rare X-linked disorder that is due to loss of the red and green pigments. It has now been analyzed at the molecular level and attributed to two classes of defects in the red-green visual pigment gene cluster [Nathans et al., 1989].

3. Visual transduction. Remarkable progress has been made during the past two decades in determining the molecular basis of transduction in vertebrate photoreceptor cells [for reviews, see Stryer, 1986, 1988; Hurley, 1987; Liebman et al., 1987; Owen, 1987; Pugh, 1987; Bitensky et al., 1988; Karpen et al., 1988; Ho et al., 1989; Takemoto and Cunnick 1990]. In the vertebrate rod outer segment, the following sequence of transduction events follows the absorption of light by rhodopsin (Fig. 5). The primary photochemical event is generally believed (but see section on *Chlamydomonas*, above) to be the isomerization of the retinal chromophore from the 11-*cis* to the all-*trans* conformation [Wald, 1968; Birge, 1990]. There follows a cycle of dark reactions with spectroscopically distinguishable intermediates (Fig. 4). The chromophore of bathorhodopsin (prelumirhodopsin), the first known intermediate, is already in the all-*trans* form, the photoisomerization having occurred within a few picoseconds. In the metarhodopsin II state, which is the one that is photochemically active for the enzymatic function of rhodopsin (see below), the chromophore is transiently deprotonated.

During the photocycle, the all-*trans* retinal chromophore dissociates from the opsin apoprotein. Resynthesis of rhodopsin is a slow process (~20 min), including the following steps: reduction to all-*trans* retinol (vitamin A); transport of this species to the pigment epithelium; isomerization to 11-*cis* retinol; export back to the photoreceptor cells; oxidation to 11-*cis* retinal; and covalent attachment to the opsin apoprotein. The isomerization process in the epithelium is unusual in that membrane phospholipids serve as the energy source

a

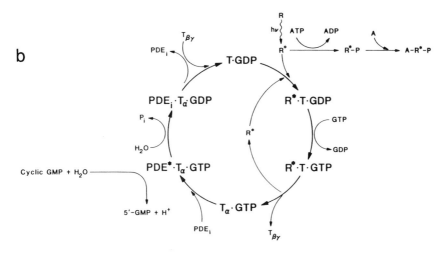

b

Fig. 5. **a:** Information flow in visual excitation processes in vertebrate photoreceptor cells. Light excites rhodopsin (R to R*), which activates the transducin α-subunit (T_α) by exchanging its bound GDP for GTP. Transducin then activates the cGMP phosphodiesterase (PDE). The hydrolysis of cGMP causes cation channels in the membrane to close and the plasma membrane to hyperpolarize. **b:** Details of transducin cycle activated by photoexcited rhodopsin. PDE_i represents inhibited phosphodiesterase and A represents arrestin. See text. (After Stryer [1988].)

by donating acyl groups to the vitamin A molecules [Trehan et al., 1990]. The all-*trans* retinyl ester thus obtained is the substrate for the isomerase [Deigner et al., 1989].

The enzymatic function of photoactivated rhodopsin (R*) is to catalyze the exchange of GTP for bound GDP on the α-subunit, T_α, of the heterotrimeric G protein (guanine nucleotide–binding protein) [Gilman, 1987; Birnbaumer, 1990; Levitzki, 1990] transducin, which then releases its activated T_α-subunit from the remaining β- and γ-subunits. The T_α-GTP in turn activates a specific phosphodiesterase that hydrolyzes cGMP. Both transducin and the phosphodiesterase are peripheral membrane proteins. The molecular weights of the transducin subunits are 39 kD for α, 36 kD for β, and 8 kD for γ [Stryer, 1988]. The subunit structure of phosphodiesterase is αβγγ [Deterre et al., 1988], with the following molecular weights: 85 kD for α, 82 kD for β, and 9.7 kD for γ. The γ-subunits of phosphodiesterase are inhibitory. By removing these inhibitory γ-subunits, the transducin T_α-GTP switches on the phosphodiesterase successively to half-maximal and full activity [Wensel and Stryer, 1990]. The remaining α- and β-subunits together constitute the catalytic moiety of phosphodiesterase. The transducin α-subunit has been found in human cone cells as well as in rods, and there are multiple genes for cone T_α [Lerea et al., 1989].

In darkness, the internal messenger cGMP opens specific cation channels in the rod outer segment plasma membrane [Owen, 1987; Karpen et al., 1988; Kaupp et al., 1989]. Depletion of cGMP therefore leads progressively to closure of these channels. Thus the dark current [Penn and Hagins, 1972], caused primarily by Na^+ influx, is reduced as a consequence of light absorption by rhodopsin, and the net effect is a graded hyperpolarization of the rod cell membrane. That signal is transmitted to horizontal and bipolar cells in the retina and, in turn, to the ganglion cells, which produce action potentials that are propagated to the lateral geniculate nucleus and from there to the primary visual cortex.

For every 100 rhodopsins in the bovine rod outer segment, there are ~10 transducin molecules and about one phosphodiesterase molecule [Liebman et al., 1987]. By means of lateral diffusion, transducins shuttle back and forth between excited rhodopsins and phosphodiesterases [Chabre et al., 1988]. In its enzyme function, photoexcited (photolyzed) rhodopsin can catalyze the exchange of GDP for GTP on several hundred transducin molecules. This represents the first stage of amplification or gain in the enzyme cascade. Under steady-state conditions, there are ~500 activated phosphodiesterases per activated rhodopsin (R*) [Hurley, 1987]. The hydrolysis of cGMP by phosphodiesterase is the second stage of amplification. The final amplification stage at the level of the rod outer segment is the reduced influx of Na^+ through the cGMP-gated channels, and this is reflected in the hyperpolarization of the rod cell membrane.

A critical part of the visual transduction process is the inactivation and recycling of the various components. To this end, activated rhodopsin becomes progressively phosphorylated by means of rhodopsin kinase (there is about one kinase per 1,000 rhodopsins). Up to nine serine and threonine sites on the carboxy-terminal tail (in the cytoplasmic space) of rhodopsin become phosphorylated. Then the 48 kD protein arrestin (also known as S-antigen) binds to phosphorylated rhodopsin, competitively to the transducin-binding site. In this way arrestin inhibits rhodopsin activation of transducin. In another stage of the inactivation process, transducin autocatalytically hydrolyzes the bound GTP to produce the inactive GDP form of transducin.

The cGMP-gated cation channels, which are normally open in darkness, permit the entry mainly of Na^+, but also of Ca^{2+}. To maintain a low level of internal Ca^{2+}, an exchanger (antiport) pumps out Ca^{2+} against its steep gradient while K^+ flows out and Na^+ flows in, each down their concentration gradients; the stoichiometry is 4 Na^+:1 Ca^{2+}, 1 K^+ [Cervetto et al., 1989].

The role of calcium in vertebrate visual transduction has a long, spirited history. Hagins and coworkers [Yoshikami and Hagins, 1970; Hagins and Yoshikami, 1974, 1977] had championed the notion that calcium, sequestered in (and released from) rod disks, serves as the key internal messenger in visual excitation. However, with the eventual recognition of cGMP as the internal messenger, the question remained as to what the true role of calcium is. It has become evident that its main role is to control the sensitivity of rods, i.e., to govern the aspects of visual adaptation that occur at the level of the rod outer segment [Hodgkin and Nunn, 1988; Koch and Stryer, 1988; Matthews et al., 1988; Nakatani and Yau, 1988; Pugh and Altman, 1988].

The mode of action of calcium appears to be negative regulation of the enzyme guanylate cyclase [Koch and Stryer, 1988; Hakki and Sitaramayya, 1990] that catalyzes the synthesis of cGMP, which in turn controls the cation channels in the rod outer segment membrane. The regulation of guanylate cyclase by calcium is mediated by a modulator protein that is not calmodulin [Koch and Stryer, 1988]. The light-induced decline in Ca^{2+} mediates both termination of response and the adaptation process. When light closes the cGMP-gated cation channels, the Ca^{2+} influx is thereby blocked, but extrusion of Ca^{2+} by the Na:Ca,K antiporter persists. The resulting reduction of Ca^{2+} concentration inside the rod outer segment leads to accelerated enzymatic reactions there, including increased cyclization of GMP to cGMP via guanylate cyclase; this counteracts the light-induced decline in cGMP and thereby promotes adaptation with an appropriate time lag.

The G protein–based visual enzyme cascade shares significant homology with hormone-based cascades—in particular, with respect to the three-segment architecture linking receptor, G protein, phosphodiesterase, and cGMP [Bitensky et al., 1988]. The β-adrenergic receptor is actually homologous with rhodopsin in terms of gene sequence and amino acid sequence [Dixon et al., 1986; Lefkowitz et al., 1986; Tsendina et al., 1988; Iwabe et al., 1989]. Both membrane proteins have seven transmembrane helices and both activate G proteins with associated enzyme cascades, although there are significant differences in the subsequent details. In visual systems, rhodopsin is the analog of the hormone receptor, and the photoexcited retinal chromophore plays the role of the hormone as activating ligand. Additionally, the transducin α-subunit is homologous with those of other G proteins, including the *ras* oncogene product and elongation factors of protein synthesis [Hurley et al., 1984; Lochrie et al., 1985].

E. Invertebrate Visual Systems and Pigments

In terms of both structure and function, invertebrate visual systems are considerably more diverse than vertebrate visual systems. The following brief and selective treatment of invertebrate photoreception and transduction primarily addresses differences with vertebrate visual systems. For more general and thorough coverage of invertebrate vision, see the reviews by Autrum [1979], Fein and Szuts [1982], Tsuda [1987], Goldsmith and Bernard [1985], and Stieve [1985b]. Some earlier reviews on invertebrate photoreception are cited by Dratz [1989].

Although invertebrates employ rhodopsin and related pigments for vision, the anatomical structures and the photochemical and physiological processes differ markedly from those found in vertebrate vision [Fein and Szuts, 1982; Tsuda, 1987]. Instead of rod and cone type structures, which are elaborated cilia, invertebrate photoreceptors usually employ arrays of microvilli; thus the receptor pigment resides in the plasma membrane, unlike the situation with vertebrate rods, where most of the rhodopsin is contained in the internal disk membranes. Image-forming eyes similar to those of vertebrates are found in mollusks—specifically, in cephalopods such as squid and octopus. Compound eyes with ommatidia are found in arthropods.

Unlike vertebrate photoreceptor cells, which hyperpolarize upon light excitation (see above), invertebrate photoreceptors depolarize. Such depolarization after stimulation is the more typical mode of operation of sensory receptor cells and excitable cells.

The main arthropod visual systems that have been studied for visual transduction processes include the ventral and lateral eyes of the horseshoe crab *Limulus* and the compound eyes of flies, notably *Drosophila* and *Musca*. In *Drosophila*, the availability of behavioral mutants and receptor potential mutants has been of immense value, especially in conjunction with molecular biology techniques [Pak and O'Tousa, 1988; Montell, 1989].

1. Invertebrate visual pigments. Amino acid sequences have been determined for visual pigments in *Drosophila* [O'Tousa et al., 1985; Zuker et al., 1985, 1987; Cowman et al., 1986; Montell et al., 1987] and in octopus [Ovchinnikov et al., 1988]. On the basis of gene sequences and deduced amino acid sequences, these pigments are homologous with one another and with the vertebrate pigments, as well as hormone receptors that couple to G proteins.

In insects, the main visual pigment chromophore is not retinal but rather 3-hydroxyretinal (Fig. 1) [Vogt and Kirschfeld, 1984; Kirschfeld, 1985]. This pigment has been named "xanthopsin."[3] In close proximity to the insect visual pigments with their 3-hydroxyretinal chromophores, there reside sensitizing pigments that employ a novel chromophore: 3-hydroxyretinol [Kirschfeld, 1985]. Analysis of the quantum efficiency of photosensitization according to resonance energy transfer theory [Förster, 1951] indicates that the sensitizing chro-

---

[3]Not because it is yellow itself (generally it is not), but rather because it is derived from the yellow pigment xanthophyll.

mophore is located within 25 Å of the 3-hydroxyretinal chromophore of the xanthopsin visual pigment [Vogt and Kirschfeld, 1984; Kirschfeld, 1985]. The quantum efficiency of this energy transfer exceeds 0.8.

Light absorption by vertebrate rhodopsin leads to dissociation (photolysis) of the chromophore from the opsin apoprotein. When invertebrate xanthopsin (P) becomes excited, though, the chromophore remains bound to the opsin. Photoexcitation of P converts it to an alternative thermostable form, metaxanthopsin (M), which can be photoreverted to P. Thus xanthopsin operates as a photochromic switch, analogous to the plant photomorphogenic sensor pigment phytochrome (see below) and to SR-I. In flies, P absorbs maximally at ~490 nm and M at ~570 nm. Conversion of a substantial proportion of P to M leads to a so-called prolonged depolarizing afterpotential that can persist for hours. It can be suppressed, though, by photochromic conversion of M back to P.

In flies, fluorescence measurements have revealed another metaxanthopsin-like form: M′ [Franceschini et al., 1981]. In the blowfly, M and M′ have similar emission spectra (660 nm maximum) but different excitation spectra (maxima at 584 nm for M and at 568 nm for M′) Kruizinga and Stavenga, 1990].

Cephalopods, including octopus and squid, employ a dual pigment system [Seki, 1984]. In addition to the rhodopsin pigment with its 11-*cis* retinal chromophore there is a "retinochrome" pigment with an all-*trans* retinal chromophore, not implicated as a photosignal transducer. Light activation switches rhodopsin to the all-*trans* metarhodopsin and conversely switches retinochrome to the 11-*cis* metaretinochrome form. After these reciprocal photoisomerizations, the pigments can regnerate each other by exchanging chromophores [Seki, 1984].

2. Invertebrate visual transduction. The transduction processes that occur in invertebrate photoreceptors differ considerably from those in vertebrates. Although excitation of invertebrate visual pigments does lead similarly to activation of G proteins [Tsuda, 1987], the subsequent events use a different signaling pathway than the cGMP phosphodiesterase pathway employed in vertebrate photoreceptors. Instead, the well-studied and widespread phosphoinositide pathway [Berridge and Irvine, 1984; 1989; Berridge, 1987; Berridge and Taylor, 1988] plays a central role in invertebrate visual transduction [Brown et al., 1984; Fein et al., 1984; Payne et al., 1990].

In inositol lipid hydrolysis, the complex sequence of events begins with hormonal or light activation of a membrane receptor that in turn activates a G protein. This G protein then activates a phospholipase C that hydrolyzes inositol-4,5-bisphosphate, producing two second messengers: inositol-1,4,5-trisphosphate (IP_3) and diacylglycerol (DG). The IP_3 molecules, which are soluble, diffuse and bind to specific membrane receptors that control Ca^{2+}

release from internal stores. The DG, on the other hand, remains in the plasma membrane and activates a protein kinase C, so called because it is sensitive to calcium, which then activates other enzymes by phosphorylation.

Interestingly, the eyes of a *Drosophila* receptor potential mutant called *norpA* (for "no receptor potential") lack phospholipase C activity, and the *norpA* gene is homologous to that for bovine brain phospholipase C [Bloomquist et al., 1988]. Thus, *norpA* is probably the gene for the phospholipase C that plays a key role in phototransduction, in accordance with the inositol cascade described above.

As a consequence of the characteristic action of the internal messenger IP_3, light increases the internal calcium concentration of invertebrate photoreceptor cells. Conversely, in vertebrate photoreceptors, light decreases internal calcium by closing the cGMP-gated cation channels at the end of the transducin-based cascade.

In invertebrate visual transduction, extensive evidence has accumulated in favor of the inositol cascade with its dual internal messengers (IP_3 and DG). Nevertheless, there is some evidence also for the participation of cGMP as an internal messenger in invertebrate photoreceptors [Tsuda, 1987].

In *Limulus* ventral photoreceptors, quantum bumps (discrete waves of depolarization, normally caused by absorption of single photons, or occurring spontaneously) are due to activation of a G protein [Kirkwood et al., 1989]. The gain of the first amplification stage, namely, G-protein activation by rhodopsin, has been estimated to be eightfold. This gain is much lower than that estimated for bovine rhodopsin and transducin ($\sim 100–500$-fold).

III. TETRAPYRROLES

A. Phytochrome

1. Photophysiology. Plants make use of light not only as a source of energy, but also to obtain information. Growth and development of plants adapt to the fluence rate, spectral quality, and direction of light. The action spectra for germination of photosensitive seeds and for the induction of flowering predicted the discovery of phytochrome [Butler et al., 1959; Borthwick and Hendricks, 1960]. This pigment is the best characterized of the plant photoreceptors, with the exception, of course, of the photosynthetic pigments, whose primarily energy transducing role will not be discussed here. Like chlorophylls, phytochrome absorbs strongly in the red region of the spectrum, but has only a weak absorption band in the blue. As its name implies, and in contrast to chlorophyll, phytochrome is photochromic: Upon absorption of red light by the Pr form, a new stable species, Pfr, is produced. The absorption maximum of Pfr is red-shifted by ~ 70 nm with respect to Pr (Fig. 6). Far-red light drives the photoequilibrium back toward Pr. The biological activity of phytochrome

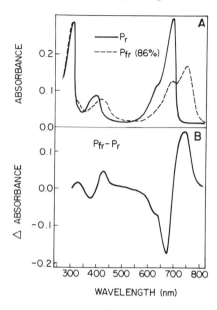

Fig. 6. Absorption spectra of purified oat phytochrome. **A:** The dashed line (Pfr) is the photoequilibrium mixture obtained by irradiation of Pr with red light, approximately 88% Pfr and 12% Pr. **B:** Difference spectrum calculated by subtraction of the spectra in A. (Calculated and redrawn from Lagarias et al. [1987].)

is closely related to its photochromicity. Pr, present in dark-grown seedlings, is presumably inactive, while production of even small amounts of Pfr can markedly alter development. Far-red light can often partially or completely reverse the effects of red light by removing the active species Pfr. Phytochrome thus acts like a molecular switch controlling development.

The photochromicity of phytochrome has also been a highly useful tool. Red, far-red reversible photoconversion produces a characteristic difference spectrum (Fig. 6). This spectrum, when matched with the action spectra, was the biochemical assay that led to the isolation of phytochrome. The initial success in isolation of the pigment was followed by much progress in the study of the molecule [see Lagarias, 1985], though we still do not know how Pfr acts in the cell.

Plants, unlike animals, "see" in a myriad of ways, so that phytochrome modulates many seemingly different aspects of development. Dark-grown seedlings are perhaps found most often in the laboratory, but may be a good representation of what occurs when a seed germinates deep in the soil. Phytochrome, to a large extent, is responsible for the striking difference in appearance of light and dark-grown seedlings (Fig. 7). This and many other photoresponses

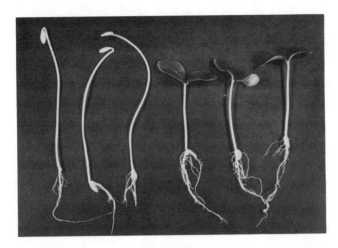

Fig. 7. Photocontrol of morphogenesis. Cucumber seedlings were grown for 6 days in total darkness (left) or 30 μmol m⁻²sec⁻¹light (measured in the 400–700 nm range) from a cool-white fluorescent tube. Note the small cotyledons (first, embryonic, leaves) and long hypocotyls (stem below the cotyledons) and in the dark-grown (etiolated) seedling.

have been studied in great detail [Shropshire and Mohr, 1983; Kendrick and Kronenberg, 1986; Furuya, 1987; Pratt and Cordonnier, 1989; Wada and Kadota, 1989]. To list a few examples, phytochrome modulates seed germination in many species, interacts with the circadian clock to time flowering according to day length, and modulates growth rate and pigment synthesis. Phytochrome is the main photoreceptor controlling chloroplast movement in some algae [Haupt, 1982], and phototropism in mosses [Hartmann and Weber, 1988]. In gametophytes of some ferns, blue and red light have opposite effects, red promoting linear and blue promoting planar growth. A major role of phytochrome in light-grown plants is to sense light quality, in particular the red to far-red ratio [Casal and Smith, 1989]. Perception of the red to far-red ratio can reveal the proximity of, or light blocking by, other plants and is clearly of ecological importance [Smith et al., 1990].

Phytochrome responses include those induced by a brief pulse of light, generally obeying Bunsen-Roscoe reciprocity, and those preferentially induced by long irradiation periods. The latter are referred to as "high irradiance responses" (HIR) [Mancinelli and Rabino, 1978; Drumm-Herrel, 1987]. HIR in the red part of the spectrum can be explained by phytochrome kinetics [Hartmann 1966; Schäfer, 1975]. When blue light is more effective than would be predicted from phytochrome alone, additional photoreceptors must contribute. This reasoning has been applied to anthocyanin synthesis [Sponga et al., 1986]. It should not be overlooked, in kinetic analysis, that the photo-chemical conversion constants may be different for purified phytochrome and intact tissue [Mancinelli, 1986]. The pulse-induced phenomena include those for which the threshold approaches the theoretical limit of a few molecules of Pfr per cell (very low fluence [VLF]) and the classic, photoreversible, low fluence (LF) responses [see Briggs et al., 1985; Schäfer and Briggs, 1986].

2. Phytochrome and gene expression. Phytochrome modulates enzyme activities, and the methods to test the gene expression model for phytochrome action [Mohr, 1972] have been available for some time. Phytochrome even exerts feedback control on its own concentration in the cell by both protein stability and transcriptional regulation [Colbert et al., 1983; Otto et al., 1983; Lissemore and Quail, 1988]. Particularly during seedling development, expression of several nuclear genes encoding chloroplast proteins is under phyto-chrome control [for reviews, see Thompson et al., 1985; Tobin and Silverthorne, 1985; Schäfer and Briggs, 1986; Kuhlemeier et al., 1987; Jenkins, 1988; Nagy et al., 1988]. Recent rapid progress was possible because techniques such as transfer of genes from one species to another are now available in plants and also because some of the photoregulated genes code for abundant products. Prominent among these are gene families encoding light-harvesting chloro-phyll a/b binding proteins (*cab*) and the small subunit of ribulose bisphosphate carboxylase (*rbcS*).

Of particular relevance to the subject of this chapter is that study of gene expression may lead backward through the transduction chain to the primary action of phytochrome. The "handle" on the pathway may be the proteins (*trans*-acting factors) that bind to specific sequences (*cis*-acting elements) upstream from the coding regions of light-regulated genes [Green et al., 1987; Giuliano et al., 1988]. Lam et al. [1989b] used cycloheximide and other inhibitors to implicate synthesis of proteins (the *trans*-acting factors, perhaps) in phytochrome activation of *cab* and *rbcS* in wheat and pea. The inhibitors did not block expression of the same genes introduced into tobacco under con-trol of a constitutive promoter. Lissemore and Quail [1988], in contrast, found that Pfr repressed expression of a phytochrome gene(s) even when protein syn-thesis was blocked.

3. Chromophore and photochemistry. The chromophore of phytochrome is an open tetrapyrrole (Fig. 8). The mechanism for phototransformation is thought to be a Z,E (*cis, trans*) isomerization at the 15,16 C = C double bond [Rüdiger et al., 1983; Thümmler et al., 1983]. These conclusions, until recently, were based on work with chromopeptides rather than native Pr and Pfr. Intact phytochrome has now been studied by resonance Raman spectroscopy [Fodor et al., 1988; Farrens et al., 1989]. Surface-enhanced resonance Raman scat-tering spectra, interpreted with the help of similar studies on model compounds, confirmed the Z,E isomerization for the intact molecule [Farrens et al., 1989].

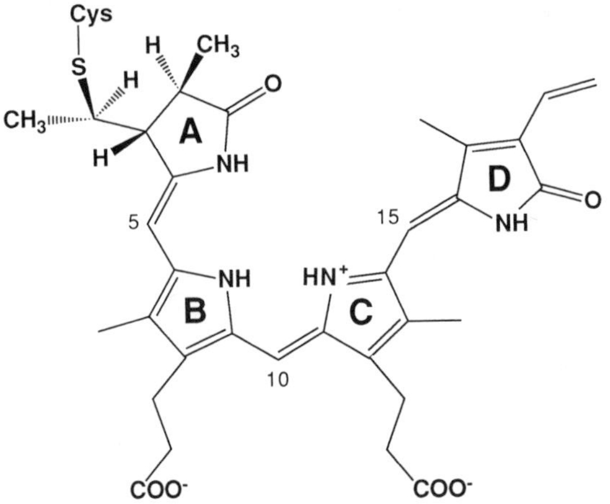

Fig. 8.   Phytochrome chromophore. **A–D** indicate the four rings of the open tetrapyrrole. Current evidence (see text) indicates that the difference between Pr and Pfr is a Z to E isomerization at the 15,16 double bond. The semiextended conformation of the chromophore and protonated state of Pr illustrated here are based on resonance Raman spectroscopy [Fodor et al., 1988; Farrens et al., 1989].

A very rapid, intramolecular proton transfer can also take place, although this is not the primary photoprocess [Song, 1988]. It may be possible to resolve the exact protonation state of both forms, as has been done for Pr [Fodor et al., 1988].

Conversion of Pr to Pfr takes place via a series of unstable photochemical intermediates [Kendrick and Spruit, 1977]. The first products, known as I_{700} or *lumi*-R, are formed within picoseconds and are photoreversible to Pr [Brock et al., 1987]. These relax within microseconds, in a dark reaction, to the next set of intermediates, known as *meta*-R or I_{bl} [Shimazaki et al., 1980; Eilfeld et al., 1987]. The *meta*-R group itself consists of several forms; in the most recent model, *meta*-R_a and *meta*-R_{ac} are in equilibrium, forming a pool that can decay to Pr, as well as to *meta*-R_c, the direct precursor of Pfr [Eilfeld et al., 1989]. Apparently, the conformational changes in the apoprotein (see below) occur at this last step. The *meta*-R_c to Pfr transition would thus mark the creation of a stable physiological signal in the cell [Eilfeld et al., 1989]. The photoconversion scheme for phytochrome can be compared, at least formally, to rhodopsin photocyles (see above).

The formation and decay of intermediates can be followed in physiological experiments with very short (submicrosecond or ns) laser pulses. A significant fraction of phytochrome is expected to be in intermediate states, at very high fluence rates or long irradiation times [Hartmann and Cohnen-Unser,

1972]. This prediction, and the known intermediates, agree with data for laser pulse induction of chloroplast rotation in *Mougeotia* [Haupt and Polacco, 1979], seed germination [Scheuerlein and Braslavsky, 1983], and fern spore germination [Scheuerlein et al., 1988; Scheuerlein and Koller, 1988]. It will also be interesting to compare theory and experiment for a continuous light, rather than pulse-induced, response. One photochemical prediction is that very bright light (sunlight in nature), which leads to a significant population of intermediates, should induce a "shade" response [Casal and Smith, 1989]. Of course this does not occur, and the study of how plants avoid this paradox should yield new information on phytochrome function in green plants.

4. Apoprotein. The photoconversion of the chromophore must be expressed in some way by the apoprotein, which then transduces the signal into the biochemical language of the cell. Immediately upon discovery of phytochrome, purification attempts began [Butler et al., 1959]. The native apoprotein from dark-grown oat seedlings has a molecular mass of 124 kD [Vierstra and Quail, 1983]. Early purification work led to a 60 kD polypeptide, but this, as well as later-purified forms of ~120 kD, were the results of partial proteolysis during isolation. The native 124 kD form, like the in vivo difference spectrum, shows a slightly longer wavelength Pfr maximum than the (approximately) 120 kD form [Everett and Briggs, 1970; Horwitz and Epel, 1977; Vierstra and Quail, 1983]. Isolation in the Pfr form in the presence of protease inhibitors prevents the Pr-specific proteolysis near the N terminus. Undenatured phytochrome can then be purified by poly(ethyleneimine) and ammonium sulfate precipitation and three chromatography steps [Smith and Daniels, 1981; Vierstra and Quail, 1983, 1986]. A modified procedure in which one of the chromatography steps is replaced by ammonium sulfate back-extraction gives high yields and requires half the time to complete [Chai et al., 1987]. Rye phytochrome has also been purified by FPLC [Ernst et al., 1987].

Analysis based on the nucleotide sequence [Hershey et al., 1985], mapping by partial proteolysis and monoclonal antibodies, and the sequence of chromopeptides has established a clear picture of the primary structure of 124 kD *Avena* phytochrome [Vierstra and Quail, 1986]. The polypeptide is 1,128 amino acids long, and the chromophore is attached at Cys-321 via a covalent thioether bond. The distribution of hydrophobic and hydrophilic residues is consistent with the observation that phytochrome behaves as a soluble protein. There is no evidence for transmembrane segments, though there is a hydrophobic "pocket" around the chromophore; the 6 kD peptide that is removed from the N-terminal end by partial proteolysis is hydrophilic and may shield and interact with the chromophore in the Pfr form [Song, 1988].

Although phytochrome is a soluble protein, no one has yet succeeded in crystallizing it so that its structure could be determined by X-ray diffraction. The structure has been visualized at the resolution that can be reached by elec-

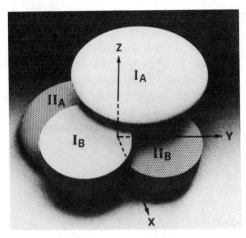

Fig. 9. Model for quaternary structure of phytochrome. Pea phytochrome (Pr form) was studied by small-angle X-ray scattering and by electron microscopy of rotary-shadowed preparations. **I** and **II** represent the two identical polypeptides forming the dimer; **A** is the 59 kD chromophoric, N-terminal domain, and **B** is the 55 kD nonchromophoric domain [Tokutomi et al., 1989]; original print kindly supplied by Dr. S. Tokutomi.

tron microscopy [Jones and Erickson, 1989]. Phytochrome forms dimers in solution, and the most detailed picture thus far of the dimeric structure of phytochrome (Fig. 9) has been obtained by small-angle X-ray scattering [Tokutomi et al., 1989].

Photoconversion leads to a significant conformational change in the apoprotein. Pfr appears just slightly larger than Pr on a size-exclusion column and displays different sensitivities to partial proteolysis, various reagents, and phosphorylation by protein kinases [Wong et al., 1986]. Furthermore, Pfr, under some conditions, can be pelleted from plant extracts [Quail et al., 1973]. While the physiological significance of this pelletability is unclear [see Pratt and Cordonnier, 1989], it does, at the very least, indicate some difference in physical properties. There are monoclonal antibodies with different affinities for the two forms of phytochrome [Cordonnier et al., 1985; Thomas and Penn, 1986], including one very specific for Pr [Holdsworth and Whitelam, 1987]. This implies that different antigenic domains are exposed in Pr and Pfr, again showing that the conformation is different. One of the changes that might be occurring is that the Pfr chromophore is more exposed compared with Pr [Song, 1988; Sommer and Song, 1990]. Evidence for a change in secondary structure comes from far-UV circular dichroism (CD) spectra: A photoreversible increase in ellipticity is observed upon conversion of Pr to Pfr. This corresponds to an increase in α-helicity of the protein, probably in the N-terminal region, which interacts with the chromophore. Chelation of the chromophore with Zn^{2+} reduces the ellipticity [Sommer and Song, 1990]; because the secondary structure modification depends so strongly on the chromophore, it may be functionally significant.

5. Light-labile and light-stable phytochromes. Upon transfer of dark-grown plants to light, a large proportion of phytochrome disappears. Photoconversion to Pfr evidently triggers specific proteolysis of the apoprotein through the ubiquitin pathway [Shanklin et al., 1987]. Not all phytochrome, though, is unstable upon transfer to light. The population of stable phytochrome molecules in green plants differs from the bulk phytochrome of dark-grown seedlings [Shimazaki and Pratt, 1985; Tokuhisa et al., 1985; Tokuhisa and Quail, 1989]. The primary structures of stable and unstable phytochromes are distinct, according to amino acid sequence data for pea [Abe et al., 1989] and gene-specific DNA probes for *Arabidopsis* [Sharrock and Quail, 1989]. In *Arabidopsis,* there are three distinct genes, two of which are expressed in the dark and in the light. It will soon be possible to determine whether the members of the phytochrome gene family encode photoreceptors with different functions, as with human visual pigments (see above). The *Arabidopsis* phytochrome gene expressed in the dark is more homologous to the ''dark'' phytochrome gene from other plants than to the other gene family members in *Arabidopsis* [Sharrock and Quail, 1989].

Mutants affected in specific phytochrome genes would permit one to assign a function to each member of the gene family. Although such mutants have yet to be isolated, certain photomorphogenic mutants are thought to be defective in either the ''etiolated'' or ''green'' phytochromes [Adamse et al., 1988a–c; Chory et al., 1989]. Lower plants may contain different light-stable phytochrome species; phytochrome purification methods have been developed recently for green algae [Kidd and Lagarias, 1990] and for a moss [Lindemann et al., 1989]. There is new evidence for phytochrome control in algal groups not previously studied [Lopez-Figueroa et al., 1989].

6. Transduction following phytochrome photoconversion. The molecular events following formation of Pfr remain to be elucidated. Processes that have been implicated include 1) action at the membrane, 2) action in the nucleus, and 3) signaling via internal messengers. Phytochrome exerts rapid effects on membrane potentials [for reviews, see Quail, 1983; Racusen and Galston, 1983]. The lag times, on the order of seconds, preclude slow biochemical processes between the photoevents and electrical changes. Phytochrome-mediated potential changes are easiest to detect in the etiolated tissues of dark-grown plants [Racusen, 1976]. Red, far-red reversible potential changes would be good indicators of phytochrome function in green tissue were it not for the difficulty in sorting out photosynthetic from phytochrome control [Loppert et al., 1978; Montavon et al., 1983].

Direct action in the nucleus could account for the many influences of phytochrome on gene expression. Animal cell receptors for steroid hormones suggest a model for action in the nucleus [for an introduction to this subject, see Alberts et al., 1989]. An observation that supports such a model for phytochrome action is that purified, undegraded Pfr can activate transcription in nuclei isolated from dark-grown plants [Ernst and Oesterhelt, 1984]. Mösinger et al. [1987] carried this analysis further. In experiments on isolated nuclei, a pulse of red light in vivo induced transient changes in transcription rates for specific genes. A second pulse, given after the effect of the first had begun to decay, increased the duration of the changes in transcription. Exogenously added oat phytochrome (Pfr) simulated the second in vivo irradiation: Transcription of light-harvesting chlorophyll a/b-binding protein (LHCP) sequences increased, and transcription of NADPH-protochlorophyllide oxidoreductase sequences decreased. Positive and negative modulation of these two genes in the same assay provides the strongest evidence for physiological relevance of results obtained with isolated nuclei. Subcellular localization experiments, however, have not demonstrated the presence of phytochrome in nuclei [Nagatani et al., 1988; Mackenzie et al., 1975; Speth et al., 1986].

Signaling pathways that function in animal cells have been proposed to act in photomorphogenesis, notably the phosphoinositide pathway, Ca^{2+} transport, and protein phosphorylation [see Horwitz, 1989]. Turnover of inositol lipids after illumination was detected in isolated pulvini of the tropical tree *Samanea* [Morse et al., 1987]. There was an increase in the level of IP_3, and, correspondingly, a transient decrease in the membrane phosphoinositides phosphatidylinositol 4-phosphate (PIP) and phosphatidylinositol 4,5-bisphosphate (PIP_2). The turgor pressure in pulvini of *Samanea* adjusts the angle of the leaflets and is controlled, at least in part, by phytochrome [Satter et al., 1974]. Phosphoinositide turnover has not been definitively associated with phytochrome, because only white light was used in these studies. In the moss *Ceratodon purpureus*, phytochrome modulated the activity of a phosphoinositide-specific phospholipase C [Hartmann and Pfaffmann, 1990].

Much data have already been presented in favor of the participation of calcium in phytochrome transduction, in particular for unicellular (or filamentous) organisms, which are the most amenable to such experiments [Blatt, 1987]. Examples are chloroplast rotation in the filamentous green alga *Mougeotia* [Haupt, 1982; Wagner and Grolig, 1985; Grolig and Wagner, 1989] and fern spore germination [Wayne and Hepler, 1984]. *Mougeotia* is aquatic, so the flux between inside and outside can be measured [Dreyer and Weisenseel, 1979], and inhibitors can be applied in the bathing solution. Local application of a calcium-specific ionophore to *Mougeotia* filaments promoted chloroplast rotation, replacing red light [Serlin and Roux, 1984]. This experiment provides strong evidence for Ca^{2+} serving as a second messenger. Nevertheless, influx of calcium ions from outside the cell may not be the normal route to an increase in cytosolic free Ca^{2+}. Ca^{2+} entry blockers did not affect light-induced chloroplast movement in *Mougeotia* [Schönbohm et al., 1990]. Evidence in favor of the Ca^{2+} hypothesis in higher plants is provided by studies with wheat protoplasts [Bossen et al., 1988]; red, far-red reversible swelling requires Ca^{2+} and a calcium ionophore mimics the effect of red light. Another system amenable to this kind of experiment is a photoautotrophic soybean cell suspension culture: Expression of chlorophyll a/b binding protein LHC(II) genes is induced by red light and at least partially reversed by far-red light in these cells [Lam et al., 1989a]. Calmodulin antagonists could block the response, yet Ca^{2+} and an ionophore, in this case, substituted only to a very limited extent for red light, so that additional light-dependent steps are likely to be required [Lam et al., 1989a].

The phosphorylation status of several proteins in dark-grown oat seedlings is rapidly modulated by phytochrome [Otto and Schäfer, 1988]. Furthermore, phytochrome can be phosphorylated in vitro by a variety of kinases. There is also evidence, presently controversial, that phytochrome itself has protein kinase activity [Wong et al., 1986; Kim and Song, 1989]. Three mammalian protein kinases, as well as an endogenous polycation-dependent protein kinase, catalyzed phosphorylation of *Avena* phytochrome in vitro [Wong et al., 1986]. The endogenous kinase copurified with phytochrome. The protein kinase activity, however, was separated from phytochrome in two studies [Kim and Song, 1989; Grimm et al., 1989]. The possibility remains that the discrepancy is the result of different purification and assay conditions [Wong et al., 1989]. In any case, the close association of phytochrome and kinase could suggest a functional connection.

B. Phycobiliproteins

The phycobiliproteins may not actually have a sensory role but, because such a role has been proposed in the past, they will be mentioned here. The chromophores, like those of phytochrome, are open tetrapyrroles. In cyanobacteria (prokaryotic, blue-green ''algae'') and in the eukaryotic red algae, macromolecular light-harvesting complexes, the phycobilisomes, contribute to photosynthesis. The phycobiliproteins in the complex, allophycocyanin (APC), phycocyanin (PC), and phycoerythrin (PE), transfer energy to chlorophyll with high efficiency. Many cyanobacteria have the capacity to adjust the levels of PC and PE in such a way that absorption of the incident light is maximized [Bogorad, 1975; Grossman et al., 1986]. In some species, such as *Fremyella diplosiphon*, this complementary chromatic adaptation involves changes in both PC and PE: Red light promotes synthesis of PC, which absorbs maximally at 620 nm, and inhibits PE (absorption maximum 560 nm). Green light has just the reverse effect, inducing PE and repressing PC. Until about

10 years ago, a number of reports accumulated suggesting that the photoreceptor for chromatic adaptation is a photochromic form of APC. In contrast to phytochrome, though, such a photoreversible species could only be detected after denaturation or partial degradation. The controversy [reviewed by Grossman 1990] has been put aside during the recent rapid progress in the study of chromatic adaptation at the molecular level [Oelmueller et al., 1988a,b]. The hypothesis of a single reversible "phycochrome" has still not been excluded, though it is probably not APC. The action spectra, and analogy with phytochrome (though the details differ [Oelmuller et al., 1988a,b]), are compatable with a tetrapyrrole chromophore. Isolation of photomutant cyanobacteria [Cobley and Miranda, 1983; Bruns et al., 1989] should be very helpful in this prokaryotic system: Cloning the gene(s) for the photoreceptor(s) and transducers by phenotypic complementation may be easier than it would be in a plant, as new vectors for gene transfer become available.

C. Chlorophylls

1. Photosynthetic photosystems. Only the sensory, as opposed to energy, converting role of the photosynthetic pigments will be discussed here. Photosystems I and II (PSI and PSII) sense light quality in plants and algae, adjusting their state to optimize photosynthesis. Several thylakoid proteins become phosphorylated when isolated intact chloroplasts are incubated in the light [Bennett, 1983]. The 24 kD and 26 kD light-harvesting chlorophyll a/b–binding proteins of PSII, designated LHC(II), are among the major phosphoproteins, and their surface charge is thought to influence the topography of the photosynthetic membrane [Staehelin and Arntzen, 1983; Canaani et al., 1984]. Phosphorylation of the LHC(II) is sensitive to the redox state of the plastoquinone pool, which is in turn a measure of light quality, because the pigments transferring energy to PSI absorb, on the average, at longer wavelengths than those of PSII. As with phytochrome, red and far-red light have opposing effects; plants appear to have evolved more than one way to measure the red/far-red light ratio. There is evidence that light quality can also modulate gene expression in this way [Glick et al., 1986]. The transduction mechanism is not known, but it has recently been proposed that thylakoid membranes possess a G protein that can respond to the redox state [Millner and Clarkson, 1989]. Another recent, suggestive finding is that LHC(II) kinase activity, as well as a 64 kD polypeptide immune cross-reactive with a G-protein β-subunit, copurified with the cytochrome b_6f complex [Gal et al., 1989].

Cyanobacteria are capable of movements that optimize photosynthesis while avoiding photodamage [Nultsch, 1985]. The two photosystems of photosynthesis, along with their accessory pigments PC and PE, play a sensory role, as indicated by the action spectrum (Fig. 10). The photophobic step-down response of *Phormidium uncinatum* is coupled directly to the photosynthetic

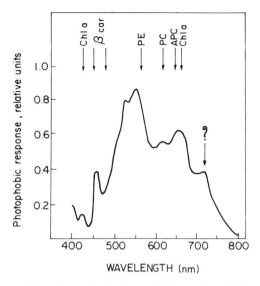

Fig. 10. A sensory role for photosynthetic pigments. The wavelength dependence of the step-down photophobic response of the cyanobacterium *Phormidium uncinatum* is shown, with the positions of the absorption maxima of photosynthetic pigments (in solution) indicated. The shoulder in the far-red does not correspond to any characterized photoreceptor. Chl a, chlorophyll a; PE, phycoerythrin; PC, phycocyanin; APC, allophycocyanin. (Modified from Nultsch, 1985.)

electron transport chain at plastoquinone, via electrical polarization of the cell [Häder, 1974, 1981, 1982; Häder and Poff, 1982]. It will be interesting to see whether any of the transduction pathways in eukaryotes resemble this one. The action spectra do not point to common photoreceptors for photo-movement and for chromatic adaptation (see above). In plants, likewise, chlorophylls are the sensor pigments for energy "spillover" from PSII to PSI, while phototropism and photomorphogenesis are controlled by cryptochrome(s) and phytochrome.

2. Protochlorophyll photoconversion. In the early stages of greening in flowering plants, protochlorophyllide (PChl) serves as the photoreceptor for its own conversion to chlorophyll. The conversion is catalyzed by PChl NADPH oxidoreductase, which binds PChl and can be considered its apoprotein. Chloroplast development requires cooperation of the nuclear and chloroplast genetic compartments, as well as chlorophyll, the photoproduct of PChl [Harpster and Apel, 1985; Batschauer et al., 1986; Oelmuller and Mohr, 1986; Rajasekhar and Mohr, 1986; Taylor, 1989]. Chlorophyll is required for accumulation of at least one nuclear-encoded chloroplast component, LHC(II) [Bennett, 1981]. Thus, at least formally, PChl is a photoreceptor that controls the accumulation of the LHC(II). Whether PChl has other sensory roles, direct or indirect, remains to be seen.

It should not be overlooked that chlorophyll and phytochrome both have tetrapyrrole chromophores, suggesting multiple possibilities for feedback controls. Huang and Castelfranco [1990] propose that there are two pools of the precursor δ-aminolevulinic acid (ALA) and that chlorophyll and the phytochrome chromophore are each derived from a separate pool.

IV. FLAVINS AND PTERINS

A. DNA Photolyase

Although DNA photolyases do not actually intiate a sensory response, it is nevertheless appropriate to open this section with a discussion of these enzymes. As will be apparent from the discussion below [Galland and Senger, 1988b], DNA photolyases confirm the plausibility of some of the speculations and models proposed for the elusive sensory receptors for blue and near-UV light. DNA photolyases catalyze, with high quantum yield, the photo-splitting of pyrimidine dimers to monomers, an important mechanism for DNA repair. The enzyme isolated from *E. coli* contains both flavin [Heelis et al., 1987; Sancar et al., 1987] and a pterin derivative [Wang et al., 1988; Jorns et al., 1990] as chromophores (Figs. 11, 12). The highest quantum yield was found when the flavin was reduced, i.e., in its normal redox state in the cell [Sancar et al., 1987]. It has been proposed that the first singlet state of reduced flavin, $^1FADH_2^*$, functions in catalysis, donating an electron to the pyrimidine dimer. This transfer generates an unstable radical anion that monomerizes, and $FADH_2$ is regenerated following collision with the radical member of the pair of monomers. The excited singlet of the pterin probably serves to harvest light and transfer excitation energy to the flavin [Jorns et al., 1990]. The high efficiency of this transfer, despite the relatively small wavelength shift between pterin and reduced flavin, has not been fully explained. It will be interesting to see whether gene sequence homology searches will uncover any similarities between DNA photolyase and cryptochromes. Flavins and pterins could be used both for DNA photorepair and for photosensory transduction, an elegant, but still speculative, example of Delbrück's "short list" (see Introduction).

B. Cryptochromes (Blue Light Photoreceptors)

1. Chromophore candidates: flavins, pterins, and carotenoids. The blue region of the visible spectrum controls a wide range of events in plants and fungi [Presti and Delbrück, 1978; Senger, 1980, 1984, 1987; Briggs and Iino, 1983; Schmidt, 1984b]. Prominent examples are phototropism in fungi and most plants [Pohl and Russo, 1984; Firn, 1986; Briggs and Baskin, 1988], extension growth rate in plants and fungi [Foster and Lipson, 1973; Gaba and Black, 1985; Cosgrove, 1986, 1988; Cerdá-Olmedo and Lipson, 1987], and

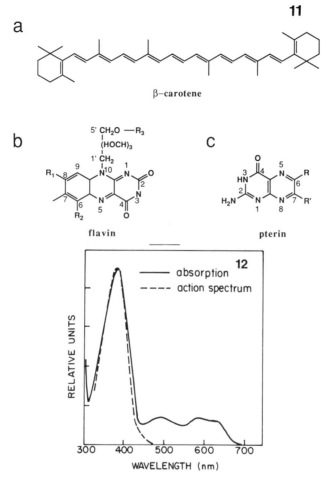

Fig. 11. Structures of chromophores proposed for blue-light photoreceptors (cryptochromes). **a:** β-Carotene. The structure shown (all-*trans*) lacks the UV-A peak found in cryptochrome action spectra. The 15,15′-*cis* isomer has a UV-A band, but it has not been shown to be present in organisms that respond to blue light. **b:** Flavins. In riboflavin, $R_1 = CH_3$, $R_2 = H$, $R_3 = H$. The forms usually found in the cell are riboflavin 5′-phosphate (FMN) or flavin adenine dinucleotide (FMN), in which R_3 is adenosine attached by a phosphodiester linkage. Various natural and synthetic derivatives have substituents at positions 6 or 8. **c:** Pterins. Naturally occurring derivatives of 2-amino-3H-pteridinone (for simplicity, referred to as "pterin") differ mostly in their substituents at positions 6 and 7. In folic acid, for example, $R = p$-amino-benzoylglutamate and $R' = H$. Some derivatives are alkylated at position N(5). The fully oxidized form is shown; successive reduction, to the 7,8-dihydro and 5,6,7,8-tetrahydro forms, alters the UV absorption spectrum.

Fig. 12. Spectra of *E. coli* DNA photolyase. The action spectrum for photorepair of thymidine dimers (dashed line, redrawn from Sancar et al. [1987]) indicates primarily absorption by the pterin chromophore. The absorption spectrum of the purified apoenzyme (redrawn from Jorns et al. [1990]) shows contributions of flavin (reduced and semiquinone forms) and pterin chromophores.

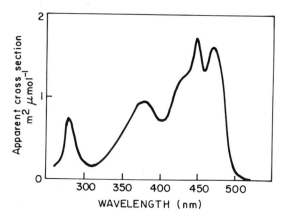

Fig. 13. Typical blue-light action spectrum. This spectrum, for first positive phototropic curvature of alfalfa seedlings, has maxima corresponding to the definition of cryptochrome. Above threshold, first positive curvature increases ("ascending" region, shown here), then decreases ("descending" region). The action spectra for the two regions are similar, but show slightly different fine structure. (Redrawn from Baskin and Iino, 1987.)

carotenoid synthesis and sporulation in fungi [Cerdá-Olmedo, 1985; Gressel and Rau, 1983]. Many action spectra fit into the pigment class known as cryptochrome(s). Typically (Fig. 13), these action spectra have a broad band peaking near 450 nm, with shoulders near 425 and 480 nm and very low activity above 520 nm. An additional broad band near 370 nm has often been found when measurements were extended into the near-UV. These action spectra serve as an operational definition for the pigment class [Gressel, 1980]. Cryptochrome, hidden as its name implies under the large Soret bands of the cytochromes present in any cell, and the nearly ubiquitous carotenoids (not to mention chlorophyll in green plants), has eluded identification by simple comparison of action spectra with absorption spectra. Flavins and carotenoids have been proposed as chromophores, and both can fit the action spectra in the blue [see Galland and Senger, 1988a]. The flavin–carotenoid controversy has been much reviewed [Presti and Delbrück, 1978; Senger, 1980, 1984; Schmidt, 1984b] and, though not completely resolved, will not be repeated here. Most evidence, from carotenoidless mutants, action spectra, and the use of analogs, favors flavins in most, but not all, systems [Schmidt, 1984b; Galland and Senger, 1988a]. For flavins, the fine structure of the action spectra suggests a chromophore environment that enhances the contribution of vibrational levels. In certain blue-light–sensitive organisms, *Phycomyces* in particular, multiple receptor pigments may be operating [Galland and Lipson, 1985].

Both the excited singlet and triplet states of flavins have long enough lifetimes to allow opportunities for photochemistry. Furthermore, the pK of the proton at N5 (see Fig. 11) is increased several units upon excitation from the ground state to the first triplet state [Song, 1968; Schreiner et al., 1975]. Among the reactions that could occur are photosensitized oxidations, electron transfer without the participation of molecular oxygen, and proton exchange [Schmidt, 1987; Song, 1987]. For comparison, it is worth noting that the current view for photocatalysis by DNA photolyase is electron transfer from the excited singlet of (reduced, and thus lacking the blue part of the cryptochrome spectrum) flavin to the pyrimidine dimer [Jorns et al., 1990]. Also suggestive are model systems in which blue light can generate redox or pH gradients across a membrane containing lipid-anchored flavins [Schmidt, 1983, 1984a]. The model consisted of artificial membrane vesicles to which flavins were incorporated by attaching them covalently to hydrocarbon chains. The vesicles were loaded with an electron acceptor (cytochrome c), and an electron donor was supplied outside. Upon illumination with blue light, redox equivalents were carried across the membrane.

Carotenoids (Fig. 11) have fewer possibilities of being primary photoreceptors than flavins. Song [1987] assessed the possibilities based on the most recent assignment of electronic states in carotenoids. His prediction is that carotenoids that act as blue-light photoreceptors should show an action spectrum peak in the red as well. This prediction has not yet been tested systematically by searching for carotenoid photoreceptors in some red/blue-sensitive organisms like the slime mold *Physarum* [Poetsch et al., 1989]. Carotenoids, of course, could act as antenna pigments, as they do in photosynthesis, transferring excitation energy to the photochemically active pigment.

The need to widen the search for chromophores beyond flavins or carotenoids has often been emphasized [Horwitz and Gressel, 1986]. Many blue, near-UV action spectra do not agree with either a flavin or carotenoid cryptochrome spectrum. Blue and near-UV light may be perceived by different chromophores, particularly as they sometimes have opposite effects [Kumagai, 1988]. The reversibility of such systems led to the name "mycochrome," though the blue, near-UV reversibility is probably not a single photochromic system analogous to phytochrome. The blue and near-UV responses in fact have different kinetics and temperature dependence [Kumagai, 1989]. In *Phycomyces* extracts, blue and near-UV caused light-induced absorbance changes in opposite directions, and the effect of near-UV did not decrease with successive exposures, yet near-UV potentiated the effect of a subsequent blue irradiation [Trad et al., 1987]. Hertel [1980] has proposed photoreversible interconversion of the semiquinone and oxidized forms of flavoenzymes; such a photochrome might explain some of the complexities of phototropism.

Galland and Senger [1988b] have recently put forward in detail a hypothesis in which flavin and pterin chromophores could explain many properties of the action spectra for effects of blue and near-UV on plants and microorganisms. The photoreactions catalyzed by DNA photolyase (above) certainly support this idea. Another enzyme containing both flavin and pterin is nitrate reductase [Johnson et al., 1980; Siefermann-Harms et al., 1985]. Nitrate reductase is a large complex that acts as a complete electron transport chain from NADH or NADPH to nitrate. Here, there is no light-driven reaction like in DNA photolyase, but the activity of the dark reaction catalyzed by the enzyme can be photoregulated [Ninnemann, 1987]. Although there is no direct evidence for the participation of the pterin in photoactivation of nitrate reductase, its presence in a light-regulated enzyme is most suggestive. Nitrate reductase is a candidate for cryptochrome in *Neurospora* [Klemm and Ninnemann, 1979], but nitrate reductase–deficient mutants show at least some of the photoresponses [Paietta and Sargent, 1982], raising the usual questions about the specificity of light-induced absorbance changes (see below). The paraflagellar body of the phytoflagellate *Euglena gracilis* is presumed to be its photoreceptor organelle. It has recently been shown that the paraflagellar body contains a pterin chromophore [Galland et al., 1990] in addition to flavin [Benedetti and Lenci, 1977; Lenci and Ghetti, 1989]. Furthermore, four chromoproteins, three pterin-binding and one flavin-binding, were detected by FPLC separation and fluorescence spectra of a paraflagellar body preparation solubilized with 9 M urea [Brodhun and Häder, 1990].

Compared with flavins, relatively little photochemical work has been done for pterins, though this situation may change rapidly. The spectroscopic properties and excited-state chemistry of 2-amino-3H-pteridinone ("pterin"; Fig. 11) have been studied in some detail [Chahidi et al., 1981]. The pterin triplet energy is high enough to allow production of singlet oxygen and to react directly with hydrogen donors such as amino acids. As photosensitizers, pterins are approximately as effective as flavins [Chahidi et al., 1981; Aubailly and Santus, 1986].

2. Blue-light modulation of gene expression. Blue and UV light have been shown to modulate gene expression in a variety of organisms [see Horwitz and Gressel, 1987]. The enzymes of the phenylpropanoid pathway in parsley cell cultures are induced by unknown UV-B receptors, and this was one of the first photoresponses for which transcriptional control was clearly shown [Chappell and Hahlbrock, 1984; Ohl et al., 1989]. These genes are also photoregulated in cell cultures and in intact plants of *Petunia* [Koes et al., 1989]. Several photoreceptors seem to be involved in the intact plant. Changes in gene expression, particularly genes encoding cytoskeletal proteins, precede or accompany morphogenesis in the slime mold *Physarum* [Poetsch et al., 1989]. The carotenogenic enzyme system is induced by blue light in the Ascomycete *Neurospora crassa* [Rau and Rau-Hund, 1977], and a number of unidentified genes are also rapidly photoinduced [Sommer et al., 1989]. The level of mRNA encoded by the recently cloned *al-3* gene in *Neurospora* increased 15-fold within 30 min after exposure to blue light [Nelson et al., 1989]. The *al-3* gene product is one of the carotenoid biosynthetic enzymes: geranylgeranyl pyrophosphate synthetase. In higher plants, of course, analysis of blue-light effects is complicated by phytochrome. Expression of the plastid gene *psbA* in greening *Spirodela* is primarily under blue-light control [Gressel, 1978]. Fluhr and Chua [1986] found that blue light was more effective than red in photoinduction of *rbcS* mRNA in regreening petunia. Blue-light modulation of several nuclear encoded genes, specifically detected against a constant red background light, has been reported for tomato [Oelmuller et al., 1989] and pea [Marrs and Kaufman, 1989; Warpeha et al., 1989]. As for phytochrome, current molecular genetic work is aimed at elucidating the steps between blue-light reception and gene expression. Molecular studies need not await definitive identification of the photoreceptors. The fungal systems are particularly amenable to genetic analysis; *Neurospora*, in particular, is an organism for which much molecular information is already available.

3. Transduction in blue-light responses. All of the transduction and second-messenger possibilities discussed above for phytochrome are under consideration for cryptochrome as well. Unlike phytochrome, speculation as to the mode of action of cryptochromes and other blue/UV photoreceptors is not limited by any knowledge of the apoprotein's amino acid sequence. Indeed, despite the maxima near 280 nm in some action spectra, it is not even certain that there is always an apoprotein. A recent model for phase shifting of the circadian clock in *Neurospora* is that free riboflavin in the cytosol acts as a photosensitizer [Fritz et al., 1989]. Despite our lack of knowledge of what cryptochrome(s) are, some of the blue light-sensitive systems may be excellent models for the study of the transduction chain. Prominent among these are phototropism and the other responses of the Zygomycete fungus *Phycomyces blakesleeanus* [Cerdá-Olmedo and Lipson, 1987]. Phototropism and the light-growth response of *Phycomyces* functions over a wide range of fluences, comparable to that of vision (see above). Adaptation, probably at both the input (photoreceptor) and output (growth), make this possible [Lipson and Block, 1983; Galland, 1989]. As components of the transduction chain for blue light are identified, the biochemical mechanisms of adaptation should be revealed as well. In *Phycomyces* [Galland and Lipson, 1985; Bejarano et al., 1990], as well as in the *Neurospora* [Harding and Turner, 1981; Harding and Melles, 1983; Degli-Innocenti and Russo, 1984] and *Trichoderma harzianum* (Fungi Imperfecti, probably Ascomycete) [Horwitz et al., 1986], there are mutants in photobehavior. Cloning the defective gene in a photoresponse mutant should identify the defective component. While this approach is formally elegant, we note that no phototransduction component has yet been identified in this way in any of the blue light–sensitive organisms. Stomatal guard cells of higher plants have become a model system of choice [Serrano and Zeiger, 1989], in which specific effects of cryptochrome, as well as phytochrome, and photo-synthetic pigments can be studied. The latter two red-light photoreceptors must be carefully distinguished [Holmes and Klein, 1986]. Evidence for a few possible transduction mechanisms is given below, with emphasis on recent data.

a. Membrane action. Blue light has many effects on membrane potentials and extracellular currents in plants, algae, and fungi [for reviews, see Weisenseel and Kicherer, 1981; Blatt, 1987; Horwitz and Gressel, 1987]. Patch-clamp and other studies on stomatal guard cell protoplasts [Assmann et al., 1985; Shimazaki et al., 1986; Serrano et al., 1988] point to a (blue and red) light-modulated electrogenic proton pump in the plasma membrane. A recent study [Spalding and Cosgrove, 1989] suggests that a blue light–induced potential change might transduce photoinhibition of growth in cucumber hypocotyls. Genetic evidence for a link between a membrane potential change and photo-transduction comes from work with *Neurospora*: Electrical properties of mycelia of the photobehavioral mutant *wc-1* were different from those of the wild type, and the mutant lacked the hyperpolarization that normally occurs upon exposure to light [Levina et al., 1988].

b. Redox reactions. Intense blue irradiation can mediate redox reactions, which, with some exceptions, can be attributed to flavin-mediated cytochrome b reduction. Such photoresponses are detected by light-minus-dark difference spectroscopy in vivo or in vitro and are thus referred to as light-induced absorbance changes (LIAC) [Poff and Butler, 1974; Widell and Björn, 1976; Lipson and Presti, 1977; Leong and Briggs, 1982; for reviews, see Senger and Briggs, 1981; Gressel and Rau, 1983; Horwitz, 1989]. LIACs are fairly universal in extracts and indeed in in vitro models; it is difficult to propose that such a general photoreaction is a unique phototransducer [Schmidt, 1984b]. Modification of LIAC spectra or kinetics in mutants, as in *Trichoderma* [Horwitz et al., 1986] may point out the LIACs that are specific to photoreception. If LIACs can be shown to be physiologically relevant, it will be important to identify the next step in transduction. The first clue to such a step might come from the finding that a *ras*-related protein is associated with cytochrome b in human neutrophils [Quinn et al., 1989]. Photoreduction of a b-type cytochrome might trigger a signaling protein (homologous to the *ras* or other G protein classes). The evidence (see above) for G proteins associated with the thyla-koid cytochrome b_6f complex also lends circumstantial support to this speculation. Purification of LIAC components like the b-type cytochromes in plant plasma membranes [Asard et al., 1989] is essential for biochemical identification and confirmation of the importance of LIACs in transduction.

c. Protein phosphorylation. As noted above, second-messenger suggestions for blue-light transduction are parallel to those for phytochrome. One of the pathways for which there has been recent progress is protein phosphorylation. When a membrane fraction from pea stem segments was incubated in vitro with $\gamma\text{-}^{32}$P-ATP, several polypeptides were phosphorylated. A prominent phosphorylated band at 120 kD was not detected when the intact stem segments had received blue light prior to extraction [Gallagher et al., 1988; Short and Briggs, 1990]. The fluence and time dependence suggest that this event is an early step in blue-light transduction. Such events may occur in other blue light–sensitive organisms. When *Trichoderma* extracts were phosphorylated in the light or in the dark, two light-specific species appeared [Gresik et al., 1989]. In *Neurospora* mycelia, in this case radiolabeled in vivo, light induced the dephosphorylation of a 33 kD polypeptide. Photomutants *wc-1* and *wc-2* had altered phosphorylation patterns: in *wc-2*, the 33 kD polypeptide was already dephosphorylated in the dark, while in *wc-1*, two polypeptides, the 33 kD one and a second one of 23 kD, lost their phosphate label following illumination [Lauter and Russo, 1990]. These findings are genetic evidence for involvement of protein phosphorylation in phototransduction, though it is not clear yet how the *wc* gene products are involved, and whether all the phosphoprotein bands migrating at 33 kD are indeed identical polypeptide species.

V. RECEPTOR PIGMENTS IN PROTOZOA

A. Hypericin Pigments: Blepharismin and Stentorin

A novel class of photoreceptor pigments was discovered in the protozoan *Stentor coeruleus* [Walker et al., 1979; Song, 1981, 1983; Song and Poff, 1989] and in *Blepharisma* sp. [Sevenants, 1965; Lenci and Ghetti, 1989; Lenci et al., 1989; Colombetti, 1990]. These pigments, which employ hypericin (Fig. 14) [Durán and Song, 1986] as chromophore, are respectively, stentorin and blepharismin. They serve as the photoreceptors for phototaxis and photophobic responses in these microorganisms. They reside in pigment granules beneath the cell surface. Under strong illumination, these pigments act as photosensitizers for photodynamic action [Yang et al., 1986]. The photoresponses thus help the cells avoid harmful light exposures.

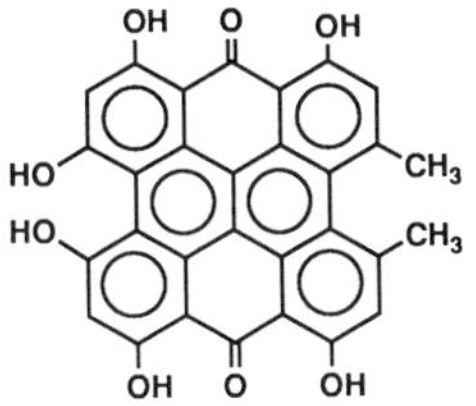

Fig. 14.   Structure of hypericin, the chromophore of stentorin and blepharismin pigments in protozoa. (After Durán and Song [1986].)

In *Stentor*, there are now known to be two forms of the pigment, stentorin I and stentorin II [Kim et al., 1990; Song et al., 1990]. Stentorin I may serve as an antenna pigment or may be nonactive metabolite. Stentorin II, a molecular complex with several polypeptides, is probably the primary photoreceptor. Its absorption and fluorescence spectra correspond to the behavioral action spectra. In this system, there is no evidence to date of photochemical cycles with spectroscopically distinguishable intermediates. The primary photochemical process has been hypothesized to be a proton dissociation leading to proton release to the cytoplasm. The intracellular and/or intraciliary reduction in pH causes a depolarization effect that activates voltage-sensitive calcium channels in the plasma and ciliary membranes. The process is regenerative, because the resulting calcium influx further depolarizes the plasma membrane. Such calcium action potentials are commonly found in ciliated protozoa [Eckert and Naitoh, 1972; Eckert and Brehm, 1979] and generally lead to a reversal of the ciliary beating. In *Stentor*, this is manifested by a photophobic response following light stimulation. The cycle is completed by the extrusion of calcium ions by a calcium pump.

The general photophysiology of *Blepharisma* and the spectroscopy of blepharismin are similar to those for *Stentor* and stentorin. For further details, the reader should consult the reviews cited above.

B. Unidentified Pigments in Protozoa

Colombetti [1990] has recently reviewed photomovement in ciliated protozoa, including *Paramecium* species and *Loxodes*, as well as *Blepharisma*, which was recently reviewed along with *Stentor* by Lenci and Ghetti [1989]. The main photobehaviors studied in these ciliated protozoa are photophobic and photokinetic responses. A particularly interesting case is that of *Paramecium bursaria*, which owes its photosensitivity to a symbiotic species of the photosynthetic alga *Chlorella*. In general, *Paramecium* has been an excellent model microorganism for sensory transduction studies in view of the ability to perform electrophysiological recordings on single cells [Eckert and Naitoh, 1972; Eckert and Brehm, 1979; Kung and Saimi, 1982]. A key feature found in *Paramecium* and related protozoa is a graded calcium action potential (depolarizing) that is closely associated with the reversal of ciliary beating. The avoiding (of obstacles) reaction of *Paramecium tetraurelia*, in particular, has been extensively studied in wild-type and behavioral mutant strains [Kung and Eckert, 1972; Kung et al., 1975; Nelson and Kung, 1978; Saimi et al., 1988]. The relatively limited photobehavioral work on *Paramecium* has yielded a variety of action spectra. The identity of the receptors is unknown. It is unknown too whether the pigments are photochemically active themselves or whether they serve strictly as photosensitizers.

The ciliate *Loxodes* responds both to oxygen gradients and to light. Actually, the photoresponses require oxygen and are inhibited by cyanide (CN^-). The superoxide anion radical (O_2^-) is generated when the pigment of *Loxodes* is illuminated in the presence of oxygen [Colombetti, 1990] and may well play a role in phototransduction.

VI. CONCLUSION

In the Introduction, the short list of photochemically active chromophores found in living systems was given in the form enunciated by Delbrück [1976] and then in an updated version with but four entries: retinal pigments, tetrapyrroles, cryptochromes (flavin and pterin), and hypericin pigments. It is remarkable that the known sensory pigments—as well as energy transducing pigments—can be subsumed in this modest list. Delbrück [1976] termed this situation the "paradox of the short list."

Among the photosensory systems discussed in this chapter, vertebrate visual transduction is the best understood. Visual systems in vertebrate and invertebrate systems employ homologous rhodopsin-like pigments, but the respective transduction processes are notably different. In particular, invertebrate systems exploit the phosphoinositide cascade as opposed to the cGMP-based cascade found universally in the vertebrate photoreceptors. Plants rely on light not only for photosynthesis but also for control of gene expression, growth, and development. The photochemical and molecular properties of phytochrome, the major sensory pigment in higher plants, are now almost as well understood as are those of rhodopsin. The transduction pathways for photomorphogenesis, however, are only beginning to be unraveled. Blue and UV light are sensed by still-unidentified photoreceptors, though flavins are the most likely chromophores for the blue region, with pterins cooperating as photosensitizers in the near-UV.

In the dark reactions following photoexcitation, the transduction processes that have been investigated typically include one or more of the following elements: G proteins, enzyme cascades, internal messengers, gated ion channels, and gene activation. These types of pathways afford ample opportunities for amplification and control. Ancillary processes including sensory adaptation and other forms of feedback regulation confer special advantages in sensory signal handling, especially the ability to manage enormous operating ranges of sensitivity.

It is evident that not only is there an economy of photochemically active receptor pigments, but also there appears to be a limited number of strategies of ancient origin that are used repeatedly for the transduction processes following photoexcitation. Those processes are not unique to phototransduction.

The commonality between phototransduction and signal transduction in general has been made abundantly clear by the surprising discovery that rhodopsin and the β-adrenergic receptor are homologous and therefore of common evolutionary origin. This finding is reinforced by the similarities in the signaling pathways for these light and hormone receptors.

ACKNOWLEDGMENTS

Both authors wish to acknowledge support from a grant from the United States–Israel Binational Science Foundation. E.L. is grateful to the Compton Fund of the Technion for support during a semester in Israel when this chapter was written. We are indebted to Kenneth Foster, Pill-Soon Song, and Walther Stoeckenius for comments on the manuscript and to Robert Birge for providing computer assistance for some of the figures.

VII. REFERENCES

Abe H, Takio K, Titani K, Furuya M (1989) Amino-terminal amino acid sequence analysis of pea phytochrome II fragments obtained by limited proteolysis. Plant Cell Physiol 30:1089–1097.

Adamse P, Jaspers P, Bakker J, Kendrick R, Koornneef M (1988a) Photophysiology and phytochrome content of long-hypocotyl mutant and wild-type cucumber seedlings. Plant Physiol 87:264–268.

Adamse P, Jaspers P, Bakker J, Wesselius J, Heeringa G, Kendrick R, Koornneef M (1988b) Photophysiology of a tomato mutant deficient in labile phytochrome. J Plant Physiol 133:436–440.

Adamse P, Kendrick RE, Koornneef M (1988c) Photomorphogenetic mutants of higher plants. Photochem Photobiol 48:833–841.

Alam M, Lebert M, Oesterhelt D, Hazelbauer GL (1989) Methyl-accepting taxis proteins in *Halobacterium halobium*. EMBO J 8:631–639.

Alberts B, Bray D, Lewis J, Raff M, Roberts K, Watson JD (1989) Cell signalling. In Alberts B, Bray D, Lewis J, Raff M, Roberts K, Watson JD (eds): Molecular Biology of the Cell. New York: Garland, pp 681–726.

Applebury ML, Hargrave PA (1986) Molecular biology of the visual pigments. Vision Res 26:1881–1895.

Asard H, Venken M, Caubergs R, Reijinders W, Oltmann FL, DeGreef JA (1989) *b*-Type cytochromes in higher plant plasma membranes. Plant Physiol 90:1077–1083.

Assmann SM, Simoncini L, Schroeder JI (1985) Blue light activates electrogenic ion pumping in guard cell protoplasts of *Vicia faba*. Nature 318:285–287.

Aubailly M, Santus R (1986) Oxidations photosensitized by pterins and diaminopterins. In Cooper BA, Whitehead VM (eds): Chemistry and Biology of Pterines 1986. Pteridines and Folic Acid Derivatives. Berlin: de Gruyter, pp 99–102.

Autrum H (1979) Introduction. In Autrum H (ed): Comparative Physiology and Evolution of Vision in Invertebrates. Handbook of Sensory Physiology, Volume 7, No. 6A. Berlin: Springer-Verlag, pp 1–22.

Baehr W, Falk JD, Bugra K, Triantafyllos JT, McGinnis JF (1988) Isolation and analysis of the mouse opsin gene. FEBS Lett 238:253–256.

Bagley KA, Eisenstein L, Ebrey TG (1989) A comparative study of the infrared difference spectra for octopus and bovine rhodopsins and their bathorhodopsin photointermediates. Biochemistry 28:3366–3372.

Baskin TI, Iino M (1987) An action spectrum in the blue and ultraviolet for phototropism in alfalfa. Photochem Photobiol 46:127–136.

Batschauer A, Mosinger E, Kreuz K, Dorr I, Apel K (1986) The implication of a plastid-derived factor in the transcriptional control of nuclear genes encoding the light-harvesting chlorophyll a/b protein. Eur J Biochem 154:625–634.

Baylor DA, Lamb TD, Yau K-W (1979) Responses of retinal rods to single photons. J Physiol 288:613–634.

Becker RS (1988) The visual process: Photophysics and photoisomerization of model visual pigments and the primary reaction. Photochem Photobiol 48:369–399.

Bejarano ER, Avalos J, Lipson ED, Cerdá-Olmedo E (1990) Photoinduced accumulation of carotene in Phycomyces. Planta 183:1–9.

Bendich A, Olson JA (1989) Biological actions of carotenoids. FASEB J 3:1927–1932.

Benedetti PA, Lenci F (1977) In vivo microspectrofluorometry of photoreceptor pigments in *Euglena gracilis*. Photochem Photobiol 26:315–318.

Bennett J (1981) Biosynthesis of the light-harvesting chlorophyll a/b protein. Eur J Biochem 118:61–70.

Bennett J (1983). Regulation of photosynthesis by reversible phosphorylation of the light-harvesting chlorophyll a/b protein. Biochem J 212:1–13.

Berg HC (1988) A physicist looks at bacterial chemotaxis. Cold Spring Harbor Symp Quant Biol 53:1–9.

Berridge MJ (1987) Inositol trisphosphate and diacylglycerol: Two interacting second messengers. Annu Rev Biochem 56:159–193.

Berridge MJ, Irvine RF (1984) Inositol trisphosphate, a novel second messenger in cellular signal transduction. Nature 312:315–321.

Berridge MJ, Irvine RF (1989) Inositol phosphates and cell signalling. Nature 341:197–205.

Berridge MJ, Taylor CW (1988) Inositol trisphosphate and calcium signaling. Cold Spring Harbor Symp Quant Biol 53:927–933.

Birge RB (1990) Nature of the primary photochemical events in rhodopsin and bacteriorhodopsin. Biochim Biophys Acta 1016:293–327.

Birnbaumer L (1990) G proteins in signal transduction. Annu Rev Pharmacol Toxicol 30:675–705.

Bitensky MW, Whalen MM, Torney DC (1988) Life, evolution, and the pursuit of single photon sensitivity. Cold Spring Harbor Symp Quant Biology 53:303–311.

Blanck A, Oesterhelt D, Ferrando E, Schegk ES, Lottspeich F (1989) Primary structure of sensory rhodopsin I, a prokaryotic photoreceptor. EMBO J 8:3963–3971.

Blatt MR (1987) Toward the link between membranes, transport and photoperception in plants. Photochem Photobiol 45:933–938.

Bloomquist B, Shortridge R, Schneuwly S, Perdew M, Montell C, Steller H, Rubin G, Pak W (1988) Isolation of a putative phospholipase C gene of Drosophila *norpA*, and its role in phototransduction. Cell 54:723–733.

Bogomolni RA, Spudich JL (1982) Identification of a third rhodopsin-like pigment in phototactic *Halobacterium halobium*. Proc Natl Acad Sci USA 79:6250–6254.

Bogomolni RA, Taylor ME, Stoeckenius W (1984) Reconstitution of purified halorhodopsin. Proc Natl Acad Sci USA 81:5408–5411.

Bogorad L (1975) Phycobiliproteins and complementary chromatic adaptation. Annu Rev Plant Physiol 26:369–401.

Borthwick HA, Hendricks SB (1960) Photoperiodism in plants. Science 132:1223–1228.

Bossen M, Dassen H, Kendrick R, Vredenberg W (1988) The role of calcium ions in phytochrome-controlled swelling of etiolated wheat (*Triticum aestivum* L.) protoplasts. Planta 174:94–100.

Boynton R (1979) Human Color Vision. New York: Holt, Rinehart and Winston.

Brainman MS, Rothschild KJ (1988) Fourier transform infrared techniques for probing membrane protein structure. Annu Rev Biophys Bioeng 17:541–570.

Briggs WR, Baskin TI (1988) Phototropism in higher plants—Controversies and caveats. Botan Acta 101:133–139.

Briggs WR, Iino M (1983) Blue light-absorbing photoreceptor in plants. Philos Trans R Soc Lond [Biol] 303:347–359.

Briggs WR, Mandoli DF, Shinkle JR, Kaufman LS, Watson JC, Thompson WF (1985) Phytochrome regulation of plant development at the whole plant, physiological, and molecular levels. In Colombetti G, Lenci F, Song P-S (eds): Sensory Perception and Transduction in Aneural Organisms. New York: Plenum, pp 265–280.

Brock H, Ruzsicska BP, Arai T, Schlammann W, Holzwarth AR, Braslavsky SE, Schaffner K (1987) Fluorescence lifetimes and relative quantum yields of 124-kilodalton oat phytochrome in H_2O and D_2O solutions. Biochemistry 26:1412–1417.

Brodhun B, Häder D-P (1990) Photoreceptor proteins and pigments in the paraflagellular body of the flagellate, *Euglena gracilis*. Photochem Photobiol 52:865–871.

Brown JE, Rubin LJ, Ghalayini AJ, Tarver AP, Irvine RF, Berridge MJ, Anderson RE (1984) *myo*-Inositol polyphosphate may be a messenger for visual excitation in *Limulus* photoreceptors. Nature 311:160–163.

Bruns BU, Briggs WR, Grossman AR (1989) Molecular characterization of phycobilisome regulatory mutants of *Fremyella diplosiphon*. J Bacteriol 171:901–908.

Butler WL, Norris KH, Siegelman HW, Hendricks SB (1959) Detection, assay, and preliminary purification of the pigment controlling photoresponsive development of plants. Proc Natl Acad Sci USA 45:1703–1708.

Callender R (1982) An introduction to visual pigments and purple membranes and their primary processes. In Alfano RR (ed): Biological Events Probed by Ultrafast Laser Spectroscopy. New York: Academic Press, pp 239–258.

Callender R, Honig B (1977) Resonance Raman studies of visual pigments. Annu Rev Biophys Bioeng 6:33–55.

Canaani O, Barber J, Malkin S (1984) Evidence that phosphorylation and dephosphorylation regulate the distribution of excitation energy between the two photosystems of photosynthesis in vivo: Photoacoustic and fluorimetric study of an intact leaf. Proc Natl Acad Sci USA 81:1614–1618.

Casal JJ, Smith H (1989) The function, action and adaptive significance of phytochrome in light-grown plants. Plant Cell Environ 12:855–862.

Cerdá-Olmedo E (1985) Carotene mutants of *Phycomyces*. Methods Enzymol 110:220–243.

Cerdá-Olmedo E, Lipson ED (eds) (1987) *Phycomyces*. Cold Spring Harbor, NY: Cold Spring Harbor Laboratory.

Cervetto L, Lagnado L, Perry RJ, Robinson DW, McNaughton PA (1989) Extrusion of calcium from rod outer segments is driven by both sodium and potassium gradients. Nature 337:740–743.

Chabre M, Bigay J, Bruckert F, Bornancin F, Deterre P, Pfister C, Vuong TM (1988) Visual signal transduction: The cycle of transducin shuttling between rhodopsin and cGMP phosphodiesterase. Cold Spring Harbor Symp Quant Biol 53:313–324.

Chahidi C, Aubailly A, Momzikoff A, Bazin M, Santus R (1981) Photophysical and photosensitizing properties of 2-amino-4-pteridinone: A natural pigment. Photochem Photobiol 33:641–649.

Chai YG, Singh BR, Song PS, Lee J, Robinson GW (1987) Purification and spectroscopic properties of 124-kda oat phytochrome. Anal Biochem 163:322–330.

Chappell J, Hahlbrock K (1984) Transcription of plant defence genes in response to UV light or fungal elicitor. Nature 311:76–78.

Chory J, Peto CA, Ashbaugh M, Saganich R, Pratt L, Ausubel F (1989) Different roles for phytochrome in etiolated and green plants deduced from characterization of *Arabidopsis thaliana* mutants. Plant Cell 1:867–880.

Cobley JG, Miranda RD (1983) Mutations affecting chromatic adaptation in the cyanobacterium *Fremyella diplosiphon*. J Bacteriol 153:1486–1492.

Colbert JT, Hershey HP, Quail PH (1983) Autoregulatory control of translatable phytochrome mRNA levels. Proc Natl Acad Sci USA 80:2248–2252.

Colombetti G (1990) New trends in photobiology: Photomotile responses in ciliated protozoa. J Photochem Photobiol, [Biol]4:243–259.

Colombetti G, Lenci F, Song P-S (eds.) (1985) Sensory Perception and Transduction in Aneural Organisms. New York: Plenum Press.

Cordonnier M-M, Greppin H, Pratt LH (1985) Monoclonal antibodies with differing affinities to the red absorbing and far-red absorbing forms of phytochrome. Biochemistry 24:3246–3253.

Cosgrove DJ (1986) Photomodulation of growth. In Kendrick RE, Kronenberg GHM (eds): Photomorphogenesis in Plants. Dordrecht, Netherlands: Martinus Nijhoff/Junk, pp 159–183.

Cosgrove DJ (1988) Mechanism of rapid suppression of cell expansion in cucumber hypocotyls after blue-light irradiation. Planta 176:109–116.

Cowman AF, Zuker CS, Rubin GM (1986) An opsin gene expressed in only one photoreceptor cell type of the *Drosophila* eye. Cell 44:705–710.

Crouch RK (1986) Studies of rhodopsin and bacteriorhodopsin using modified retinals. Photochem Photobiol 44:803–808.

Degli-Innocenti F, Russo VEA (1984) Isolation of new white collar mutants of *Neurospora crassa* and studies on their behavior in the blue light-induced formation of protoperithecia. J Bacteriol 159:757–761.

DeGrip WJ (1988) Recent chemical studies related to vision. Photochem Photobiol 48:799–810.

DeGrip WJ, Gray D, Gillespie J, Bovee PHM, Van den Berg EMM, Lugtenberg J, Rothschild KJ (1988) Photoexcitation of rhodopsin: Conformation changes in the chromophore, protein and associated lipids as determined by FTIR difference spectroscopy. Photochem Photobiol 48:497–504.

Deigner PS, Law WC, Rando RR (1989) Membrane as the energy source in the endergonic transformation of vitamin A to 11-*cis*-retinol. Science 244:968–971.

Delbrück M (1976) Light and life III. Carlsberg Res Commun 41:299–309.

Deterre P, Bigay J, Forquet F, Robert M, Chabre M (1988) cGMP phosphodiesterase of retinal rods is regulated by two inhibitory subunits. Proc Natl Acad Sci USA 85:2424–2428.

Dixon RAF, Kobilka BK, Strader DJ, Benovic JL, Dohlman HG, Frielle T, Bolanowski MA, Bennett CD, Rands E, Diehl RE, Mumford RA, Slater EE, Sigal IS, Caron MG, Lefkowitz RJ, Strader CD (1986) Cloning of the gene and cDNA for mammalian β-adrenergic receptor and homology with rhodopsin. Nature 321:75–79.

Doukas AG, Junnarkar MR, Alfano RR, Callender RH, Balogh-Nair V (1985) The primary event in vision investigated by time-resolved fluorescence spectroscopy. Biophys J 47:795–798.

Dratz EA (1989) Vision. In Smith KC (ed): The Science of Photobiology. New York: Plenum Press, pp 231–271.

Dratz EA, Hargrave PA (1983) The structure of rhodopsin and the rod outer segment disk membrane. Trends Biochem Sci 8:128–131.

Dreyer EM, Weisenseel MH (1979) Phytochrome-mediated uptake of calcium in *Mougeotia* cells. Planta 146:31–39.

Drumm-Herrel H (1987) Blue light control of pigment biosynthesis–anthocyanin biosynthesis. In Senger H (ed): Blue Light Responses: Phenomena and Occurrence in Plants and Microorganisms. Boca Raton, FL: CRC Press, Inc., pp 65–74.

Dryja TP, McGee TL, Reichel E, Hahn LB, Cowley GS, Yandell DW, Sandberg MA, Berson EL (1990) A point mutation of the rhodopsin in one form of retinitis pigmentosa. Nature 343:364–366.

Dumler IL, Korolkov SN, Garnovskaya MN, Parfenova DV, Etingof RN (1989) The systems of photo- and pheremone signal transduction in unicellular eukaryotes. J Protein Chem 8:387–389.

Durán N, Song P-S (1986) Hypericin and its photodynamic action. Photochem Photobiol 43:677–680.

Ebrey TG, Frauenfelder H, Honig B, Nakanishi K (eds) (1987) Biophysical studies of retinal proteins. Urbana: University of Illinois Press.

Eckert R, Brehm P (1979) Ionic mechanisms of excitation in Paramecium. Annu Rev Biophys Bioeng 8:353–358.

Eckert R, Naitoh Y (1972) Bioelectric control of locomotion in the ciliates. J Protozool 19:237–243.

Eilfeld PH, Eilfeld PG, Vogel J, Maurer R (1987) Evidence for a sequential pathway from P_r to P_{fr} of the phototransformation of 124-kDa oat phytochrome. Photochem Photobiol 45:825–830.

Eilfeld P, Eilfeld P, Vogel J, Maurer R (1989) Laser-flash photolysis of 124 kDa oat phytochrome: Studies concerning the late steps of P_{fr} formation. J Photochem Photobiol [Biol] 3:209–222.

Ernst D, Oesterhelt D (1984) Purified phytochrome influences in vitro transcription in rye nuclei. EMBO J 3:3075–3078.

Ernst D, Vojacek R, Oesterhelt D (1987) Purification of phytochrome from rye by fast protein liquid chromatography. Photochem Photobiol 45:859–862.

Everett MS, Briggs WR (1970) Some spectral properties of pea phytochrome in vivo and in vitro. Plant Physiol 45:679–683.

Eyring G, Mathies R (1979) Resonance Raman studies of bathorhodopsin: Evidence for a protonated Schiff base linkage. Proc Natl Acad Sci USA 76:33–37.

Farrens DL, Holt RE, Rospendowski BN, Song PS, Cotton TM (1989) Surface-enhanced resonance Raman scattering spectroscopy applied to phytochrome and its model compounds. 2. Phytochrome and phycocyanin chromophores. J Am Chem Soc 111:9162–9169.

Fein A, Payne R, Corson DW, Berridge MJ, Irvine RF (1984) Photoreceptor excitation and adaptation by inositol 1,4,5-triphosphate. Nature 311:157–160.

Fein A, Szuts EZ (1982) Photoreceptors: Their Role in Vision. Cambridge: Cambridge University Press.

Firn RD (1968) Phototropism. In Kendrick RE, Kronenberg GHM (eds): Photomorphogenesis in Plants. Dordrecht, Netherlands: Martinus Nijhoff/Junk, pp 367–388.

Fluhr R, Chua N-H (1986) Developmental regulation of two genes encoding ribulose-bisphosphate carboxylase small subunit in pea and transgenic petunia plants: Phytochrome response and blue-light induction. Proc Natl Acad Sci USA 83:2358–2362.

Fodor SPA, Lagarias JC, Mathies RA (1988) Resonance Raman spectra of the P_r-form of phytochrome. Photochem Photobiol 48:129–136.

Förster T (1951) Fluoreszenz organischer Verbindungen. Göttingen: Vandenhoeck und Ruprecht.

Foster KW, Lipson E (1973) The light growth response of Phycomyces. J Gen Physiol 62:590–617.

Foster K, Saranak J, Derguini F, Jayathirtha V, Zarrilli G, Okabe M, Fang J-M, Shimizu N, Nakanishi K (1988a) Rhodopsin activation: A novel view suggested by in vivo Chlamydomonas experiments. J Am Chem Soc 110:6588–6589.

Foster K, Saranak J, Derguini F, Zarilli G, Johnson R, Okabe M, Nakanishi K (1989) Activation of Chlamydomonas rhodopsin in vivo does not require isomerization of retinal. Biochemistry 28:819–824.

Foster KW, Saranak J, Dowben PA (1991) Spectral sensitivity, structure, amd activation of eukaryotic rhodopsins: Activation spectroscopy of rhodopsin analogs in Chlamydomonas. J Photochem Photobiol [Biol] 8:385–408.

Foster KW, Saranak J, Patel N, Zarilli G, Okabe M, Kline T, Nakanishi K (1984) A rhodopsin is the functional protoreceptor for phototaxis in the unicellular eukaryote *Chlamydomonas*. Nature 311:756–759.

Foster K, Saranak J, Zarrilli G (1988b) Autoregulation of rhodopsin in *Chlamydomonas reinhardtii*. Proc Natl Acad Sci USA 85:6379–6383.

Foster KW, Smyth RD (1980) Light antennas in phototactic algae. Microbiol Rev 44:572–630.

Franceschini N, Kirschfeld K, Minke B (1981) Fluorescence of photoreceptor cells observed in vivo. Science 213:1264–1267.

Fritz BJ, Kasai S, Matsui K (1989) Free cellular riboflavin is involved in phase shifting by light of the circadian clock in *Neurospora crassa*. Plant Cell Physiol 30:557–564.

Furuya M (ed) (1987) Phytochrome and Photoregulation in Plants. Tokyo: Academic Press.

Gaba V, Black M (1985) Photocontrol of hypocotyl elongation in light-grown *Cucumis satiavus* L. Planta 164:264–271.

Gal A, Mor TS, Hauska G, Ohad I (1989) LHCII kinase activity associated with isolated b6f complex. Physiol Plant 76:A154.

Gallagher S, Short TW, Ray PM, Pratt LH, Briggs WR (1988) Light-mediated changes in two proteins found associated with plasma membrane fractions from pea stem sections. Proc Natl Acad Sci USA 85:8003–8007.

Galland P (1989) Photosensory adaptation in plants. Botan Acta 102:11–20.

Galland P (1990) Phototropism of the *Phycomyces* sporangiophore: A comparison with higher plants. Photochem Photobiol 52:233–248.

Galland P, Keiner P, Dornemann D, Senger H, Brodhun B, Hader DP (1990) Pterin-like and flavin-like fluorescence associated with isolated flagella of *Euglena gracilis*. Photochem Photobiol 51:675–680.

Galland P, Lipson ED (1985) Modified action spectra of photogeotropic equilibrium in *Phycomyces blakesleeanus* mutants with defects in genes *madA*, *madB*, *madC*, and *madH*. Photochem Photobiol 41:331–335.

Galland P, Senger H (1988a) The role of flavins as photoreceptors. J Photochem Photobiol [Biol] 1:277–294.

Galland P, Senger H (1988b) The role of pterins in the photoreception and metabolism of plants. Photochem Photobiol 48:811–820.

Gilbert W (1978) Why genes in pieces? Nature 271:501.

Gilbert W (1987) The exon theory of genes. Cold Spring Harbor Symp Quant Biol 52:901–905.

Gilman AG (1987) G proteins: Transducers of receptor-generated signals. Annu Rev Biochem 56:615–649.

Giuliano G, Pichersky E, Malik VS, Timko MP, Scolnik PA, Cashmore AR (1988) An evolutionarily conserved protein binding sequence upstream of a plant light-regulated gene. Proc Natl Acad Sci USA 85:7089–7093.

Glick RE, McCauley SW, Gruissem W, Melis A (1986) Light quality regulates expression of chloroplast genes and assembly of photosynthetic membrane complexes. Proc Natl Acad Sci USA 83:4287–4291.

Goldsmith TH, Bernard GD (1985) Visual pigments of invertebrates. Photochem Photobiol 42:805–810.

Green PJ, Kay SA, Chua N-H (1987) Sequence-specific interactions of a pea nuclear factor with light-responsive elements upstream of the rbcS-3A gene. EMBO J 6:2543–2549.

Gresik M, Kolarova N, Farkas V (1989) Light-stimulated phosphorylation of proteins in cell-free extracts from *Trichoderma viride*. FEBS Lett 248:185–187.

Gressel J (1978) Light requirements for the enhanced synthesis of a plastid mRNA during *Spirodela* greening. Photochem Photobiol 27:167–169.

Gressel J (1980) Blue light and transcription. In Senger H (ed): The Blue Light Syndrome. Berlin: Springer-Verlag, pp 133–153.

Gressel J, Rau W (1983) Photocontrol of fungal development. In Shropshire W Jr, Mohr H (eds): Photomorphogenesis. Springer-Verlag, pp 603–639.

Grimm R, Gast D, Rüdiger W (1989) Characterization of a protein kinase activity associated with phytochrome from etiolated oat (*Avena sativa* L.) seedlings. Planta 178:199–206.

Grolig F, Wagner G (1989) Characterization of the isolated calcium-binding vesicles from the green alga *Mougeotic scalaris,* and their relevance to chloroplast movement. Planta 177:169–177.

Grossman AR (1990) Chromatic adaptation and the events involved in phycobilisome biosynthesis. Plant Cell Environ 13:651–666.

Grossweiner LI (1989a) Photochemistry. In Smith KC (ed): The Science of Photobiology. New York: Plenum Press, pp 47–78.

Grossweiner LI (1989b) Photophysics. In Smith KC (ed): The Science of Photobiology. New York: Plenum Press, pp 1–45.

Häder D-P (1974) Participation of two photosystems in the photo-phobotaxis of *Phormidium uncinatum.* Arch Microbiol 96:255–266.

Häder D-P (1981) Electrical and proton gradients in the sensory transduction of photophobic responses in the blue-green alga, *Phormidium uncinatum.* Arch Microbiol 130:83–86.

Häder D-P (1982) Gated ion fluxes involved in photophobic responses of the blue-green alga, *Phormidium uncinatum.* Arch Microbiol 131:77–80.

Häder D-P, Poff KL (1982) Spectrophotometric measurement of plastoquinone photoreduction in the blue-green alga, *Phormidium uncinatum.* Arch Microbiol 131:347–350.

Häder D-P, Tevini M (1987) General Photobiology. Oxford: Pergamon Press.

Hagins WA, Yoshikami S (1974) A role for Ca^{++} in excitation of retinal rods and cones. Exp Eye Res 18:299–305.

Hagins WA, Yoshikami S (1977) Intracellular transmission of visual excitation in photoreceptors: Electrical effects of chelating agents introduced into rods by vesicle fusion. In Barlow HB, Fatt P (eds): Vertebrate Photoreception. New York: Academic Press, pp 97–138.

Hakki S, Sitaramayya A (1990) Guanylate cyclase from bovine rod outer segments: Solubilization, partial purification, and regulation by inorganic pyrophosphate. Biochemistry 29:1088–1094, 1990.

Hall ZW (1987) Three of a kind: The β-adrenergic receptor, the muscarinic acetylcholine receptor, and rhodopsin. Trends Neurosci 10:99–101.

Hara T (ed) (1988) Molecular physiology of Retinal Proteins. Osaka, Japan: Yamada Science Foundation.

Harding RW, Melles S (1983) Genetic analysis of phototropism of *Neurospora crassa* perithecial beaks using white collar and albino mutants. Plant Physiol 72:996–1000.

Harding RW, Turner RV (1981) Photoregulation of the carotenoid biosynthetic pathway in albino and white collar mutants of *Neurospora crassa.* Plant Physiol 68:745–749.

Hargrave PA, McDowell JH, Curtis DR, Wang JK, Juszczak E, Fong E, Mohana SL, Rao JK, Argos P (1983) The structure of bovine rhodopsin. Biophys Struct Mech 9:235–244.

Harpster M, Apel K (1985) The light-dependent regulation of gene expression during plastid development in higher plants. Physiol Plant 64:147–152.

Hartmann E, Pfaffmann H (1990) Phosphatidylinositol and phytochrome-mediated phototropism of moss protonemal tip cells. In Morre DJ, Boss WF, Loewus (eds): Inositol Metabolism in Plants. New York: Wiley-Liss, pp 259–275.

Hartmann E, Weber M (1988) Storage of the phytochrome-mediated phototropic stimulus of moss protonemal tip cells. Planta 175:39–49.

Hartmann KM (1966) A general hypothesis to interpret "high energy phenomena" of photomorphogenesis on the basis of phytochrome. Photochem Photobiol 5:349–366.

Hartmann KM, Cohnen-Unser I (1972) Analytical action spectroscopy with living systems: Photochemical aspects and attenuance. Ber Deut Bot Ges 85:481–551.

Haupt W (1982) Light-mediated movement of chloroplasts. Annu Rev Plant Physiol 33:205–233.

Haupt W, Feinleib ME (eds) (1979) Physiology of Movements. Berlin: Springer-Verlag.

Haupt W, Polacco E (1979) Phytochrome-mediated response in *Mougeotia* to very short laser flashes. Plant Sci Lett 17:67–73.

Hecht S, Schlaer S, Pirenne MH (1942) Energy, quanta and vision. J Gen Physiol 25:819–840.

Heelis PF, Payne G, Sancar A (1987) Photochemical properties of *Escherichia coli* DNA photolyase: Selective photodecomposition of the second chromophore. Biochemistry 26:4634–4640.

Hegemann P, Marwan W (1988) Single photons are sufficient to trigger movement responses in *Chlamydomonas reinhardtii*. Photochem Photobiol 48:99–106.

Henderson R, Baldwin JM, Downing KH, Lepault J, Zemlin F (1986) Structure of purple membrane from *Halobacterium halobium*: Recording, measurement, and evaluation of electron micrographs at 3.5 Å resolution. Ultramicroscopy 19:147–178.

Henderson R, Unwin PNT (1975) Three-dimensional model of purple membrane obtained by electron microscopy. Nature 257:28–32.

Hepler PK, Wayne RO (1985) Calcium and plant development. Ann Rev Plant Physiol 36:397–439.

Hershey HP, Barker RF, Idler KB, Lissermore JL, Quail PH (1985) Analysis of cloned cDNA and genomic sequences for phytochrome: Complete amino acid sequences for two gene products expressed in etiolated *Avena*. Nucleic Acids Res 13:8543–8558.

Hertel R (1980) Phototropism of lower plants. In Lenci F, Colombetti G (eds): Photoreception and Sensory Transduction in Aneural Organisms. New York: Plenum Press, pp 89–105.

Hildebrand E, Schimz A (1990) The lifetime of photosensory signals in *Halobacterium halobium* and its dependence on protein methylation. Biochim Biophys Acta 1052:96–105.

Ho YK, Hingorani VN, Navon SE, Fung BKK (1989) Transducin—A signaling switch regulated by guanine nucleotides. Curr Topics Cell Regul 30:171–202.

Hodgkin AL, Nunn BJ (1988) Control of light-sensitive current in salamander rods. J Physiol [Lond] 403:439–471.

Holdsworth ML, Whitelam GC (1987) A monoclonal antibody specific for the red-absorbing form of phytochrome. Planta 172:539–547.

Holmes MG, Klein WH (1986) Photocontrol of dark circadian rhythms in stomata of *Phaseolus vulgaris* L. Plant Physiol 82:28–33.

Horwitz BA (1989) 12. The potential for second messengers in light signaling. In Boss WF, Morre DJ (eds): Second Messengers in Plant Growth and Development. New York: Alan R. Liss, Inc., pp 289–313.

Horwitz BA, Epel BL (1977) A far-red form of phytochrome exhibiting in vivo spectral properties: Studies with crude extracts of oats and squash. Plant Sci Lett 9:205–210.

Horwitz BA, Gressel J (1986) Properties and working mechanisms of the photoreceptors. In Kendrick RE, Kronenberg GH (eds): Photomorphogenesis in Plants. Dordrecht, Netherlands: Martinus Nijhoff/Junk, pp 159–183.

Horwitz BA, Gressel J (1987) First measurable effects following photoinduction of morphogenesis. In Senger H (ed): Blue Light Responses: Phenomena and Occurrence in Plants and Microorganisms. Boca Raton, FL: CRC Press, Inc., pp 53–70.

Horwitz BA, Trad CH, Lipson ED (1986) Modified light-induced absorbance changes in *dimY* photoresponse mutants of *Trichoderma*. Plant Physiol 81:726–730.

Huang L, Castelfranco PA (1990) Regulation of 5-aminolevulinic acid (ALA) synthesis in developing chloroplasts. Plant Physiol 92:172–178.

Hurley J (1987) Molecular properties of the cGMP cascade of vertebrate photoreceptors. Annu Rev Physiol 49:793–812.

Hurley JB, Simon MI, Teplow DB, Robishaw JD, Gilman AG (1984) Homologies between signal transducing G proteins and *ras* gene products. Science 226:860–862.

Iwabe N, Kuma K, Saitou N, Tsuda M, Miyata T (1989) Evolution of rhodopsin supergene

54   Lipson and Horwitz

family: Independent divergence of visual pigments in vertebrates and insects and possibly in mollusks. Proc Jpn Acad Ser B 65:195–198.

Jenkins GI (1988) Photoregulation of gene expression in plants. Photochem Photobiol 48:821–832.

Johnson JC, Hainlive BE, Rajagopalan KV (1980) Characterization of the molybdenum cofactor of sulfite oxidase, xanthine oxidase and nitrate reductase: Identification of a pteridine as a structural component. J Biol Chem 255:1783–1786.

Jones AM, Erickson HP (1989) Domain structure of phytochrome from *Avena sativa* visualized by electron microscopy. Photochem Photobiol 49:479–483.

Jorns MS, Wang BY, Jordan SP, Chanderkar LP (1990) Chromophore function and interaction in *Escherichia coli* DNA photolyase: Reconstitution of the apoenzyme with pterin and/or flavin derivatives. Biochemistry 29:552–561.

Karpen JW, Zimmerman AL, Stryer L, Baylor DA (1988) Molecular mechanics of the cyclic-GMP–activated channel of retinal rods. Cold Spring Harbor Symp Quant Biol 53:325–332.

Kaupp UB, Niidome T, Tanabe T, Terada S, Bönigk W, Stühmer W, Cook N, Kangawa K, Matsuo H, Hirose T, Miyata T, Numa S (1989) Primary structure and functional expression from complementary DNA of the rod photoreceptor cyclic GMP-gated channel. Nature 342:762–766.

Kendrick RE, Kronenberg GHM (eds) (1986) Photomorphogenesis in Plants. Dordrecht, Netherlands: Martinus Nijhoff.

Kendrick RE, Spruit CJP (1977) Phototransformations of phytochrome. Photochem Photobiol 26:201–214, 1977.

Kidd DG, Lagarias JC (1990) Phytochrome from the green alga *Mesotaenium caldariorum*—purification and preliminary characterization. J Biol Chem 265:7029–7035.

Kim I-H, Rhee JS, Huh JW, Florell S, Faure B, Lee KW, Kahsai T, Song P-S, Tamai N, Yamazaki T, Yamazaki I (1990) Structure and function of the photoreceptor stentorins in *Stentor coeruleus*. I. Partial characterization of the photoreceptor organelle and stentorins. Biochim Biophys Acta 1040:43–57.

Kim IS, Song P-S (1989) A purified 124-kDa oat phytochrome does not possess a protein kinase activity. Photochem Photobiol 49:319–324.

Kirkwood A, Weiner D, Lisman JE (1989) An estimate of the number of G regulatory proteins activated per excited rhodopsin in living *Limulus* ventral photoreceptors. Proc Natl Acad Sci USA 86:3872–3876.

Kirschfeld K (1985) Sensitizing pigments and their significance for vision. In Gilles R, Balthazart J (eds): Neurobiology. Berlin: Springer-Verlag, pp 375–386.

Kitagawa T, Maeda A (1989) Vibrational structure of rhodopsin and bacteriorhodopsin. Photochem Photobiol 50:883–894.

Klemm E, Ninnemann H (1979) Nitrate reductase—A key enzyme in blue light-promoted conidiation and absorbance change of *Neurospora*. Photochem Photobiol 29:629–632.

Koch K-W, Stryer L (1988) Highly cooperative feedback control of retinal guanylate cyclase by calcium ions. Nature 334:64–66.

Koes RE, Spelt CE, Mol JNM (1989) The chalcone synthase multigene family of *Petunia hybrida* (V30): Differential, light-regulated expression during flower development and UV light induction. Plant Mol Biol 12:213–225.

Koutalos Y, Ebrey TG (1986) Recent progress in vertebrate photoreception. Photochem Photobiol 44:809–817.

Krinsky NI (1989) β-Carotene—Functions. In Spiller GA, Scala J (eds): New Protective Roles for Selected Nutrients. New York: Alan R. Liss, Inc., pp 1–15.

Kruizinga B, Stavenga DG (1990) Fluorescence spectra of blowfly metaxanthopsins. Photochem Photobiol 51:197–201.

Kuhlemeier C, Green PJ, Chua N-H (1987) Regulation of gene expression in higher plants. Annu Rev Plant Physiol 38:221–257.

Kumagai T (1988) Photocontrol of fungal development. Photochem Photobiol 47:889–896.

Kumagai T (1989) Temperature and mycochrome system in near-UV light inducible and blue light reversible photoinduction of conidiation in *Alternaria tomato*. Photochem Photobiol 50:793–798.

Kung C, Chang SY, Satow Y, Van Houten J, Hansma H (1975) Genetic dissection of behavior in *Paramecium*. Science 188:898–904.

Kung C, Eckert R (1972) Genetic modification of electric properties in an excitable membrane. Proc Natl Acad Sci USA 69:93–97.

Kung C, Saimi Y (1982) The physiological basis of taxes in *Paramecium*. Annu Rev Physiol 44:519–534.

Lagarias JC (1985) Progress in the molecular analysis of phytochrome. Photochem Photobiol 42:811–820.

Lagarias JC, Kelly JM, Cyr KL, Smith WO Jr (1987) Comparative photochemical analysis of highly purified 124 kilodalton oat and rye phytochromes in vitro. Photochem Photobiol 46:5–13.

Lam E, Benedyk M, Chua N-H (1989a) Characterization of phytochrome-regulated gene expression in a photoautotrophic cell suspension: Possible role for calmodulin. Mol Cell Biol 9:4819–4823.

Lam E, Green PJ, Wong M, Chua N-H (1989b) Phytochrome activation of two nuclear genes requires cytoplasmic protein synthesis. EMBO J 8:2777–2783.

Lanyi JK (1984) Bacteriorhodopsin and related light-energy converters. In Ernster L (ed): Bioenergetics. Amsterdam: Elsevier, pp 315–335.

Lanyi JK (1990) Halorhodopsin, a light-driven electrogenic chloride-transport system. Physiol Rev 70:319–330.

Lauter FR, Russo VEA (1990) Light-induced dephosphorylation of a 33-kDa protein in the wild-type strain of *Neurospora crassa*—The regulatory mutants *wc-1* and *wc-2* are abnormal. J Photochem Photobiol [Biol] 5:95–103.

Lefkowitz RJ, Benovic JL, Kobilka B, Caron MG (1986) β-Adrenergic receptors and rhodopsin: Shedding new light on an old subject. Trends Pharmac Sci 7:444–448.

Lenci F, Colombetti G (eds) (1980) Photoreception and Sensory Transduction in Aneural Organisms. New York: Plenum Press.

Lenci F, Ghetti F (1989) Photoreceptor pigments for photomovement of microorganisms: Some spectroscopic and related studies. J Photochem Photobiol [Biol] 3:1–6.

Lenci F, Ghetti F, Gioffré D, Passarelli V, Heelis PF, Thomas B, Phillips GO, Song P-S (1989) Effects of the molecular environment on some spectroscopic properties of *Blepharisma* photoreceptor pigment. J Photochem Photobiol [Biol] 3:449–454.

Leong T, Briggs WR (1982) Evidence from studies with acifluorfen for participation of a flavincytochrome complex in blue light photoreception for phototropism of oat coleoptiles. Plant Physiol 70:875–881.

Lerea CL, Buntmilam AH, Hurley JB (1989) α-Transducin is present in blue-sensitive greensensitive and red-sensitive cone photoreceptors in the human retina. Neuron 3:367–376.

Levina N, Belozerskaya T, Kritsky M, Potapova T (1988) Photoelectrical responses of *Neurospora crassa* mutant white collar 1. Exp Mycol 12:77–79.

Levitzki A (1990) GTP–GDP exchange proteins. Science 248:794.

Liebman PA, Parker KR, Dratz EA (1987) The molecular mechanism of visual excitation and its relation to the structure and composition of the rod outer segment. Annu Rev Physiol 49:765–791.

Lindemann P, Braslavsky SE, Hartmann E, Schaffner K (1989) Partial purification and initial characterization of phytochrome from the moss *Atrichum undulatum* P. Beauv. grown in the light. Planta 178:436–442.

Lipson ED, Block SM (1983) Light and dark adaptation in *Phycomyces* light-growth response. J Gen Physiol 81:845–859.

Lipson ED, Presti D (1977) Light-induced absorbance changes in *Phycomyces* photomutants. Photochem Photobiol 25:203–208.

Lissemore JL, Quail PH (1988) Rapid transcriptional regulation by phytochrome of the genes for phytochrome and chlorophyll a/b-binding protein in *Avena sativa*. Mol Cell Biol 8:4840–4850.

Lochrie MA, Hurley JB, Simon MI (1985) Sequence of the α subunit of photoreceptor G protein: Homologies between transducin, *ras*, and elongation factors. Science 228:96–100.

Lopez-Figueroa F, Perez R, Niell FX (1989) Effects of red and far-red light pulses on the chlorophyll and biliprotein accumulation in the red alga *Corallina elongata*. J Photochem Photobiol [Biol] 4:185–194.

Loppert H, Kronberger W, Kandeler R (1978) Phytochrome-mediated changes in the membrane potential of subepidermal cells of *Lemna paucicostata* 6746. Planta 138:133–136.

Mackenzie JMJ, Coleman RA, Briggs WR, Pratt LH (1975) Reversible redistribution of phytochrome within the cell upon conversion to its physiologically active form. Proc Natl Acad Sci USA 72:799–803.

Mancinello AL (1986) Comparison of spectral properties of phytochromes from different preparations. Plant Physiol 82:956–961.

Mancinelli AL, Rabino I (1978) The "high irradiance responses" of plant photomorphogenesis. Botan Rev 44:129–180.

Marrs KA, Kaufman LS (1989) Blue-light regulation of transcription for nuclear genes in pea. Proc Natl Acad Sci USA 86:4492–4495.

Martin RL, Wood C, Baehr W, Applebury ML (1986) Visual pigment homologies revealed by DNA hybridization. Science 232:1266–1269.

Marwan W, Schäfer W, Oesterhelt D (1990) Signal transduction in *Halobacterium* depends on fumarate. EMBO J 9:355–362.

Matthews HR, Murphy RL, Fain GL, Lamb TD (1988) Photoreceptor light adaptation is mediated by cytoplasmic calcium concentration. Nature 334:67–69.

McRee DE, Tainer JA, Meyer TE, Beeumen JV, Cusanovich MA, Getzoff ED (1989) Crystallographic structure of a photoreceptor protein at 2.4 Å resolution. Proc Natl Acad Sci USA 86:6533–6537.

Melkonian M, Robenek H (1980) Eyespot membranes of *Chlamydomonas reinhardtii*: A freeze-fracture study. J Ultrastruc Res 72:90–102.

Melkonian M, Robenek H (1984) The eyespot apparatus of flagellated green algae: A critical review. In Round F, Chapman DJ (eds): "Progress in Phycological Research." Bristol: Biopress, pp 193–268.

Meyer TE, Fitch JC, Bartsch RG, Tollin G, Cusanovich MA (1990) Soluble cytochromes and a photoactive yellow protein isolated from the moderately halophilic purple phototrophic bacterium, *Rhodospirillum salexigens*. Biochim Biophys Acta 1016:364–370.

Meyer TE, Yakali E, Cusanovich MA, Golin G (1987) Properties of a water-soluble, yellow protein isolated from a halophilic phototrophic bacterium that has photochemical activity analogous to sensory rhodopsin. Biochemistry 26:418–423.

Millner PA, Clarkson J (1989) Characterisation of a guanine nucleotide binding protein associated with the thylakoid membrane. Physiol Plant 76:A174.

Mohr H (1972) Lectures on Photomorphogenesis. Berlin: Springer.

Mollon JD, Sharpe LT (1983) Colour Vision. New York: Academic Press.

Montavon M, Horwitz BA, Greppin H (1983) Far-red light-induced changes in intracellular potentials of spinach mesophyll cells. Plant Physiol 73:671–676.

Montell C (1989) Molecular genetics of *Drosophila* vision. BioEssays 11:43–48.

Montell C, Jones K, Zuker C, Rubin GM (1987) A second opsin gene expressed in the ultraviolet-sensitive R7 photoreceptor cells of *Drosophila melanogaster*. J Neurosci 7:1558–1566.

Morse MJ, Crain RC, Satter RL (1987) Light-stimulated phosphatidylinositol turnover in *Samanea saman* leaf pulvini. Proc Natl Acad Sci USA 84:7075–7078.

Mösinger E, Batschauer A, Vierstra R, Apel K, Schäfer E (1987) Comparison of the effects of exogenous native phytochrome and in-vivo irradiation on in-vitro transcription in isolated nuclei from barley (*Hordeum vulgare*). Planta 170:505–514.

Nagatani A, Jenkins GI, Furuya M (1988) Non-specific association of phytochrome to nuclei during isolation from dark-grown pea (*Pisum sativum* cv. Alaska) plumules. Plant Cell Physiol 29:1141–1145.

Nagy F, Kay SA, Chua N-H (1988) Gene regulation by phytochrome. Trends Genet 4:37–42.

Nakatani K, Yau K-W (1988) Calcium and light adaptation in retinal rods and cones. Nature 334:69–71.

Nathans J (1989a) Molecular biology of visual pigments. Annu Rev Neurosci 10:163–194.

Nathans J (1989b) The genes for color vision. Sci Am 260:42–49.

Nathans J (1990) Determinants of visual pigment absorbance—Role of charged amino acids in the putative transmembrane segments. Biochemistry 29:937–942.

Nathans J, Davenport DM, Maumenee IH, Lewis RA, Hejtmancik JF, Litt M, Lovrien E, Weleber R, Bachynski B, Zwas F, et al. (1989) Molecular genetics of blue cone monochromaticity. Science 245:831–838.

Nathans J, Hogness D (1983) Isolation, sequence analysis, and intron–exon arrangement of the gene encoding bovine rhodopsin. Cell 34:807–814.

Nathans J, Hogness D (1984) Isolation and nucleotide sequence of the gene encoding human rhodopsin. Proc Natl Acad Sci USA 81:4851–4855.

Nathans J, Piantanida TP, Eddy RL, Shows TB, Hogness DS (1986a) Molecular genetics of inherited variation in human color vision. Science 232:203–210.

Nathans J, Thomas D, Hogness DS (1986b) Molecular genetics of human color vision: The genes encoding blue, green, and red pigments. Science 232:193–210.

Nelson DL, Kung C (1978) Behavior of *Paramecium*: Chemical, physiological and genetic studies. In Hazelbauer GL (ed): Taxis and Behavior. London: Chapman and Hall, pp 77–100.

Nelson MA, Morelli G, Caratolli A, Romano N, Macino G (1989) Molecular cloning of a *Neurospora crassa* carotenoid biosynthetic gene (Albino-3) regulated by blue light and the products of the white collar genes. Mol Cell Biol 9:1271–1276.

Ninnemann H (1987) Photoregulation of eukaryotic nitrate reductase. In Senger H (ed): Blue Light Responses: Phenomena and Occurrence in Plants and Microorganisms. Boca Raton, FL: CRC Press, pp 17–29.

Nultsch W (1983) The photocontrol of movement in *Chlamydomonas*. In Cosens DJ, Vince-Prue D (eds): The Society for Experimental Biology Symposium XXXVI. Cambridge: Cambridge University Press, pp 521–539.

Nultsch W (1985) Photosensing in cyanobacteria. In Colombetti G, Lenci F, Song P-S (eds): Sensory Perception and Transduction in Aneural Organisms. New York: Plenum Press, pp 147–165.

58   Lipson and Horwitz

Nultsch W, Häder D-P (1988) Photomovement in motile microorganisms—II. Photochem Photobiol 47:837–869.

Nultsch W, Throm G, von Rimscha I (1971) Phototaktische Untersuchungen an *Chlamydomonas reinhardtii* Dangeard in homokontinuierlicher Kultur. Arch Microbiol 90:47–58.

Oelmueller R, Conley PB, Federspiel N, Briggs WR, Grossman AR (1988a) Changes in accumulation and synthesis of transcripts encoding phycobilisome components during acclimation of *Fremyella diplosiphon* to different light qualities. Plant Physiol 88:1077–1083.

Oelmuller R, Grossman A, Briggs W (1988b) Photoreversibility of the effect of red and green light pulses on the accumulation in darkness of mRNAs coding for phycocyanin and phycoerythrin in *Fremyella diplosiphon*. Plant Physiol 88:1084–1091.

Oelmuller R, Kendrick RE, Briggs WR (1989) Blue-light mediated accumulation of nuclear-encoded transcripts coding for proteins of the thylakoid membrane is absent in the phytochrome-deficient *aurea* mutant of tomato. Plant Mol Biol 13:223–232.

Oelmuller R, Mohr H (1986) Photooxidative destruction of chloroplasts and its consequences for expression of nuclear genes. Planta 167:106–113.

Oesterhelt D, Stoeckenius W (1971) Rhodopsin-like protein from the purple membrane of *Halobacterium holobium*. Nature 133:149–152.

Oesterhelt D, Stoeckenius W (1973) Functions of a new photoreceptor membrane. Proc Natl Acad Sci USA 70:2853–2857.

Oesterhelt D, Tittor J (1989) Two pumps, one principle: Light-driven ion transport in Halobacteria. Trends Biochem Sci 14:57–61.

Ohl S, Hahlbrock K, Schafer E (1989) A stable blue-light-derived signal modulates ultraviolet-light–induced activation of the chalcone-synthase gene in cultured parsley cells. Planta 177:228–236.

O'Tousa, Baehr W, Martin RL, Hirsh J, Pak WL, Applebury MW (1985) The *Drosophila ninaE* gene codes an opsin. Cell 40:839–850.

Otto V, Schäfer E (1988) Rapid phytochrome-controlled protein phosphorylation and dephosphorylation in *Avena sativa* L. Plant Cell Physiol 29:1115–1121.

Otto V, Mösinger E, Sauter M, Schäfer E (1983) Phytochrome control of its own synthesis in *Sorghum vulgare* and *Avena sativa*. Photochem Photobiol 38:693–700.

Ovchinnikov YA, Abduaev NG, Feigina MY, Artamonov ID, Bogachuk ID, Zolotarev AS, Eganyan ER, Kostetkii PV (1983) Visual rhodopsin. 3. Total amino-acid sequence and arrangement in the membrane. Bioorg Khim 9:1331–1340.

Ovchinnikov YA, Abdulaev NG, Zolotarev AS, Artamonov ID, Bespalov IA, Dergachev AE, Tsuda M (1988) Octopus rhodopsin: Amino acid sequence deduced from cDNA. FEBS Lett 232:69–72.

Ovchinnikov YuA (ed) (1987a) Retinal Proteins. Utrecht: VSP.

Ovchinnikov YuA (1987b) Structure of rhodopsin and bacteriorhodopsin. Photochem Photobiol 45:909–914.

Owen WG (1987) Ionic conductances in rod photoreceptors. Annu Rev Physiol 49:743–764.

Paietta J, Sargent ML (1982) Blue light responses in nitrate reductase mutants of *Neurospora crassa*. Photochem Photobiol 35:853–855.

Pak W, O'Tousa J (1988) Molecular analysis of visual pigment genes. Photochem Photobiol 47:877–882.

Payne R, Flores TM, Fein A (1990) Feedback inhibition by calcium limits the release of calcium by inositol trisphosphate in *Limulus* ventral photoreceptors. Neuron 4:547–555.

Penn RD, Hagins WA (1972) Kinetics of the photocurrent of retinal rods. Biophys J 12:1073–1094.

Piantanida T (1988) The molecular genetics of color vision and color blindness. Trends Genet 4:319–323.

Poetsch B, Schreckenbach T, Werenskiold A (1989) Photomorphogenesis in *Physarum poly-*

cephalum: Temporal expression pattern of actin, α- and β-tubulin. Eur J Biochem 179:141–146.

Poff KL, Butler WL (1974) Absorbance changes induced by blue light in *Phycomyces blakesleeanus* and *Dictyostelium discoideum*. Nature 248:799–801.

Pohl U, Russo VEA (1984) Phototropism. In Colombetti G, Lenci F (eds): Membranes and Sensory Transduction. New York: Plenum, pp 231–329.

Pratt LH, Cordonnier MM (1989) Photomorphogenesis. In Smith KC (ed): The Science of Photobiology. New York: Plenum, pp 273–304.

Presti D, Delbrück M (1978) Photoreceptors for biosynthesis, energy storage and vision. Plant Cell Environ 1:81–100.

Pugh E, Altman J (1988) A role for calcium in adaptation. Nature 334:16–17.

Pugh EN (1987) The nature and identity of the internal excitational transmitter of vertebrate phototransduction. Annu Rev Physiol 49:715–741.

Quail PH (1983) Rapid action of phytochrome in photomorphogenesis. In Shropshire W Jr, Mohr H (eds): Photomorphogenesis. Berlin: pp 178–212.

Quail PH, Marme D, Schäfer E (1973) Particle-bound phytochrome from maize and pumpkin. Nature [New Biol] 245:189–191.

Quinn MT, Parkos CA, Walker L, Orkin SH, Dinauer MC, Jesaitis AJ (1989) Association of a *ras*-related protein with cytochrome b of human neutrophils. Nature 342:198–200.

Racusen RH (1976) Phytochrome control of electrical potentials and intercellular coupling in oat-coleoptile tissue. Planta 132:25–29.

Racusen RH, Galston AW (1983) Developmental significance of light-mediated electrical responses in plant tissue. In Shropshire W Jr, Mohr H (eds): Photomorphogenesis. Berlin: Springer-Verlag, pp 687–703.

Rajasekhar VK, Mohr H (1986) Appearance of nitrite reductase in cotyledons of the mustard (*Sinapsis alba* L.) seedling as affected by nitrate, phytochrome and photooxidative damage of plastids. Planta 168:369–376.

Rau W, Rau-Hund A (1977) Light-dependent carotenoid synthesis. Planta 136:49–52.

Rüdiger W, Thümmler F, Cmiel E, Schneider S (1983) Chromophore structure of the physiologically active form (P_{fr}) of phytochrome. Proc Natl Acad Sci USA 80:6244–6248.

Saimi Y, Martinac B, Gustin MC, Culbertson MR, Adler J, Kung C (1988) Ion channels in *Paramecium*, yeast, and *Escherichia coli*. Cold Spring Harbor Symp Quant Biol 53: 667–673.

Sakmar TP, Franke RR, Khorana HG (1989) Glutamic acid-113 serves as the retinylidene Schiff base counterion in bovine rhodopsin. Proc Natl Acad Sci USA 86:8309–8313.

Sancar GB, Jorns MS, Payne G, Fluke DJ, Rupert CS, Sancar A (1987) Action mechanism of *Escherichia coli* DNA photolyase. J Biol Chem 262:492–498.

Sancar A, Smith FW, Sancar GB (1984) Purification of *Escherichia coli* DNA photolyase. J Biol Chem 259:6028–6023.

Satter RL, Geballe GT, Galston AW (1974) Potassium flux and leaf movement in *Samanea saman*. II. Phytochrome-controlled movement. J Gen Physiol 64:431–442.

Schäfer E (1975) A new approach to explain the ''high irradiance responses'' of photomorphogenesis on the basis of phytochrome. J Math Biol 2:41–56.

Schäfer E, Briggs WR (1986) Photomorphogenesis from signal perception to gene expression. Photobiochem Photobiophys 12:305–320.

Schegk ES, Oesterhelt D (1988) Isolation of a prokariotic photoreceptor: Sensory rhodopsin from Halobacteria. EMBO J 7:2925–2933.

Scheuerlein R, Braslavsky SE (1983) Induction of seed germination in *Lactuca sativa* L. by nanosecond dye laser flashes. Photochem Photobiol 109:319–345.

Scheuerlein R, Inoue Y, Furuya M (1988) Intermediates in the photoconversion of functional phytochrome in fern spores of *Dryopteris*—II. In vivo kinetics of the decay of I700 and of the formation of P_{fr} studied with a double-laser apparatus. Photochem Photobiol 48:519–524.

Scheuerlein R, Koller D (1988) Intermediates in the photoconversion of functional phytochrome in fern spores of *Dryopteris*—I. Demonstration and quantitative characterization of the photochromic system P_r I700 using nanosecond-laser pulses. Photochem Photobiol 48:511–518.

Schilde C (1968) Schnelle photoelektrische Effekte der Algae *Acetabularia*. Z Naturforsch 23:1369–1376.

Schimz A (1981) Methylation of membrane proteins is involved in chemosensory and photosensory behavior of *Halobacterium halobium*. FEBS Lett 125:205–207.

Schimz A, Hildebrand E (1987) Effects of cGMP, calcium and reversible methylation on sensory signal processing in halobacteria. Biochim Biophys Acta 923:222–232.

Schmidt W (1983) Further photophysical and photochemical characterization of flavins associated with single-shelled vesicles. J Membr Biol 76:73–82.

Schmidt W (1984a) Bluelight-induced, flavin-mediated transport of redox equivalents across artificial bilayer membranes. J Membr Biol 82:113–122.

Schmidt W (1984b) Bluelight physiology. Bioscience 34:698–704.

Schmidt W (1987) Primary reactions and optical spectroscopy of blue light photoreceptors. In Senger H (ed): Blue Light Responses: Phenomena and Occurrence in Plants and Microorganisms. Boca Raton, FL: CRC Press, pp 19–36.

Schönbohm E, Meyerwegener J, Schönbohm E (1990) No evidence for Ca^{2+} influx as an essential link in the signal transduction chains of either light-oriented chloroplast movements or P_{fr}-mediated chloroplast anchorage in *Mougeotia*. J Photochem Photobiol [Biol] 5:331–341.

Schreiner S, Steiner U, Kramer HEA (1975) Determination of the pK values of the lumiflavin triplet state by flash photolysis. Photochem Photobiol 21:81–84.

Seki T (1984) Metaretinochrome in membranes as an effective donor of 11-*cis*-retinal for the synthesis of squid rhodopsin. J Gen Physiol 84:49–62.

Senger H (ed) (1980) The Blue Light Syndrome. Berlin: Springer-Verlag.

Senger H (ed) (1984) Blue Light Effects in Biological systems. Berlin: Springer-Verlag.

Senger H (ed) (1987) Blue Light Responses: Phenomena and Occurrence in Plants and Microorganisms. Vols. I. and II. Boca Raton, FL: CRC Press.

Senger H, Briggs WR (1981) The blue light receptor(s): Primary reactions and subsequent metabolic changes. In Smith KC (ed): Photochemical and Photobiological Reviews. New York: Plenum pp 1–38.

Serlin BS, Roux SJ (1984) Modulation of chloroplast movement in the green alga *Mougeotia* by the Ca^{++} ionophore A23187 and by calmodulin antagonists. Proc Natl Acad Sci USA 81:6368–6372.

Serrano E, Zeiger E, Hagiwara S (1988) Red light stimulates an electrogenic proton pump in *Vicia* guard cell protoplasts. Proc Natl Acad Sci USA 85:436–440.

Serrano EE, Zeiger E (1989) Sensory transduction and electrical signaling in guard cells. Plant Physiol 91:795–799.

Sevenants MR (1965) Pigments of *Blepharisma undulans* compared with hypericin. J Protozool 12:240–245.

Shanklin J, Jabben M, Vierstra RD (1987) Red light–induced formation of ubiquitin-phytochrome conjugates: Identification of possible intermediates of phytochrome degradation. Proc Natl Acad Sci USA 84:359–363.

Sharrock RA, Quail PH (1989) Novel phytochrome sequences in *Arabidopsis thaliana*—Structure, evolution, and differential expression of a plant regulatory photoreceptor family. Genes Dev 3:1745–1757.

Shichi H (1983) Biochemistry of Vision. New York: Academic Press.

Shimazaki K, Iino M, Zeiger E (1986) Blue light–dependent proton extrusion by guard-cell protoplasts of *Vicia faba*. Nature 319:324–326.

Shimazaki Y, Inoe Y, Yamamoto KT, Furuya M (1980) Phototransformation of the red-light–absorbing form of undegraded pea phytochrome by laser flash excitation. Plant Cell Physiol 21:1619–1625.

Shimazaki Y, Pratt LH (1985) Immunochemical detection with rabbit polyclonal and mouse monoclonal antibodies of different pools of phytochrome from etiolated and green *Avena* shoots. Planta 164:333–344.

Short TW, Briggs WR (1990) Characterization of a rapid, blue light-mediated change in detectable phosphorylation of a plasma membrane protein from etiolated pea (*Pisum sativum* L.) seedlings. Plant Physiol 92:179–185.

Shropshire W Jr, Mohr H (eds) (1983) Photomorphogenesis. Berlin: Springer-Verlag.

Siefermann-Harms D, Fritz B, Ninnemann H (1985) Evidence for a pterin-derivative associated with the molybdenum cofactor of *Neurospora crassa* nitrate reductase. Photochem Photobiol 42:771–778.

Sineshchekov OA, Litvin FF, Keszthelyi L (1990) Two components of photoreceptor potential in phototaxis of the flagellated green alga *Haematococcus pluvialis*. Biophys J 57:33–39.

Smith H, Casal JJ, Jackson GM (1990) Reflection signals and the perception by phytochrome of the proximity of neighbouring vegetation. Plant Cell Environ 13:73–78.

Smith KC (ed) (1989) The Science of Photobiology, 2nd ed. New York: Plenum Press.

Smith WO, Daniels SM (1981) Purification of phytochrome by affinity chromatography on agarose-immobilized Cibacron blue 3GA. Plant Physiol 68:443–446.

Smyth RD, Saranak J, Foster KW (1988) Algal visual systems and their photoreceptor pigments. Prog Phycol Res 6:225–286.

Sommer D, Song P-S (1990) Chromophore topography and secondary structure of 124-kilodalton *Avena* phytochrome probed by Zn^{2+}-induced chromophore modification. Biochemistry 29:1943–1948.

Sommer T, Chambers JAA, Eberle J, Lauter FR, Russo VEA (1989) Fast light-regulated genes of *Neurospora crassa*. Nucleic Acids Res 17:5713–5723.

Song P-S (1968) On the basicity of the excited state of flavins. Photochem Photobiol 7:311–313.

Song P-S (1981) Photosensory transduction in *Stentor coeruleus* and related organisms. Biochim Biophys Acta 639:1–29.

Song P-S (1983) Protozoan and related photoreceptors: Molecular aspects. Annu Rev Biophys Bioeng 12:35–68.

Song P-S (1987) Possible primary photoreceptors. In Senger H (ed): Blue Light Responses: Phenomena and Occurrence in Plants and Microorganisms. Boca Raton, FL: CRC Press, pp 3–17.

Song P-S (1988) The molecular topography of phytochrome: Chromophore and apoprotein. J Photochem Photobiol [Biol] 2:43–57.

Song P-S, Kim I-H, Florell S, Tamai N, Yamazaki T, Yamazaki I (1990) Structure and function of the photoreceptor stentorins in *Stentor coeruleus*. II. Primary photoprocess and picosecond time-resolved fluorescence. Biochim Biophys Acta 1040:58–65.

Song P-S, Poff KL (1989) Photomovement. In Smith KC (ed): The Science of Photobiology. New York: Plenum Press, pp 305–345.

Spalding EP, Cosgrove DJ: Large plasma-membrane depolarization precedes rapid blue-light–induced growth inhibition in cucumber. Planta 178:407–410.

Speth V, Otto V, Schäfer E (1986) Intracellular localisation of phytochrome in oat coleoptiles by electron microscopy. Planta 168:299–304.

Spikes JD (1989) Photosensitization. In Smith KC (ed): The Science of Photobiology. New York: Plenum, pp 79–110.

Sponga F, Deitzer GF, Mancinelli AL (1986) Cryptochrome, phytochrome, and the photoregulation of anthocyanin production under blue light. Plant Physiol 82:952–955.

Springer MS, Goy MF, Adler J (1979) Protein methylation in behavioural control mechanisms and in signal transduction. Nature 280:279–284.

Spudich EN, Hasselbacher CA, Spudich JL (1988) Methyl-accepting protein associated with bacterial sensory rhodopsin I. J Bacteriol 170:4280–4285.

Spudich EN, Spudich JL (1982) Control of transmembrane ion fluxes to select halorhodopsin-deficient and other energy-transduction mutants of *Halobacterium halobium*. Proc Natl Acad Sci USA 79:4308–4312.

Spudich EN, Sundberg SA, Manor D, Spudich JL (1986) Properties of a second sensory receptor protein in *Halobacterium halobium* phototaxis. Protein 1:239–246.

Spudich EN, Takahashi T, Spudich JL (1989) Sensory rhodopsin-I and rhodopsin-II modulate a methylation demethylation system in *Halobacterium halobium* phototaxis. Proc Natl Acad Sci USA 86:7746–7750.

Spudich JL (1984) Genetic demonstration of a sensory rhodopsin in bacteria. In Liana BC, Helmreich EJM, Passow H (eds): Information and Energy Transduction in Biological Membranes. New York: Alan R. Liss, pp 221–229.

Spudich JL, Bogomolni RA (1984) The mechanism of colour discrimination by a bacterial sensory rhodopsin. Nature 312:509–513.

Spudich JL, Bogomolni RA (1988) Sensory rhodopsins of halobacteria. Annu Rev Biophys Bioeng 17:193–215.

Staehelin LA, Arntzen CJ (1983) Regulation of chloroplast membrane function: Protein phosphorylation changes the spatial organization of membrane components. J Cell Biol 97:1327–1337.

Stewart RC, Dahlquist FW (1987) Molecular components of bacterial chemotaxis. Chem Rev 87:997–1025.

Stieve H (ed) (1985a) Molecular mechanism of photoreception. Berlin: Springer-Verlag.

Stieve H (1985b) Phototransduction in invertebrate visual cells. The present state of research exemplified and discussed through the *Limulus* photoreceptor cell. In Gilles R, Balthazart J (eds): Neurobiology. Berlin: Springer-Verlag, pp 346–362.

Stock JB, Stock AM, Mottonem JM (1990) Signal transduction in bacteria. Nature 344:395–400.

Stoeckenius W (1985) The rhodopsin-like pigments of halobacteria: Light-energy and signal transducers in an archaebacterium. Trends Biochem Sci 10:483–486.

Stoeckenius W, Bogomolni RA (1982) Bacteriorhodopsin and related pigments of halobacteria. Annu Rev Biochem 52:587–616.

Stryer L (1986) Cyclic GMP cascade of vision. Annu Rev Neurosci 9:87–119.

Stryer L (1988) Molecular basis of visual excitation. Cold Spring Harbor Symp Quant Biol 53:283–294.

Takahashi T, Kamo N, Kobatake Y (1986) Sensory rhodopsinlike proteins in *Halobacterium halobium*. Membrane 11:126–136, 1986.

Takao M, Yasui A, Tokunaga F (1988) Isolation and sequence determination of the chicken rhodopsin gene. Vision Res 28:471–480.

Takemoto DJ, Cunnick JM (1990) Visual transduction in rod outer segments. Cell Signal 2:99–104.

Taylor WC (1989) Regulatory interactions between nuclear and plastid genomes. Annu Rev Plant Physiol Plant Mol Biol 40:211–233.

Thomas B, Penn SE (1986) Monoclonal antibody ARC MAC 50.1 binds to a site on the phytochrome molecule, which undergoes a photoreversible conformational change. FEBS Lett 1985:174–148.

Thompson WF, Kaufman LS, Watson JC (1985) Induction of plant gene expression by light. BioEssays 3:153–159.

Thümmler F, Rüdiger W, Cmiel E, Schneider S (1983) Chromopeptides from phytochrome and phycocyanin, NMR studies of the P_{fr} and P_r chromophores of phytochrome and E,Z isomeric chromophores of phycocyanin. Z Naturforsch 38c:359–368.

Tobin EM, Silverthorne J (1985) Light regulation of gene expression in higher plants. Annu Rev Plant Physiol 36:569–593.

Tokuhisa JG, Daniels SM, Quail PH (1985) Phytochrome in green tissue: Spectral and immunochemical evidence for two distinct molecular species of phytochrome in light-grown *Avena sativa* L. Planta 164:321–332.

Tokuhisa JG, Quail PH (1989) Phytochrome in green-tissue: Partial purification and characterization of the 118-kilodalton phytochrome species from light-grown *Avena sativa* L. Photochem Photobiol 50:143–152.

Tokutomi S, Nakasako M, Sakai J, Kataoka M, Yamamoto KT, Wada M, Tokunaga F, Furuya M (1989) A model for the dimeric molecular structure of phytochrome based on small-angle X-ray scattering. FEBS Lett 247:139–142.

Tomioka H, Takahashi T, Kamo N, Kobatake Y (1986) Flash spectrophotometric identification of a fourth rhodopsin-like pigment in *Halobacterium halobium*. Biochem Biophys Res Commun 139:389–395.

Trad CH, Horwitz BA, Lipson ED (1987) Light-induced absorbance changes in extracts of *Phycomyces* sporangiophores: Modifications in night-blind mutants. J Photochem Photobiol [Biol] 1:305–313.

Trehan A, Cañada FJ, Rando RR (1990) Inhibitors of retinyl ester formation also prevent the biosynthesis of 11-*cis*-retinol. Biochemistry 29:309–312.

Tsendina MB, Frishman DI, Levchenko VF, Berman AL (1988) Similarity of primary structures and homology of rhodopsin, β-adrenoreceptor and muscarinic cholinoreceptors. J Evol Biochem Physiol 24:600–609.

Tsuda M (1987) Photoreception and phototransduction in invertebrate photoreceptors. Photochem Photobiol 45:915–932.

Vierstra RD, Quail PH (1983) Purification and initial characterization of 124-kilodalton phytochrome from *Avena*. Biochemistry 22:2498–2505.

Vierstra RD, Quail PH (1986) The protein [phytochrome]. In Kendrick RE, Kronenberg GHM (eds): Photomorphogenesis in Plants. Dordrecht, Netherlands: Martinus Nijhoff/Junk, pp 35–60.

Vogt K, Kirschfeld K (1984) Chemical identity of the chromophores of fly visual pigment. Naturwissen 71:211–213.

Wada M, Kadota A (1989) Photomorphogenesis in lower green plants. Annu Rev Plant Physiol Plant Mol Biol 40:169–191.

Wagner G, Grolig F (1985) Molecular mechanisms of photoinduced chloroplasts movements. In Colombetti G, Lenci F, Song P-S (eds): Sensory Perception and Transduction in Aneural Organisms. New York: Plenum Press, pp 281–298.

Wald G (1968) The molecular basis of visual excitation. Nature 219:800–807.

Walker EB, Lee TY, Song P-S (1979) Spectroscopic characterization of the *Stentor* photoreceptor. Biochim Biophys Acta 587:129–144.

Wang B, Jordan S, Schuman Jorns M (1988) Identification of a pterin derivative in *Escherichia coli* DNA photolyase. Biochemistry 27:4222–4226.

Warpeha KMF, Marrs KA, Kaufman LS (1989) Blue-light regulation of specific transcript levels in *Pisum sativum*. Plant Physiol 91:1030–1035.

Weisenseel MH, Kicherer RM (1981) Ionic currents as control mechanism in cytomorphogenesis. In Kiermeyer O (ed): Cell Biology Monographs, Cytomorphogenesis in Plants. Vienna: Springer-Verlag, pp 379–399.

Wensel TG, Stryer L (1976) Activation mechanism of retinal rod cyclic GMP phosphodiesterase probed by fluorescein-labeled inhibitory subunit. Biochemistry 29:2155–2161.

Widell S, Björn LO (1976) Light-induced absorption changes in etiolated coleoptiles. Physiol Plant 36:305–309.

Wong YS, Cheng HC, Walsh DA, Lagarias JC (1986) Phosphorylation of *Avena* phytochrome in vitro as a probe of light-induced conformational changes. J Biol Chem 261:12089–12097.

Wong YS, McMichael RWJ, Lagarias JC (1989) Properties of a polycation-stimulated protein kinase associated with purified *Avena* phytochrome. Plant Physiol 91:709–718.

Yan B, Takahashi T, Johnson R, Derguini F, Nakanishi K, Spudich JL (1990) All-*trans*/13-*cis* isomerization of retinal is required for phototaxis signaling by sensory rhodopsins in *Halobacterium halobium*. Biophys J 57:807–814.

Yang K-C, Prusti RK, Walker EB, Song P-S, Watanabe M, Furuya M (1986) Photodynamic action in *Stentor coeruleus* sensitized by endogenous pigment stentorin. Photochem Photobiol 43:305–310.

Yoshikami S, Hagins WA (1970) Ionic basis of dark current and photocurrent of retinal rods. Biophys J 10:60a.

Young T (1802) On the theory of light and colours. Philos Trans R Soc Lond 92:12–48.

Zhukovsky EA, Oprian DD (1989) Effect of carboxylic acid side chains on the absorption maximum of visual pigments. Science 246:928–930.

Zuker CS, Cowman AF, Rubin GM (1985) Isolation and structure of a rhodopsin gene from *D. melanogaster*. Cell 40:851–858.

Zuker CS, Montell C, Jones K, Laverty T, Rubin GM (1987) A rhodopsin gene expressed in photoreceptor cell R7 of the *Drosophila eye:* Homologies with other signal transducing molecules. J Neurosci 7:1550–1557.

Sensory Receptors and Signal Transduction: 65–136
© 1991 Wiley-Liss, Inc.

Signal Transduction in Chemoreception

Judith Van Houten

Department of Zoology, University of Vermont, Burlington, Vermont 05405

I. INTRODUCTION

Every organism has sensory systems designed to extract information from its environment and to transduce this information into a useful form that triggers a response. When the external information is a chemical or a mixture of chemical cues, the sensory process is referred to as "chemoreception" and can range from taste and smell, familiar to all of us, to the attraction of motile bacteria. The incentive for reviewing chemoreception in this chapter comes from the relatively recent, rapid developments in the understanding of signal transduction in a multitude of systems, including photoreception, mitogenesis, and chemoreception. Therefore this chapter is devoted to chemosensory signal transduction, i.e., the conversion of chemical cues into intracellular messengers that provide useful information to the receptor cell and hence to the organism about its chemical environment.

A. Chemicals as Primary Messengers

There is no overall unifying theme among the chemical stimuli that are utilized in chemosensory transduction, but within this confusion of compounds there is order because each stimulus fits into the context of the life of the organism: Sugars attract bacteria that ferment them; folic acid attracts paramecia and slime mold amoebae that feed on the stimulus source, bacteria; amino acids attract lobsters and catfish that prey on muscle; pheromones (or pheromone blends) unique to insect or protozoan species attract their own for mating.

The participation of chemical compounds as primary messengers subjects chemosensory transduction to constraints that do not exist for photosensory or mechanosensory transduction. For a stimulus to be effective it must be transient [Atema, 1987]. If a stimulus remains in place too long, the sensory system will adapt, become insensitive to the presence of the stimulus, and stop responding. Unlike light or touch, when the source of the stimulus is removed, chemical stimuli remain. Therefore, there must be a means of destroying the signal, including enzymes to degrade the chemical stimulus, proteins to bind it, and the endocytosis of receptor–ligand complexes (see section II.F.)

B. Diverse Chemosensory Systems and Responses

The chemosensory systems commonly studied are diverse and their responses varied. In unicellular organisms, detection and transduction of chemical signals brings about the changes in the cells' motility apparatuses that allow bacteria and protozoa to accumulate at sources of nutrients or to escape nonoptimal environments; allow slime mold amoebae to crawl to seek food or to aggregate for development into a multicellular slug; facilitate the meeting of sperm and egg or cells of different mating type; or, considering circulating blood cells as honorary unicellular systems, mediate the migration of leukocytes to sites of infection. In metazoans, chemoreception underlies the sensory processes of taste, smell, and common chemical sense that in turn facilitate the processes of identifying (safe) food sources, mates, and sites for settling on substrates. The behavioral mechanisms by which the organisms achieve the same ends of the chemosensory pathway—location of food, for example—can range from indirect movement by biased random walk (klinokinesis) to direct crawling or swimming up a gradient of chemical stimulus (chemotaxis).

One solution to covering sensory transduction with all this diversity would be to focus on general, common aspects. Therefore this chapter attempts to survey many of these systems in order to make emerging, common themes apparent.

C. Common Pathways of Reception and Transduction

While wide-ranging, chemoreception systems do have many aspects in common, particularly at the cellular and molecular levels. They all appear to be initiated at the membrane surface of a receptor cell by the interaction of a stimulus with a receptor molecule (or perhaps in some cases the membrane directly) and subsequent transduction of this interaction into intracellular messengers. The second and third messengers are limited in number and for the most part are recruited from cyclic nucleotides, permeant ions, phosphoinositides, diacylglycerol, arachidonic acid, and internal pH levels. It is becoming increasingly apparent that GTP-binding proteins (G proteins) mediate at least some of this transduction. Therefore receptors, internal messengers, and transduction mechanisms are discussed in turn in order to examine common themes with variations among diverse chemosensory systems.

II. RECEPTORS
A. Bacteria

Bacterial chemoreceptors mediate a change in flagellar motion that biases the individual cell's random walk and indirectly causes a population of bacteria to accumulate in attractant stimuli or disperse away from repellents. In the most extensively studied bacteria, *Escherichia coli, Salmonella typhimurium*, and *Bacillus subtilis*, the cells swim smoothly in response to attractants (with flagella rotating counterclockwise) and in a "tumbly," frequently turning response to repellents (with flagella rotating clockwise with each tumble). The general scheme of things is shown in Figure 1, taken from an overview by Parkinson [1988]. Bacterial chemoresponse is treated in depth in this volume

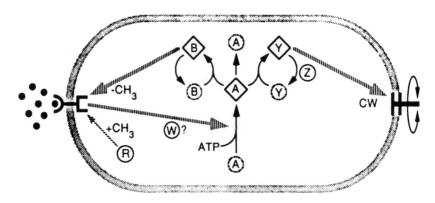

Fig. 1. Schematic of information transfer in bacterial chemoresponse. Ligand (•) binds to receptor, which signals the presence of ligand by way of *cheW* to *cheA* by enhancing the autophosphorylation of A (nonphosphorylated states are ○ and phosphorylated states are ◇). The phosphates on A proteins are then physically transferred from A to Y and B. Activated (phosphorylated) Y interacts with the motor to promote clockwise (CW) rotation and tumbling. Z functions to inactivate the signal by receiving phosphates from Y (or A, not shown). *cheB* and *cheR* affect the adaptation state of the receptor by adding or removing methyl groups. [Reproduced from Parkinson, 1988, with permission of the publisher.]

by M. Eisenbach. However, because such a great deal is known about protein components of the bacterial chemoresponse pathway, bacterial chemoreception is also included in this chapter, especially for the purposes of comparison to other, often lesser known systems.

The 20 or so receptors for *Esch. coli* and the highly homologous receptors in *Sal. typhimurium* fall into two classes: those carrier proteins loosely associated with the membrane and found in the periplasmic space and those intrinsic membrane proteins that also serve as transducers. Within this latter group are four proteins that have been referred to as "MCPs" (methyl-accepting chemotaxis proteins) and are known as the products of the *tsr*, *tar*, *trg*, and *tap* genes (Fig. 2). The aspartate receptor (MCP II) serves as a good example from which to generalize. This one MCP mediates both aspartate and maltose chemoresponse by slightly different mechanisms.

The aspartate receptor resides in the membrane as a dimer of Tar proteins [Milligan and Koshland, 1988], each with two membrane-spanning groups, a periplasmic domain with ligand-binding sites and a cytoplasmic domain with its sites for signal transduction and covalent modification [Russo and Koshland, 1983]. The bacterial aspartate and other MCP receptors fall into a family of "simple" receptors, including the epidermal growth factor (EGF), nerve growth factor (NGF), low-density lipoprotein (LDL), and insulin receptors based on the small number of transmembrane-spanning regions through which information about binding of ligand to the extracellular domain must be conveyed to the interior of the cell [Mowbray and Koshland, 1987]. Using site-directed muta-

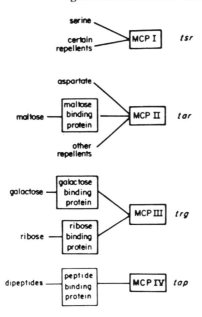

Fig. 2. The receptors and membrane signal transducing proteins of *E. coli*. The gene names for the methyl-accepting chemotaxis proteins (MCPs) are given in italics. (The sensory transduction pathway for phosphotransferase sugars joins with these transduction pathways downstream of the MCPs). [Reproduced from Adler, 1987, with permission of the publisher.]

genesis to create sites of disulfide crosslinking, Falke and Koshland [1987] have manipulated the aspartate receptor. From their studies, the protein appears to be flexible, and the binding of aspartate directly to the Tar protein induces ''global'' conformation changes from the periplasmic domain through the membrane-spanning region to the cytoplasmic domain to facilitate intracellular signalling and adaptation. (The nature of the signalling is discussed in section IV.)

Adaptation is thought to occur through the methylation of the glutamate moieties of the receptor's cytoplasmic domain. A truncated aspartate receptor that is missing these residues can signal but cannot adapt [Russo and Koshland, 1983]. These glutamate residues become accessible to a methyltransferase following the binding-induced conformation change [see Adler, 1987, for a review]. The number of methyl groups on the MCP is a function of the nature of the stimulus (attractant stimuli increase the number of methyl groups over basal levels; repellent stimuli decrease this number) and the concentration of the stimulus. With the addition of more (but not saturating) stimulus such as the attractant aspartate, the number of methyl groups increases in an additive fashion [Mowbray and Koshland, 1987], with the consequences that the MCP stops transducing and the response adapts. Removal of aspartate leads to a rapid removal of methyl groups until basal levels are again attained (Fig. 3). In the

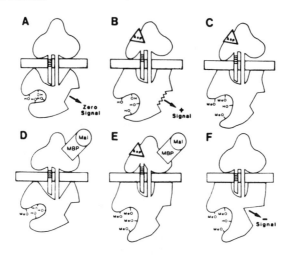

Fig. 3. Schematic of signaling and adaptation with maltose and aspartate: a vertical slide model. **A:** The unstimulated receptor is shown with an external domain that is responsible for ligand binding, two transmembrane segments, and a cytoplasmic domain that can send a signal and be methylated. The glutamic acid groups are symbolized here by the unmethylated OH groups to emphasize the net change of methylation in the following steps. **B:** The conformational change induced by the binding of aspartate causes the transmembrane region to be pulled up slightly (shown as three notches) into the external space. This in turn causes an alteration of the cytoplasmic portions (shown here as a compression against the membrane), which brings about changes in the signaling region (indicated by the jagged line) and in the methylation region (indicated by the exposure of the OH groups of the relevant glutamic acids). As a result, the aspartate-bound receptor becomes more highly methylated, which somehow releases the stress at the signaling site caused by binding of aspartate. **C:** At the new steady state, the methylation sites are sufficiently modified to bring the structure back to the nonsignaling mode, even though aspartate remains bound to the protein. **D:** The receptor adapted to maltose is shown here. The binding of maltose-binding protein, charged with its own ligand, at a different site has effects similar to those of aspartate, but smaller in degree (e.g., the transmembrane segment is moved only one notch). **E:** When both maltose and aspartate are bound, the effects are greatest (four notches), with adaptation occurring at the highest levels of methylation. An additional state, shown in **F,** exists when the attractant is removed from the methylated protein. This receptor sends a signal that is opposite in polarity to the one previously described. [Reproduced from Mowbray and Koshland, 1987, with permission of the publisher.]

interim, the cell responds behaviorally as though it has been exposed to a negative or repellent stimulus. This titration of methyl groups is thought to reset the system in an unchanging environment so that it is poised to respond to a *change* in stimulus concentration, even a change riding on top of a background level of stimulus.

The number of methyl groups on MCPs is kept in balance by the actions of a methyltransferase (*CheR* product) and an esterase (*CheB* product). A mutant in either *cheR* or *cheB* genes renders a bacterium defective in chemoresponse.

Curiously, the double mutant does retain some chemoresponse, bringing into question the role of methylation and adaptation in chemoresponse [Stock and Stock, 1987]. In particular, double mutants accumulate in capillaries of aspartate where they arrive by diffusion and move by smooth swimming and methylation-independent partial adaptation up the steep concentration gradient at the mouth of the capillary [Weiss et al., 1990]. Serine, which does not elicit any adaptation, also does not elicit any accumulation of the double mutant in capillaries, despite the presence of functional receptors and other sensory transduction components in the double mutant. It appears that the methylation-dependent adaptation that resets the response system is required for the chemoresponse to shallow gradients of stimuli and that without methylation only weak responses to very steep gradients of a few stimuli, such as aspartate, are operative.

The *Esch. coli* aspartate receptor also mediates the response to the attractant maltose. Maltose binds to its receptor, maltose-binding protein (MBP), one of the class of receptors that is found in the periplasmic space [see Brass, 1986, for a review of such proteins]. The ligand–receptor complex in turn binds to the aspartate receptor at a site probably distinct from that for aspartate binding [Mowbray and Koshland, 1987]. From a study of combined and separate responses to aspartate and maltose, Mowbray and Koshland [1987] conclude that there most likely is only one population of receptors that mediates both responses. Maltose-MBP, like aspartate, induces global MCP conformation changes that signal to the cell interior and make glutamates available for methylation. However, the number of methyl groups added under saturating stimulus conditions is lower and the order of priority of the methylation of sites is different from the aspartate response. A model that takes the conclusions of Mowbray and Koshland into account is shown in Figure 3.

As mentioned above, the MCPs fall into the class of chemoreceptors that includes intrinsic membrane proteins. Joining this class are the phosphotransferase sugar transport proteins that mediate both the transport of and chemoresponse to mannose and glucose [Lengeler et al., 1981]. The as yet unknown adaptation mechanism of these receptors does not involve methylation, and one prospect is the phosphorylation that regulates their transport function [Postma and Lengeler, 1985; Taylor et al., 1988]. The MCP-dependent and -independent systems do seem to share common requirements for the *che Y, che W*, and *che A* proteins and presumably a significant portion of the chemosensory transduction pathway [Taylor et al., 1988].

Like *Esch. coli, Bac. subtilis* is attracted to aspartate and phosphotransferase (PTS) sugars. However, there are many significant differences between the two bacterial systems [Thoekle et al., 1990]. The PTS sugars act through MCPs in *B. subtilis* and elicit a turnover of methyl groups on all the MCPs concurrently and fairly uniformly. Aspartate, which in *Esch. coli* affects the methylation state of its MCP receptor only, causes changes in methyl distribution on the three MCP species, but not uniformly as do the PTS sugars. The methylation/ adaptation of *Bac. subtilis* differs from that of *Esch. coli* in that attractants stimulate demethylation and repellents stimulate no methylation change in MCPs. Additionally, there can be methyltransfer among one class of MCPs and between intermediates and other classes of MCPs [Thoelke et al., 1987; Beadle et al., 1988]. These observations hint that the methylation modifications may subserve different or additional functions from originally envisioned.

There are still other interesting chemoresponses of bacteria to oxygen, for example [Shioi et al., 1987; Taylor et al., 1988], that cannot be dealt with here. Likewise there are other bacteria with equally interesting responses, such as *Caulobacter* in which MCP synthesis is controlled in time and space within the cell [Nathan et al., 1986] and photosynthetic bacteria such as *Rhodobacter sphaeroides* and *Rhodospirillum rubrum* in which there are methylation-independent and -dependent chemoresponses and a role for transport in chemoreception [Ingham and Armitage, 1987; Sockett et al., 1987; Armitage, 1988, 1990]. *Rhodob. sphaeroides* offers an interesting contrast to the enteric bacteria, because its chemoattraction is limited to chemoeffectors and cations that are transported and do not interact with MCPs [Armitage, 1990]. The attractant stimuli (no repellents have been identified) induce increased swimming speed and decreased stopping not directly by alteration of proton motive force or pH_i, but the responses do require transport and metabolism of the stimuli, implying interaction of the metabolic intermediates with the flagellar motor or acting as second messengers.

B. Neutrophils

Polymorphonuclear neutrophil leukocytes (PMNs) crawl their way to sites of inflammation from infection or wounds. They use as chemotactic stimuli fragments of complement such as C5a and fragments of bacterial proteins such as *N*-formyl-methionyl-leucyl-phenylalanine (FMLP); leukotriene B4; and a multitude of other endogenous and exogenous factors that diffuse from the inflammation site and set up a concentration gradient for the cells to follow [see Allen et al., 1988, for a review of stimuli]. At the site, in response to a higher concentration of stimuli than elicits chemotaxis, the PMNs release hydrolytic enzymes and superoxide that serve both to kill the infectious agent and to release more attractant stimuli. Most research on leukocyte chemotaxis has centered around FMLP and C5a as ligands, and therefore this discussion focuses primarily on the FMLP and the analogous C5a receptor-mediated transduction that causes cells to orient, polarize, migrate up concentration gradients, and secrete cytotoxic agents.

Receptors for FMLP and C5a have been identified by affinity crosslinking as integral membrane proteins of 50,000–60,000 and 40,000 M_r, respectively

[Niedel and Cuatrecasas, 1980a,b; Rollins and Springer, 1985; see Allen et al., 1988, and Painter et al., 1984, for reviews]. There are ~60,000 FMLP receptors elaborated on the plasma membrane and at least as many inside the cell. These glycoproteins are found minimally in two isoforms that can be separated by M_r (50,000 and 60,000) and by pI (6.0 and 6.5, respectively), even when their substantial component of carbohydrate is removed. There may be even more isoforms within the two pI classes, because affinity labeling of receptor with radioiodinated FMLP characteristically results in a broad band of labeled protein from 50,000 to 60,000 M_r on gels [see Allen et al., 1988, and Sha'afi and Molski, 1988, for reviews].

Apparently one heterogeneous set of FMLP receptors (K_d 0.6 nM [Sklar et al., 1984a,b]) mediates both chemotaxis and superoxide release, even though these responses differ in ED_{50} by one order of magnitude or more [Allen et al., 1988; Lohr and Snyderman, 1982; Yuli et al., 1982]. This difference in concentration dependence may reflect the different percentages of occupied receptors necessary to elicit each response [Painter et al., 1984; Sklar et al., 1987]. There is an alternative view that the different ED_{50}s reflect the two receptor affinity states and that the receptors in the high-affinity state mediate chemotaxis and those in the low-affinity state mediate other responses [Lohr and Snyderman, 1982; see Sklar et al., 1987, for discussion]. Both views allow for receptor affinity modulation with ligand binding, but the percent occupancy view would have the high-affinity state uncoupled from response, preparatory to down-regulation.

The different views arise in part because the FMLP-binding sites are highly dynamic, changing affinity, number, mobility, and distribution with ligand occupancy, guanine nucleotides, and methylation. Figure 4 represents a model that accounts for the effects of stimulation on receptor affinity and distribution. Upon stimulation with FMLP, bound receptors release the associated G protein in an active form that continues the signal transduction process (see section III). The receptor–ligand complex now changes affinity to become a very slowly dissociating, almost irreversibly bound form that is no longer coupled to the G protein, but is associated with the cytoskeleton [Painter et al., 1987; Jesaitis et al., 1984]. Its lateral movement to a different lipid domain and its association with the cytoskeleton are sensitive to cytochalasin D but not to pertussis toxin (a G protein inhibitor) or to guanyl nucleotides [Painter et al., 1987; Jesaitis et al., 1984]. The high-affinity receptors of the cytoskeleton-enriched fraction are still capable of interaction with G proteins, and the lateral segregation of these receptors into membrane regions poor in G proteins suggests a mechanism for desensitization and response termination [Jesaitis et al., 1989]. These desensitized receptors should correspond to the form Sklar et al. [1989] measure in real time as "LRX." These receptors are high affinity, not G associated, insensitive to pertussis toxin, and derived from "LR,"

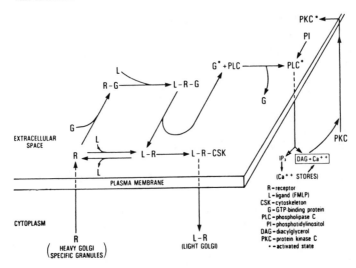

Fig. 4. A schematic of chemoattractant (e.g., FMLP) stimulation of neutrophils. Note the multiple states of receptors, including association with the cytoskeleton, G protein interactions with PLC and generation of multiple second messengers, many of which are not shown here as less than essential for activation. (From Allen et al., 1988, with permission.)

a lower affinity form that is generated when the G protein subunits rapidly dissociate from the receptor once it is bound with ligand ("LRG").

Dissociation of the G proteins from the LRG complex is essential for the rapid (<1 min) segregation of the receptors to the cytoskeleton-associated, G protein–depleted membrane domain, because toxins have no effect while the GDP analog GDPβS drastically reduces association of receptor with cytoskeleton [Sarndahl et al., 1989]. Presumably, dissociation of the G proteins reveals an actin-binding site that allows association of the receptor with the actin filaments of the cytoskeleton. The half-life of the transient association of the receptor with the cytoskeleton is ~50 sec, similar to that for the internalization of receptor [Jesaitiset al., 1984; Painter et al., 1984]. There is a loss of receptor number and sensitivity during chemotaxis for which this internalization may be responsible in part. Likewise, internalization may be a necessary process in the orientation of receptors during chemotaxis by replacing external receptors with new or cryptic ones primarily at the leading edge of the cell [Zigmond and Sullivan, 1979; Sullivan and Zigmond, 1982].

The model is based on acute stimulation with 1 nM FMLP for 2 min. Chronic stimulation, i.e., stimulation at lower temperatures that prevent endocytosis and secretion with 100 nM FMLP for 20–60 min, renders cells desensitized, unresponsive to FMLP yet still able to produce superoxide in response to phorbol ester [Jesaitis et al., 1986, 1988a,b]. As with acute stimulation, the occupied receptors of desensitized cells convert to a high-affinity, very slowly dissociating form, still at the cell surface but now associated with cytoskeleton and in a different membrane domain from the G proteins. The relationship of these high-affinity binding sites in desensitized cells to the receptor isoforms discussed above is not yet clear, although in acutely stimulated cells the high-affinity sites associated with the cytoskeleton seem to be the 50,000–60,000 M_r proteins [Painter et al., 1987].

Homologous desensitization in chronically stimulated neutrophils appears to result from the physical separation of the surface receptor from the G proteins that are essential for transduction. Certainly internalization of receptors also is occurring, but the conversion of surface receptors to an almost irreversibly bound and sequestered form probably accounts for most of the desensitization process, because the ability of preincubated cells to respond to FMLP is relative to the number of surface receptors not complexed with the cytoskeleton [Jesaitis et al., 1986]. Densensitization could also involve covalent modification in addition to sequestration, as for the β-adrenergic receptor in its control of adenylate cylase [Sibley et al., 1987]. However, there is no evidence for covalent modification with desensitization of the neutrophil receptor at this time.

This model, shown in Figure 4, is only a starting point. Filling in more details will require answers to the following questions. Is receptor occupancy all important, or are there functioning, G protein–associated receptors with different affinities that mediate different responses (chemotaxis vs. superoxide production and secretion)? As sequelae: Is there only one population of receptors that interconvert by guanine nucleotides between high- and low-affinity and thereby between different functions [Painter et al., 1987]? What is the function of the unoccupied receptor found associated with the cytoskeleton in unstimulated cells? (Its K_d of 1 nM curiously correlates with the ED_{50} of chemotaxis, while the K_d of cytoskeleton-free receptors correlates with the ED_{50} of superoxide production [10 nM] [Allen et al., 1988].) Regardless of the answers, it will be important to know whether there is only one type of G protein associated with FMLP receptors and, if so, how one second effector produces several different responses to the same stimulus [see Sha'afi and Molski, 1988, for discussion].

Eventually a comprehensive model of neutrophil chemoresponse must account for the mechanism by which cells respond over several orders of magnitude of FMLP concentration and shift half-maximal responses to higher concentrations with prestimulation (somewhat similar to the bacterial adaptation system) [Sklar et al., 1984a,b; Seligmann et al., 1982]. The neutrophils detect a 1%–2% drop in FMLP concentration across the cell, and the model must take this restriction on receptor occupancy into account [Zigmond and Sullivan, 1979; Sullivan and Zigmond, 1982]. (As Zigmond [1989] points out, desensitization of receptors sets transduction and levels of second messengers back to basal levels and allows the neutrophil to detect changes in second messenger elicited by changes in receptor occupancy from 200 to 400 receptors as well as from 4,000 to 4,200 receptors.) Additionally, a model must account for potentially different roles for the two or more isoforms of the receptors and the phenomenon of priming, a receptor-mediated process by which the FMLP receptor complement in the membrane increases upon prestimulation with a variety of extrinsic or cellular factors [see Allen et al., 1988, for review]. Many questions surrounding neutrophil receptors will be better resolved now that the cloning of the FMLP and C5a receptor genes has been accomplished [Thomas et al., 1990; Coats and Navarro, 1990; Murphy et al., 1990; Gerard and Gerard, 1991; see Goldman and Goetzl, 1982; Grob et al., 1990, for still other leukocyte receptors and coexpression of C5a, CR1, CR3, Fc, and FMLP receptors; Van Epps et al., 1990].

C. Unicellular Eukaryotes

In the category of unicellular eukaryotes are protists such as *Euplotes, Blepharisma, Paramecium, Chlamydomonas*; slime molds such as *Dictyostelium discoideum*; and yeast. Among these, receptors for the slime mold and yeast mating factor have been identified, and, for the rest, putative receptors have been described [see Van Houten and Preston, 1987, and Van Houten, 1990, for reviews and Devreotes and Zigmond, 1988, for a comparison of *Dictyostelium* and neutrophils].

1. Slime mold. When amoebae of *D. discoideum* run out of bacteria to feed on, they begin the process of developing into a multicellular slug. In this process, they respond to pulses of cAMP that emanate from focal cells. The cells migrate up the pulsatile gradient of cAMP until they can touch and aggregate as a prelude to forming the slug. When each cell is stimulated with cAMP, it in turn releases a pulse of cAMP (the relay) in addition to orienting and transiently moving toward the origin of the wave of stimulus. The chemoresponse can therefore be divided into the orientation of the cytoskeletal motile apparatus for chemotaxis and the activation of adenylate cyclase to produce cAMP for the relay, and the two processes can be studied independently.

Upon starvation, the amoebae acquire cAMP receptors. These receptors were first studied for ligand-binding properties, and, through pharmacological studies, a fairly detailed picture of the ligand-binding site has emerged, as chronicled by Janssens and Van Haastert [1987]. The binding sites were found to be heterogeneous and positively cooperative (Table I). Those binding sites associated with chemotaxis response are likely to be the high-affinity "B" sites that are coupled to the guanylate cyclase that is responsible for the production of an internal messenger for chemotaxis (Fig. 5). The "A" sites are thought to be coupled with the adenylate cyclase of the cAMP relay system. Within both classes of sites there are high- and low-affinity or fast- and slow-dissociating sets that can interconvert in the presence of ligand, and binding to members of both classes can be modulated by the presence of guanine nucleotides (Table

TABLE I. Kinetic cAMP Receptor Forms Observed in *D. discoideum* **Cells and Isolated Membranes**

Receptor form	Apparent K_d (nM)	Dissociation rate constant $(k^{-1}, s^{-7}; 20°C)$	No. of sites per cell	Effect of guanine nucleotides on abundancy
A^H	60	4×10^{-1}	77,000	Decrease
A^L	450	10×10^{-1}		Increase
B^S	6–13	4.3×10^{-2}	2,300	Decrease
B^{SS}	6–13	4.7×10^{-3}	1,100	Decrease

Reproduced from Janssens and Van Haastert [1987], with permission of the publisher.

I). As with the neutrophil chemoattractant receptor [Sklar et al., 1984a,b], the rate of ligand binding rather than occupancy alone may be significant for transduction [Van Haastert et al., 1981].

Two groups have identified the protein counterpart of a cAMP receptor by photoaffinity labeling cells with ^{32}P-N_3-cAMP [Klein et al., 1985b; Juliani and Klein, 1981; Thiebert et al., 1984]. The protein is ~40,000 in M_r, and, despite the lack of consensus about the size, it is agreed that the protein is a phosphoprotein existing in two phosphorylation states [Klein et al., 1986,

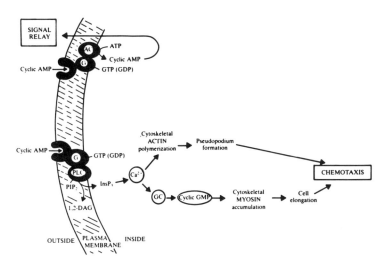

Fig. 5. Signal transduction pathways in *Dictyostelium discoideum* leading from cell surface cAMP receptors to the regeneration of the cAMP signal (signal relay) and to events of chemotaxis. More recent findings could add action of *synag 7* gene product at the G protein (G) and adenylate cyclase (AC) interaction and the *frgA* gene product as the G protein for chemotaxis [Snaar-Jaglaska and Van Haastert, 1988; Kesbeke et al., 1988]. [Reproduced from Newell et al., 1988, with permission of the publisher.]

1987b]. Once bound with cAMP, the receptors become phosphorylated (approximately seven phosphates per peptide) [Klein et al., 1987b] and consequently shift to lower mobility on sodium dodecyl sulfate (SDS) gels.

The 40 kD protein has been purified to homogeneity [Klein et al., 1987a], and this phosphoprotein fits several criteria for the receptor: 1) specificity for labeling by the photoaffinity cAMP analog that parallels potency or affinity of analogs for chemoreceptor binding; 2) appearance at the expected time in development; 3) presence in membranes and not cytosol; and 4) nonidentity with the phosphodiesterase that is responsible for degradation of the extracellular stimulus [Klein et al., 1987b]. An additional 70 kD protein has been identified by photoaffinity labeling [Meyers-Hutchins and Frazier, 1984]. It is not clear how this protein relates to the 40 kD protein, but it is possible that this represents an aggregation product of the 40 kD protein [Janssens and Van Haastert, 1987].

As mentioned above, the adenylate cyclase of the relay and the guanylate cyclase that produces an internal messenger for chemotaxis appear to be activated by separate sets of receptors (Fig. 5). Judging from the kinetics of the high- to low-mobility transitions of the 40 kD protein on gels, this phosphoprotein could qualify for the receptor involved with *adaptation* of adenylate cyclase, but not with activation of the adenylate cyclase or either activation or adaptation of guanylate cyclase [Janssens and Van Haastert, 1987]. Therefore, as in the bacteria, a covalent modification of the receptor is coincident with adaptation, a common theme of vertebrate receptors as well [Sibley and Lefkowitz, 1985; Sibley et al., 1987].

The relationship of the phosphoprotein to the identified binding sites (Table I) is not known at this time [Janssens and Van Haastert, 1987]. cAMP is thought to activate the relay adenylate cyclase through the "A" sites, and the abundance of the phosphoproteins would suggest that they represent the majority of cAMP-binding sites, i.e., the "A" sites. One could extrapolate that the phosphorylation of the 40 kD protein corresponds to the transition of "A" sites from high- to low-affinity forms and that the low-affinity form no longer activates the adenylate cyclase and thereby is responsible for adaptation of the relay. However, the time course of transitions of the high- to low-affinity "A"-binding sites and the high- to low-mobility phosphoprotein do not match [Van Haastert and De Wit, 1984; Devreotes and Sherring, 1985]. A correspondence of the phosphoprotein with the "B" sites that govern chemotaxis seems unlikely, but has not yet been ruled out. Indeed, it is not clear whether the forms of the surface receptor (two A and two B) represent states of the same protein [Van Ments-Cohen and Van Haastert, 1989].

Relatively recently, screening of a cDNA library yielded cloned genes corresponding to cAMP receptors [Klein et al., 1988; Saxe et al., 1988; Saxe, personal communication]. A primary amino acid sequence deduced from one DNA clone predicts seven transmembrane-spanning regions, a G protein interaction site, and phosphorylation sites on the C-terminal cytoplasmic tail, all characteristics of a new member of the superfamily of receptors typified by rhodopsin and β-adrenergic receptors. *Dictyostelium* transformed with antisense constructs of the receptor gene do not express the mRNA for the receptor protein and fail to aggregate and proceed through development [Klein et al., 1988]. By following the appearance of mRNAs from the cloned genes during *Dictyostelium* development, the receptors for chemotaxis, relay, and developmental gene expression will be identified, and the discussions of the number and coincidence of receptors with binding states will soon be settled by molecular genetics. (See Section V for new additions to this gene family.)

The *Dictyostelium* amoebae when feeding on bacteria and not starved are responsive to folic acid and pteridines. Like the cAMP receptor, the folate receptor was first characterized among the membrane folate-binding proteins for its binding kinetics [see Janssens and Van Haastert, 1987, for review]. There are a total of five kinetic binding site forms, and among these three ''B'' sites have a selective binding that corresponds to the specificity of chemoresponse and therefore are likely to be the ones coupled with the guanylate cyclase for signal transduction in chemotaxis. (The two ''A'' sites probably couple with the adenylate cyclase and account for the ability of folic acid to induce cAMP in early aggregative cells.) The three ''B'' sites are interconvertible with ligand binding. As with the cAMP receptors, G proteins are implicated in receptor function because guanine nucleotides modulate the binding to all five binding subtypes and folic acid modulates the binding of GTP to cell membranes. The availability of chemoresponse mutants should facilitate the search for the still-elusive folate receptor [Segall et al., 1987]; however, it appears that no folate mutants to date are null mutants [Segall et al., 1988], and it remains for techniques of gene disruption and homologous recombination to produce the necessary cell lines [Segall and Gerisch, 1989]. Alternatively, the folate receptor gene may be identified among the growing number of cAMP receptor genes [Saxe et al., 1991].

2. Chlamydomonas. *Chlamydomonas* gametes begin by sticking to cells of the complementary mating type as a prelude to mating. This sticking at first is random, later is confined to the flagella, and then in *Chlamydomonas reinhardtii* is further limited to the tips of these organelles. The species-specific agglutinin molecules that mediate this process in *Chlamydomonas* and *C. reinhardtii* are large ($>10^3$ kD, 228–320 nm) glycoproteins, rich in hydroxyproline, with characteristic shaft, hook, and globular head regions [Goodenough et al., 1985; Adair et al., 1983; Crabbendam et al., 1986]. The hook anchors the molecule in the membrane. It is the head that shows morphological differences between + and − mating type gametes and is essential for the agglutination mating response [Goodenough et al., 1985; Crabbendam et al., 1986]. The + and − *C. reinhardtii* mating type cells each express the corresponding + or − agglutinin along the long axis of the flagella. After contact with the complementary gamete, the agglutinins accumulate at the tip, hence the ''tipping'' process in which the cells contact each other only at the flagellar ends. The + cell of the pair puts out a fertilization tube filled with polymerized actin. This tube contacts the − cell at a swelling specifically prepared for this contact, and fusion of the cells occurs here. The cells secrete autolysin to loosen or shed their cell walls in preparation to cell fusion [see Pasquale and Goodenough, 1987, and Musgrave and van den Ende, 1987, for reviews and Van Ende et al., 1990, for differences between species].

The agglutination process has set in motion a series of events. It is not clear how the agglutinin membrane proteins signal to the cell that this series should commence, but the adenylate cyclase is activated early in the process, and an increase in internal cAMP is sufficient to trigger the cascade of mating responses [Pasquale and Goodenough, 1987]. Crosslinking of the agglutinins in place on the membrane seems essential; solubilized agglutinins or isolated flagella interact weakly if at all [Musgrave and van den Ende, 1987]. Studies with antibodies to the agglutinins imply that crosslinking of complementary agglutinins is sufficient and that invoking the binding of agglutinins to yet other unknown surface receptors is not necessary [Homan et al., 1987]. The N-glucosamine sugars of the + mating type agglutinin and the O-linked oligosaccharide with terminal galactose residues of the − mating type agglutinin of C. eugametos are obligatory for mating-specific binding domains [Musgrave and van den Ende, 1987]. There is still much to discover about these agglutinins that mediate this contact chemoresponse that is reminiscent of immune cell and sperm–egg receptor-mediated interactions.

3. Ciliates. Paramecium tetraurelia responds to chemicals in solution around it. In particular, fermentation and other bacterial products are attractants, probably signifying the presence of food [Van Houten, 1978; Van Houten and Preston, 1988]. Stimuli such as folic acid, acetate, and cAMP hyperpolarize the cells [Van Houten, 1979], and thereby causing changes in ciliary beating: The cells move more smoothly and turn less frequently as a consequence. This in turn causes populations of cells to accumulate indirectly by a biased random walk, not unlike that of the bacterial chemoresponse [Van Houten, 1978; Van Houten and Van Houten, 1982]. The stimuli are thought to interact with the cell at specific receptor sites, because radiolabeled stimuli bind specifically and saturably to the cells [Schulz et al., 1984; Smith et al., 1987] and single-site mutations eliminate both binding and chemoresponse [DiNallo et al., 1982; Schulz et al., 1984; Smith et al., 1987; Isaksen and Van Houten, unpublished results]. Cilia are not essential for chemoreception: Deciliated cells show the characteristic hyperpolarization in attractants [Preston and Van Houten, 1987a,b], and only a small minority of binding sites are on the cilia [Schulz et al., 1984; Smith et al., 1987]. An exception to this may be the response to L-glutamate [Preston and Usherwood, 1988].

One candidate receptor has been partially purified. A doublet of cAMP-binding proteins from cell body membranes shows an elution profile from cAMP affinity columns that would be expected for the receptor [Van Houten et al., 1990]. A protein of the same M_r (48,000) can be labeled by ^{32}P-N$_3$-cAMP photolysis of whole cells. Covalent linking of N$_3$-cAMP to whole cells specifically eliminates chemoresponse to cAMP and not to other stimuli, implying that the receptor should be among the proteins crosslinked with this photoaffinity analog [Van Houten et al., 1991]. Both bands of the doublet are glycosylated, and other covalent modifications remain to be determined, as does the relationship between the two proteins. Total amino acid analysis is consistent with the two proteins having one origin at the gene level. Most importantly, polyclonal antibodies produced against this doublet specifically block chemoresponse to folate, and the preimmune serum does not (Baez and Van Houten, unpublished results). Other receptors for folate are being identified by similar approaches [Sasner and Van Houten, 1989]. There is a gradient of responsiveness to folate from anterior to posterior, and it will be interesting to determine whether receptors follow this gradient [Preston and Van Houten, 1987b].

As *Chlamydomonas*, ciliates have different mating types, but, unlike *Chlamydomonas*, some ciliates signal their presence to complementary mating types by *soluble* pheromones. These pheromones cause physiological changes in cells in preparation for mating. The two mating types of *Blepharisma japonicum* each have a soluble "gamone." Type I cells secrete blepharmone (gamone I, a glycoprotein of 20,000 M_r), and type II cells put out blepharisomone (gamone II, a tryptophan derivative) [see Van Houten and Preston, 1987, and Nobili, 1987, for reviews]. Blepharisomone is a chemoattractant to cells of mating type I and is a common gamone to all *Blepharisma* species. In contrast, gamone 1 is species specific. Binding studies using ^{125}I-gamone II imply that there is a specific binding site, perhaps a receptor on the cell surface. However, receptor proteins for these interesting stimuli have not been identified.

Species of another ciliate, *Euplotes*, have multiple mating types. The genetic analysis implicates three to four codominant alleles of the mating type locus, depending on the species. The expression of a homozygous or heterozygous state determines the cell's mating type and, presumably, both the pheromones released and receptors displayed at the cell surface. At present there is no agreement about the nature of this complex system: whether cells synthesize receptors for the pheromones they produce or only for the pheromones they do not produce [see Beale, 1990, for overview; Nobili et al., 1987; Heckmann and Kuhlmann, 1986].

In the self-recognition model for *Euplotes raikovi*, a homozygous cell expresses a single receptor to which homologous (self)-pheromone or nonself-pheromones from cells of other mating types can bind. If there is sufficient nonself-pheromone to displace the self-pheromone from the receptor, the mating process will commence. This model is supported by competition binding studies of purified pheromones [Luporini and Miceli, 1986]. An interesting prediction of this model is that the receptor and pheromone ($\sim$ 14kD) will be closely related, indeed identical, except for the portion of the receptor necessary to anchor it in the membrane. The cDNA for one pheromone has been characterized [Miceli et al., 1989], and cloning of the receptor gene will determine whether the receptor and pheromone are related. The M_r of the dimeric pheromone–receptor complex is ~28 kD in molecular mass, which is compatible with this model [Beale, 1990].

A different model for *Euplotes octocarinatus* predicts not one but many receptors per cell recognizing all pheromones but the ones produced by the cell itself [Heckmann and Kuhlmann, 1986]. Genetics of *Eup. octocarinatus* lend support to this model, and the recent cloning of the pheromone genes will help to clarify the details [Meyer et al., 1991, and personal communication; see Van Houten et al., 1981, for overview of protozoan chemoresponse].

4. Yeast. There are two mating types, *a* and α, of haploid cells of the yeast *Saccharomyces cerevisiae*. Each mating type produces a pheromone that arrests cells of the complementary mating type in G1, induces changes in the cell wall and the characteristic shmoo shape, and alters gene expression as a prelude to mating. The pheromones *a* and α are small peptides of 12 and 13 amino acids each [Thorner, 1981]. The α-factor binds to approximately 8,000 sites on an *MATa* cell with a K_d of 6×10^{-9} [Jenness et al., 1986, 1987]. A haploid cell will express the *a* or α-receptor gene, but not both, and likewise secretes only the pheromone to which it will not respond. The mechanism by which the *a*-factor is secreted is unconventional and may involve a specific ATPase pump [see Featherstone, 1990, for review]. Diploid cells that result from mating are not responsive to either pheromone. The genetics of mating types in yeast is fascinating [Nasmyth, 1982], but here only the genes for the receptors are the focus of attention [see Fields, 1990, for a short review of the entire pheromone response].

The receptor for α-factor is coded for by the *STE2* gene and for *a*-factor by the *STE3* gene [Burkholder and Hartwell, 1985; Nakayama et al., 1985; Hagen et al., 1986]. The amino acid sequence that is inferred from the DNA sequence gives a picture of two receptors that are similar in structure. It is curious that while their hydropathy plots are virtually superimposable with seven potential membrane-spanning regions, the proteins are utterly different in primary amino acid sequence [Hagen et al., 1986]. However, their deduced structures resemble those of members of the class of receptors that interact with G proteins: the rhodopsin/β-adrenergic, muscarinic acetylcholine family [Herskowitz and Marsh, 1987; Marx, 1987; Marsh and Herskowitz, 1988]. This classification based on structure is supported by recent reports of G protein involvement in the mating process (see below).

D. Invertebrates

This section focuses on chemoreception in sea urchin spermatozoa and arthropods, to the exclusion of other interesting, but less well-characterized invertebrate receptor systems [see Ache, 1987, for a review].

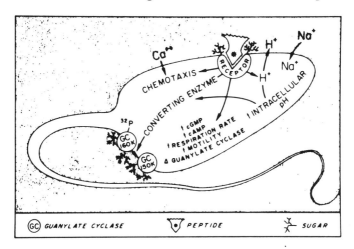

Fig. 6. Summary of events that occur upon an egg peptide interacting with its receptor on the sea urchin sperm cell. [Reproduced from Garbers et al., 1986, with permission of the publisher.]

Secretions from the eggs of the sea urchins *Strongylocentrotus purpuratus* and *Arbacia punctulata* stimulate spermatozoan motility and metabolism to facilitate fertilization [Trimmer and Vacquier, 1986]. Upon stimulation, internal levels of cAMP and cGMP increase, there is a net H^+ and K^+ efflux and calcium influx, and guanylate cyclase is dephosphorylated (Fig. 6). The stimulus activity comes from two peptides, speract and resact, consisting of 10 and 14 amino acids each [Dangott and Garbers, 1984].

Speract and resact stimulate spermatozoa in a species-specific manner through receptor proteins in spermatozoan membranes. Speract- and resact-binding proteins have been identified through crosslinking studies as proteins of M_r 77,000 and 160,000, respectively [Dangott and Garbers, 1984; Shimomura et al., 1986; Bentley et al., 1987]. The 160,000 M_r resact receptor and the guanylate cyclase are the same protein [Shimomura et al., 1986] and represent one example of a new paradigm for second-messenger signal transduction [Bentley et al., 1986b; Paul et al., 1987; Thorpe and Garbers, 1989; Garbers, 1989a,b; Schulz et al., 1989]. The speract peptide of *Strong. purpuratus* likewise activates a guanylate cyclase, but it is not yet evident whether the 77 kD protein to which speract binds is the receptor or a subunit thereof or how it relates to the guanylate cyclase [Schulz et al., 1989]. When spermatozoa are incubated with egg jelly or resact, the guanylate cyclase is first transiently activated and then inactivated by dephosphorylation [Bentley et al., 1986a,b]. This loss of phosphates coincides with a change in mobility of the enzyme on gels from 160,000 to 150,000 M_r. Therefore, like receptors in bacteria and *Dictyostelium*, spermatozoan receptors may undergo covalent modification, and like *Bac. subtilis* in particular, attractant receptor occupancy would be associated with *removal* of covalently attached groups. Whether this modification in spermatozoa is part of the adaptation process is not yet known. The spermatozoan resact receptor serves as a model for the mammalian atriopeptide factor receptors, which similarly are guanylate cyclases and therefore represent yet other members of this relatively newly described signal transduction receptor family that crosses phyla [Lowe et al., 1989; Schulz et al., 1989; see Paul et al., 1987, and Bentley et al., 1986b, for discussions).

Among the arthropods, lobsters (both spiny and American) and insects share very similar structures and receptor cell mechanisms for taste and smell, even though the medium by which the stimuli arrive is in water for crustacea and air for insects [Atema, 1987]. The long, aesthetasc sensilla on the lobsters antennules and the sensilla trichodea of moth antennae subserve olfaction. Both have permeable chitinous coverings over the dendrites of the bipolar receptor neurons that send information about odors in trains of impulses to the central nervous system (CNS) [Ache, 1987; Kaissling, 1987]. The thick hedgehog sensilla on the lobster walking legs and the tarsal sensilla of insect feet are chitin-covered dendrites of receptor and mechanosensory cells with access to taste stimuli only through one tip pore. The animals taste as stimuli enter the sensilla, usually upon direct contact with food. As in olfaction, information about stimuli is sent to the CNS in trains of action potentials from the receptor neurons.

Sensilla on insect legs respond to contact with sugar solutions [Dethier, 1978] and those on insect antennae are tuned to components of pheromones [Vogt, 1987; Kaissling, 1987], while the lobster and other crustacea find amino acids, nucleotides, and peptides to be stimulatory [Ache, 1987; Carr et al., 1987]. The spectrum of stimulatory amino acids is large and overlaps between antennules and legs, characteristically with glutamate receptors prominent on legs and hydroxyproline and taurine receptors prominent on antennules [Atema, 1987].

As Atema [1985] notes, signals must not persist. They must be removed from the area of the receptor cell if fresh information is to be processed. The female pheromone is rapidly degraded by the abundant esterase in the lymph that surrounds the receptor dendrites in the male silk moth sensillum [Vogt et al., 1985; Vogt, 1987]. It is possible that the stimulus survives on its traverse from pores in the chitin covering to the receptor cell, because it is promptly bound to a lymph protein that protects it until it can stimulate the receptor [Vogt, 1987; Vogt et al., 1989]. The lobster, likewise, has a system for degradation of signal in the aesthetasc sensilla (Fig. 7). Here a primary stimulus, ATP, is degraded to ADP, AMP, and, finally, adenosine, all of which are active as weaker stimuli or inhibitors of the degradation enzymes or are actively transported into the receptor cell [Trapido-Rosenthal et al., 1987]. One end result of this cascade is the removal of stimulus from the receptor interaction, but certainly there are other modulatory effects as well.

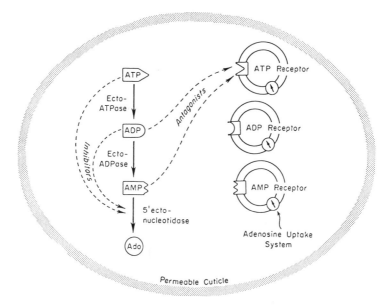

Fig. 7. Multiple receptors and signal degrading enzymes of the lobster olfactory sensilla. The cross section through the sensillum shows lymph surrounding dendrites, on which are separate receptors for adenine nucleotides and a ubiquitous adenosine uptake system. ATP, ADP, and AMP are stimulatory while adenosine is not, and ADP and AMP are antagonists of the ATP response. In the sensillar lymph surrounding the dendrites are enzymes that rapidly degrade ATP to adenosine and, by doing so, create complex mixtures of stimuli and ultimately adenosine that is removed by uptake. (There is no evidence that the classes of receptors always reside on separate dendrites.) [Reproduced from Trapido-Rosenthal et al., 1989, with permission of the publisher.]

Insects and crustacea have very low thresholds for response of a receptor cell [Kaissling, 1987; Ache, 1987]. It is estimated that one molecule of pheromone can elicit an action potential [Kaissling, 1987]. The action potentials originate in either dendrite or soma [Ache, 1987; Kaissling, 1987], and their ionic mechanism(s) are not yet fully characterized [Schmiedel-Jakob et al., 1989; McClintock and Ache, 1988, 1989a,b]. A cell can be specialized to respond best to one stimulus, or it can be a more generalist in its response. In either case, the rate of discharge is a function of stimulus concentration, but a unique pattern of discharge does not code each individual stimulus in the cell's response spectrum [Ache, 1987]. Therefore, when odorant stimuli from natural sources arrive at the receptor cells in mixtures, it is thought that the collective pattern of depolarized cells across the olfactory sensillum provide the CNS with information about the quality and quantity of the odor. However, it is now clear (for vertebrates as well as invertebrates) that components of odorant mixtures can be excitatory to one cell and inhibitory to another, and, while both individual cells are depolarized by the mixture, the inhibitory components can reduce the magnitude and delay the onset of the evoked depolarization [McClintock and Ache, 1989; Michel and Ache, 1990; Dionne, 1990]. Therefore, the first level of integration of information is at the level of the receptor cell [Michel and Ache, 1990] and not in the CNS, as previously believed.

The lobster responds over many orders of magnitude of stimulus concentration [Ache, 1987; Atema, 1987]. A means of expanding the dynamic range of a cell is the shift up of the entire stimulus–response curve of leg ammonium receptor cells after adaptation to background amounts of ammonium [Borroni and Atema, 1987]. (This is very reminiscent of the neutrophil's ability to respond to an increase in 200 receptors occupied regardless of whether the change is 200 to 400 or 4,000 to 4,200 [Zigmond, 1989]; see section II.B.) Adaptation may allow these cells to distinguish signal from background ammonium, which ranges from 10^{-6} M in seawater to 10^{-2} M in prey tissues [Atema, 1987]. The molecular mechanism of adaptation is not yet understood, but must somehow be accounted for in the receptor function or the transduction mechanism [see Atema, 1985; Derby and Atema, 1987; Schmitt and Ache, 1979; and Ache, 1987, for consideration of adaptation and section II.G. for other means of expanding a cell's dynamic range].

The receptor proteins of arthropod sensilla have been elusive, even though moths provide reasonable amounts of membrane for receptor biochemistry. Recently, however, Vogt et al. [1988] used a photoaffinity analog of the *Antheraea polyphemus* pheromone (E,Z)6,11-^{3}H-hexadecaniehyl diazoacetate to label not only the soluble receptor lymph-binding protein but also a 69 kD protein from dendrite membranes. This protein is labeled specifically by the photoaffinity probe and is found in dendritic membrane only and in male moths only [Vogt et al., 1988].

E. Vertebrates

Vertebrates monitor their chemical environment through taste, smell, and common chemical sense. In all these sensory modalities, neurons or neuroepithelial cells serve as receptor cells.

1. Taste. Taste buds generally are comprised of 50–150 neuroepithelial cells in pear- or spindle-shaped clusters [Kinnamon, 1987]. They make contact with the environment at their apical end with the microvilli that protrude through the taste pore. The receptor cells are innervated by fibers that penetrate or abut the bud. Generally, sweet, saline, sour, and bitter tastants are detected by receptor cells that are not particularly finely tuned, but do respond best to one tastant class [Teeter and Brand, 1987b]. Amino acids are taste stimuli, particularly in fish. As in crustacea, the spectrum of amino acids overlaps for taste and smell [Caprio, 1988; Atema, 1987].

Upon stimulation, a taste receptor cell will release neurotransmitter and alter the rate of spontaneous firing of primary nerve fibers that traverse to the CNS. In this case, interaction of stimulus with the apical membrane of the receptor cell is transduced into signals for neurotransmitter release and generally not into active electrogenic response as in taste receptors in invertebrates and all olfactory receptor cells (although some taste cells have been shown to be capable of generating action potentials [Roper, 1989]).

There is no unifying mechanism for taste stimulus transduction. The ion movements and second messengers in response to saline, sweet, bitter, sour, and amino acid tastants are still being deciphered [Kinnamon, 1988; Teeter and Brand 1987b]. However, some generalizations can be made, and all of the following mechanisms are likely to work (Fig. 8): The release of neurotransmitter is a calcium-dependent process, and a tastant could increase internal calcium by one of several ways. 1) Depolarization would open calcium channels and allow an influx of internal calcium. The depolarization could be a direct consequence of the tastant, e.g., salt entering the cell through voltage-insensitive amiloride blockable channels [DeSimone et al., 1981; DeSimone and Ferrell, 1985; Schiffmann, 1990]; H^+ transiently blocking resting K^+ conductance, thus decreasing a hyperpolarizing conductance [Kinnamon and Roper, 1988]; or a tastant binding to receptor that in turn opens a channel or activates a transport system [Mierson et al., 1988; Teeter et al., 1990]. 2) Alternatively, no depolarization is needed if a tastant alters surface potential and consequently opens channels in the membrane, or if the tastant, through a receptor such as the sugar receptor or the catfish alanine receptor, generates internal messengers that liberate calcium from internal stores [see Teeter and Brand, 1987b; Teeter et al., 1987, 1989; and Roper, 1989, for reviews].

There is evidence for receptors in the mediation only of sweet and amino acid taste [Sato, 1987; Teeter and Brand, 1987b; Cagan and Boyle, 1984; Dionne, 1988]. Perhaps the best characterized are the catfish receptors for alanine and arginine for which binding kinetics have been measured and blocking antibodies have been produced [Cagan, 1981; Brand et al., 1987; Bryant et al., 1987; Kalinoski et al., 1987a,b]. A heterogeneous group of proteins of 110,000 daltons exclusively from taste tissues are recognized on immunoblots by an antibody that blocks alanine binding [Bryant et al., 1987, 1989]. The receptor among these proteins has yet to be purified or cloned, but it is expected that the arginine receptor will be a ligand-gated cation channel and the alanine receptor will be a G protein–associated, transmembrane receptor [Teeter et al., 1990].

The only other partially characterized taste receptors are for sapid stimuli [Persaud et al., 1988] and the sweet-tasting protein thaumatin [see Sato, 1987 for a review]. A ^{3}H-photoaffinity analog of thaumatin was used to label specifically a 50,000 dalton protein in taste but not other papillae. Likewise, proteins eluting from a thaumatin affinity column included one of $\simeq 50,000$ daltons.

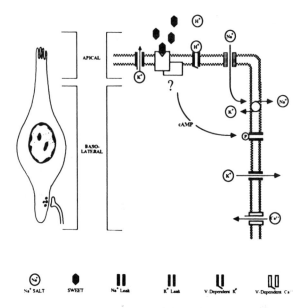

Fig. 8. Diagrammatic representation of taste transduction mechanisms. Sour transduction involves acid block of voltage-dependent K^+ channels, which are restricted to the apical membrane. Na^+ transduction involves the passage of Na^+ into taste cells through passive, amiloride-blockable Na^+ channels on the apical membrane of taste cells; Na^+ is then pumped out by an Na^+,K^+-ATPase on the basolateral membrane. Sweet transduction involves receptor-mediated stimulation of adenylate cyclase; voltage-independent K^+ channels on the basolateral membrane are then closed in response to cAMP-dependent phosphorylation. However, the link between increased adenylate cyclase activity in response to sweet stimuli and closure of K^+ channels by cAMP-dependent phosphorylation has not yet been shown in the same taste receptor cells. Transduction by all these pathways involves one final common pathway: depolarization and influx of Ca^{2+} through voltage-dependent Ca^{2+} channels. Transduction mechanisms for other taste modalities have not been illustrated and include ligand or cyclic nucleotide activated cation channels. It is not yet clear if all these mechanisms are present on a single taste cell, as illustrated here, or if different taste cells are specialized to detect particular taste modalities. [Reproduced from Kinnamon, 1988, with permission of the publisher.]

2. Olfaction. Olfactory receptor cells are bipolar primary neurons. The cilia (or, less commonly, microvilli) at the apical ends make contact with the immediate environment, the mucous layer that sweeps across the olfactory and respiratory epithelia. The mucus is secreted in part by sustentacular cells that along with the receptor and basal cells make up the epithelium. Odorants partition into the mucus, where at least some kinds are bound by an olfactory-binding protein (OBP) [Pevsner et al., 1985; Bignetti et al., 1985] that is secreted into the mucus [Pevsner et al., 1986]. It is likely that this OBP from cow and mouse as well as a newly described protein from frog [Lee et al., 1987] are analogous to the insect lymph pheromone-binding protein and protect odorant until it contacts the cilia, the site of olfactory transduction [Adamek et al., 1984; Rhein and Cagan, 1981]. Alternatively, the OBP may function to clear odor from the mucus [see Getchell and Getchell, 1987, and Getchell et al., 1984, for review]. As the intake of air washes odorants over the epithelium, the odorants partition into the mucus as a function of their solubility, imposing a differential distribution of odorants on the epithelium. Superimposed on this is the inherent pattern of receptor cells. Individual receptor neurons are broadly tuned with a spectrum of response that overlaps that of other cells [Gesteland, 1986; Sicard and Holley, 1984]. However, receptor cells are not evenly distributed across the epithelium. Maps of activity across the epithelium show differential clusters of activity to different odorants [Edwards et al., 1988]. The axons of the receptor cells project to the olfactory bulb, and the pattern of activity across the axons must encode the quantity and quality of the odor [see Kauer, 1987, for a review].

A receptor cell will respond to an excitatory odorant stimulus with a decrease in input resistance, current flow of monovalent cations, and subsequent depolarization receptor potential that is responsible for opening voltage-dependent channels of the axon hillock [Gesteland, 1986; Persaud et al., 1987]. The opening of these channels converts the transducing receptor current into action potentials that are transmitted to the CNS [see Getchell and Getchell, 1987, for review]. The important questions in olfactory transduction regard the generation of a receptor current and depolarization by the interaction of stimulus with dendritic ciliary membrane.

Because olfactory receptor cells are broadly tuned, it is possible that each has many receptors for different stimuli. The number of stimuli that a human can detect is thought to be 10^4 [Dionne, 1988], and therefore the number of receptors necessary for this detection could be very high. There could be many gene products of similar size but with different odorant-binding capacities, perhaps generated through differential gene rearrangement analogous to the immune system or through differential splicing of one transcript or transcription of a family of genes. Minimally there appear to be two transduction mechanisms (see below) and therefore at least two sets of receptor types. However, to date no vertebrate olfactory receptor protein has been isolated, although there are some candidates (see next paragraph). This failure to identify an external olfactory chemoreceptor may be due in part to the difficulties of dealing with low abundance membrane proteins of relatively low binding affinity [Price, 1981]. Alternatively, there may be mechanisms of olfaction that do not require receptors, in which volatile lipophilic molecules interact directly with the membrane [Dionne, 1988; Anholt, 1987; Lerner et al., 1988]. The recent cloning of putative receptor genes will help to resolve these issues [Buck and Axel, 1991; Nef and Dionne, personal communication; see section V].

Candidates for receptors are the anisole- and benzaldehyde-binding proteins identified by affinity chromatography of dog epithelium [Price and Willey,

1987, 1988]. These proteins are found in the olfactory but not respiratory epithelium. Antibodies against the anisole proteins block electrical responses to anisole stimulation best, but block all odorant stimulation to some degree, perhaps reflecting epitopes common to all receptors. This idea is supported by studies of electro-olfactograms (EOGs) in the presence of monoclonal antibodies against the same proteins [Price and Willey, 1988]. Some of the monoclonal antibodies were specific in their inhibition of the electrical stimulation by anisole or benzaldehyde, but others were nonspecific. It is curious that the anisole- and benzaldehyde-binding proteins are of the same M_r (62,000) and perhaps share an epitope in common to a family of olfactory receptors.

Lancet and coworkers have found a membrane glycoprotein of 95 kD (gp95) from frog olfactory epithelium that is of particular interest because antibodies against it coprecipitate the ciliary adenylate cyclase, which they argue is an important component in sensory transduction [Lancet et al., 1987; Lancet and Pace, 1987; Chen et al., 1986]. While this protein has the tissue specificity and location in ciliary membrane to qualify for a receptor, it has not been demonstrated to bind odorant and appears to be secreted into the mucus [Menco, 1991].

Fesenko et al. [1987] reported odorant binding to a membrane glycoprotein specific to the olfactory epithelium. However, as Vogt et al. [1988] point out, there is no demonstration that this protein is enriched in the ciliary fraction. In other examples, binding sites for ^{3}H-alanine [Rhein and Cagan, 1981; Cagan, 1981], amino acids on skate olfactory epithelium [Novoselov et al., 1988], and pyrazine [Pelosi et al., 1982] are described, but the protein moieties are at best only partially purified and characterized.

3. Common chemical sense. In common chemical sense, chemosensation is due to the stimulation of epithelial or mucosal free nerve endings from branches of the trigeminal nerve [Silver, 1987]. Receptor studies lag behind those in taste and olfaction and will not be treated further here.

F. Perireceptor Events

Ligand binding to receptor is thought to begin the transduction process that leads to the second messengers and ion conductance changes that are essential for chemoreception. However, there are essential events that occur prior to and after binding, the so-called perireceptor events that play a significant role in the chemoreception process [Getchell et al., 1984]. As mentioned for insect pheromone and vertebrate olfaction, there are molecules that are likely to be carriers, i.e., protectors, of the odorant molecule until it binds to receptor. Stengl et al. [1990] have shown that pheromone complexed with pheromone-binding protein is less effective than pheromone alone at opening ion channels in cultured insect cells, and therefore pheromone-binding proteins may also function to sequester stimulus in preparation for the next wave. Recently, an mRNA for a protein analogous to the OBP has been demonstrated in von Ebner's glands, salivary glands located directly beneath and ducting into a trough at the base of rat taste bud papillae [Schmale et al., 1990]. The protein is a member of the same carrier protein superfamily to which OBP belongs, suggesting that this salivary protein might function in the concentration or delivery of sapid molecules to the taste receptor. Whether these binding proteins can act to facilitate diffusion or cause concentration of stimulus [Pevsner et al., 1986] is a matter of discussion [Snyder et al., 1988; Pelosi and Dal Monte, 1990]. However, there clearly are other mechanisms to remove the stimulus from the region of the receptor: phosphodiesterase of *Dictyostelium* degrades extracellular cAMP; neutrophil enzymes degrade the attractant stimulus FMLP; phosphatase, and nucleotidases in lobster, destroy nucleotide stimuli; the movement of mucus and active and facilitated transport remove stimuli from the area of receptors in vertebrates and crustaceans; and intracellular degradation by cytochrome P-450 and UDP-glucuronosyltransferase prevent the diffusion of hydrophobic odorants back out of cells where they can be confused with newly arriving stimuli [Lancet et al., 1989; Lazard et al., 1990, 1991; see Burchell, 1991, for review]. The relative rates of these reactions greatly influence the sensitivity, duration, and adaptation of receptor-mediated events and therefore indirectly affect sensory transduction [see Getchell et al., 1984; Getchell and Getchell, 1987; Carr, 1989; and Trapido-Rosenthal et al., 1989, for reviews].

G. Reception in Mixtures

Stimuli rarely come singly, but more usually in a bouquet with other components. Mixtures are the most effective stimuli in eliciting behavioral responses in crustacea [Carr et al., 1984] and insects [Linn and Roelofs, 1989; Linn et al., 1985; O'Connell, 1986; Vogt, 1987]. The components of natural stimulatory mixtures for these organisms are not generally equimolar or equipotent; some components act additively or synergistically to stimulate, and others suppress the behavioral response [see Derby and Atema, 1987; Caprio 1987a,b; Ache, 1987, 1989; and Derby et al., 1989, for discussion].

The individual receptor cells inside both taste and olfactory sensilla can be finely tuned to only one component of the mixture, and indeed narrow tuning predominates in the lobster taste and smell [Atema, 1985] and insect olfaction [Kaissling, 1987]. However, despite the narrow tuning, these receptor cells do not extract information about their "best" stimulus to the exclusion of other components of a mixture. Indeed, mixture components, to which the finely tuned cell will not respond individually, often suppress the receptor cell impulse output from its "best" stimulus [Derby and Atema, 1987]. This mixture suppression is thought to allow the cell a large concentration range for response [Atema, 1987; Johnson et al., 1989]. The lobster receptor cell response saturates over two to three orders of magnitude, but the receptor populations must be able to respond over a range of $10^{-8}–10^{-2}$ M amino acids, for example [Atema, 1985; Ache, 1987]. Not all stimuli in mixtures are excitatory or neutral. As discussed under invertebrate olfaction (section II.D.2.), stimuli can be excitatory to some cells and inhibitory to others by hyperpolarizing the cell. Mixtures of the hyperpolarizing stimuli can influence the time of onset and the magnitude of the evoked depolarization, thus allowing for integration of mixture information at the periphery as well as at the CNS.

Lobsters and insects are not the only organisms to show mixture suppression and synergy, but they serve to point out that, when examining receptor function and receptor-mediated transduction, one must be aware of mixture effects. Additionally, mixture suppression occurs in the CNS as well as the periphery and therefore should not be interpreted solely as a modification of receptor or receptor cell function [Derby et al., 1984; Derby and Ache, 1984].

III. SECOND MESSENGERS IN CHEMORECEPTION

A. Overview of Second Messengers

Now that several chemoreceptor systems have been introduced, it is time to discuss their common aspects of signal transduction. None of these transduction pathways are known from ligand to response end, but there is clear evidence for each system that one or more second messengers are involved. There are a limited number of second messengers, and, as Margolis [1987] notes for olfaction, there is no reason to suspect that any of these organisms have had to utilize a completely novel pathway to deal with the fairly common process of signally the presence of an external ligand to the interior of a cell. It is important to recognize that there can be two or more "second" messengers in series. To avoid confusion, these will be referred to generally as "internal" messengers and more specifically as "second" and "third" messengers if this hierarchy has been established.

B. Cyclic Nucleotides

Changes in levels of intracellular cAMP or cGMP have been identified as responses to ligand binding in *Chlamydomonas* agglutination [Pasquale and Goodenough, 1987; Musgrave and van den Ende, 1987], *D. discoideum* aggregation [Janssens and Van Haastert, 1987], sperm chemotaxis [Garbers et al., 1986], neutrophil chemotaxis [Sha'afi and Molski, 1988], and vertebrate olfaction and gustation [see Teeter and Gold, 1988; Lancet and Pace, 1987; and Anholt, 1987, for overviews]. In *Chlamydomonas* and *D. discoideum* it is most clearly established that cyclic nucleotides are internal messengers that function as links in the sensory transduction pathways.

In *Chlamydomonas*, intracellular cAMP is increased 10-fold upon flagellar agglutination [Pasquale and Goodenough, 1987]. Permeable dibutyrl-cAMP and phosphodiesterase inhibitors will elicit flagellar tip activation, cell wall loss, and mating structure activation with actin polymerization in gametes of a single mating type, and an inhibitor of cAMP protein kinase, H8, antago-nizes these effects. The flagella have adenylate cyclase (albeit different from vertebrate enzymes) and phosphodiesterase activity [Pasquale and Goodenough, 1987]. Therefore the site of signal transduction that controls second-messenger levels could be either of these enzymes.

In *D. discoideum*, cGMP is not the only internal messenger generated as a result of receptor binding (Fig. 5), but it does indeed appear to be a causative agent in the half of the bifurcated response pathway that mediates chemo-taxis. The transient increases in internal cGMP in response to external cAMP or folic acid stimuli occur over the time course expected for the second-messenger response for initiation of chemotaxis, and for some time cGMP was considered the second messenger in chemotaxis [Mato et al., 1977; Wurster et al., 1977; see Van Houten and Preston, 1987, for an overview]. Now it is clear that increases in inositol phosphates, in particular inositol-1,4,5-tris-phosphate (IP$_3$), and Ca^{2+}, precede the stimulation of guanylate cyclase and the rise in cGMP (Fig. 5) [Small et al., 1987; Europe-Finner and Newell, 1985, 1986]. Therefore cGMP may be considered a later, perhaps fourth, mes-senger and functions in the accumulation of myosin in the cytoskeleton of the *Dictyostelium* cell that is preparing for a change in cell shape and orientated movement [Liu and Newell, 1988; Newell et al., 1988]. Actin polymerization likewise is implicated in change of cell shape and as a driving force in pseudo-pod extension [Newell, 1986; Condeelis et al., 1988]. The "B" receptor, mediated chemotaxis pathway that couples through G$_{2\alpha}$ to phospholipase C (PLC) can be examined separately from the "A"-mediated relay pathway that is coupled through the G$_s$ protein to the adenylate cyclase, and it appears that G$_{2\alpha}$ is directly or indirectly responsible for transduction of stimulus by cAMP to actin nucleation centers [Hall et al., 1989]. Intracellular Ca^{2+}, not cGMP, appears to be the second messenger for actin polymerization, although both second messengers are the consequences of "B"-receptor activation of PLC [Newell, 1986]. Mutants with defective phosphodiesterase and hence abnormally elevated and prolonged rises in cGMP are defective in chemotaxis [Ross and Newell, 1981; Van Haastert et al., 1982]. In these mutants, myosin associa-tion with the cytoskeleton but not actin polymerization is affected [Newell, 1986; Liu and Newell, 1988].

In *sea urchin sperm* chemotaxis, the stimulus resact increases cAMP levels 300-fold [Garbers and Kopf, 1980] and alters cGMP levels by transiently stim-ulating and then inhibiting the receptor guanylate cyclase [Bentley et al., 1986a]. The adenylate cyclase requires an influx of calcium for its activation (Fig. 6), and cAMP in turn activates the cAMP-dependent protein kinase that figures into the stimulatory effects of resact on respiration and motility [Garbers et al., 1980; Garbers, 1986; see Satir, 1985, Bonini and Nelson, 1988, and Tash et al., 1987, for effects of cyclic nucleotides on flagellar motility]. Because the guanylate cyclase is both resact receptor and generator of internal messenger, it seems safe to assume that either the absolute increase or decrease (as in vision) or the changes in cGMP figure into the chemotaxis signal transduction pathway.

Olfactory cilia have a very high adenylate cyclase activity [Lancet, 1986], and this activity is stimulated 1.5–2.5-fold with some odorants in a GTP-dependent manner [Pace and Lancet, 1986; Sklar et al., 1986; Shirley et al., 1986]. At present, odorants are categorized by their ability or inability to stimulate adenylate cyclase. The latter class is thought possibly to work by stimulation of phosphoinositol lipid (PIP$_2$) hydrolysis to generate internal messengers [Lancet and Pace, 1987]. (cGMP is not a candidate as an internal messenger here because its levels do not change with odorant stimulation [Shirley et al., 1986].)

What has not been apparent is the role of the cAMP that clearly increases in response to some odorants: Is cAMP a second messenger that opens ion channels in receptor cells either directly or by way of a protein kinase A activity, or is it outside the sensory transduction pathway and functions to desensitize the receptor or close ion channels by processes such as phosphorylation (Fig. 9)? The time course of the adenylate cyclase stimulation in some systems would suggest that it functions in a slower process such as adaptation/desensitization [Bruch and Teeter, 1988; Bruch et al., 1987a,b, 1989; Anholt, 1987]. Also, there are ion conductances that are directly odorant stimulated, obviating the need for a second messenger to open channels [Labarca et al., 1988]. However, cyclic nucleotide–sensitive conductances have also been identified by voltage- and patch-clamping of receptor cells. These conductances respond equally well to cAMP or cGMP [Nakamura and Gold, 1987; Kolesnikov et al., 1990; Bruch and Teeter, 1990]. The magnitude of the EOG, a summed response of olfactory epithelial cells elicited by an odorant, correlates with the magnitude of adenylate cyclase activity, possibly implying a transduction and not adaptation role for cAMP [Lowe et al., 1988]. Which one or more of these nucleotide-dependent and -independent conductances is involved in sensory transduction and generation of the receptor potential in the olfactory receptor cells remains to be established. However, it seems clear that cAMP gating of channels will be among the mechanisms [Firestein and Shepherd, 1989, 1990].

Recently, stop-flow kinetics analyses have provided evidence that cAMP can indeed increase and drop off sufficiently rapidly in a GTP-dependent manner to qualify as a second messenger for a set of odorants [Breer and Boekoff, 1991; Breer et al., 1990a,b]. It appears that odorants stimulate *either* cAMP *or* IP$_3$ production in rat olfactory cilia on a subsecond time scale. In comparison, a moth pheromone stimulates second-messenger production on a time scale sufficiently fast to be involved in conductance changes, but only IP$_3$ is generated in the antennal preparations. In all cases, the effects on second messengers are GTP dependent, reinforcing the idea that odorant receptors will eventually be isolated. Excitable cells other than olfactory receptor cells did not respond to odorants

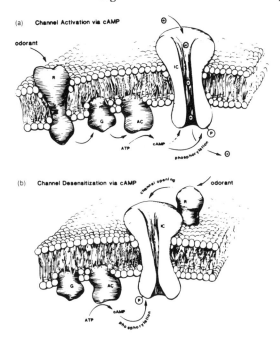

Fig. 9. Schematic of two alternative working hypotheses for signal transduction at the olfactory membrane. **a:** Linkage of an odorant receptor (R) via a G protein (G) to adenylate cyclase (AC) results in the generation of cAMP, which, either directly or via phosphorylation, activated an ion channel (IC). **b:** Linkage of an odorant recognition site to a channel causes opening of the channel directly. In this model, cAMP-dependent phosphorylation would lead to inactivation (desensitization) of the channel. Activation by the odorant of the olfactory adenylate cyclase may either be mediated via a distinct receptor protein or via direct activation (i.e., partial dissociation) of the G protein as a result of partitioning of the odorant in the membrane. There now is evidence that in some systems cyclic nucleotides can activate conductances as part of the sensory transduction pathway. [Reproduced from Anholt, 1987, with permission of the publisher.]

with increases in second messengers, helping to discount some of the concern that the lipophilic nature of some odorants would allow them to induce conductance changes by direct membrane interactions without benefit of receptors or specific binding sites on channels [Dionne, 1988; Lerner et al., 1988; Kashiwayanagi et al., 1990].

There may be a second mechanism by which odorants stimulate the adenylate cyclase [Anholt and Rivers, 1990]. In frog epithelium, adenylate cyclase is stimulated not only by odorants, but also by Ca^{2+}-calmodulin in a GTP-dependent manner [Anholt and Rivers, 1990]. The two modes of stimulation are additive, providing for alternate mechanisms by which odorants can produce second messengers and for "cross-talk" between pathways. In particular, Anholt and Rivers [1990] propose that low concentrations of odorants directly open Ca^{2+} channels to provide the Ca^{2+} for calmodulin stimulation of adenylate cyclase and that, at high concentrations of odorants, the olfactory specific G protein (G_{olf}) is activated, resulting in further stimulation of adenylate cyclase. This model implies that receptor cells could have the potential for crosstalk between these pathways to add a dimension of integration of information about quantities of stimuli in mixtures, for example. (See next section for parallel pathways for cAMP and IP_3 in catfish.)

Similarly in *taste cells*, cyclic nucleotide internal messengers are implicated in the depolarization of the receptor cell. Reports of GTP-dependent cAMP synthesis in response to sugars in rat taste tissue [Lancet et al., 1987; Striem et al., 1989] and to amino acids by catfish [Bruch and Teeter, 1988, 1989; Kalinoski et al., 1988; Bruch et al., 1989] are further supported by direct measurements of depolarizing conductance changes mediated by cyclic nucleotides. Rat taste cells injected with cGMP (and to a lesser extent with cAMP) depolarize the cells by decreasing K^+ conductance, the same conductance that decreases during depolarization with a sugar stimulus [Tonosaki and Funakoshi, 1988]. Frog taste cells under patch-clamp likewise decrease K^+ conductance with cAMP (cGMP was not tested), and in this case the conductance decrease has been traced to a cAMP-dependent protein phosphorylation [Avenet et al., 1988].

The stimulation of taste adenylate cyclase may be sufficiently fast to allow cAMP levels to participate in transduction [Kalinoski et al., 1988,1989], but not all tastants in catfish activate adenylate cyclase, thereby requiring at least a second transduction mechanism. (The recent reports of tastants L-arginine and L-proline activating ion channels directly neatly provides one answer [Teeter et al., 1990; Kumazawa et al., 1990; Kohbara et al., 1990]; see section IV.D.). The modulation of ion channel gating by cAMP-dependent protein kinase is a departure of the gustatory from the olfactory system with its direct gating by cyclic nucleotides [Nakamura and Gold, 1987], but there are bound to be multiple mechanisms of transduction in taste cells, perhaps some of which will include direct gating by cyclic nucleotides, calcium, inositol phosphates, and other internal messengers (see Teeter and Gold, 1988, for an overview; also see sections III.C. and IV.B.).

Neutrophils experience transient increases in cAMP with chemotactic peptide stimulation not as a result of activation of the adenylate cyclase, but probably through inhibition of the phosphodiesterase [Jackowski and Sha'afi, 1979; Sha'afi and Molski, 1988; Smollen et al., 1980; Keller et al., 1970; Verghese et al., 1985]. However, exogenously applied cAMP, epinephrine, PGE_1, cholera toxin, and isoproterenol inhibit chemotaxis, phagocytosis, and degranulation [see Sha'afi and Molski, 1988, for an overview].

Interestingly, dibutyrl-cAMP inhibits the FMLP-stimulated phosphoinositol lipid hydrolysis [Della Bianca et al., 1986; Takenawa et al., 1986; Kato et al., 1986] and may do so indirectly through the action of the cAMP-dependent protein kinase A on either the FMLP receptor or the sensory transduction G protein characteristic of neutrophils and associated with the receptor [Sha'afi and Molski, 1988]. Taken together, these observations suggest an indirect, modulatory role for the FMLP-induced transient rise in cAMP as opposed to a role of an internal messenger in the sensory transduction pathway.

C. Phosphoinositol Lipid Hydrolysis and Sequelae

There is a renewed appreciation of the role of lipids and lipid metabolites in receptor functioning. In particular, arachiodonic acic (AA) and the inositol phospholipid hydrolysis products $1,4,5$-IP_3 and diacylglycerol (DAG) have been found to figure into a diverse range of sensory transduction pathway steps [Berridge, 1987; Kikkawa and Nishizuka, 1986; Piomelli et al., 1987; Axelrod et al., 1988], many of which have been documented to be mediated by G proteins [Gilman, 1987; Berridge, 1987; Stryer and Bourne, 1986; Axelrod et al., 1988]. $1,4,5$-IP_3 and DAG are generated by the action of phospholipase C (PLC) on PIP_2, although DAG can be derived from other sources as well. AA is generated by the action of DAG lipase on DAG or phospholipase A_2 on membrane lipids. Therefore, AA synthesis can be linked to or separate from the PIP_2 metabolism. The functions of IP_3 and DAG appear to be the liberation of calcium from internal, nonmitochondrial stores [Berridge, 1987] and the activation of protein kinase C, respectively [Kikkawa and Nishizuka, 1986]. The direct site of interaction of AA or its metabolites is not yet clear. It is clear, however, that IP_3, DAG, and/or AA are produced as a result of ligand–receptor interactions in *Dictyostelium*, neutrophils, and olfactory and taste cells.

A neutrophil's response to FMLP is many faceted and mediated by several different internal messengers. The facets of the response differ in concentration of stimulus and time: Chemotaxis requires a lower concentration of FMLP, and changes in cytoskeleton preparatory to oriented movement occur immediately; activation of NADPH oxidase that is seminal in the oxidative burst requires a 10–50-fold high stimulus concentration [Snyderman, 1984] and occurs later in the process of activating the cell [Truett et al., 1988]. Therefore, to simplify the discussion and yet touch upon the major issues of neutrophil activation, two aspects will be examined, i.e., actin polymerization in preparation for chemotaxis and NADPH oxidase activation for the oxidative burst that produces bactericidal O_2^- and H_2O_2.

Receptor–FMLP binding through the intervention of a G protein stimulates PLC activity and thereby increases the cellular content of $1,4,5$-IP_3 and DAG [Dillon et al., 1987a]. $1,4,5$-IP_3 affects internal calcium stores and also serves as a precursor to $1,3,4,5$-IP (IP_4), a potential stimulus for opening calcium channels [Irvine and Moor, 1986; Houslay, 1987]. (External Ca^{2+} entry appears to be essential for some sustained responses to stimuli, but the mechanism by which surface membrane calcium channels open after the initial stimulation of IP_3 production is a matter of debate [Putney, 1987; Petersen, 1989; Schulz et al., 1989]. Additionally, the source of this secondary Ca^{2+} for sustained response need not be external [Krause et al., 1989].

The metabolism of 1,4,5-IP_3 follows two separate routes: 1) At ambient intracellular Ca, it is dephosphorylated to 1,4-IP_2, 4-IP, and inositol; and 2) at increased calcium levels, it is phosphorylated to 1,3,4,5-IP_4, which is then dephosphorylated through a different sequence of intermediates. The differential dependence on calcium implies different functions for the inositol polyphosphates in neutrophil activation. There undoubtedly are other levels of control, as the finding of S-adenosylhomocysteine as a competitive inhibitor of phosphatidylinositol kinase implies [Pike and DeMeester, 1988]. The activation of protein kinase C by DAG appears to feed back and inhibit phosphatidylinositol hydrolysis by a yet undefined interaction with the G protein that intervenes between receptor and PLC [Dillon et al., 1987a]. DAG also serves as an important source of AA that in turn serves many functions by providing a precursor to leukotrienes (also chemoattractants), prostaglandins, and thromboxanes [Balsinde et al., 1988] and by liberating internal calcium pools [Nasmith and Grinstein, 1987a,b; Beaumier et al., 1987]. Additionally, phospholipase A_2 can produce AA from sources other than DAG, and activation of phospholipase A_2 is an early event in activation of neutrophils by ionophore [Lackie, 1988; Balsinde et al., 1988].

Upon stimulation, a neutrophil immediately changes shape by extending pseudopods and lamellepodia along the edge in contact with the highest stimulus concentration. Subsequently, it reorients its cytoskeleton to produce the characteristic polar shape and moves up the gradient of attractant [Cochrane, 1984]. Underlying the shape change and motility are rearrangements of the cytoskeleton, including a rapid polymerization, slower depolymerization, and redistribution of actin within the cell [Howard and Wang, 1987; Sha'afi and Molski, 1988; Cassimeris et al., 1990]. There appear to be two populations of actin in the cell: one stable, cortical population that is unaffected by attractants and a second labile population rapidly turning over in the lamellipodia, where chemoattractants stimulate polymerization for oriented movement and removal of attractants triggers rapid depolymerization [Cassimeris et al., 1990]. In contrast to *Dictyostelium*, PIP_3 and not PIP_2 seems to be involved in the modulation of actin after receptor binding [Eberle et al., 1990].

There are roles for both calcium and protein kinase in chemotaxis as evidenced by studies of oriented locomotion using ionophores, internal calcium buffers and chelators, calmodulin inhibitors, and inhibitors and activators of protein kinase [Wright et al., 1988; Harvath et al., 1989; Roos et al., 1987; Sha'afi and Molski, 1988; Laskin et al., 1987]. The roles must be complex, because manipulations of protein kinase C and intracellular Ca alone or in combination are not sufficient to account for the in vivo changes in F-actin that precede chemotaxis [Howard and Wang, 1987]. However, there are complications in the interpretation of the results with phorbol myristate acetate (PMA) treatment [Webster et al., 1986; Roos et al., 1987] that do not satisfactorily mimic the pertussis toxin–sensitive, presumably gelsolin-mediated [Yin, 1987] changes in F-actin stimulated by FMLP [Sha'afi and Molski, 1987; Howard and Wang, 1987]. The pertussis toxin sensitivity may come in part from the G protein–mediated activation of phospholipase A_2 [Burgoyne et al., 1987]. The participation of AA generated by phospholipase A_2 in early stimulus-induced changes such as actin polymerization could account for some of the failures of phorbol esters to mimic more of the FMLP response [Lackie, 1988].

The oxidative burst, as chemotaxis, appears to involve multiple pathways [see Bagglioni and Wymann, 1990, for review] and is initiated through the receptor-mediated stimulation of PIP_2 metabolism with consequent increases in internal calcium levels. One emerging scenario for regulation of the oxidative burst is that NADPH oxidase is activated by three mechanisms, all of which may be active under normal physiological conditions. The first is a calcium-dependent mechanism that is part of the "classic" signal transduction liberating DAG and calcium via IP_3 and possibly IP_4. This mechanism is supported by the observation of calcium ionophore A23187 and ionomycin stimulation of the oxidative burst and the inhibition of this stimulation by trifluoperazine [see Sha'afi and Molski, 1988; and Grinstein and Furuya, 1988, for details].

The second is a protein kinase C–dependent mechanism that requires a minimum but not a change in the internal levels of calcium [Wymann et al., 1987; Grinstein and Furuya, 1988]. Indeed, some of the strongest evidence comes from PMA induction of the oxidative burst and inhibition of this induction by protein kinase C inhibitors [Grinstein aand Furuya, 1988; Sha'afi and Molski, 1988]. Additionally, PMA pretreatment can circumvent this inhibition of the oxidative burst, PLC activation, and production of IP_3 and DAG brought about by buffering internal calcium with Quin-2 [Lew et al., 1984]. The presence of these first two mechanisms, one calcium dependent and the other protein kinase dependent, would fit with the observed synergism of calcium and DAG or permeable analogs [White et al., 1984; Volpi et al., 1985].

The third pathway is a very rapid NADPH oxidase activation that is not dependent on calcium and may be an effect of the lipid environment on the membrane-bound enzyme [Grinstein and Furuyma, 1988].

Truett et al. [1988] and Reibmann et al. [1988] have compared leukotriene B4 and FMLP for their internal messenger production, because, while they are equipotent as chemotaxis stimuli, they are very different in their ability to stimulate the oxidative burst. In these comparisons, leukotriene B4 and FMLP elicited similar initial increases in calcium, IP_3, IP_4, and DAG (<30 sec), but FMLP sustained the increased calcium and IP_3 levels and elicited a second peak of DAG (at ~120 sec). This second peak of DAG was not derived from phosphoinositol lipid hydrolysis and probably was dependent on the sustained higher calcium levels. These results predict that a stimulus that supports a sustained phosphoinositol lipid hydrolysis will also sustain increased calcium levels not only by liberating internal stores but also by stimulating influx from external sources (possibly mediated by calcium-stimulated calcium conductance or possibly IP_3-gated channel [Bagglioni and Wymann, 1990]. This prolonged new high level of internal calcium will elicit a second wave of DAG production perhaps from phosphatidylcholine. The DAG may participate in protein kinase C membrane translocation for the oxidative burst, because leukotriene B4 that fails to elicit much of a burst also fails to stimulate much translocation [Nishihara et al., 1986].

The substrates of protein kinase C are being cataloged and include a 60 kD protein that is associated with the activation of the Na^+/H^+ antiporter by FMLP, possibly the α-subunit of the G protein that activates PLC; a 47 kD protein associated with degranulation; and several membrane- and cytoskeleton-associated proteins [White et al., 1984; Suzuki et al., 1990]. These substrates will be the next components of the multiple pathways to be fit into the puzzle of the neutrophil sensory transduction.

Activation of the calcium–phospholipid-dependent protein kinase C includes its translocation from cytosolic to membrane compartments of the cell. The binding to the DAG that is transiently present because of hydrolysis of phosphoinositol lipids brings the enzyme in contact with the membrane and lowers the calcium requirement [Sha'afi and Molski, 1988]. It is tempting to speculate that priming of neutrophils (i.e., synergistic enhancement of respiratory burst by pretreatment with low concentrations of agonists) also could be due to the translocation of the protein kinase C to the membrane, where it stands ready for immediate response to stimulus. This would fit with Alkon and Rasmussen's idea [1988] of biochemical memory. However, priming as with all aspects of neutrophil physiology, is not simply accounted for by protein kinase C translocation, but alternatively may be due to protein kinase C activation in the cytosol by increased calcium or possibly to the actions of AA [Bass et al., 1987; Costa-Casnellie et al., 1986; Korchak et al., 1984].

As depicted in Figure 5, the *D. discoideum* transduction systems are twofold, with one set of receptors (A sites) associated with the adenylate cyclase of the relay and another set of receptors (B sites) poised to activate the cytoskeletal alterations necessary for chemotaxis by way of PIP_2 hydrolysis, calcium liberation, and production of cGMP. The implication of IP_3 comes from its mobilization of calcium from internal stores and polymerization of actin when applied to permeable cells [Newell et al., 1988]. Additionally, ^3H-inositol was used to trace the increased cycling of phosphoinositol lipids through IP_3 with cAMP stimulation [Europe-Finner and Newell, 1987a]. The liberation of calcium was found to be downstream from the phosphoinositol lipid step in the transduction pathway; calcium mimicked cAMP-induced actin polymerization and cGMP formation in permeabilized cells without stimulation of IP_3 formation [Newell et al., 1988]. The actin polymerization in slime mold amoebae is not sustained [Newell et al., 1988], but exhibits a cyclical change in polymerization–depolymerization–repolymerization that corresponds to the initial pseudopod extension, rounding up (cringing), and cell elongation necessary for oriented movement. Calcium seems to be directly responsible for these cycles of F-actin formation [Newell, 1986]. Calcium also activates the guanylate cyclase, and the resultant cGMP in turn regulates the association of myosin with the cytoskeleton, independent of calcium [Liu and Newell, 1988]. Presumably the actin and myosin associate with the cytoskeleton and contribute to orientation and motility. Chemotaxis, although not completely normal, occurs in the absence of myosin II heavy chain [Knecht and Loomis, 1987; DeLozanne and Spudich, 1987; Wessels et al., 1988], while actin polymerization correlates with pseudopod extension in *Dictyostelium* and neutrophils [Devreotes and Zigmond, 1988]. In light of redundant functions within cells, interpretation of these results are suggestive but not conclusive that actin and not myosin II is necessary for chemotaxis.

The phosphatidylinositol metabolism of slime molds is being determined by Van Haastert's group in as much detail as in neutrophils, and it is indeed an integral part of the sensory transduction in *Dictyostelium*. It is interesting that both the neutrophil and *D. disoideum* amoebae polymerize actin in preparation for chemotaxis, but that in *D. discoideum* the internal levels of calcium appear to be sufficient to account for the state of F-actin [Newell, 1986], whereas in neutrophils acidification may also be necessary [Yuli and Oplatka, 1987].

To account for the *odorants* that do not activate adenylate cyclase and other considerations of the adenylate cyclase as transducer [Anholt, 1987], the PIP_2 hydrolysis in olfactory epithelium has been scrutinized. GTP and odorants stimulate IP_3 production in ciliary preparations of catfish olfactory tissue [Huque and Bruch, 1986; Bruch and Huque, 1987] and do so more than additively when odorant is combined with GTP [Bruch et al., 1987]. L-alanine and L-arginine bind to distinctly separate receptor sites whose affinities are regulated by guanine nucleotides [Kalinoski and Bruch, 1987], and both amino acids elicit rapid (<15 sec) two-to threefold increases in IP_3 in a GTP-dependent manner [Bruch et al., 1989]. (The catfish olfactory PLC that is responsible for generating IP_3 is being characterized [Boyle et al., 1987].)

The L-amino acid–stimulated EOG of catfish olfactory receptor cells is abolished with the removal of external Ca^{2+}, and Ca^{2+} channel blockers and patch-clamping of the receptor cell membranes reveal an IP_3-gated calcium channel [Restrepo et al., 1990]. Therefore in catfish two parallel receptor–G protein pathways exist, one coupled to PLC that increases IP_3 and thereby directly activates Ca channels and another coupled to adenylate cyclase that increases cAMP and thereby activates cation channels [Restrepo et al., 1990; Bruch and Teeter, 1989]. The relationship of the receptors, G proteins, and channels within a single cell is of great interest because of the extra latitude multiple pathways provide for integration of information at the periphery and for cross-talk between pathways.

The IP_3 pathway in olfaction promises to be a common theme across phyla. In rat olfactory cilia and in moth antennae, odorants or pheromones can elicit an extremely rapid, GTP-dependent peak of IP_3 [Breer et al., 1990a,b], qualifying IP_3 as a second messenger. However, unlike in catfish, the set of odorants that stimulate IP_3 in rat olfactory cilia is not overlapping with the set that activate adenylate cyclase, and the rate of cAMP accumulation is clearly fast enough to qualify it as a second messenger [Breer et al., 1990a,b; Breer and Buekoff, 1991; see Restrepo et al., 1990, and Bruch and Teeter, 1989].

Similarly, in catfish *taste tissues*, the tastant L-alanine rapidly stimulates IP_3 formation, as does Na-fluoride (NaF) [Huque et al., 1987; Huque and Brand, 1988], implicating a GTP-dependent system for taste. Bitter stimuli elicit increases in internal calcium from internal stores [Akabas et al., 1987, 1988], also indirectly pointing to IP_3 as an internal messenger [see Teeter and Gold, 1988, for a review]. The details of the involvement of PLC in taste and olfaction remain to be elaborated.

D. Calcium, pH, and Membrane Potential

Calcium, pH, and membrane potential are grouped together because often changes in one are inseparable from changes in the other two. Calcium has been described in some detail earlier (see sections II.B. and III.C.). Briefly, calcium figures into cytoskeletal changes in F-actin for neutrophil chemotaxis and into at least one pathway in oxidative burst. Lamellepodia are the sites of F-actin formation for pseudopod extension and also the site of at least some of the elevated Ca^{2+} during chemotaxis [Sawyer et al., 1985; Jaconi et al., 1988]. However, calcium-sensitive dyes over very short sampling times (0.5 sec) show no consistent localization of Ca^{2+} during chemotaxis [Marks and Maxfield, 1990a,b].

H^+ content and membrane potential (Vm) have been shown to change rapidly with FMLP stimulation [see Sha'afi and Molski, 1988, for review]. There is a rapid (maximal in <10 sec) K^+-dependent hyperpolarization that usually is masked by a subsequent depolarization when FMLP exceeds $10^{-9}\overline{M}$ [Lazzari et al., 1990]; a rapid acidification follows the depolarization time course and is in turn followed by a more slowly developing H^+ extrusion by an Na^+/H^+ antiporter that is activated probably by protein kinase C [see Sha'afi and Molski, 1988, and Fletcher and Seligmann, 1986, for discussion]. Yuli and Oplatka [1987] suggest that the transient rapid acidification is responsible for triggering the rearrangement of the cytoskeleton in preparation for actin polymerization and chemotaxis. Fletcher and Seligmann [1986] [although not others; see Lazzari et al., 1990] have found a correlation between the depolarization, which varies greatly in individual cells from a neutrophil population, and the oxidative burst. The slower alkalinization caused by the activity of the Na^+/H^+, amiloride-sensitive antiporter can be inhibited with no significant effect on the stimulated cell responses [Sha'afi and Molski, 1988].

Calcium figures prominently in the *D. discoideum* sensory transduction pathway that results in chemotaxis (Fig. 5). The source of this calcium is internal, nonmitochondrial stores, and apparently calcium is mobilized from these stores by IP_3 [Newell, 1986]. Calcium levels correlate with the polymerization of actin [Newell, 1986], and, as in neutrophils [Cassimeris et al., 1990], it is not quite clear how the polymerization is controlled and localized for pseudopod formation and motility. Calcium also acts to stimulate guanylate cyclase activity. The enzyme in vitro is not sensitive to calcium levels; therefore the details of how calcium regulates this enzyme are not yet clear [see Newell et al., 1988, for discussion]. Depolarizing changes can be made membrane potential with no consequences for chemotaxis or cGMP accumulation with stimulation by cAMP [Van Duijn et al., 1990], and therefore membrane potential seems to have no role in the chemotaxis sensory transduction pathways of these amoebae.

In *spermatozoan* activation by resact, there must be a calcium influx from external sources both to activate the adenylate cyclase and to elicit chemotaxis (Fig. 6). Calcium and not a receptor– or G protein–adenylate cyclase interaction modulates the enzyme activity. Although the sources of calcium may differ, there are interesting parallels of the calcium regulation of guanylate cyclase activity in *D. discoideum* amoebae with the direct calcium activation of adenylate cyclase in spermatozoa and *Chlamydomonas*. Calcium influx is an absolute requirement for chemotaxis in spermatozoa. Although there also is a resact stimulation of H^+ efflux, this alkalinization is slow and cannot account for some of the initial response of sperm to ligand binding. However, there may be yet undescribed roles for the ligand-activated H^+ efflux, because internal pH correlates with activation of motility and exposure of sea urchin sperm to pH 9 buffers causes reversible dephosphorylation of the guanylate cyclase–resact receptor similar to that caused by resact [Trimmer and Vacquier, 1986, for review; Garbers et al., 1986; Garbers, 1989a,b].

On a similar note, the cAMP that serves as a second messenger in *Chlamydomonas* agglutination responses is generated by a calcium–calmodulin (CM)-dependent adenylate cyclase [Pasquale and Goodenough, 1987]. CM inhibitors block postadhesion responses; cAMP relieves this block. The inhibitors also reduce adenylate cyclase activity in vitro. Calcium ionophores do not elicit the agglutination responses, implying that perhaps a minimum level of calcium is necessary for enzyme activation and that sensory transduction does not include an increase in internal calcium.

Taste cells function by releasing neurotransmitters that in turn stimulate the synapsing neurons. Calcium presumably is a requirement for neurotransmitter release, and there are several potential mechanisms by which internal cal-cium levels are raised preparatory to release: Voltage-sensitive calcium channels are opened by cell depolarization through an increased influx of cation through passive or ligand-gated channels, increased membrane resistance or surface potential, or ligand–receptor interactions that result in second messengers that inhibit ion pumps. Alternatively, in the instances when cells do not change input resistance, second messengers may be liberating calcium from internal stores [see Teeter and Brand, 1987a,b for discussion]. Only in the case of sour taste is calcium thought both to carry the depolarizing current and to stimulate release of neurotransmitter [Sato et al., 1987]. Taste cell transduc-tion varies greatly with cell type, and it is likely that all these mechanisms of increasing internal calcium are at work.

Paramecia respond to chemical stimuli with a change in membrane potential that is predictable from their change in swimming, hence ciliary beating patterns [Van Houten, 1979]. Ciliary beating frequency and angle (hence efficiency of swimming) are controlled by Vm [Machemer, 1976, 1989]. The electrophysio-logical bases of the change in Vm have been elusive; the hyperpolarization in response to folate or acetate is not dependent on either external K^+ or Na^+, has no reversal potential, correlates with a small increase (for folic acid) or decrease (for acetate) in membrane resistance, and is perhaps due to the activation of a calcium pump activity [Preston and Van Houten, 1987a]. Cal-cium efflux has been implicated in yet other ways: Lithium, which causes an inhibition of chemoresponse, reduces the normal calcium efflux and appar-ently the normal functioning of the surface Ca^{2+}-ATPase pump [Wright and Van Houten, 1988, 1990; Van Houten et al., 1991b]; a mutant, *K-shy* [Evans et al., 1987], with defects in calcium homeostasis is not responsive to most stim-uli [Van Houten, 1990]. Not all responses to attractant stimuli are affected by lithium, and the stimuli have been divided into groups based on this lithium effect [Van Houten et al., 1991b]. Interestingly, the stimuli that are thought to stimulate the Ca^{2+}-ATPase to generate the hyperpolarization elicit a lithium-sensitive response and are not attractants to mutant *K-shy*, while NH_4Cl, for example, that is thought to affect internal pH and not affect Ca^{2+}-ATPase through a receptor-mediated mechanism, does not elicit a lithium-sensitive response, and serves as a good stimulus for *K-shy* [Van Houten, 1990]. There-fore the working hypothesis is that the 0.2 namp current that is elicited by folate stimulation of cells, for example, could be accounted for by a voltage-insensitive calcium pump current (Van Houten and Preston, unpublished data).

The Ca^{2+}-ATPase activities of the complex surface membranes (pellicle) of *Paramecium* have been partially characterized [Wright and Van Houten, 1990], and a corresponding protein has been identified both as a phosphoenzyme intermediate and as a calmodulin-binding protein [Wright and Van Houten, 1990, and unpublished data), but a definitive demonstration of its role in chemokinesis has yet to be made. Calcium pump fluxes may also contribute to the calcium fluxes of FMLP-stimulated neutrophils and *Dictyostelium* [Foder et al., 1989; Böhme et al., 1987].

Both pH and Vm contribute to the proton motive force (PMF) that is the energy source for the gram-negative *bacterial flagella* [Boyd and Simon, 1982]. Levels of PMF also appear to be sensed by the flagellar switch that is responsible for the bacterial chemoresponse. In particular, oxygen concentrations affect *Sal. typhimurium* swimming; the "aerotaxis" pathway by-passes the MCPs and other membrane receptors but does converge with the other chemoresponse pathways at the flagellar switch for clockwise and counterclockwise rotation. Shioi and Taylor [1984] find that "aerotaxis" is mediated not by pH or Vm alone but by the PMF. Likewise in the photosynthetic bacteria *Rhodob. sphaeroides*, the response of the cells to light or O_2 depend on the PMF generated by electron transport, but not on the electron transport directly [Armitage et al., 1985].

E. Integrating Multiple Messengers

It should be evident from the descriptions of neutrophils, *D. discoideum*, olfaction, and taste systems that multiple internal messengers are set loose upon chemostimulation. Some are necessarily generated together, as in PLC action on PIP_2 to produce IP_3 and DAG. However, DAG can come from other sources and apparently does in neutrophils. Others are generated separately, like cAMP and calcium, but work either synergistically or in opposition to control physiological responses [Rasmussen, 1981; Alkon and Rasmussen, 1988]. While control by and presence of multiple messengers is not new [Belardetti and Siegelbaum, 1988; Imagawa et al., 1987; Rasmussen, 1981], it complicates the neat dissection of the sensory transduction pathways, particularly if the pathways are not parallel but interactive.

Multiple messengers can be generated by separate sets of receptors or the same set causing a cascade of sequential messenger production. The sensory transduction pathways in *D. discoideum* appear to have two sets of cAMP receptors coupled with different G proteins (*frgA* product vs. G_s) that stimulate PLC and adenylate cyclase, respectively, along two separate sensory transduction pathways. Within the PLC pathway, IP_3, calcium, and cGMP all are generated and calcium, in particular, has further multiple effects. In neutrophils, it still is debatable whether multiple receptors or one population of receptors associated with different G proteins or other effectors allows the cells to respond differentially to a range of concentrations of stimuli or over different time courses and to have such a large repertoire of intracellular effects. Likewise, in olfaction and taste it is becoming clear that the cell population is heterogeneous and that several transduction pathways can exist within one cell with responsiveness to more than one stimulus, i.e., more than one receptor (see section IV.C. for a discussion of the interactions of cyclic nucleotides and Vm).

IV. TRANSDUCTION MECHANISMS

A. An Overview

Signal transduction begins with the stimulus–receptor interaction and ends in a response such as directed motility or synaptic transmission. The signal is first an external chemical cue and is transformed into an internal, diffusible messenger. The transfer of information from receptor to effector enzyme that produces the internal messenger very often is mediated by a G protein. G proteins are implicated in activation of adenylate cyclase, PLC, and phospholipase A_2 and in opening ion channels directly [Gilman, 1987; Axelrod et al., 1988; Dunlap et al., 1987; Miller, 1988]. However, G proteins are not the exclusive agents that trrransfer information to enzymes or ion channels. Calcium can do this directly [Hockberger and Swandulla, 1987], as can Vm (see section III.D.). Cyclic nucleotides interact with some ion channels directly [Hockberger and Swandulla, 1987] or indirectly influence the activity of enzymes and channels through protein kinases [Edelman et al., 1987; Hanks et al., 1988]. Likewise, there are calcium- and CM-dependent protein kinases. An interesting exception to this pattern of diffusible internal messengers is the bacterial chemoresponse system. Here information is passed from protein to protein as a phosphorylation without intervention of a diffusible messenger. The yeast mating system may involve G proteins without diffusible messengers and be yet another interesting exception in sensory transduction.

B. G Proteins

In receptor-mediated sensory transduction, often a G protein is interfaced between the receptor and effector enzyme that generates the internal messenger. The control adenylate cyclase by stimulatory (G_s) and inhibitory (G_i) G proteins is now a classic example, as is transducin inhibition of the cGMP-phosphodiesterase in retinal cells [Stryer and Bourne, 1986] (the reader is referred to one of several reviews of G protein function for details [Stryer and Bourne, 1986; Gilman, 1987; Neer and Clapham, 1988]). A brief sketch of G protein function is as follows: G proteins are multimeric, consisting of α-, β-, and γ-subunits. GDP is bound to the α-subunit, and upon ligand binding to receptor there is a conformational change transduced to the α-subunit facilitating its binding of GTP. In this bound form, the α-subunit dissociates from the β- and γ-subunits and is active in stimulating or inhibiting its target enzyme or channel. The α-subunit also has GTPase activity, and, upon hydrolyzing GTP to GDP, the α-subunit becomes inactive and reassociates with the β- and γ-subunits and the receptor. The complexity of control of G proteins is becoming evident as accessory proteins that influence G protein function (e.g., by activating GTPase activity) are being characterized [Parsons, 1990]. Additionally, there are increasing numbers of reports of functions for the β- and γ-subunits in transduction, but these are controversial at present [Neer and Clapham, 1988; Dunlap et al., 1987]. Cholera and pertussis toxins ADP-ribosylate and thereby perturb the functions of the α-subunit [Neer and Clapham, 1988].

The criteria for the involvement of G proteins in a sensory transduction process are [Gilman, 1987] 1) both ligand and GTP are required to initiate the response; 2) nonhydrolyzable analogs or NaF should provoke the response; 3) there should be a decreased affinity in ligand binding in the presence of GTP, and, conversely, ligand should enhance the binding of GTP to membranes; 4) cholera or pertussis toxin or antibodies against G proteins could perturb the response; and 5) reconstitution of the pathway in vitro and dependence on GTP and a G protein for the response are the ultimate criteria.

Both calcium and protein kinase C are heavily implicated in neutrophil chemotaxis and oxidative burst (see above). Both calcium and protein kinase C are modulated by PIP_2 metabolism, calcium by IP_3, IP_4, and AA, and protein kinase C by DAG and calcium. Therefore the major second messengers are IP_3 and DAG and third messengers are calcium, AA, and possibly IP_4. The generation of these messengers is dependent on G proteins at several levels.

Neutrophil receptors are coupled to PLC through G proteins. The evidence for this includes the requirement for GTP and FMLP to stimulate PIP_2 hydrolysis in membrane preparations; the same hydrolysis is inhibited by pertussis toxin; guanine nucleotides regulate receptor affinity; FMLP stimulates GTP binding and GTPase activity in membranes [Dillon et al., 1987a,b; Cockroft, 1987; Sklar et al., 1987]. The α-subunit involved is not the same as that in G_i or G_o, but instead is a smaller G_c α-subunit that is substrate for both pertussis and cholera toxins [Cockroft, 1987; Polakis et al., 1988; Sha'afi and Molski, 1988]. A pertussis toxin substrate that can be copurified with the receptor decreases affinity of receptor for FMLP upon GTP binding [Polakis et al., 1988]. This 40 kD protein is the likely candidate for G_c α-subunit.

Neutrophil phospholipase A_2 apparently is regulated by interactions with a G protein [Burgoyne, 1987]. Additionally, the sustained high calcium levels from calcium influx may be mediated by a G protein interaction separate from the one regulating PLC [Nasmith and Grinstein, 1987a,b; Lu and Grinstein, 1990], as may some of the other aspects of neutrophil activation that Sha'afi and Molski [1988] have cataloged as pertussis toxin sensitive: chemotaxis; degranulation; oxidative burst; aggregation; rise in intracellular Ca^{2+}; actin polymerization; PI, PIP, and PIP_2 hydrolysis; Na^+ influx; increase in intracellular H^+; increase in internal pH; protein phosphorylation; membrane potential change; GTPase activity; AA release; and generation of phosphatidic acid, phosphatidylinositol, IP_2, and IP_3.

There are several lines of evidence that G proteins are integral parts of the *D. discoideum* sensory transduction. At the receptor level, GTP affects the

binding of cAMP to the cell surface receptors of both the relay and chemotaxis pathways [Janssens and Van Haastert, 1987], and cAMP and folic acid
increase binding of GTP to membranes [Janssens and Van Haastert, 1987;
Snaar-Jaglaska et al., 1988]. In the relay pathway, GTP modulates activity of
the adenylate cyclase [Thiebert et al., 1984; Van Haastert et al., 1987a,b]. In
the chemotaxis pathways, GTP and analogs stimulate IP_3 formation, as does
the stimulus cAMP [Europe-Finner and Newell, 1987a,b]. Synchronized cells
exhibit oscillations of IP_3 and cGMP with cAMP stimulation and likewise
with GTPγS treatment.

An interesting study of the *D. discoideum ras* protein (an oncogene product
member of the family of smaller GTP-binding protein) implicates separate G
proteins in the chemotaxis and relay sensory transductions [Europe-Finner et
al., 1988; Van Haastert et al., 1987a,b]. *Dictyostelium* cells transformed with
the homolog of the normal, human protooncogene (gly-12) aggregated normally, while those transformed with the homolog of the human activated
oncogene (thr-12) showed abnormal chemotaxis, probably because of IP_3 levels
elevated two to three times over basal levels. The oscillation in IP_3 normally
induced by cAMP was aberrant and started from a higher basal level in trans-
formants. In the same cells, the adenylate cyclase relay was not affected.

A modification of the G protein–receptor interaction appears to be responsible
for adaptation, i.e., the unresponsiveness of cells to a second pulse of cAMP
given within 30 sec of the first. There is no adaptation apparent if GTPγS, IP_3,
or calcium is used to bypass the receptor and start the transduction pathway downstream from the ligand–receptor interaction [Small et al., 1987]. However, GTP
γS cannot circumvent adaptation produced by cAMP binding to receptor. Therefore, adaptation must somehow involve the G protein–receptor interaction.

An interesting question for both neutrophils and *D. discoideum* regards the
number of G proteins associated with receptors. There are separate G proteins
coupled to the cAMP and folate receptors [Kesbeke et al., 1990]. Are there two
or more classes of G proteins to account for the divergent pathways? If, as Sklar
argues for neutrophils, all receptors are functionally coupled, how can the number
of receptors occupied translate into chemotaxis vs. oxidative burst and degranulation responses? Alternatively, are receptor populations different? If so, are
the G proteins associated with them different? The availability of mutants has
contributed significantly to the dissection of G protein function in *Dictyostelium*.
Synag mutants are defective in interactions between G protein and the relay
adenylate cyclase, but the defects probably do not lie in the G protein itself [Snaar-
Jaglaska and Van Haastert, 1988], while *fgdA*, mutants in a different gene, are
no longer able to couple receptor to G protein properly yet GTP can activate
their adenylate cyclase [Kesbeke et al., 1988]. Therefore the two transduction
pathways (Fig. 5) appear to be mediated by separate G proteins, and the receptor-
coupled G protein α-subunit has been identified among several cDNA clones

for G proteins as $G_{2\alpha}$ [Johnson et al., 1989]. Small *ras*-like G proteins are present in *Dictyostelium*, and their overexpression or alteration affects chemosensory transduction possibly through the activation of protein kinase C [Robbins et al., 1989; Luderus et al., 1988]. However, it is not yet clear how these *ras* G proteins fit into the normal transductions pathways, if at all.

In both *olfaction and taste* there are two effector enzymes (adenylate cyclase and PLC) that are coupled to G proteins. Either or both are activated in a stimulated cell; both enzymes may function in sensory transduction and perhaps adenylate cyclase adaptation [Anholt, 1987]. It is clear, however, that G proteins play major roles in sensory transduction in olfaction and taste tissues. The lines of evidence for G proteins in olfaction are 1) GTP dependence of adenylate cyclase and PLC, 2) presence of G proteins in appropriate tissues, and 3) influence of GTP on stimulus binding. Only GTP dependence of adenylate cyclase and PLC has been established for taste [see Bruch, 1990a,b, for reviews].

1. In *olfactory epithelium*, from all sources, the adenylate cyclase is GTP dependent, and in frogs and mammals in particular the activation of adenylate cyclase by odorants requires GTP [Sklar et al., 1986; Lancet and Pace, 1987; Pace and Lancet, 1986]. The adenylate cyclase of catfish olfactory cilia also is activated by GTP, but Bruch and Teeter [1988] have found that odorant stimulation is not likely to work through the classic G_s mechanism, despite the presence of G_s in both catfish and other olfactory cilia [Bruch et al., 1987]. In pseudoparathyroidism patients, the G_s is defective, making modulation of adenylate cyclase by some hormones impossible [Carter et al., 1987; Weinstock et al., 1986]. Because such patients have deficits in olfactory function, there may be a role for G_s in mammalian and perhaps frog adenylate cyclase, while a different mechanism is at work in the catfish.

In *taste* tissues from catfish, the adenylate cyclase is GTP dependent and rapidly activated by tastant [Kalinoski et al., 1989a; Bruch et al., 1987]. Likewise, in rat the adenylate cyclase is activated by sugar in a GTP-dependent manner [Lancet et al., 1987].

The alternative transduction pathway in taste and smell is similarly dependent on GTP. The PLC of both *olfactory* and *taste* tissues of the catfish are both stimulus and GTP dependent [Bruch et al., 1987, 1989; Huque and Bruch, 1986, Huque et al., 1987].

2. Five cDNA clones for different GTP-binding proteins and the protein counterparts of G_s, G_i, and G_o have been identified with molecular genetic and immunological probes in rat and frog olfactory epithelium [Jones and Reed, 1987; Anholt et al., 1987]. A sixth cDNA clone was found to code for a G protein specific to the olfactory epithelium (G_{olf}) [Jones and Reed, 1989]. In a comparison of three species, Pace and Lancet [1986] isolated a 42 kD G protein and demonstrated that this G protein activates the adenylate cyclase and can be ADP-ribosylated by cholera toxin. Similarly, in catfish olfactory cilia, a G_s α-subunit cholera toxin substrate (45 kD) and a pertussis toxin substrate of 40

kD have been identified [Bruch et al., 1987]. However, the only G protein that has been identified in taste tissues are the catfish α- and β-subunits of G_s and the 41 kD form of G_i [Bruch and Kalinoski, 1990; Bruch, 1990a].

3. Bruch and Kalinoski [1987] measured binding of L-arginine and L-alanine that serve as both odorants and tastants to catfish and found that GTP decreases affinity of binding to the separate receptors by 1 order of magnitude in olfactory but not taste membranes. L-arginine opens channels from taste membranes directly [Teeter and Brand, 1987a; Teeter et al., 1987b], thereby obviating the need for a G-coupled receptor. However, the mechanism of the L-alanine stimulation of adenylate cyclase and PLC in a GTP-dependent manner in the apparent absence of a G-coupled taste receptor remains unclear.

The two lines of evidence for G protein interaction in the *yeast* mating type system are indirect yet compelling. First, the receptors resemble rhodopsin in their structure and therefore have been assigned to the family of receptors that are G protein coupled (Fig. 10). Second, two investigative groups have cloned the yeast gene for a protein homologous to the G_s α-subunit. Disruption of this gene leads to growth arrest in G_1, which is characteristic of haploid cells

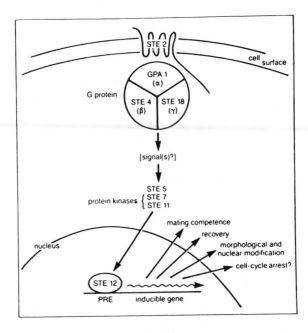

Fig. 10. Schematic of the response pathway in a cells to α-factor. The genes shown are involved in the response to pheromone that leads to transcriptional induction. The pathway apart from pheromone and receptor appears to be the same in α-cells. [Reproduced from Fields, 1990, with permission of the publisher.]

exposed to mating pheromone [Dietzel and Kurjan, 1987; Miyajima et al., 1987]. Diploid cells are unaffected by mating pheromones and are also not growth arrested by the disruption of the G protein gene. No second messenger such as calcium or cAMP seems to evolve from interaction of G protein with effector enzyme [Herskowitz and Marsh, 1987]. Instead, it has been proposed that, in the absence of mating factor, the G protein is in the trimeric GDP-bound form and upon mating factor stimulation it is bound with GTP [Dietzel and Kurjan, 1987; Miyajima et al., 1987]. Dietzel and Kurjan [1987] proposed that the GDP-bound form of the G protein acts as an inhibitor of some effector, allowing the cell to traverse the cell cycle. When mating factor is bound to receptor, and the GTP-bound form G protein predominates, the affinity for effector is reduced and the effector is free to produce the cell cycle arrest; and the effector could be the β- and γ-subunits. Additional genetic and biochemical information is necessary to sort through the multiple models that are proposed for G protein function in yeast mating response [see Kurjan, 1990, for review].

C. Cyclic Nucleotides and Membrane Potential

The response of paramecia to organic, chemical stimuli includes an immediate hyperpolarization and a change to smoother, faster swimming [Van Houten, 1978, 1979]. Presumably the cilia are beating faster and at an angle that facilitates movement. Both membrane potential and cyclic nucleotides are implicated in the control of ciliary beating [Bonini et al., 1986; Gustin and Nelson, 1987; Bonini and Nelson, 1988; Nakoaka and Ooi, 1985; Majima et al., 1986; Klumpp et al., 1984; Schultz et al., 1984]. The induction of faster ciliary beating by hyperpolarization (without the complication of altered surface charge) or by cAMP is not in dispute; it is the causal relationship between the two that is complex and not yet clear.

cAMP injected into paramecia hyperpolarizes them, and their cilia increase beating frequency [Hennessey et al., 1985]. Voltage-clamping of the membrane prevents this increased frequency, and yet experiments with permeabilized cells (hence with no means of altering their membrane potential) show that cyclic nucleotides can increase the frequency of ciliary beating directly [Bonini et al., 1986; Bonini and Nelson, 1988; Majima et al., 1986]. It is significant that not all the modulation of speed can be attributed to internal cAMP levels; in an intact cell where membrane potential was regulated by external K^+ levels, increases in internal cAMP (attained by incubation in permeant analogs of cAMP) did increase swimming speed, but the absolute speed was a function of both the Vm and cAMP levels [Bonini et al., 1986]. Therefore, it will be important to sort out the contributions of nucleotide-dependent phosphorylation of axonemal proteins and the effects of both hyper- and depolarizing membrane potential changes on the function of the cilium, both as the motor end of the *Paramecium* chemosensory response pathway and for its relevance to yet other systems including sperm [Tash et al., 1986] and ciliated epithelium [Nelson and Wright, 1974; Satir, 1985; Brokaw, 1987], and perhaps ciliated olfactory epithelium.

D. Cyclic Nucleotide- and Ligand-Gating of Ion Channels

There are examples in the literature of ligands that activate one of the family of G protein–coupled receptors that activate ion channels indirectly [Dohlman et al., 1987] and of other ligands that activate channels directly [Stevens, 1987; Barnard et al., 1987]. Likewise, the second messengers that are generated in the G protein–associated systems can activate channels directly [Hockberger and Swandulla, 1987; Kuo and Gardner, 1987] or indirectly through protein kinase activities [Edelman et al., 1987; Hanks et al., 1988; Kikkawa and Nishizuka, 1986]. In olfactory systems and taste, there are observations of stimulus activation of G protein–dependent adenylate cyclase and PLC, cyclic nucleotide–and IP_3-activated conductances, direct odorant activation of conductances, and even direct odorant activation of adenylate cyclase, presumably through perturbation of lipid environment around the enzyme, in melanocytes that ought not to have odorant receptors [Lerner et al., 1988]. Therefore it remains to be seen which of these mechanisms is at work in olfaction and taste or, more aptly perhaps, how they are distributed across receptor cell types and whether they are associated with specific stimuli.

E. Bacterial CheY Protein

The bacterial chemoresponse systems seem to function without the internal messengers and components of the eukaryotes: cyclic nucleotides, calcium, Vm, IP_3, DAG, or G proteins. Indeed, no prokaryotic G proteins that control enzyme activity have been identified [Janssens, 1987]. Instead, the bacterial pathways seem to pass on the signal from protein to protein until it reaches the CheY protein that can interact directly with the switch to promote clockwise rotation (Fig. 3) [Ravid et al., 1986; Eisenbach and Matsumura, 1988]. The information passes from receptor–MCP to CheA as a phosphorylation, possibly mediated by CheW (Fig. 3) [Parkinson, 1988; Hess et al., 1988; Oosawa et al., 1988; Gegner and Dahlquist, 1991]. CheA in turn can be found in a complex with CheZ and CheY, and the CheA phosphate is rapidly passed on to CheY (and also to CheB). Upon phosphorylation of CheY, the phosphate has reached the protein that interacts directly with the flagellar switch. CheY can directly promote clockwise rotation in bacterial envelopes with flagella attached. CheZ acts as an antagonist to CheY and promotes counterclockwise rotation, but the flagella of envelopes will rotate counterclockwise without the presence of CheZ, implying that CheZ interacts with CheY to achieve the antagonism and does not interact directly with the flagellar switch. Presumably the phosphorylated form of

CheY is active in the switching function; the phosphate of CheY is rapidly transferred to CheZ, which accounts for the antagonism by CheZ. An important aspect yet being clarified is the nature of the CheA and MCP interaction that starts this phosphorylation cascade.

A common signalling motif is emerging for prokaryotes [Parkinson, 1988; Stock et al., 1989; Stock, 1987; Ronson et al., 1987]. Bacterial proteins with known "transmitter" modes and those with known "receiver" modes in signal transduction are being compared among themselves. It appears that CheA is one of the transmitter family, with CheY receiving its signal in the form of a phosphorylation. The transmitters have kinase domains, and the receivers have phosphate acceptor sites. Phosphorylation has been developed to a high degree in prokaryotes to serve in sensory transduction processes.

V. FUTURE DIRECTIONS

One challenge for future research in chemosensory transduction is the isolation and characterization of receptors. To date only four receptors from unicellular organisms have been purified and cloned. Peripheral receptors have remained technically difficult to isolate, but their isolation and characterization will be important in understanding their structure and function. Molecular genetics, which has been used successfully to clone neurohormone receptors [Koblika et al., 1988; Kerlavage et al., 1987; Boulter et al., 1986; Barnard et al., 1987], will be employed in this task, as will more immunological techniques [Fraser and Lindstrom, 1984; Bryant et al., 1987; Kalinoski et al., 1987; Price and Willey, 1988]. Because many receptors appear to fall into classes based on amino acid sequence (e.g., G-coupled vs. direct ion channel–gating), the gene sequence of a chemosensory receptor could give clues about its regions of potential G protein interactions or functions as ion channels [Koblika et al., 1988; Barnard et al., 1987] and uncover some consensus features unique to peripheral chemoreceptors.

A necessary process that is currently underway is the cataloging of stimulus-related G proteins, protein kinases [Meier and Klein, 1988], and protein kinase substrates that first must be identified before their roles in sensory transduction can be elucidated. Likewise, second messenger– and ligand-activated conductances of receptor neurons are being sorted out prior to understanding where they fit into sensory transduction.

Another challenge for the future will be to untangle the relationships of the messengers in these overlapping and interacting pathways using pharmacological agents and, when possible, mutants. A catchword for future transduction studies is "cross-talk," and it is just this cross-talk between pathways and interactions between the internal messengers that allows chemosensory cells such a rich repertoire of responses and makes chemosensory transduction so complex in its control.

VI. NOTE ADDED IN PROOF

This chapter is like a snapshot of the field of chemical sensing, but the subject is moving rapidly and the picture is necessarily blurry. Since the writing of this chapter, more components of vertebrate olfactory transduction pathways can be studied at the gene level with the cloning of an olfactory specific adenylate cyclase [Bakalyar and Reed, 1990] and nucleotide gated channels [Ludwig et al., 1990; Dhallan et al., 1990]. These genes, along with those for a G protein (G_{olf}) [Jones and Reed, 1989] and degradative enzymes [Lazard et al., 1990, 1991; Ding et al., 1991] specific to olfactory epithelium almost complete the picture of major sensory transduction components. The receptor proteins have remained elusive, but now some of a family of genes may have been cloned [Buck and Axel, 1991; Nef and Dionne, personal communication]. These genes appear to comprise a large branch of the superfamily of rhodopsin-like proteins and await functional assays to verify their identity. The oocyte systems that have been patiently developed [Getchell et al., 1990] can serve as an important technique for screening genes and providing functional assays of odorant responsiveness of gene products. While the olfactory binding protein or its counterpart are being identified and cloned in more species [Krieger et al., 1991; Vandenberg and Zeilgelberger, 1991; Vogt et al., 1990a], its functions still are not agreed upon [see Vogt et al., 1990b, for discussion].

Olfactory cells in culture from vertebrates, insects, and lobsters are a welcome development that will greatly facilitate the biochemical approaches to second messengers [Ronnett et al., 1990; Zufall et al., 1991; Fadool et al., 1991]. For example, while it was established that the lobster olfactory receptor cells do not utilize the cAMP transduction system for excitatory amino acids [McClintock et al., 1989], patch clamping of the cultured cells made it possible to identify IP_3 as the second messenger [Fadool et al., 1991]. Similarly, the second messengers for the inhibitory stimuli that activate K conductances [Michel et al., 1991] can now be deciphered.

On other fronts, the purification and cloning of the olfactory IP_3 gated calcium channel is in progress [Kalinoski, Restrepo, and Teeter, personal communication] and the electrophysiology of the olfactory receptor cells continues to develop [Firestein et al., 1990; Kleene and Gesteland, 1990; Lowe and Gold, 1990; O'Connell et al., 1990; Kaissling et al., 1991]. Additionally, the temporal nature of the stimulus at the receptor cells is being described in unprecedented detail [Moore et al., 1989].

Perhaps the greatest advances in olfaction have come from improved technology. Whole cell patch clamping, rapid kinetic systems [Breer and Boekhoff, 1991] for the analysis of second messengers, and molecular genetics (polymerase chain reaction, in particular) have greatly clarified the roles of second messengers and advanced the identification of the elusive receptors. As techniques continue to evolve, the molecular genetic approach that began with olfactory marker protein [Danciger et al., 1989] will accelerate. The ability to measure second messengers on millisecond time scales has helped to sort out fast and slow responses to stimuli and, hence, potential for participation in transduction or slower processes like adaptation. From the second messenger biochemistry, it appears that "diversity" will be the operative word as it is in taste systems and that there will be multiple, cross-talking transduction pathways to unravel.

Taste cells, likewise, are yielding new information, particularly through voltage and patch clamping [Sugimoto and Teeter, 1990; Bigiani and Roper, 1991; among others] and cytochemistry [Dockstader et al., 1991; Oakley et al., 1990; Finger and Bottjer, 1990; among others]. Even questions of integration at the periphery can now be approached [Ewald and Roper, 1990]. Kinnamon [1988] brought the diversity of taste transduction mechanisms to our attention and the diverse second messenger systems involved in sweet and bitter taste can now be pursued through a combinatin of electrophysiology [Cummings et al., 1991; Avenet et al., 1991; Behe et al., 1990; Herness, 1990] and fast kinetic biochemistry. The catfish taste system is providing a set of contrasting mechanisms of taste transduction including ligand gated channels with valuable behavioral correlates [Kohbara et al., 1990; Kumazawa et al., 1990].

On the unicellular side, the yeast story continues to evolve [Jackson and Hartwell, 1990; Stone and Reed, 1990; Cartwright and Tipper, 1991], and the members of the receptor guanylate cyclase and *Dictyostelium* cAMP receptor family continue to grow in number [Schulz et al., 1990; Saxe et al., 1991]. Along with the receptors, the other components of *Dictyostelium* pathway are being teased apart [Tao and Klein, 1990a,b]. The cloning of leukocyte receptors has provided a major advance that will provide sequences, derived protein structures, and an opportunity for producing and systematically altering the proteins [Thomas et al., 1990; Murphy et al., 1990; Coats and Navarro, 1990; Gerard and Gerard, 1991]. The ciliates, similarly, are amenable to the cloning of component parts of their transduction pathways, and such cloning offers now hope to sort out the mechanisms of mating type recognition among other processes [Meyer et al., 1991; Anderson et al., 1990; Ortenzi et al., 1990]. Progress continues in the bacterial systems, particularly in the non-methylating chemoresponse pathways [Armitage et al., 1990] and *B. subtilis* [Zuberi et al., 1991]. For the bacteria, as for several of the other unicellular eukaryotic systems, the reader is directed to the volume by Armitage and Lackie [1990] for overviews.

The field of chemical sensing as a whole is experiencing a time of rapid advances and longstanding questions about peripheral and central systems should be resolved. The scope of this chapter is limited to transduction pathways of peripheral receptor cells and unicellular organisms and, even with this limitation, the chapter cannot touch upon structural, developmental, and coding aspects of olfactory and gustatory receptor cells, for example [see Farbman, 1990; Hill and Mistretta, 1990; Scott and Giza, 1990]. Therefore, (with apologies for the necessary oversights) for more of an update on olfaction and *Dictyostelium* and to discover some of the excitement surrounding the recent developments in chemical sensing, the reader should consult Lewis [1991], Taylor [1991], and Lancet [1991].

VII. REFERENCES

Ache B (1987) Chemoreception in invertebrates. In Finger T, Silver W (eds): Neurobiology of Taste and Smell. New York: John Wiley & Sons, pp 39–64.

Ache BW (1989) Central and peripheral bases for mixture suppression in olfaction: A crustacean model. In Laing DG, Cain WS, McBride RL, Ache BW (eds): Perception of Complex Smells. Sydney: Academic Press, pp 101–114.

Adair WS, Hwang C, Goodenough U (1983) Identification and visualization of the sexual agglutinin from the mating-type plus flagellar membrane of *Chlamydomonas*. Cell 33:183–193.

Adamek GD, Gesteland RC, Mair RG, Oakley B (1984) Transduction physiology of olfactory receptor cilia. Brain Res 310:87–97.

Adler J (1987) How motile bacteria are attracted and repelled by chemicals: An approach to neurobiology. Biol Chem Hoppe-Seyler 368:163–173.

Akabas MH, Dodd J, Al-Awqati Q (1987) Mechanism of transduction of bitter taste in rat taste bud cells. Soc Neurosci Abstr 13:361.

Akabas MJ, Dodd J, Al-Awqati Q (1988) A bitter substance induces a rise in intracellular calcium in a subpopulation of rat taste cells. Science 242:1047–1050.

Alkon DL, Rasmussen H (1988) A spatial–temporal model of cell activation. Science 239:998–1004.

Allen RA, Traynor AE, Omann GM, Jesaitis AJ (1988) The chemotactic peptide receptor: A model for future understanding of chemotactic disorders. In Curnutte JT (ed): Phagocytic Defects: Abnormalities Outside of the Respiratory Burst. Philadelphia: WB Saunders, pp 33–59.

Anderson D, Raffioni S, Luporini P, Bradshaw RA, Eisenberg D (1990) Crystallization of the *Euplotes raikovi* mating pheromone Er-1. J Molec Biol 216:1–2.

Anholt R (1987) Primary events in olfactory reception. TIBS 12:58–62.

Anholt RH, Mumby SM, Stoffers DA, Girard PR, Kuo JF, Snyder SH (1987) Transduction proteins of olfactory receptor cells: Identification of guanine nucleotide binding proteins and protein kinase C. Biochemistry 26:788–795.

Anholt RH, Rivers AM (1990) Olfactory transduction: Cross-talk between second-messenger systems. Biochemistry 1990:4049–4054.

Armitage A, Havelka WA, Sockett RE (1990) Methylation-independent taxis in bacteria. In Armitage JP, Lackie JM (eds): Biology of the Chemotactic Response. Cambridge: Cambridge University Press, pp 177–198.

Armitage J (1988) Tactic responses in photosynthetic bacteria. Can J Microbiol 34:475–481.

Armitage J (1990) Sensory signalling in *Rhodobacter sphaeroides*. In Drews G (ed): Molecular Biology of Membrane Protein Complexes in Phototrophic Bacteria. New York: Plenum Press (in press).

Armitage J, Ingham C, Evans MCW (1985) Role of proton motive force in phototactic and aerotactic responses of *Rhodopseudomonas sphaeroides*. J Bacteriol 161:967–972.

Armitage JP, Lackie JM (eds) (1990) Biology of the Chemotactic Response. Cambridge: Cambridge University Press, pp 1–404.

Atema J (1985) Chemoreception in the sea: Adaptations of chemoreceptors and behavior to aquatic stimulus conditions. In Laverack AS (ed): Physiological Adaptations of Marine Animals. Society of Experimental Biology, Great Britain, pp 387–423.

Atema J (1987) Aquatic and terrestrial chemoreceptor organs: Morphological and physiological designs for interfacing with chemical stimuli. In Dejours P, Bolis L, Taylor CR, Weibel ER (eds): Comparative Physiology: Life in Water and on Land. Fidia Research Series, Padova: IX Liviana Press, pp 303–316.

Avenet P, Hofmann F, Lindemann B (1988) Patch-clamp study of isolated taste receptor cells of the frog. J Membr Biol 97:223–240.

Avenet P, Kinnamon S, Roper S (1991) In situ recording from hamster taste cells: Responses to salt, sweet and sour. Chem Senses 16 (in press).

Axelrod J, Burch RM, Jelsma CL (1988) Receptor-mediated activation of phospholipase A_2 via GTP-binding proteins: arachidonic acid and its metabolites as second messengers. TINS 11:117–122.

Bagglioni M, and Wymann MP (1990) Turning on the respiratory burst. Trends Boichem Sci 15:69–72.

Bakalyar H, Reed R (1990) Identification of a specialized adenylate cyclase that may mediate odorant detection. Science 250:1403–1405.

Balsinde J, Diez E, Schüller A, Mollinedo F (1988) Phospholipase A_2 activity in resting and activated human neutrophils. J Biol Chem 263:1929–1936.

Barnard EA, Darlison MG, Seeburg P (1987) Molecular biology of the $GABA_A$ receptor: The receptor/channel superfamily. TINS 10:502–509.

Bass DA, Gerard C, Olbrantz P, Wilson J, McCall CE, McPhail LC (1987) Priming of the respiratory burst of neutrophils by diacylglycerol. J Biol Chem 262:6643–6649.

Beale G (1990) Self- and nonself recognition in the ciliate protozoan *Euplotes*. Trends in Genet 6:137–139.

Beaumier L, Faucher N, Naccache PH (1987) Arachidonic acid–induced release of calcium in permeabilized human neutrophils. FEBS Lett 221:289–292.

Bedale WA, Nettleton DO, Sopata CS, Thoekle MS, Ordal GW (1988) Evidence for methyl-group transfer between the methyl-accepting chemotaxis proteins in *Bacillus subtilis*. J Bacteriol 170:223–227.

Behe P, DeSimone JA, Avenet P, Lindemann (1990) Membrane currents in taste cells of the rat fungiform papilla—Evidence for two types of Ca currents and inhibition of K- currents by saccharin. J Gen Physiol 96:1061–1084.

Belardetti F, Siegelbaum SA (1988) Up- and down-modulation of single K^+ channel function by distinct second messengers. TINS 11:232–238.

Bentley JK, Khatra AS, Garbers DL (1987) Receptor-mediated phosphorylation of spermato-zoa proteins. J Biol Chem 262:15708–15713.

Bentley JK, Shimomura H, Garbers DL (1986a) Retention of a functional resact receptor in isolated sperm plasma membranes. Cell 45:281–288.

Bentley JK, Tubb DJ, Garbers DL (1986b) Receptor-mediated activation of spermatozoan guanylate cyclase. J Biol Chem 261:14859–14862.

Berridge MJ (1987) Inositol triphosphate and diacylglycerol: Two interacting second messen-gers. Annu Rev Biochem 56:159–194.

Bigiani A, Roper S (1991) Mediation of responses to calcium in taste cells by modulation of a K conductance. Science 252:126–128.

Bignetti E, Cavaggioni A, Pelosi P, Persaud KL, Sorbi RT, Tirindelli R (1985) Purification and characterization of an odorant binding protein from cow nasal tissue. Eur J Biochem 149:227–231.

Böhme R, Bumann J, Aeckerle S, Malchow D (1987) A high-affinity plasma membrane Ca^{2+}-ATPase in *Dictyostelium discoideum*: Its relation to cAMP-induced Ca^{2+} fluxes. Biochim Biophys Acta 904:125–130.

Bonini NM, Gustin M, Nelson DL (1986) Regulation of ciliary motility by membrane potential in *Paramecium*: A role for cAMP. Cell Motil Cytoskel 6:256–272.

Bonini NM, Nelson DL (1988) Differential regulation of *Paramecium* ciliary motility by cAMP and cGMP. J Cell Biol 106:1615–1623.

Borroni PF, Atema J (1987) Self- and cross-adaptation of single chemoreceptor cells in the taste organs of the lobster, *Homarus americanus*. In Roper S, Atema J (eds): "Olfaction and Taste IX." New York: New York Academy of Sciences, pp 184–186.

Boulter J, Evans K, Goldman D, Martin G, Treco D, Heinemann S, Patrick S (1986) Isolation of a cDNA clone coding for a possible neural nicotinic acetylcholine receptor α-subunit. Nature 319:368–374.

Boyd A, Simon M (1982) Bacterial chemotaxis. Annu Rev Physiol 44:501–517.

Boyle AG, Park YS, Huque T, Bruch RC (1987) Properties of phospholipase C in isolated olfactory cilia from the channel catfish (*Ictalurus punctatus*). Comp Biochem Physiol 88B: 767–775.

Brass JM (1986) The cell envelope of gram-negative bacteria: New aspects of its function in transport and chemotaxis. Curr Top Microbiol Immunol 129:1–92.

Breer H, Boekoff I (1991) Odorants of the same odor class activate different second messenger pathways. Chem Senses 16:16–29.

Breer H, Boekhoff I, Tareilus E (1990a) Rapid kinetics of second-messenger signalling in olfaction. Chem Senses 15:553.

Breer H, Boekhoff I, Tareilus E (1990b) Rapid kinetics of second-messenger formation in olfactory transduction. Nature 345:65–68.

Brokaw C (1987) A lithium sensitive regulator of sperm flagellar oscillations is activated by cyclic AMP-dependent phosphorylation. J Cell Biol 105:1789–1798.

Bruch RC (1990a) Signal transduction in olfaction and taste. In Inyegar R, Birnbaumer L (eds): G-Proteins. New York: Academic Press, pp 411–428.

Bruch RC (1990b) Signal transducing GTP-binding proteins in olfaction. Comp Biochem Physiol 95A:27–29.

Bruch RC, Huque T (1987) Odorant- and guanine nucleotide–stimulated phosphoinositide turnover in olfactory cilia. In Roper S, Atema J (eds): Olfaction and Taste IX. New York: New York Academy of Sciences, pp 205–207.

Bruch RC, Kalinoski DL (1987) Interaction of GTP-binding regulatory proteins with chemosensory receptors. J Biol Chem 262:2401–2404.

Bruch RC, Kalinoski DL, Huque T (1987a) Role of GTP-binding regulatory proteins in receptor-mediated phosphoinositide turnover in olfactory cilia. Chem Senses 12:173.

Bruch RC, Rulli RD, Boyle AG (1987b) Olfactory L-amino acid receptor specificity and stimulation of potential second messengers. Chem Senses 12:642–643.

Bruch RC, Teeter JH (1989) Second-messenger signalling mechanisms in olfaction. In Brand JG, Teeter JH, Cagan RH, Kare MR (eds): Chemical Senses, Vol 1. New York: Marcel Dekker, pp 283–298.

Bruch RC, Teeter JH (1990) Cyclic AMP links amino acid chemoreceptors to ion channels in olfactory cilia. Chem Senses 15:419–430.

Burchell B (1991) Turning on and turning off the sense of smell. Nature 350:16–17.

Bryant BP, Brand JG, Kalinoski DL (1989) Receptor site specificity in taste. In Brand JG, Teeter JH, Cagan RH, Kare MR (eds): Chemical Senses, Vol 1. New York: Marcel Dekker, pp 35–53.

Bryant B, Brand JG, Kalinoski DL, Bruch RC, Cagan RH (1987) Use of monoclonal antibodies to characterize amino acid taste receptors in catfish: Effects on binding and neural responses. In Roper R, Atema J (eds): Olfaction and Taste IX. New York: New York Academy of Sciences, pp 208–209.

Buck L, Axel R (1991) A novel multigene family may encode odorant receptors: A molecular basis for odor recognition. Cell 65:175–187.

Burgoyne RD, Cheek TR, O'Sullivan AJ (1987) Receptor-activation of phospholipase A_2 in cellular signalling. Trends Bioch 12:332–333.

Burkholder AC, Hartwell LH (1985) The yeast *a*-factor receptor: Structural properties deduced from the sequence of the STE2 gene. Nucleic Acids Res 13:8463–8473.

Cagan RH (1981) Recognition of taste stimuli at the initial binding interaction. In Cagan RH, Kare MR (eds): Biochemistry of Taste and Olfaction. New York: Academic Press, pp 175–204.

Cagan RH, Boyle AG (1984) Biochemical studies of taste sensation XI. Isolation, characterization and taste ligand binding activity of plasma membranes from catfish taste tissue. Biochim Biophys Acta 799:230–237.

Caprio J (1987a) Olfactory receptor responses to binary mixtures of amino acids in the channel catfish, *Ictalurus punctatus*. In Miller IS (ed): LM Beidler Symposium on Taste and Smell (in press).

Caprio J (1987b) Peripheral filters and chemoreceptor cells in fishes. In Atema J, Fay R, Popper A, Tavolga W (eds): Sensory Biology of Aquatic Animals. New York: Springer-Verlag, pp 311–336.

Caprio J (1988) Peripheral filters and chemoreceptor cells in fishes. In Atema J, Fay RR, Popper AN, Tavoiga WN (eds): Sensory Biology of Aquatic Animals. Berlin: Springer Verlag, pp 313–338.

Carr WES (1989) Chemical signaling systems in lower organisms. In Anderson PAV (ed): Evolution of the First Nervous System. New York: Plenun Press, pp. 81–94.

Carr WES, Ache BW, Gleeson RA (1987) Chemoreceptors of crustaceans: Similarities to receptors for neuroactive substances in internal tissues. Environ Health Perspect 71:31–46.

Carr WES, Netherton JC, Milstead ML (1984) Chemoattractants of the shrimp, *Palamemonetes pugio*. Comp Biochem Physiol 77A:469–474.

Carter A, Bardin C, Colins R, Simons C, Bray P, Spiegel A (1987) Reduced expression of multiple forms of the α-subunit of the stimulatory GTP-binding protein in pseudohypoparathyroidism type Ia. Proc Natl Acad Sci USA 84:7266–7269.

Cartwright CP, Tipper DJ (1991) In vivo topological analysis of Ste2, a yeast plasma membrane protein, by using beta-lactamase gene fusions. Mol Cell Biol 11:2620–2628.

Cassimeris H, McNeill H, Zigmond SH (1990) Chemoattractant-stimulated polymorphonuclear leukocytes contain two populations of actin filaments that differ in their spatial distributions and relative stabilities. J Cell Biol 110:1067–1075.

Chen Z, Pace U, Ronen D, Lancet D (1986) Polypeptide gp95, a unique glycoprotein of olfactory cilia with transmembrane receptor properties. J Biol Chem 261:1299–1305.

Coats WD, Navarro J (1990) Functional reconstitution of the f-met-leu-phe receptor in *Xenopus laevis* oocytes. J Biol Chem 265:5964–5966.

Cochrane CG (1984) Mechanisms coupling stimulation and function in leukocytes. Fed Proc 43:2729–2731.

Cockroft S (1987) Polyphosphoinositide phosphodiesterase: Regulation by a novel guanine nucleotide binding protein. G_p. TIBS 12:75–78.

Condeelis J, Hall A, Bresnick A, Warren V, Hock R, Bennett H, Ogihara S (1988) Actin polymerization and pseudopod extension during amoeboid chemotaxis. Cell Motil Cystoskel 10:77–90.

Costa-Casnellie MR, Segel GB, Lichtman MA (1986) Signal transduction in human monocytes: Relationship between superoxide production and the level of kinase C in the membrane. J Cell Physiol 129:336–342.

Crabbendam KJ, Klis FM, Musgrave A, van den Ende H (1986) Ultrastructure of the plus and minus mating-type sexual agglutinins of *Chlamydomonas eugametos*, as visualized by negative staining. J Ultrastruct Mol Struct Res 96:151–159.

Cummings TA, Avenet P, Roper SD, Kinnamon SC (1991) Patch-clamp recordings of hamster taste cells: Effects of saccharin and cAMP. Chem Senses (in press).

Danciger E, Mettling C, Vidal M, Morris R, Margolis F (1989) Olfactory marker protein gene: Its structure and olfactory neuron-specific expression in transgenic mice. Proc Natl Acad Sci USA 86:8565–8569.

Dangott LJ, Garbers DL (1984) Identification and partial purification of the receptor for speract. J Biol Chem 259:13712–13716.

Della Bianca V, Grzeskowiak M, Cassatella MA, Zeni L, Rossi F (1986) Inhibition by verapamil of neutrophil responses to f-met-leu-phe and phorbol myristate acetate. Biochem Biophys Res Commun. 135:556–567.

DeLozanne A, Spudich JA (1987) Disruption of the *Dictyostelium* myosin heavy chain gene by homolgous recombination. Science 236:1086–1091.

Derby CD, Ache BW (1984) Quality coding of a complex odorant in an invertebrate. J Neurophys 51:906–924.

Derby CD, Atema J (1987) Chemoreceptor cells in aquatic invertebrates: Peripheral mechanisms of chemical signal processing in decapod crustaceans. In Atema J, Fay RR, Popper AN, Tavolga WN (eds): Sensory Biology of Aquatic Animals. New York: Springer-Verlag, pp 365–385.

Derby CD, Giraradot M-N, Daniel P, Fine-Levy JB (1989) Olfactory discrimination of mixtures: Behavioral electrophysiological and theoretical studies using the spiny lobster *Panulirus argus*. In Laing DG, Cain WS, McBride RL, Ache BW (eds): Perception of Complex Smells. Sydney: Academic Press, pp 65–82.

Derby CD, Hamilton KA, Ache BW (1984) Processing of olfactory information at three neuronal levels in the spiny lobster. Brain Res 300:311–319.

DeSimone JA, Ferrell F (1985) Analysis of amiloride inhibition of chorda tympani taste response of rat to NaCl. J Physiol 369:R52–R61.

DeSimone JA, Heck GL, DeSimone SK (1981) Active ion transport in dog tongue: A possible role in taste. Science 214:1039–1041.

Dethier V (1978) Other tastes, other worlds. Sci 201:224–228.

Devreotes PN, Sherring JA (1985) Kinetics and concentration dependence of reversible cAMP-induced modification of the surface cAMP receptor in *Dictyostelium*. J Biol Chem 260:6378–6384.

Devreotes PN, Zigmond SH (1988) Chemotaxis in eukaryotic cells. Annu Rev Cell Biol 4:649–686.

Dhallan RS, Yau K, Schrader KA, Reed RR (1990) Primary structure and function expression of a cyclic nucleotide-activated channel from olfactory neurons. Nature 347:184–186.

Dietzel C, Kurjan J (1987) The yeast SCG1 gene: A G_a-like protein implicated in the a and a-factor response pathway. Cell 50:1001–1010.

Dillon SB, Murray JJ, Uhing RJ, Snyderman R (1987a) Regulation of inositol phospholipid and inositol phosphate metabolism in chemoattractant-activated human polymorphonuclear leukocytes. J Cell Biochem 35:345–359.

Dillon SB, Murray JJ, Verghese MW, Snyderman R (1987b) Regulation of inositol phosphate metabolism in chemoattractant-stimulated human polymorphonuclear leukocytes. J Biol Chem 262:11546–11552.

DiNallo M, Wohlford M, Van Houten J (1982) Mutants of *Paramecium* defective in chemoreception of folate. Genetics 103:453–468.

Ding XX, Porter TD, Peng HM, Coon MJ, (1991) cDNA and derived amino acid sequence of rabbit nasal cytochrome P450NMb, a unique isozyme possibly involved in olfaction. Arch Biochem Biophys 285:120–125.

Dionne V (1988) How do you smell? Principle in question. Trends Neurol Sci 11:188–189.

Dionne V (1990) Excitatory and inhibitory responses induced by amino acids in isolated mudpuppy olfactory receptor neurons. Chem Senses 15:566.

Dockstader KC, Dunwiddie TV, Finger TE (1991) Glutamate in NOT the neurotransmitter of primary gustatory afferent fibers. Chem Senses 16 (in press).

Dohlman HG, Caron MG, Lefkowitz R (1987) A family of receptors coupled to guanine nucleo-tide regulatory proteins. Biochemistry 26:2657–2664.

Dunlap K, Holz GG, Rane SG (1987) G proteins as regulators of ion channel function. TINS 10:241–244.

Eberle M, Traynorcaplan AE, Sklar L, Norgauer J (1990) Is there a relationship between phos-phatidylinositol trisphosphate and F-actin polymerization in human neutrophils? J Biol Chem 265:16725–16728.

Edelman AM, Blumenthal DK, Krebs EG (1987) Protein serine/threonine kinases. Annu Rev Biochem 56:567–614.

Edwards DA, Mather RA, Dodd GH (1988) Spatial variation in response to odorants on the rat olfactory epithelium. Experientia 44:208–211.

Eisenbach M, Matsumura P (1988) In vitro approach to bacterial chemotaxis. Botan Acta 101:93–99.

Europe-Finner GN, Luderus MEE, Small NV, Van Driel R, Reymond CD, Firtel RA, Newell PC (1988) Mutant *ras* gene induces elevated levels of inositol *tris-* and hexakisphosphates in *Distyostelium*. J Cell Sci 89:13–20.

Europe-Finner GN, Newell PC (1985) Inositol 1,4,5-trisphosphate induces cGMP formation in *Dictyostelium discoideum*. Biochem Biophys Res Commun 130:1115–1122.

Europe-Finner GN, Newell PC (1986) Inositol 1,4,5-trisphosphate induces calcium release from a non-mitochondrial pool in amoebae of *Dictyostelium*. Biochim Biophys Acta 887:335–340.

Europe-Finner GN, Newell PC (1987a) GTP analogues stimulate inositol trisphosphate forma-tion transiently in *Dictyostelium*. J Cell Sci 87:513–518.

Europe-Finner GN, Newell PC (1987b) Cyclic AMP stimulates accumulation of inositol trisphos-phate in *Dictyostelium*. J Cell Sci 87:221–229.

Evans TC, Hennessey T, Nelson DL (1987) Electrophysiological evidence suggests a defective Ca^{2+} control mechanism in a new *Paramecium* mutant. J Membr Biol 98:275–283.

Ewald DA, Roper SD (1990) Delayed depolarizing responses of *Necturus* taste cells to chemical and electrical stimuli at the apical pore of taste buds. Soc Neurosci Abstr 16:25.

Fadool DA, Michel WC, Ache BW (1991) G-proteins and inositol-phospholipid metabolism implicated in odor response of cultured lobster olfactory neurons. Chem Senses 16 (in press).

Falke JJ, Koshland DE (1987) Global flexibility in a sensory receptor: A site-directed cross-linking approach. Science 237:1596–1600.

Farbman AI (1990) Olfactory neurogenesis—Genetic or environmental controls. Trends in Neurosci 13:362–365.

Featherstone C (1990) An ATP-driven pump for secretion of yeast mating factor. Trends Biochem Sci 15:169–170.

Fesenko EE, Novoselov VI, Bystrova MF (1987) The subunits of specific odor-binding glyco-proteins from rat olfactory epithelium. FEB Lett 219:224–226.

Fields S (1990) Pheromone response in yeast. Trends Biochem Sci 15:270–273.

Finger TE, Bottjer B (1990) Transcellular labeling of taste bud cells by carbocyanine dye (DiI) applied to peripheral nerves in the barbels of the catfish, Ictalurus-punctatus. J Compar Neurol 302:884–892.

Firestein S, Shepherd GM (1989) Olfactory transduction is mediated by the action of cAMP. Soc Neurosci Abstracts 19:749.

Firestein S, Shepherd GM (1990) The role of cAMP as a second messenger in vertebrate olfactory transduction. Chem Senses 15:574.

Firestein S, Shepherd G, Werblin FS (1990) Time course of the membrane current underlying sensory transduction in salamander olfactory receptor neurones. J Physiol (London) 430:135–158.

Firestein S, Werblin F (1987) Electrophysiological basis of the response of olfactory receptors to odorant and current stimuli. In Roper S, Atema J (eds): Olfaction and Taste IX. New York: New York Academy of Sciences, pp 287–289.

Fletcher MP, Seligmann BE (1986) PMN heterogeneity: Long-term stability of fluorescent membrane potential responses to the chemoattractant N-formyl-methionyl-leucyl-phenylalanine in healthy adults and correlation with respiratory burst activity. Blood 68:611–618.

Foder B, Scharff O, Thastrup O (1989) Ca^{2+}-transcients and Mn^{2+} entry in human neutrophils induced by thapsigargin. Cell Calcium 10:477–490.

Fraser CM, Lindstrom J (1984) The use of monoclonal antibodies in receptor characterization and purification. In Venter JC, Harrison LC (eds): Molecular and Chemical Characterization of Membrane Receptors. New York: Alan R. Liss, pp 1–30.

Garbers DL (1989a) Guanylate cyclase, a cell surface receptor. J Biol Chem 264:9103–9106.

Garbers DL (1989b) Molecular basis of signalling in the spermatozoon. J Androl 10:99–107.

Garbers DL, Kopf GS (1980) The regulation of spermatozoa by calcium and cyclic nucleotides. Adv Cyclic Nucleotide Res 13:251–306.

Garbers DL, Noland TD, Dangott LJ, Ramarao CS, Bentley JK (1986) The interaction of egg peptides with spermatozoa. In Dhindsa DS, Bahl Om P (eds): Molecular and Cellular Aspects of Reproduction. New York: Plenum, pp 145–163.

Gegner JA, Dahlquist FW (1991) Signal transduction in bacteria—CheW forms a reversible complex with protein kinase CheA. Proc Natl Acad Sci USA 88:750–754.

Gerard N, Gerard C (1991) The chemotactic receptor for human C5a and phylatoxin. Nature 349:614–617.

Gesteland RC (1986) Speculation on receptor cells as analyzers and filters. Experientia 42:287–291.

Getchell TV, Getchell ML (1987) Peripheral mechanisms of olfaction: Biochemistry and neurophysiology. In Finger TE, Siver WL (eds): Neurobiology of Taste and Smell. New York: John Wiley & Sons, pp 91–123.

Getchell TV, Grillo M, Tate SS, Urade R, Teeter J, Margolis FL (1990) Expression of catfish amino acid taste receptors in Xenopus oocytes. Neurochem Res 15:449–456.

Getchell TV, Margolis FL, Getchell ML (1984) Perireceptor and receptor events in vertebrate olfaction. Prog Neurobiol 23:317–345.

Gilman AG (1987) G proteins: Transducers of receptor-generated signals. Annu Rev Biochem 56:615–650.

Golman DW, Goetzl EJ (1982) Specific binding of leukotriene B_4 to receptors on human polymorphonuclear leukocytes. J Immunol 129:1600.

Goodenough U, Adair WS, Collin-Osdoby P, Heuser JE (1985) Structure of the Chlamydomonas agglutinin and related flagellar surface proteins in vitro and in situ. J Cell Biol 101:924–941.

Grinstein S, Furuya W (1988) Receptor-mediated activation of electropermeabilized neutrophils. J Biol Chem 263:1779–1783.

Grob PM, David E, Warren TC, DeLeon RP, Farina PR, Homon CA (1990) Characterization of a receptor for human monocyte-derived neutrophil chemotactic factor/interleukin-8. J Biol Chem 265:8311–8316.

Gustin MC, Nelson DL (1987) Regulation of ciliary adenylate cyclase by Ca^{2+} in Paramecium. Biochem J 246:337–345.

Hagan DC, McCafrey G, Sprague GF (1986) Evidence the yeast STE3 gene encodes a receptor for the peptide pheromone a factor: Gene sequence and implications for the structure of the presumed receptor. Proc Natl Acad Sci USA 83:1418–1422.

Hall AL, Watten V, Condeelis J (1989) Transduction of the chemotactic signal to the actin cytoskeleton of Dictyostelium discoideum. Dev Biol 136:517–525.

Hanks SK, Quinn AM, Hunter T (1988) The protein kinase family: Conserved features and deduced phylogeny of the catalytic domains. Science 241:42–52.

Hanley MR, Jackson T (1987) Return of the magnificent seven. Nature 329:766–767.

Harvath L (1989) Regulation of neutrophil chemotaxis. Ann Reports Med Chem 24:233–241.

Heckmann K, Kuhlmann H-W (1986) Mating types and mating substances in *Euplotes octocarinatus*. J Exp Zool 237:87–96.

Hennessey T, Machemer H, Nelson DL (1985) Injected cAMP increases ciliary beat frequency in conjunction with membrane hyperpolarization. Eur J Cell Biol 36:153–156.

Herness MS (1990) Sucrose stimulation of rat taste cells can increase membrane potassium conductance. Soc Neurosci Abstr 16:25.

Herskowitz I, Marsh L (1987) Conservation of a receptor/signal transduction system. Cell 50:995–996.

Hess JF, Oosawa K, Kaplan N, Simon M (1988) Phosphorylation of three proteins in the signaling pathway of bacterial chemotaxis. Cell 53:79–87.

Hill DL, Mistretta CM (1990) Developmental neurobiology of salt taste sensation. Trends in Neurosci 13:188–195.

Hockberger PE, Swandulla D (1987) Direct ion channel gating: A new function for intracellular messengers. Cell Mol Neurobiol 7:229–236.

Homan W, Sigon C, van den Briel W, Wagter R, de Nobel H, Mesland D, Musgrave A, van den Ende H (1987) Transport of membrane receptors and the mechanics of sexual cell fusion in *Chlamydomonas eugametos*. FEBS Lett 215:323–326.

Houslay MD (1987) Egg activation unscrambles a potential role for IP_4. TIBS 12:1–2.

Howard TH, Wang D (1987) Calcium ionophore, phorbol ester, and chemotactic peptide-induced cytoskeleton reorganization in human neutrophils. J Clin Invest 79:1359–1364.

Huque T, Brand JG (1988) Phosphatidylinositol-4,5-bisphosphate phosphodiesterase (PIP_2-PDE) activity of catfish taste tissue. Chem Senses 13:698.

Huque T, Brand JG, Rabinowitz JL, Bayley DL (1987) Phospholipid turnover is catfish barbel (taste) epithelium with special reference to phosphatidylinositol-4,5-bisphosphate. Chem Senses 12:666–667.

Huque T, Bruch RC (1986) Odorant- and guanine nucleotide–stimulated phosphoinositide turnover in olfactory cilia. Biochem Biophys Res Commun 137:36–42.

Ingham CJ, Armitage JP (1987) Involvement of transport in *Rhodobacter shpaeroides* chemotaxis. J Bacteriol 169:5801–5807.

Imagawa M, Chium R, Karin M (1987) Transcription factor AP-2 mediates induction by two different signal transduction pathways: Protein kinase C and cAMP. Cell 51:251–260.

Irvine RF, Moor RM (1986) Microinjection of inositol 1,3,4,5-tetrakisphosphate activates sea urchin eggs by a mechanism dependent on extenal Ca^{2+}. Biochem J 240:917–920.

Jackowski S, Sha'afi RI (1979) Response of adenosine cyclic-3′ 5′ monophosphate level in rabbit neutrophils to the chemotactic peptide formyl methionyl-leucyl-phenyl alanine. Mol Pharmacol 16:473–481.

Jackson C, Hartwell L (1990) Courtship in *Saccharomyces cerivisiae:* Both cell types choose mating partners by responding to the strongest pheromone signal. Cell 63:1039–1051.

Jaconi MEE, Rivest RW, Schlegel W, Wollheim CG, Pittet D, Lew PD (1988) Spontaneous and chemoattractant-induced oscillations of cytosolic free calcium in single adherent human neutrophils. J Biol Chem 263:10557–10560.

Janssens PMW (1987) Did vertebrate signal transduction mechanisms originate in eukaryotic microbes? TIBS 12:456–459.

Janssens PMW, Van Haastert PJM (1987) Molecular basis of transmembrane signal transduction in *Dictyostelium discoideum*. Microbiol Rev 51:396–418.

Jenness DD, Burkholder AC, Hartwell LH (1986) Binding of a-factor pheromone to *Saccharomyces cerevisiae* a cells: Dissociation constant and number of binding sites. Mol Cell Biol 6:318–320.

Jenness DD, Goldman BS, Hartwell LH (1987) *Saccharomyces cerevisiae* mutants unresponsive to a-factor pheromone: *a*-Factor binding and extragenic suppression. Mol Cell Biol 7:1311–1319.

Jesaitis AJ, Bokoch GM, Allen RA (1988a) Regulation of signal transduction in human neutrophils by cytoskeleton-mediated reorganization of the plasma membrane chemoattractant receptors. In Condeelis J, Satir P, Lazarides E (eds): Signal Transduction in Cytoplasmic Organization and Cell Motility. New York: Alan R. Liss, pp 325–337.

Jesaitis AJ, Bokoch GM, Tolley JO, Allen RA (1988b) Lateral segregation of occupied chemotactic receptors into actin and fodrin-rich plasma membrane microdomains depleted in guanyl nucleotide proteins. J Cell Biol 107:921–928.

Jesaitis AJ, Naemura JR, Sklar LA, Cochrane CG, Painter RG (1984) Rapid modulation of N-formyl chemotactic peptide receptors on the surface of human granulocytes: Formation of high-affinity ligand–receptor complexes in transient association with cytoskeleton. J Cell Biol 98:1378–1387.

Jesaitis AJ, Tolley JO, Allen RA (1986) Receptor–cytoskeleton interactions and membrane traffic may regulate chemoattractant-induced superoxide production in human granulocytes. J Biol Chem 261:13662–13669.

Jesaitis AJ, Tolley JO, Bokoch GM, Allen RA (1989) Regulation of chemoattractant receptor interaction with transducing proteins by organizational control in the plasma membrane of human neutrophils. J Cell Biol 109:2783–2790.

Johnson BR, Voigt R, Atema J (1989) Response properties of lobster chemoreceptor cells: Response modulation by stimulus mixtures. Physiol Zool 62:559–579.

Johnson RL, Gundersen R, Lilly P, Pitt GS, Pupillo M, Sun TJ, Vaughan RA, Devreotes PN (1989) G-protein–linked signal transduction systems control development in *Dictyostelium*. Development S1989:75–80.

Jones DT, Reed RR (1987) Molecular cloning of five GTP-binding protein cDNA species from rat olfactory neuroepithelium. J Biol Chem 262:14241–14249.

Jones DT, Reed RR (1989) G_{olf}: An olfactory neuron specific G-protein involved in odorant signal transduction. Science 244:790–795.

Juliani MH, Klein C (1981) Photoaffinity labeling of the cell surface adenosine 3′:5′-monophosphate receptor of *Dictyostelium discoideum* and its modification in down-regulated cells. J Biol Chem 256:613–619.

Kaissling K-E (1987) In Colbow K (ed): RH Wright Lectures on Insect Olfaction. Simon Fraser University, Burnaby, British Columbia.

Kaissling K-E, Keil TA, Williams JLD (1991) Pheromone stimulation in perfused sensory hairs of the moth *Antheraea polyphemus*. J Insect Physiol 37:71–78.

Kalinoski DL, Huque T, LaMorte VJ, Brand JG (1989a) Second-messenger events in taste. In Brand JG, Teeter JH, Cagan RH, Kare MR (eds): Chemical Senses, Vol 1. New York: Marcel Dekker, pp 85–101.

Kalinoski DL, La Morte VJ, Johnson LC, Brand JG (1988) L-amino acid stimulated adenylate cyclase in catfish barbel epithelium: Specificity and characterization. Chem Senses 13:700.

Kashiwayanagi M, Swenaga A, Enomoto S, Kurihara K (1990) Membrane fluidity changes of liposomes in response to various odorants. Biophys J 58:887–895.

Kato H, Ishitoya J, Takenawa T (1986) Inhibition of inositol phospholipids metabolism and calcium mobilization by cyclic AMP-increasing agents and phorbol ester in neutrophils. Biochem Biophys Res Commun 139:1272–1278.

Kauer JS (1987) Coding in the olfactory system. In Finger TE, Silver WL (eds): Neurobiology of Taste and Smell. New York: John Wiley & Sons, pp 205–231.

Keller H. Gerisch G, Wissler JH (1979) A transient rise in cAMP levels following chemotactic stimulation of neutrophil granulocytes. Cell Biol Int Rep 3:759–765.

Kerlavage AR, Fraser CM, Venter JC (1987) Muscarinic cholinergic receptor structure: Molecular biological support for subtypes. TIPS 8:426–431.

Kesbeke F, Snaar-Jagalska BW, Van Haastert P (1988) Signal transduction in *Dictyostelium* fgd A mutants with a defective interaction between surface cAMP receptors and a GTP-binding regulatory protein. J Cell Biol 107:521–528.

Kesbeke F, Van Haastert PJM, DeWit RJW, Shaar-Jagalska BE (1990) Chemotaxis to cAMP and folic acid is mediated by different G-proteins in *Dictyostelium discoideum*. J Cell Sci 96:669–673.

Kikkawa U, Nishizuka Y (1986) The role of protein kinase C in transmembrane signalling. Annu Rev Cell Biol 2:149–178.

Kinnamon J (1987) Organization and innervation of taste buds. In Finger TE, Silver WL (eds): Neurobiology of Taste and Smell. New York: John Wiley & Sons, pp 277–297.

Kinnamon S, Roper S (1988) Evidence for a role of voltage-sensitive apical K$^+$ channels in sour and salt taste transduction. Chem Senses 13:115–121.

Kinnamon SC (1988) Taste transduction: A diversity of mechanisms. Trends in Neurosci 11:491–496.

Kleene SJ, Gesteland RC (1990) Transmembrane currents in frog olfactory cilia. J Membr Biol 120:75–81.

Klein C, Lubs-Haukeness J, Simons S (1985a) cAMP induces a rapid and reversible modification of the chemotactic receptor in *Dictyostelium discoideum*. J Cell Biol 100:715–730.

Klein C, Sadeghi H, Simons S (1986) Immunological analysis of the chemotactic receptor of *Dictyostelium discoideum*. J Biol Chem 261:15192–15196.

Klein P, Knox B, Borleis J, Devreotes P (1987a) Purification of the surface cAMP receptor in *Dictyostelium*. J Biol Chem 262:352–357.

Klein PS, Sun TJ, Saxe CL, Kimmel AR, Johnson RL, Devreotes PN (1988) A chemoattractant receptor controls development in *Dictyostelium discoideum*. Science 241:1467–1472.

Klein P, Theibert A, Fontana D, Devreotes PN (1985b) Identification and cyclic AMP–induced modification of the cyclic AMP receptor in *Dictyostelium discoideum*. J Biol Chem 260:1757–1764.

Klein P, Vaughan R, Borleis J, Devreotes P (1987b) The surface cyclic AMP receptor in *Dictyostelium*. J Biol Chem 262:358–364.

Klumpp S, Gierlich D, Schultz JE (1984) Adenylate cyclase and guanylate cyclase in the excitable ciliary membrane from *Paramecium*: Separation and regulation. FEBS Lett 171:95–99.

Knecht DA, Loomis WF (1987) Antisense RNA inactivation of myosin heavy chain gene expression in *Dictyostelium discoideum*. Science 236:1081–1086.

Koblika BK, Koblika TS, Daniel K, Regan JW, Caron MG, Lefkowitz FJ (1988) Chimeric a$_2$-, β_2-adrenergic receptors: Delineation of domains involved in effector coupling and ligand binding specificity. Science 240:1310–1316.

Kohbara J, Wegert S, Caprio J (1990) Two types of arginine-best taste units in the channel catfish. Chem Senses 15:601.

Kolesnikov SS, Zhainazarov AB, Kosolapov AV (1990) Cyclic nucleotide–activated channels in the frog olfactory receptor plasma membrane. FEBS Lett 266:96–98.

Korchak HM, Vienne K, Rutherford LE, Weissmann G (1984) Neutrophil stimulation: Receptor, membrane and metabolic events. Fed Proc 43:2749–2754.

Krause K-H, Pittet D, Volpe D, Pozzan T, Meldolesi J, Leco D (1989) Calciosome, a sarcoplasmic reticulum-like organelle involved in intracellular Ca^{2+}-handling by non-muscle cells: Studies in human neutrophils and HL-60 cells. Cell Calcium 10:351–361.

Krieger J, Raming K, Breer H (1991) Cloning of genomic and complementary DNA encoding insect pheromone binding proteins—Evidence for microdiversity. Biochim Biophys Acta 1088:277–284.

Kumazawa T, Teeter JH, Brand JG (1990) L-proline activates cation channels different from those activated by L-arginine in reconstituted taste epithelial membranes from channel catfish. Chem Senses 15:8603.

Kuo M, Gardner P (1987) Ion channels activated by inositol 1,4,5-trisphosphate in plasma membrane of human T-lymphocytes. Nature 326:301–304.

Kurja J (1990) G proteins in yeast *Saccharomyces cerevisiae*. In Iyenar R, Birnbaumer L (eds): G-Proteins. New York: Academic Press, pp 571–599.

Labarca P, Simon SA, Anholt RH (1988) Activation by odorants of a multistate cation channel from olfactory cilia. Proc Natl Acad Sci USA 85:944–947.

Lackie JM (1988) The behavioural repertoire of neutrophils requires multiple signal transduction pathways. J Cell Sci 89:449–452.

Lancet D (1991) The strong scent of success. Nature 351:275–276.

Lancet D, Pace U (1987) The molecular bases of odor recognition. TIBS 12:63–66.

Lancet D, Helman J, Khen M, Lazard D, Lazarovits J, Margalit T, Poria Y, Aupko K (1989) Molecular cloning and localization of novel olfactory-specific enzymes possibly involved in signal termination: A new role for supporting cells. Soc Neurosci Abstr 15:749.

Lancet D, Striem BJ, Pace U, Zehavi U, Naim M (1987) Adenylate cyclase and GTP binding protein in rat sweet taste transduction. Soc Neurosci Abstr 13:361.

Laskin DL, Gardner CR, Laskin JD (1987) Induction of chemotaxis in mouse peritoneal macrophages by activators of protein kinase C. J Leukocyte Biol 41:474–480.

Lazard D, Tal N, Rubinstein M, Khen M, Lancet D, Zupko K (1990) Identification and biochemical analysis of novel olfactory-specific cytochrome-P-450IIa and UDP-glucuronosyl transferase. Biochem 29:7433–7440.

Lazard D, Zupko K, Poria Y, Nef P, Lazarovits J, Horn S, Khen M, Lancet D (1991) Odorant signal termination by olfactory UDP glucuronosyl transferase. Nature 349:790–793.

Lazzari KG, Proto P, Simons ER (1990) Neutrophil hyperpolarization in response to a chemotactic peptide. J Biol Chem 265:10959–10967.

Lee K-H, Wells RG, Reed RR (1987) Isolation of an olfactory cDNA: Similarity to retinol-binding protein suggests a role in olfaction. Science 235:1053–1056.

Lengeler J, Auburger AJ, Mayer R, Pecher A (1981) The phosphoenolpyruvate dependent carbohydrate: Phosphotransferase system enzymes II as chemoreceptors in chemotaxis of *Escherichia coli* K12. Mol Gen Genet 183:163–170.

Lerner MR, Reagan J, Gyorgyi T, Roby A (1988) Olfaction by melanophores: What does it mean? Proc Natl Acad Sci USA 85:261–264.

Lew D, Wollheim C, Waldvogel F, Pozzan T (1984) Modulation of cytosolic-free calcium transients by changes in intracellular buffering capacity: Correlation with exocytosis and O_2 production in human neutrophils. J Cell Biol 99:1208.

Lewis R (1991) A family of cAMP receptor subtypes helps solve a slime mold mystery. J NIH Research 3:59–62.

Linn CE, Campbell MG, Roelofs WL (1985) Male moth sensitivity to multicomponent pheromones: Critical role of female-released blend in determining the functional role of components and active space of the pheromone. J Chem Ecol 12:659–668.

Linn CE, Roelofs WL (1989) Response specificity of male moths to multicomponent pheromones. Chem Senses 14:421–437.

Liu G, Newell PC (1988) Evidence that cyclic GMP regulates myosin interaction with the cytoskeleton during chemotaxis of *Dictyostelium*. J Cell Sci 90:123–129.

Lohr KM, Snyderman R (1982) Amphotericin B alters the affinity and functional activity of the oligopeptide chemotactic factor receptor on human polymorphonuclear leukocytes. J Immunol 129:1594–1599.

Lowe DG, Chang M-S, Hellmiss R, Chen E, Singh S, Garbers DL, Goeddel DV (1989) Human atrial natriuretic peptide receptor defines a new paradigm for second messenger signal transduction. EMBO J 8:1377–1384.

Lowe G, Gold GH (1990) Cilia are the site of olfactory transduction. Soc Neurosci Abstr 16:25.

Lowe G, Nakamura T, Gold GH (1988) EOG amplitude is correlated with odor-stimulated adenylate cyclase activity in the bullfrog olfactory epithelium. Chem Senses 13:710.

Lu DJ, Grinstein S (1990) ATP and guanine nucleotide dependence of neutrophil activation—Evidence for the involvement of two distinct GTP-binding proteins. J Biol Chem 265:13721–13729.

Luderus MEE, Reymond CD, Van Haastert PJM, Van Driel R (1988) Expression of a mutated *ras* gene in *Dictyostelium discoideum* alters the binding of cyclic AMP to its chemotactic receptor. J Cell Sci 90:701–706.

Ludwig J, Margalit T, Eismann E, Lancet D, Kaupp UB (1990) Primary structure of cAMP-gated channel from bovine olfactory epithelium. FEBS Lett 270:24–29.

Luporini P, Miceli C (1986) Mating pheromones. In Gall J (ed): Molecular Biology of Ciliated Protozoa. New York: Academic Press, pp 263–299.

Machemer H (1976) Interactions of membrane potential and cations in regulation of ciliary activity in *Paramecium*. J Exp Biol 65:427–448.

Machemer H (1989) Cellular behaviour modulated by ions: Electrophysiological implications. J Protozool 36:463–487.

Majima T, Hamasaki T, Arai T (1986) Increase in cellular cyclic GMP level by potassium stimulation and its relation to ciliary orientation in *Paramecium*. Experientia 42:62–64.

Margolis FL (1987) Chemical senses: Overview of the peripheral olfactory system and the molecular biology of the olfactory marker protein. Discussions in Neurosci 4:47–52.

Marks PW, Maxfield FR (1990a) Transient increases in cytosolic free calcium appear to be required for the migration of adherent human neutrophils. J Cell Biol 110:43–52.

Marks PW, Maxfield FR (1990b) Local and global changes in cytosolic free calcium in neutrophils during chemotaxis and phagocytosis. Cell Calcium 11:181–190.

Marsh L, Herskowitz I (1988) STE2 protein of *Saccharomyces kluyveri* is a member of the rhodopsin/β-adrenergic receptor family and is responsible for recognition of the peptide ligand a factor. Proc Natl Acad Sci USA 85:3844–3859.

Marx JL (1987) Receptor gene family is growing. Science 238:615–616.

Mato JM, Krens FA, van Haastert PJM, Konijn TM (1977) Cyclic AMP dependent cGMP accumulation in *Dictyostelium discoideum*. Proc Natl Acad Sci 74:2348–2351.

McClintock TS, Schutte K, Ache BW (1989) Failure to implicate cAMP in transduction in lobster olfactory receptor cells. Chem Senses 14:817–827.

McClintock TS, Ache B (1989a) Hyperpolarizing receptor potentials in lobster olfactory receptor cells. Chem Senses 14:637–648.

McClintock TS, Ache BW (1989b) Ionic currents and ion channels of lobster olfactory receptor neurons J Gen Physiol 94:1085–1099.

Meier K, Klein C (1988) An unusual protein kinase phosphorylates the chemotactic receptor of *Dictyostelium discoideum*. Proc Natl Acad Sci USA 85:2181–2185.

Menco B (1991) Ultrastructural localization of antibodies to olfactory epithelial-specific glycoprotein gp95, olfactomedin, and 90E and 50E antigens in the frog's olfactory epithelium. Chem Senses 16 [Abstr] (in press).

Meyer F, Schmidt HJ, Plümper E, Hasilik A, Mersmann G, Meyer H, Engström A, Heckmann K (1991) UGA is translated as cysteine in pheromone 3 of *Euplotes octocarinatus*. Proc Natl Acad Sci USA 88:3758–3761.

Meyers-Hutchins BL, Frazier WA (1984) Purification and characterization of a membrane associated cAMP-binding protein from developing *Dictyostelium discoideum*. J Biol Chem 256: 4379–4388.

Miceli C, LaTerza A, Melli M (1989) Isolation and structural characterization of cDNA clones encoding the mating pheromone Er-1 secreted by the ciliate *Euplotes raikovi*. Proc Natl Acad Sci USA 86:3016–3020.

Michel WC, Ache B (1990) Odor-activated conductance inhibits lobster olfactory receptor cells. Chem Senses 15:619–620.

Michel WC, McClintock TS, Ache BW (1991) Inhibition of lobster receptor cells by an odor-activated potassium conductance. J Neurophysiol (in press).

Mierson S, DeSimone SK, Heck GL, DeSimone JA (1988) Sugar-activated ion transport in canine lingual epithelium: Implications for sugar taste transduction. J Gen Physiol (in press).

Miller RJ (1988) G proteins flex their muscles. TINS 11:3–8.

Milligan DL, Koshland DE (1988) Site-directed crosslinking: Establishing the dimer structure of the aspartate receptor of bacterial chemotaxis. J Biol Chem 263:6268–6275.

Miyajima I, Nakafuku M, Nakayama N, Brenner C, Miyajima A, Kaibuchi K, Arai K-I, Kaziro Y, Matsumoto K (1987) GPA1, a haploid-specific essential gene, encodes a yeast homolog of mammalian G protein which may be involved in mating factor signal transduction. Cell 50:1011–1019.

Moore PA, Gerhardt GA, Atema J (1989) High resolution spatio-temporal analysis of aquatic chemical signals using microelectrochemical electrodes. Chem Senses 14:829–840.

Mowbray SL, Koshland DE (1987) Additive and independent responses in a single receptor: Aspartate and maltose stimuli on the Tar protein. Cell 50:171–180.

Murphy PM, Gallen EK, Tiffany HL, Malech HZ (1990) The formyl peptide chemoattractant receptor is encoded by a 2 kilobase mRNA. FEBS Lett 261:353–357.

Musgrave A, van den Ende H (1987) How *Chlamydomonas* court their partners. TIBS 12:469–473.

Nakamura T, Gold GH (1987) A cyclic nucleotide–gated conductance in olfactory receptor cilia. Nature 325:442–444.

Nakayama N, Miyajima A, Arai K (1985) Nucleotide sequences of *STE2* and *STE3*, cell type-specific sterile genes from *Saccharomyces cerevisiae*. EMBO J 4:2643–2648.

Nakoaka Y, Ooi H (1985) Regulation of ciliary reversal in Triton-extracted *Paramecium* by calcium and cyclic adenosine monophosphate. J Cell Sci 77:195–195.

Nasmith PE, Grinstein S (1987a) Phorbol ester-induced changes in cytoplasmic Ca^{2+} in human neutrophils. J Biol Chem 262:13558–13566.

Nasmith PE, Grinstein S (1987b) Are Ca^{2+} channels in neutrophils activated by a rise in cytosolic free Ca^{2+}? FEBS Lett 221:95–100.

Nasmyth K (1982) Molecular genetics of yeast mating types. Annu Rev Genet 16:439–450.

Nathan P, Hahnenberger A, Newton A, Shapiro L (1986) Differential localization of membrane receptor chemotaxis protein in the *Caulobacter* predivisional cell. J Mol Biol 191:433–440.

Neer EJ, Clapham DE (1988) Roles of G protein subunits in transmembrane signalling. Nature 333:129–139.

Nelson DJ, Wright EM (1974) The distribution, activity, and function of the cilia in the frog brain. J Physiol [Lond] 243:63–78.

Newell PC (1986) The role of actin polymerization in amoebal chemotaxis. BioEssays 5:208–211.

Newell PC, Europe-Finner GN, Small NV, Liu G (1988) Inositol phosphates, G-proteins, and *ras* genes involved in chemotactic signal transduction in *Distyostelium*. J Cell Sci 89:123–127.

Niedel JE, Cuatrecasas P (1980a) Covalent affinity labeling of formyl peptide chemotactic receptors. J Biol Chem 255:7063–7066.

Niedel JE, Cuatrecasas P (1980b) Formyl peptide chemotactic reception of leukocytes and macrophages. Curr Top Cell Regul 17:137–170.

Nishihara J, McPhail LC, O'Flaherty JT (1986) Stimulus-dependent mobilization of protein kinase C. Biochem Biophys Res Commun 134:587–594.

Nobili R, Luporini P, Esposito F (1987) Compatibility systems in ciliates. In Greenberk AH (ed): Invertebrate Models: Cell Receptors and Cell Communication. Basel: Karger, pp 1–28.

Novoselov VI, Krapivinskaya LD, Fesenko EE (1988) Amino acid binding glycoproteins from the olfactory epithelium of skate (*Dasyatis partinaca*). Chem Senses 13:267–279.

Oakley B, Lawton A, Wong L (1990) Rabbit gustatory epithelium expresses keratin 6-like immunoreactivity. Soc Neurosci Abstr 16:25.

O'Connell RJ (1986) Responses to pheromone blends in insect olfactory receptor neurons. J Comp Physiol 156:747–761.

O'Connell RJ, Costanzo RM, Hildebrandt JD (1990) Adenylyl cyclase activation and electrophysiological responses elicited in male hamster olfactory receptor neurons by components of female pheromones. Chem Senses 15:725–739.

Oosawa K, Hess J, Simon M (1988) Mutants defective in bacterial chemotaxis show modified protein phosphorylation. Cell 53:89–96.

Ortenzi C, Miceli C, Bradshaw RA, Luporini P (1990) Identification and initial characterization of an autocrine pheromone receptor in the protozoan ciliate *Euplotes raikovi*. J Cell Biol 111:607–614.

Pace U, Lancet D (1986) Olfactory GTP-binding protein: Signal-transducing polypeptide of vertebrate chemosensory neurons. Proc Natl Acad Sci USA 83:4947–4951.

Painter RG, Sklar LA, Jesaitis AJ, Schmitt M, Cochrane CG (1984) Activation of neutrophils by *N*-formyl chemotactic peptides. Fed Proc 43:2737–2742.

Painter RG, Zahler-Bentz K, Dukes RE (1987): Regulation of the affinity state of the *N*-formylated peptide receptor on neutrophils: Role of guanine nucleotide–binding proteins and the cytoskeleton. J Cell Biol 105:2959–2971.

Parkinson JA (1988) Protein phosphorylation in bacterial chemotaxis. Cell 53:1–2.

Parsons JT (1990) Closing the GAP in signal transduction pathway. Trends Genet 6:169–171.

Pasquale SM, Goodenough U (1987) Cyclic AMP functions as a primary sexual signal in gametes of *Chlamydomonas reinhardtii*. J Cell Biol 105:2279–2292.

Paul A, Marala RB, Jaiswal RK, Sharma RK (1987) Coexistence of guanylate cyclase and atrial natriuretic factor receptor in a 180-kD protein. Science 235:1224–1226.

Pelosi P, Baldaccini E, Pisanelli AM (1982) Identification of a specific olfactory receptor for 2-isobutyl-3-methoxypyrazine. Biochem J 201:245–248.

Pelosi P, Dal Monte M (1990) Purification and characterization of odorant binding proteins from nasal mucosa of pig and rabbit. Chem Senses 15:624.

Persaud KC, Chiavacci L, Pelosi P (1988) Binding proteins for sweet compounds from gusta-¼ tory papillae of the cow, pig, and rat. Biochim Biophys Acta 967:65–75.

Persaud KC, DeSimone JA, Getchell ML, Heck GL, Getchell TV (1987) Ion transport across the frog olfactory mucosa: The basal and odorant-stimulated states. Biochim Biophys Acta 902:65–79.

Petersen OH (1989) Does inositol tetrakisphosphate play a role in the receptor-mediated control of calcium mobilization? Cell Calcium 10:375–383.

Pevsner J, Sklar PA, Snyder SH (1986) Odorant-binding protein: Localization to nasal glands and secretions. Proc Natl Acad Sci USA 83: 4942–4946.

Pevsner J, Trifiletti RR, Strittmatter SM, Snyder SH (1985) Isolation and characterization of an olfactory receptor protein for odorant pyrazines. Proc Natl Acad Sci USA 82:3050–3054.

Pike MC, DeMeester CA (1988) Inhibition of phosphoinositide metabolism in human polymorphonuclear leukocytes by *S*-adenosylhomocysteins. J Biol Chem 263:3592–3599.

Piomelli D, Volterra A, Dale N, Siegelbaum SA, Kandel ER, Schwartz JH, Belardetti F (1987) Lipoxygenase metabolites of arachidonic acid as second messengers for presynaptic inhibition of *Aplysia* sensory cell. Nature 328:38–43.

Polakis PG, Uhing RJ, Snyderman R (1988) The formylpeptide chemoattractant receptor copurifies with a GTP-binding protein containing a distinct 40-kDa pertussis toxin substrate. J Biol Chem 263:4969–4976.

Postma PW, Lengeler JW (1985) Phosphoenolpyruvate: Carboxyhydrate phosphotransferase system of bacteria. Microbiol Rev 49:232–269.

Preston RR, Usherwood PNR (1988) L-glutamate-induced membrane hyperpolarization and behavorial responses in *Paramecium tetraurelia*. J Comp Physiol 164:75–82.

Preston RR, Van Houten JL (1987a) Localization of the chemoreceptive properties of the surface membrane of *Paramecium tetraurelia*. J Comp Physiol [A] 160:537–541.

Preston RR, Van Houten JL (1987b) Chemoreception in *Paramecium tetraurelia:* acetate- and folate-induced membrane hyperpolarization. J Comp Physiol [A] 160:525–535.

Price S (1987) Effects of odorant mixtures on olfactory receptor cells. In Roper S, Atema J (eds): Olfaction and Taste IX. New York: New York Academy of Sciences, pp 55–60.

Price S, Willey A (1987) Benzaldehyde binding protein from dog olfactory epithelium. In Roper S, Atema J (eds): Olfaction and Taste IX. New York: New York Academy of Sciences, pp 561–564.

Price S (1981) Receptor proteins in vertebrate olfaction. In Cagan RH, Kare MR (eds): Biochemistry of Taste and Olfaction. New York: Academic Press, pp 69–84.

Price S, Willey A (1988) Effects of antibodies against odorant binding proteins on electrophysiological responses to odorants. Biochim Biophys Acta 965:127–129.

Pun R, Gesteland R (1990) Whole cell patch recordings show frog and salamander olfactory neurons are different. Chem Senses 15:628.

Putney JW (1987) Formation and actions of calcium-mobilizing messenger inositol 1,4,5-trisphosphate. Am J Physiol 252:G149–G157.

Rasmussen H (1981) Calcium and Cyclic AMP as Synarchic Messengers. New York: John Wiley & Sons.

Ravid S, Matsumura P, Eisenbach M (1986) Restoration of flagellar clockwise rotation in bacterial envelopes by insertion of the chemotaxis protein CheY. Proc Natl Acad Sci USA 83:7157–7161.

Reibmann J, Korchak HM, Vosshall LB, Haines KA, Rich AM, Weissmann G (1988) Changes in diacylglycerol labeling, cell shape, and protein phosphorylation distinguish "triggering" from "activation" of human neutrophils. J Biol Chem 263:6322–6328.

Restrepo D, Miyamoto T, Bryant BP, Teeter JH (1990) Odor stimuli trigger influx of calcium into olfactory neurons of the channel catfish. Science 249:1166–1168.

Rhein LD, Cagan RH (1981) Role of cilia in olfactory recognition. In Cagan RH, Kare MR (eds): Biochemistry of Taste and Olfaction. New York: Academic Press, pp 47–68.

Robbins SM, Williams JG, Jermyn KA, Spiegelman GB, Weeks G (1989) Growing and developing *Dictyostelium* cells express different *ras* genes. Proc Natl Acad Sci USA 86:938–942.

Rollins TE, Springer MS (1985) Identification of the polymorphonuclear leukocyte C5a receptor. J Biol Chem 260:7157–7160.

Ronnett GV, Hester LD, Snyder SH (1990) The effect of odorants of adenylate cyclase in primary cultures of rat olfactory neurons. Soc Neurosci Abstr 16:26.

Ronson CW, Nixon BT, Ausubel FM (1987) Conserved domains in bacterial regulatory proteins that respond to environmental stimuli. Cell 49:579–581.

Roos FJ, Zimmermann A, Keller HU (1987) Effect of phorbol myristate acetate and the chemotactic peptide fNLPNTL on shape and movement of human neutrophils. J Cell Sci 88:399–406.

Roper SD (1989) The cell biology of vertebrate taste receptors. Annu Rev Neurosci 12:329–353.

Ross FM, Newell PC (1981) Streamers: Chemotactic mutants of *Dictyostelium discoideum* with altered cyclic GMP metabolism. J Gen Microb 127:339–350.

Russo AF, Koshland DE (1983) Separation of signal transduction and adaptation functions of the aspartate receptor in bacterial sensing. Science 220:1016–1020.

Sarndahl E, Lindroth M, Bengsteeon T, Fallman M, Gustavsson J, Stendahl O, Andersson T (1989) Association of ligand–receptor complexes with actin filaments in human neutrophils: A possible regulatory role for the G-protein. J Cell Biol 109:2791–2799.

Sasner JM, Van Houten JL (1989) Evidence for a folate chemoreceptor in *Paramecium*. Chem Senses 14:587–595.

Satir P (1985) Switching mechanisms in the control of ciliary motility. In Satir B (ed): Modern Cell Biology, Vol 4. New York: Alan R. Liss, pp 1–46.

Sato M (1987) Taste receptor proteins. Chem Senses 12:277–284.

Sato T, Okada Y, Miyamoto T (1987) Ionic mechanism of generation of receptor potential in frog taste cells. In Roper S, Atema J (eds): Olfaction and Taste IX. New York: New York Academy of Sciences, pp 23–26.

Sawyer DW, Sullivan JA, Mandell GL (1985) Intracellular free calcium localization in neutrophils during phagocytosis. Science 230:663–666.

Saxe CL, Johnson RL, Devreotes PN, Kimmell AR (1991) Expression of a cAMP receptor gene of *Dictyostelium* and evidence for a multigene family. Genes Dev 5:129–135.

Saxe CL, Klein P, Sun TJ, Kimmel AR, Devreotes PN (1988) Structure and expression of the cAMP cell-surface receptor. Dev Genet 9:227–235.

Schiffmann S (1990) The role of sodium and potassium transport pathways in taste transduction: An overview. Chem Senses 15:366–329.

Schmale H, Holfgreve-Grez H, Heidje Christiansen J (1990) Possible role for salivary gland protein in taste reception indicated by homology to lipophilic-ligand carrier proteins. Nature 343:366–369.

Schmied el-Jakob I, Anderson PAV, Ache BW (1989) Whole cell recording from lobster olfactory receptor cells: Responses to current and odor stimulation. J Neurophys 61:994–1000.

Schmitt BC, Ache BW (1979) Olfaction: Response enhancement by flicking in a decapod crustacean. Sci 205:204–206.

Schultz JE, Grunemund R, von Hirschhausen R, Schönefeld U (1984) Ionic regulation of cyclic AMP levels in *paramecium tetraurelia* in vivo. FEBS Lett 167:113–116.

Schulz I, Thevenod F, Dehlinger-Kremer M (1989) Modulation of intracellular free Ca^{2+} concentration by IP_3-sensitive and IP_3-insensitive nonmitochondrial Ca^{2+} pools. Cell Calcium 10:325–336.

Schulz S, Chinkers M, Garbers DL (1989) The guanylate cyclase/receptor family of proteins. FASEB J 3:2026–2035.

Schulz S, Denaro M, Van Houten J (1984) Relationship of folate binding and uptake to chemoreception in *Paramecium*. J Comp Physiol [A] 155:113–119.

Schulz S, Green C, Yuen P, Garbers DL (1990) Guanylate cyclase is a heat-stable enterotoxin receptor. Cell 63:941–948.

Scott TR, Giza BK (1990) Coding channels in the taste system of the rat. Science 249:1585–1587.

Segall JE, Bominaar AA, Wallraff E, De Wit RJ (1988) Analysis of a *Dictyostelium* chemotaxis mutant with altered chemoattractant binding. J Cell Sci 91:479–489.

Segall JE, Fisher PR, Gerisch G (1987) Selection of chemotaxis mutants of *Dictyostelium discoideum*. J Cell Biol 104:151–161.

Segall JE, Gerisch G (1989) Genetic approaches to cytoskeleton function and the control of cell motility. Curr Opinion Cell Biol 1:44–50.

Seligmann BE, Fletcher MP, Gallin JI (1982) Adaptation of human neutrophil responsiveness to the chemoattractant N-formylmethionylleucylphenylalanine. J Biol Chem 257:6280–6286.

Sha'afi RI, Molski RFP (1987) Signalling for increased cytoskeletal actin in neutrophils. Biochem Biophys Res Commun 145:934–941.

Sha'afi RI, Molski RFP (1988) Activation of the neutrophil. Prog Allergy 42:1–64.

Shimomura H, Dangott LJ, Garbers DL (1986) Covalent coupling of a resact analogue to guanylate cyclase. J Biol Chem 261:15778–15782.

Shioi J, Dang CV, Taylor BL (1987) Oxygen as attractant and repellent in bacterial chemotaxis. J Bacteriol 169:3118–3123.

Shioi J, Taylor BL (1984) Oxygen taxis and proton motive force in *Salmonella typhimurium*. J Biol Chem 259:10983–10988.

Shirley SG, Robinson CJ, Dickinson K, Aujla R, Dodd GH (1986) Olfactory adenylate cyclase of the rat: Stimulation by odorants and inhibition by Ca. Biochem J 240:605–607.

Sibley DR, Benovic JL, Caron MG, Lefkowitz RJ (1987) Regulation of transmembrane signaling by receptor phosphorylation. Cell 48:913–922.

Sibley DR, Lefkowitz RJ (1985) Molecular mechanisms of receptor desensitization using the β-adrenergic receptor-coupled adenylate cyclase system as a model. Nature 317:124–129.

Sicard G, Holley A (1984) Receptor cell responses to odorants: Similarities and differences among odorants. Brain Res 292:283–296.

Silver WL (1987) The common chemical sense. In Finger TE, Silver WL (eds): Neurobiology of Taste and Smell. New York: John Wiley & Sons, pp 65–88.

Sklar LA, Bokoch GM, Button D, Smolen JE (1987) Regulation of ligand-receptor dynamics by guanine nucleotides. J Biol Chem 262:135–139.

Sklar LA, Finney DA, Oades ZG, Jesaitis AJ, Painter RG, Cochrane CG (1984a) The dynamics of ligand-receptor interactions. J Biol Chem 259:5561–5569.

Sklar L, Jesaitis AJ, Painter RG (1984b) The neutrophil N-formyl peptide receptor: Dynamics of ligand–receptor interactions and their relationship to cellular responses. In Snyderman R (ed): Contemporary Topics in Immunobiology, Vol 14. New York: Plenum Press, pp 29–82.

Sklar LA, Mueller H, Omann G, Oades Z (1989) Three states for the formyl peptide receptor on intact cells. J Biol Chem 264:8483–8486.

Sklar PB, Anholt RH, Snyder SH (1986) The odorant-sensitive adenylate cyclase of olfactory receptor cells. J Biol Chem 261:15538–15543.

Small NV, Europe-Finner GN, Newell PC (1987) Adaptation to chemotactic cyclic AMP signals in *Dictyostelium* involves the G-protein. J Cell Sci 88:537–545.

Smith R, Preston RR, Schulz S, Van Houten J (1987) Correlation of cyclic adenosine monophosphate binding and chemoresponse in *Paramecium*. Biochim Biophys Acta 928:171–178.

Smollen JE, Korchak HM, Weissman G (1980) Increased levels of cyclic AMP in human polymorphonuclear leukocytes surface stimulation. J Clin Invest 65:1077–1085.

Snaar-Jagalski BE, DeWit RJW, Van Haastert PJM (1988) Pertussis toxin inhibits cAMP surface receptor-stimulated binding of [^{35}S]GTPgS to *Dictyostelium discoideum* membranes. FEBS Lett 232:148–152.

Snaar-Jaglaska BE, Van Haastert PJM (1988) *Dictyostelium discoideum* mutant *synag 7* with altered G-protein–adenylate cyclase interaction. J Cell Sci 91:287–294.

Snyder SH, Sklar PB, Pevsner J (1988) Molecular mechanisms of olfaction. J Biol Chem 263:13871–13974.

Snyderman R (1984) Regulatory mechanisms of a chemoattractant receptor on leukocytes. Fed Proc 43:2743–2748.

Snyderman R, Pike MC, Edge S, Lane B (1984) A chemoattractant receptor on macrophages exists in two affinity states regulated by guanine nucleotides. J Cell Biol 989:444–448.

Sockett RE, Armitage JP, Evans MCW (1987) Methylation-independent and methylation-dependent chemotaxis in *Rhodobacter sphaeroides* and *Rhodospirillum rubrum*. J Bacteriol 169:5808–5814.

Stengl M, Zufall F, Hatt H, Dudel J, Hildebrand JG (1989) Patch clamp analysis of male *Manduca sexta* olfactory receptor neurons in primary cell culture. Soc Neurosci Abstr 15:365.

Stengl M, Zufall F, Hatt H, Hildebrand JG (1990) Olfactory receptor neurons from developing male *Manduca sexta* antennae respond to species-specific sex pheromone in vitro. Chem Senses 15:643–644.

Stevens C (1987) Channel families in the brain. Nature 328:198–199.

Stock A, Chen T, Welsh D, Stock J (1989) CheA protein, a central regulator of bacterial chemotaxis, belongs to a family of proteins that control gene expression in response to changing environmental conditions. Proc Natl Acad Sci USA 85:1403–1407.

Stock J (1987) Mechanisms of receptor function and the molecular biology of information processing in bacteria. BioEssays 6:199–203.

Stock J, Stock A (1987) What is the role of receptor methylation in bacterial chemotaxis? TIBS 12:371–374.

Stone DE, Reed SI (1990) G-protein mutations that alter the pheromone response in *Saccharomyces cerivisiae*. Mol Cell Biol 10:4439–4446.

Striem B, Pace U, Zehavi U, Naim M, Lancet D (1989) Sweet tastants stimulate adenylate cyclase coupled to GTP-binding proteins in rat tongue. Biochem J 260:121–126.

Stryer L, Bourne HR (1986) G proteins: A family of signal transducers. Annu Rev Cell Biol 2:391–419.

Sugimoto K, Teeter JH (1990) Voltage-dependent ionic currents in taste receptor cells of the larval tiger salamander. J Gen Physiol 96:809–834.

Sullivan SJ, Zigmond SH (1982) Asymmetric receptor distribution on PMNS. J Cell Biol 95:418a.

Suzuki K, Hazama M, Ota H, Oguro K, Uchiyama H, Fujikura T (1990) Phosphorylation of 64K-Da protein, enzyme release, and increase in intracellular cAMP level in human polymorphonuclear leukocytes induced by fmet-leu-phe stimulation. J Clin Bioch Nut 8:21–32.

Takenawa T, Ishitoya J, Nagai Y (1986) Inhibitory effect of PG EZ, forskolin and dibutyryl cAMP on arachidonic acid release and inositol phospholipid metabolism in guinea pig neutrophils. J Biol Chem 261:1092–1098.

Tao YP, Klein C (1990a) Properties of CAR-kinase—The enzyme that phosphorylates the cAMP chemotactic receptor of *D. discoideum*. J Prot Chem 9:565–572.

Tao YP, Klein C (1990b) Localization of functional domains of the cAMP chemotactic receptor of *Dictyostelium discoideum*. J Biol Chem 265:15584–15589.

Tash JS, Hidaka H, Means AR (1986) Axokinin phosphorylation by cAMP-dependent protein kinase is sufficient for activation of sperm flagellar motility. J Cell Biol 103:649–655.

Taylor BL, Johnson MS, Smith JM (1988) Signaling pathways in bacterial chemotaxis. Botan Acta 101:101–104.

Taylor R (1991) Whiff and poof: Adenylyl cyclase in olfaction. J NIH Research 3:49–53.

Teeter JH, Gold GH (1988) A taste of things to come. Nature 331:298–299.

Teeter JH, Brand JG (1987a) L-arginine–activated cation channels from the catfish taste epithelium. Soc Neurosci Abstr 13:361.

Teeter JH, Brand JG (1987b) Peripheral mechanisms of gustation: Physiology and biochemistry. In Finger TE, Silver WL (eds): Neurobiology of Taste and Smell. New York: John Wiley & Sons, pp 299–329.

Teeter JH, Brand JG, Kalinoski DL, Bryant BP (1988) Cation channels in reconstituted catfish taste epithelial membrane preparations activated by arginine in an enantiomerically specific manner. Chem Senses 13:740.

Teeter JH, Brand JG, Kumazawa T (1990) A stimulus-activated conductance in isolated taste epithelial membranes. Biophys J 58:253–259.

Teeter J, Funakoshi M, Kurihara K, Roper S, Sato T, Tonosaki K (1987) Generation of the taste cell potential. Chem Senses 12:217–234.

Teeter JH, Sugimoto K, Brand JG (1989) Ionic currents in taste cells and reconstituted taste epithelial membranes. In Brnad JG, Teeter JH, Cagan RH, Kare MR (eds): Chemical Senses, Vol 1. New York: Marcel Dekker, pp 151–170.

Thiebert A, Klein P, Devreotes PN (1984) Specific photoaffinity labeling of the cAMP surface receptor in *Dictyostelium discoideum*. J Biol Chem 259:12318–12321.

Thoelke MS, Bedale WA, Nettleton DO, Ordal GW (1987) Evidence for an intermediate methyl-acceptor for chemotaxis in *Bacillus subtilis*. J Biol Chem 262:2811–2816.

Thoelke MS, Casper JM, Ordal GW (1990) Methyl transfer in chemotaxis toward sugars by *Bacillus subtilis*. J Bacteriol 172:1148–1150.

Thomas KM, Pyun HY, Navarro J (1990) Molecular cloning of the fmet-leu-phe receptor from neutrophils. J Biol Chem 265:20061–20064.

Thorner J (1981) Pheromonal regulation of development in *Saccharomyces cerevisiae*. In Strathern JN, Jones EW, Broach JR (eds): Molecular Biology of the Yeast *Saccharomyces*. Cold Spring Harbor, NY: Cold Spring Harbor Laboratory, pp 143–180.

Thorpe DS, Garbers DL (1989) The membrane form of guanylate cyclase. J Biol Chem 264:6545–6549.

Tonosaki K, Funakoshi M (1984) Intracellular taste cell responses of mouse. Comp Bioch Physiol 78A:651–656.

Trapido-Rosenthal HG, Carr WES, Gleeson RA (1987) Biochemistry of an olfactory purinergic system: Dephosphorylation of excitatory nucleotides and uptake of adenosine. J Neurochem 49:1174–1182.

Trapido-Rosenthal HG, Carr WES, Gleeson RA (1989) Biochemistry of purinergic olfaction. In Brand JG, Teeter J, Cagan RH, Kure MR (eds): Chemical Senses, Vol. 1. New York: Marcel Dekker, pp 243–261.

Trapido-Rosenthal HG, Carr WES, Gleeson RA (1990) Ectonucleotidase activities associated with the olfactory organ of the spiny lobster. J Neurochem 54:1–9.

Trimmer JS, Vacquier VD (1986) Activation of sea urchin gametes. Annu Rev Cell Biol 2:1–26.

Truett AP, Verghese MW, Dillon SB, Snyderman R (1988) Calcium influx stimulates a second pathway for sustained diacylglycerol production in leukocytes activated by chemoattractants. Proc Natl Acad Sci USA 85:1549–1553.

van den Ende H, Musgrave A, Klis FM (1990) The role of flagella in the sexual reproduction of *Chlamydomonas* gametes. In Bloodgood R (ed): Ciliary and Flagellar Membranes. New York: Plenum Press, pp 129–148.

Vandenberg MJ, Ziegelberger G (1991) On the function of the pheromone binding protein in the olfactory hairs of *Antheraea polyphemus*. J Insect Physiol 37:79–85.

Van Duijn B, Vogelzang SA, Ypey DL, Van Der Molen LB, Van Haastert PJM (1990) Normal chemotaxis in *Dictyostelium discoideum* cells with a depolarized plasma membrane potential. J Cell Sci 95:177–183.

Van Epps DE, Bender JG, Simpson SJ, Chenoweth DE (1990) Relationship of chemotactic receptors for formyl peptide and C5a, C1, CR3 and Fc receptors on human neutrophils. J Leukocyte Biol 47:519–527.

Van Haastert PJM, De Wit R (1984) Demonstration of receptor heterogeneity and negative cooperativity by nonequilibrium binding experiments. J Biol Chem 259:13321–13328.

Van Haastert PJM, Kesbeke F, Reymond CD, Firtel RD, Luderus E, Van Driel R (1987a) Aberrant transmembrane signal transduction in *Dictyostelium* cells expressing a mutated *ras* gene. Proc Natl Acad Sci USA 84:4905–4909.

Van Haastert PJM, Snaar-Jagalska BW, Janssens PMW (1987b) The regulation of adenylate cyclase by guanine nucleotides in *Dictyostelium membranes*. Eur J Biochem 162:251–258.

Van Haastert PJM, Van Lookeven, Campagne MM, Ross FM (1982) Altered cGMP-phosphodiesterase activity in chemotactic mutants of *Dictyostelium discoideum*. FEBS Lett 147:147–152.

Van Houten J (1978) Two mechanisms of chemotaxis in *Paramecium*. J Comp Physiol [A] 127:167–174.

Van Houten J (1979) Membrane potential changes during chemokinesis in *Paramecium*. Science 249:167–174.

Van Houten J (1990) Chemosensory transduction in *Paramecium*. In Armitage J, Lackie J (eds): Motility and Taxis. Cambridge: Cambridge University Press, pp 297–322.

Van Houten J, Cote B, Zhang J, Baez J, Gagnon ML (1990) Studies of the cyclic adenosine monophosphate chemoreceptor of *Paramecium*. J Membr Biol 119:15–24.

Van Houten J, Hauser DCR, Levandowsky M (1981) Chemosensory behavior in protozoa. In Hutner SH, Levandowsky ML (eds): Biochemistry and Physiology of Protozoa, Vol 4. New York: Academic Press, pp 67–124.

Van Houten J, Preston RR (1987) Chemoreception in single-celled organisms. In Finger TE, Silver WL (eds): Neurobiology of Taste and Smell. New York: John Wiley & Sons, pp 11–38.

Van Houten J, Preston RR (1988) Chemokinesis. In Görtz H-D (ed): Paramecium. New York: Springer-Verlag, pp 282–300.

Van Houten J, Van Houten JC (1982) Computer analysis of *Paramecium* chemokinesis. J Theor Biol 98:453–468.

Van Ments-Cohen M, Van Haastert PJM (1989) The cyclic nucleotide specificity of eight cAMP-binding proteins in *Dictyostelium discoideum* is correlated into three groups. J Biol Chem 264:8717–8722.

Verghese MW, Smith CD, Snyderman R (1985) Potential role for a guanine nucleotide regulatory protein in chemoattractant receptor mediated polyphosphomosetide metabolism, Ca^{2+} mobilization and cellular response by leukocytes. Biochem Biophys Res Commun 127:450–457.

Vogt RG (1987) The molecular basis of pheromone reception: Its influence on behavior. In Prestwich GD, Blomquist GS (eds): Pheromone Biochemistry. New York: Academic Press, pp 385–431.

Vogt RG, Kohne AC, Dubnau JT, Prestwich GD (1989) Expression of pheromone binding proteins during antennal development in the gypsy moth *Lymantria dispar*. J Neurosci 9:3322–3346.

Vogt RG, Prestwich GD, Lerner MR (1990a) Odorant-binding-protein subfamilies associate with distinct classes of olfactory receptor neurons in insects. J Neurobiol 22:74–84.

Vogt RG, Prestwich GD, Riddiford LM (1988) Sex pheromone receptor proteins. J Biol Chem 263:3952–3959.

Vogt RG, Riddiford LM, Prestwich GD (1985) Kinetic properties of a pheromone degrading enzyme: The sensillar esterase of *Antheracea polyphemus*. Proc Natl Acad Sci USA 82:8827–8831.

Vogt RG, Rybczynski R, Lerner MR (1990b) The biochemistry of odorant reception and transduction. In Schild D (ed): Chemosensory Information Processing. Berlin: Springer-Verlag, pp 33–76.

Volpi M, Molski TFP, Naccache PH, Feinstein MB, Sha'afi RI (1985) Phorbol 12-myristate, 13 acetate potentiates the action of the calcium ionophore in stimulating arachidonic acid release and production of phosphatidic acid in rabbit neutrophils. Biochem Biophys Res Commun 128:594–600.

Webster RO, Wysolmerski RB, Lagunoff D (1986) Enhancement of human polymorphonuclear leukocyte adherence to plastic and endothelium by phorbol myristate acetate. Am J Pathol 125:369–378.

Weinstock RS, Wright HN, Spiegel AM, Levine MA, Moses AM (1986) Olfactory dysfunction in humans with deficient guanine nucleotide–binding protein. Nature 322:635–636.

Weiss RM, Chasalow S, Koshland DE (1990) The role of methylation in chemotaxis. J Biol Chem 265:6817–6826.

Wessels D, Soll DR, Knecht D, Loomis WF, DeLozanne A, Spudich J (1988) Cell motility and chemotaxis in *Dictyostelium* amoebae lacking myosin heavy chain. Dev Biol 128:164–177.

White JR, Huang C-K, Hill JM, Naccache PH, Becker EL, Sha'afi RI (1984) Effect of phorbol 12-myristate 13-acetate and its analogue 4α-phorbol 12,13-didecanoate on protein phosphorylation and lysosomal enzyme release in rabbit neutrophils. J Biol Chem 259:8605–8611.

Wright TM, Hoffman RD, Nishijima J, Jakoi L, Snyderman R, Shin HS (1988) Leukocyte chemoattraction by 1,2-diacylglycerol. Proc Natl Acad Sci USA 85:1869–1873.

Wright MV, Van Houten J (1988) Effects of lithium on chemoresponse and ion regulation in *Paramecium*. Chem Senses 13:748.

Wright MV, Van Houten J (1990) Characterization of putative transporting Ca^{2+}-ATPase from pellicles of *Paramecium tetraurelia*. Biochim Biophys Acta 1029:241–251.

Wurster B, Schubigerk, Wick U, Gerisch G (1977) Cyclic GMP in *Dictyostelium discoideum*: Oscillations and pulses in response to folic acid and cyclic AMP signals. FEBS Lett 76:141–144.

Wymann MP, VonTscharner V, Dernleau DA, Baggiolini M (1987) The onset of the respiratory burst in human neutrophils. J Biol Chem 262:12048–12053.

Yin HL (1987) Gelsolin: Calcium- and polyphosphoinositide-regulated actin-modulating protein. BioEssays 7:176–179.

Yuli I, Oplatka A (1987) Cytosolic acidification as an early transductory signal of human neutrophil chemotaxis. Science 235:340–342.

Yuli I, Tomonaga A, Snyderman R (1982) Chemoattractant receptor functions in human polymorphonuclear leukocytes are divergently altered by membrane fluidizers. Proc Natl Acad Sci USA 79:5906–5910.

Zigmond SH (1989) Chemotactic response of neutrophils. Am J Respir Cell Mol Biol 1:451–453.

Zigmond SH, Sullivan SJ (1979) Sensory adaptation of leukocytes to chemotactic peptides. J Cell Biol 82:517–527.

Zuberi AR, Bischoff DS, Ordal GW (1991) Nucleotide sequence and characterization of a *Bacillus subtilis* gene encoding a flagellar switch protein. J Bact 173:710–719.

Zufall F, Stengl M, Franke C, Hildebrand JG, Hatt H (1991) Ionic currents of cultured olfactory receptor neurons from antennae of male *Manduca sexta*. J Neurosci 11:956–965.

Sensory Receptors and Signal Transduction: 137–208
© 1991 Wiley-Liss, Inc.

Signal Transduction in Bacterial Chemotaxis

Michael Eisenbach

Department of Membrane Research and Biophysics,
The Weizmann Institute of Science, 76100 Rehovot, Israel

I. INTRODUCTION

The first systematic studies of bacterial chemotaxis were by Engelmann [1882] and by Pfeffer [1881–1885, 1888]. Interest in the field was strong until Metzner [1931] published his studies, after which it was all but forgotten. In 1965, Julius Adler renewed interest in this behavior [Adler, 1965], since when the studies of this topic can be divided into several relatively short research periods. The first period was devoted mainly to identification of attractants and repellents. The subsequent periods dealt with isolation of receptors for the stimulants, with identification of genes and gene products involved in chemotaxis, with the function and structure of the receptors, and with the biochemical events involved in adaptation to chemotactic stimuli. Studies of the mechanism of bacterial movement, without which chemotaxis cannot occur, were carried out in parallel. Throughout these periods, the mechanism of sensory transduction in bacterial chemotaxis was a major subject of scientific curiosity, but it remained a mystery until very recently. The current period of research, which is just at its outset, may perhaps be defined as the period of revealing the mechanism of sensory transduction.

The focus of this review is on transduction of sensory signals in bacterial chemotaxis. Other aspects of chemotaxis that are directly related to signal transduction will not be dealt with here. Adler [1987], Stewart and Dahlquist [1987], Macnab [1987b], Ordal [1985] and Simon et al. [1985] reviewed in recent years the field of bacterial motility and chemotaxis, in general. Parkinson [1981] and Parkinson and Hazelbauer [1983] reviewed the genetics of bacterial chemotaxis. Berg et al. [1982], Eisenbach [1990], Iino [1985], Macnab [1987a], Macnab and Aizawa [1984], and Macnab and DeRosier reviewed the structure and mechanism of function of the bacterial flagellar motor.

This review was completed in May 1989. Subsequent references had been submitted to me as preprints prior to this date.

II. BACKGROUND
A. Bacterial Behavior

Chemotaxis is an oriented movement toward favorable substances (attractants) and away from unfavorable ones (repellents). Bacteria such as *Escherichia coli, Salmonella typhimurium, Bacillus subtilis,* and *Streptococcus* sp. chemotax by modulation of two main swimming patterns: a run, which is a smooth swimming in rather straight lines, and a tumble, which is a chaotic angular motion with no net translational movement [Berg and Brown, 1972; Macnab and Koshland, 1972]. In the absence of a stimulus (an attractant or a repellent), the tumbles are short but frequent. (The tumbling frequency varies from strain to strain, being about one tumble per 1–5 sec.) When the bacteria sense an increase in the concentration of an attractant, the runs are prolonged and the tumbles are depressed. When they sense a large increase in the concentration of a repellent or a large decrease in the concentration of an attractant the tumbles are enhanced. (Other modulatable swimming patterns in other bacteria are forward and backward swimming, as in *Halobacterium halobium* [Hildebrand and Dencher, 1975; Spudich and Stoeckenius, 1979; Alam and Oesterhelt, 1984], or a run and a stop, as in *Rhodobacter sphaeroides* [Armitage and Macnab, 1987] or *Rhizobium meliloti* [Gotz and Schmitt, 1987].)

The swimming of the bacteria results from rotation of flagella attached to the cells [Berg and Anderson, 1973; Silverman and Simon, 1974]. Peritrichously flagellated bacteria (bacteria whose flagella are randomly distributed around the cell) usually have 5 to 12 flagella per cell. The rotation of the flagella, unlike eukaryotic flagella [Adler, 1985], is carried out by a motor located at the base of each flagellum and embedded in the cytoplasmic membrane [DePamphilis and Adler, 1971; for reviews, see Berg et al., 1982, and Macnab and Aizawa, 1984]. The primary driving force of the motor is the proton-motive force ($\Delta\bar{\mu}_H +$) [Larsen et al., 1974a; Thipayathasana and Valentine, 1974; Manson et al., 1977; Matsuura et al., 1977; Glagolev and Skulachev, 1978; Shioi et al., 1978; Khan and Macnab, 1980b; Manson et al., 1980; Berg et al., 1982; Ravid and Eisenbach, 1984b], defined as $\Delta\bar{\mu}_H + = \Delta\psi - Z\Delta pH$ (where $Z = 2.3RT/F = 59$ mV at 25°C); and $\Delta\psi$ is membrane potential). In alkalophilic *Bacillus,* sodium ions rather than protons drive the motor [Hirota et al., 1981].

By tethering bacterial cells of wild-type *E. coli* to glass by their flagella, it became clear that the motor alternates between counterclockwise rotation, clockwise rotation, and brief pauses [Silverman and Simon, 1974; Larsen et al., 1974b; Lapidus et al.,1988]. When wild-type bacteria detect an increase in the concentration of an attractant (which is equivalent to a decrease in the concentration of a repellent), their flagella rotate counterclockwise and do not pause; when they detect an increase in the concentration of a repellent (or a decrease in an attractant concentration), their flagella gain a clockwise bias and pause more frequently [Larsen et al., 1974b; Lapidus et al., 1988]. The result of counterclockwise rotation in bacteria like *E. coli* and *S. typhimurium* is a run [Anderson, 1975; Macnab, 1977], and the result of clockwise rotation [Macnab and Ornston, 1977] and of pausing [Eisenbach et al., 1990b] is a tumble. It was recently shown that a separate signal for pausing is unlikely [Eisenbach et al., 1990b]. Therefore, only signals for switching the direction of rotation will be dealt with in this review.

The attractants for *E. coli* and *S. typhimurium* are primarily amino acids, sugars, and dipeptides [see Adler, 1978, Koshland, 1980, and Macnab, 1987b, for elaborated reviews]. The receptors for most of these attractants have been identified and thoroughly investigated. The repellents for these species are weak organic acids, certain cations, certain amino acids, and other compounds such as indole and glycerol. Table I shows selected attractants and repellents of *E. coli.* Most of the *E. coli* stimulants are effective also for *S. typhimurium* [see Macnab, 1987b, for a comparison]. In this context it should be noted, however, that repellents for a given species may act as attractants for another species. A few examples are shown in Table II. Other stimuli are oxygen (acting as either an attractant or a repellent, depending on its concentration; see

TABLE I. Selected Attractants and Repellents of *E. coli*

Stimulant	Att/rep	Identity	Receptor Location	K_d or K_m*	MCP[†]	References
L-Serine	Att	MCP I	Membrane	5 μM	I	Mesibov and Adler [1972], Clarke and Koshland [1979], Hedblom and Adler [1980, 1983]
L-Alanine	Att	MCP I	Membrane	?	I	Mesibov and Adler [1972], Hedblom and Adler [1983]
L-Cysteine	Att	MCP I	Membrane	?	I	Mesibov and Adler [1972], Hedblom and Adler [1983]
Glycine	Att	MCP I	Membrane	?	I	Mesibov and Adler [1972], Hedblom and Adler [1983]
L-Aspartate	Att	MCP II	Membrane	5 μM	II	Mesibov and Adler [1972], Springer et al. [1977], Clarke and Koshland [1979], Hedblom and Adler [1983]
L-Glutamate	Att	MCP II	Membrane	?	II	Mesibov and Adler [1972], Hedblom and Adler [1983]
Maltose	Att	MBP	Periplasm	2 μM	II	Adler et al. [1973], Springer et al. [1977], Manson et al. [1985]
D-Galactose	Att	GBP	Periplasm	0.5 μM	III	Adler et al. [1973], Zukin et al. [1977b], Kondoh et al. [1979], Hazelbauer and Harayama [1979]
D-Ribose	Att	RBP	Periplasm	0.1 μM	III	Adler et al. [1973], Kondoh et al. [1979], Hazelbauer and Harayama [1979]
D-Glucose	Att	GBP	Periplasm	0.2 μM	III	Zukin et al. [1977b]

Stimulant	Att/Rep	Receptor	Location	K_d/K_m	MCP	References
D-Glucose	Att	E_{II}	Membrane	20 μM	None	Adler and Epstein [1974], Postma and Lengeler [1985]
D-Mannose	Att	E_{II}	Membrane	30 μM	None	Adler et al. [1973], Postma and Lengeler [1985]
Dipeptides	Att	MCP IV	Membrane	?	IV	Manson et al. [1986]
Oxygen	Att	cyt o and d	Membrane	0.7 μM	None	Laszlo et al [1984], Shioi et al. [1987]
Oxygen	Rep	?	?	1 mM	None	Shioi et al. [1987]
Acetate	Rep	MCP I	Membrane	pH dependent	I	Repaske and Adler [1981], Kihara and Macnab [1981]
Benzoate	Rep	MCP I	Membrane	pH dependent	I	Repaske and Adler [1981], Kihara and Macnab [1981]
Indole	Rep	MCP I	Membrane	?	I	Tso and Adler [1974], Springer et al. [1977], Eisenbach et al. [1990a]
Leucine	Rep	MCP I	Membrane	?	I	Tso and Adler [1974], Springer et al. [1977], Eisenbach et al. [1990a]
Ni^{2+}	Rep	MCP II	Membrane	?	II	Tso and Adler [1974], Springer et al. [1977], Eisenbach et al. [1990a]
Co^{2+}	Rep	MCP II	Membrane	?	II	Tso and Adler [1974], Springer et al. [1977], Eisenbach et al. [1990a]
Glycerol	Rep	?	?	0.2 M	Anyone	Oosawa and Imae [1983]
Isobutanol	Rep	MCPs?	?	~20 mM	Anyone	Tso and Adler [1974], Eisenbach et al. [1990a]

*K_d is the dissociation constant. K_m is the "behavioral Michaelis constant" [Macnab, 1987b], i.e., the stimulant concentration yielding half-maximal response. K_m is especially important in the case of repellents for which receptors have not been identified. The values of K_d and K_m are similar.

†Abbreviations: cyt, cytochrome; GBP, galactose-binding protein; MBP, maltose-binding protein; MCP, methyl-accepting chemotaxis protein; RBP, ribose-binding protein; E_{II}, enzyme II of the phosphotransferase system (PTS); att, attractant; rep, repellent.

TABLE II. Stimuli With Different Functions in Different Species

Stimulus	Attractant for	Repellent for	References
Phenol	*E. coli*	*. typhimurium*	Lederberg [1956], Tsang et al [1973] Koshland [1980], Imae et al. [1987] Tsang et al. [1973]
Leucine	*B. subtilis*	*E. coli, S. typhimurium*	Tsang et al [1973], Tso and Adler [1974], Ordal and Gibson [1977]
Valine	*B. subtilis*	*E. coli, S. typhimurium*	Tsang et al [1973], Tso and Adler [1974], Ordal and Gibson [1977]
Tryptophan	*B. subtilis, Chromatium vinosum*	*E. coli, S. typhimurium, R. sphaeroides*	Tsang et al [1973], Tso and Adler [1974], Ordal and Gibson [1977], Armitage et al. [1979]
Acetate	*C. vinosum*	*E. coli, S. typhimurium, R. sphaeroides*	Tsang et al [1973], Tso and Adler [1974], Armitage et al. [1979]
Benzoate	*Pseudomonas putida*	*E. coli*	Tso and Adler [1974], Harwood et al. [1984]

section IV.C.), pH (see section IV.D.), light (see the chapter by Bogomolni and Spudich, this volume), and temperature (see section VI.).

In the process of identifying the receptors and the other components of the chemotaxis machinery, genetics played a major role. By isolation of mutants with defects in chemotaxis toward specific or multiple chemicals, it became possible to identify genes and gene products involved in reception and in transduction of the sensory signals [see Adler, 1978, and Parkinson, 1981, for reviews]. Based on the phenomenological behavior of the so-called specifically, multiply, and generally nonchemotactic mutants, it became clear that the sensory transduction system in bacteria is a convergent system of the type shown in Figure 1. Thus the defective genes in the specifically nonchemotactic mutants code for specific receptors; the defective genes in the multiply nonchemotactic mutants code for methylatable, transmembrane proteins called methyl-accepting chemotaxis proteins (MCPs), sensory transducers, or—for some attractants (Table I)—receptors; and the generally nonchemotactic mutants have defects in the *che* genes (*che* for chemotaxis; Table III). The products of the latter genes are located predominantly in the cytoplasm [Ridgway et al., 1977].

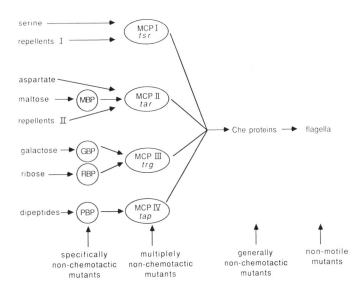

Fig. 1. Schematic representation of the information flow in chemotaxis of *E. coli*. Only MCP-mediated stimuli are drawn. The repellents are listed in Table I. MBP, GBP, RBP, and PBP are maltose-, galactose-, ribose-, and peptide-binding proteins, respectively. *tsr, tar, trg* and *tap* are the genes that encode for MCPs I–IV, respectively. The types of mutants found at each stage are marked at the bottom.

TABLE III. Cytoplasmic Che Proteins

Protein	Role in	Polymeric form	Monomeric M_r*	No. of molecules per cell[†]	References[‡]	Comments
CheA	Excitation	Dimer	71,000 60,000	?	1–4, 5, 6–8, 25	There are long and short polypeptides of CheA. The protein is a kinase
CheB	Adaptation	?	37,500	~200	1–3, 5, 9–11, 12	N-terminal of CheB is homologous to the entire length of CheY. CheB is methylesterase
CheR	Adaptation	Monomer	33,000	~200	2, 3, 5, 14–16	CheR is methyltransferase. It is a very slow enzyme
CheW	Excitation	Monomer	18,000	?	2, 3, 5, 17, 25	Has a concensus nucleotide-binding site
CheY	Clockwise rotation	Monomer	14,000	~4,000	2, 3, 5, 11, 18, 19, 20, 21	CheY is homologous to the N-terminal of CheB
CheZ	Counterclockwise rotation	Polymer (≥20 monomers)	24,000	~700	2, 3, 5, 22–24	Very acidic, methylatable protein. Has phosphatase activity

*The values given are for E. coli.

[†]Unless otherwise specified, the calculation is based on the molecular stoichiometry between tar and che gene products [DeFranco and Koshland, 1981] and the number of Tar (MCP II) molecules in a cell of E. coli [Hazelbauer et al., 1982].

[‡]Reference numbers in italics include the seqence analysis of the protein. The references are: 1, Parkinson [1976]; 2, Ridgway et al. [1977]; 3, Silverman and Simon [1977b]; 4, Smith and Parkinson [1980]; 5, Mutoh and Simon [1986]; 6, Hess et al. [1987]; 7, Macnab [1987b]; 8, Stock et al., [1988a]; 9, Stock and Koshland [1978]; 10, Yonekawa et al. [1983]; 11, A. Stock et al. [1985]; 12, Simms et al. [1985]; 13, Goy et al. [1978]; 14, Goy et al. [1977]; 15, Springer and Koshland [1977]; 16, Simms et al. [1987b]; 17, Stock et al. [1987a]; 18, Clegg and Koshland [1984]; 19, Matsumura et al. [1984]; 20, Ravid et al. [1986]; 21, Wolfe et al. [1987]; 22, A. Stock and Stock [1987]; 23, Stock et al. [1987b]; 24, Stock [1988]; 25, Gegner and Dahlquist [1991] (this information was added after completion of the manuscript).

The final target of the sensory signals is presumably the "switch" of the motor, i.e., the *fliM (cheC)*, the *fliG (cheV)*, and the *fliN* gene products [Parkinson et al., 1983; Yamaguchi et al., 1986], located at, or associated with, the cytoplasmic membrane [Ravid and Eisenbach, 1984a]. (The gene names are according to the universal nomenclature for chemotaxis [DeFranco and Koshland, 1981] and flagellar [Iino et al., 1988] genes.) These proteins were assigned as components of the presumed switch, because a mutation in any given gene of this group yielded both counterclockwise-biased and clockwise-biased mutants. This is not the case with other *che* mutants, where any defect in a given gene leads almost always to a mutant with the same bias: exclusive counterclockwise rotation (*cheA, cheR, cheW, cheY* mutants) or a predominant clockwise rotation (*cheB, cheZ*) [Parkinson, 1981]. (One exception was the isolation of a *cheZ* mutant with a counterclockwise bias [Yamaguchi et al., 1986].)

It should be noted that there may be basic differences in the chemotaxis machinery, in general, and in the mechanism of sensory transduction, in particular, among different bacterial species. This is primarily so between small (a few microns in length) and large bacterial species. In the large species, the sensory signal is expected to travel much longer distances. Because *E. coli* and *S. typhimurium* (classified as small bacteria) are the best-studied bacterial species, the information provided will be for these two species, unless otherwise mentioned. (See Ordal and Nettleton [1985] for a review of the chemotaxis machinery in *B. subtilis*.) When relevant information on large bacterial species is available, as in the case of excitatory signaling, a separate section will be devoted to those species.

B. Sensory Transduction

The chemotaxis machinery probably involves various sensory signals, and each signal may undergo several steps of transduction or be a composite of several signals. Thus, when dealing with sensory transduction, one should define the sensory signal in terms of space (from where to where in the bacterial cell the signal is transduced), cellular components (the origin and target of the signal), and function. In this review, I shall try to distinguish between the various signals spatially and functionally and then try to examine how these signals are integrated into a functional, harmonic machinery.

As shown in Figure 2, there are at least two, sometimes three, spatial regions between the receptor and the switch of the motor. For those stimuli that interact directly with the MCP or with other membrane receptors (Table I), sensory signaling involves two steps, a signal across the cytoplasmic membrane and a signal within the cytoplasm to the switch–motor complex. For those stimuli whose receptors are periplasmic binding proteins, an additional transduction step within the periplasm precedes the other steps. I shall not deal in

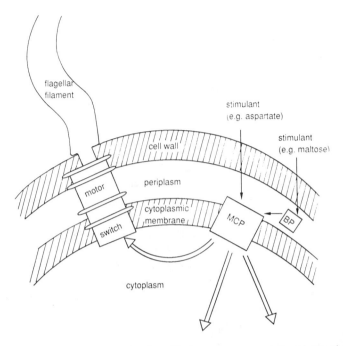

Fig. 2. Spatial regions of information flow. Single arrows represent direct interaction; double arrows, indirect interaction. BP, binding protein. The scheme is not drawn to scale.

this review with other theoretical modes of interaction between the receptors or the MCPs and the motor, such as direct interactions or signaling via lateral diffusion in the periplasm or cytoplasmic membrane. These possibilities have been reviewed elsewhere and shown to be improbable [Eisenbach et al., 1985].

Two distinct processes are known to be involved in sensory transduction in bacteria: excitation and adaptation [see Springer et al., 1979, for review]. The excitation process involves the first or the more rapid signaling process between the receptor and the switch–motor complex. In wild-type strains the excitation is observed within 0.2 sec in response to a large step change in the concentration of a stimulant [Segall et al., 1982] or within about a second in response to brief and very small changes in the concentration [Block et al., 1982; Segall et al., 1986]. The adaptation process prompts a behavior similar to the unstimulated behavior of the bacteria. The bacteria can then respond again to stimuli, even though the original stimulant is still present. In comparison with the excitation process, adaptation is a much slower process in response to a large step stimulus, but a comparable one in response to a brief and small stimulus [Block et al., 1982]. The excitation and adaptation processes might, in principle, be initiated by a single, common sensory signal, or each of them may be triggered by separate signals. These alternatives will be dealt with in detail in the following sections. Eventually, other types of taxis in bacteria will be compared with bacterial chemotaxis from the point of view of sensory transduction.

III. SENSORY SIGNALING THROUGH THE PERIPLASM

This section deals with those stimuli whose receptors are periplasmic (cf. section II and Table I). The issue of signal transduction via the periplasm is intriguing in light of evidence that the periplasmic space is rather a gel-like material [Hobot et al., 1984] and that the rate of lateral diffusion of proteins such as the maltose-binding protein (the maltose receptor) or the galactose-binding protein (the galactose receptor) in the periplasm is very low (the lateral diffusion coefficient is 100-fold lower than would be expected for such proteins in the cytoplasm and 1,000-fold lower than in aqueous medium [Brass et al., 1986]).

It seems quite established that two steps are involved in sensory transduction within the periplasm: 1) conformational changes of the periplasmic receptor (the sugar- or peptide-binding protein) as a result of attractant binding and 2) binding of the formed complex to the appropriate MCP. (This is sketched in Fig. 3 for the attractant galactose.) Evidence in support of the first step was given by Boos et al. [1972] and by Zukin et al. [1977a] for the galactose receptor and by Szmelcman et al. [1976] and by Zukin [1979] for the maltose receptor. The evidence is based on attractant- stimulated changes in the electrophoretic mobility of the binding protein, changes in the apparent dissociation constants, and changes in the fluorescence of the tryptophan residues of the receptor and in the fluorescence of an extrinsic fluorophore, 5-(iodoacetamido)fluorescein, attached at a single methionine residue of the receptor. Evidence in favor of the second step came from genetic analysis of mutants in the maltose-binding protein. Kossmann et al. [1988] found two *malE* mutants that are specifically nonchemotactic toward maltose in which residue 53 or 55 of the maltose-binding protein was replaced by another amino acid. These chemotactic defects were suppressed by point mutations in *tar*, the gene that codes for MCP II. These results indicate a physical interaction between the maltose-binding protein and MCP II. X-ray crystallography was carried out for the galactose-binding proteins from a wild-type strain and from a mutant whose receptor binds galactose normally, but the strain is nevertheless specifically nonchemotactic to galactose, presumably because of a defect in the site for binding MCP III. The analysis revealed the possible site in the galactose-binding protein for interaction with MCP III [Vyas et al., 1988]. This study also indicated that ten van der Waals contacts, a salt link, and a positive entropic effect (but no

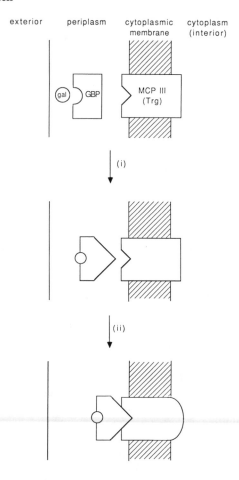

Fig. 3. Schematic representation of the first steps involved in galactose-stimulated signal transduction. Gal, galactose; GBP, galactose-binding protein. The scheme is not drawn to scale.

hydrogen bonds) comprised the interaction. Supportive evidence for both the first and second steps, i.e., conformational changes and binding, was supplied for the maltose receptor by Koiwai and Hayashi [1979]. These investigators made an affinity column containing purified maltose receptor and then used this column to chromatograph the solubilized membrane fraction of *E. coli*. They found that the receptor interacted with MCP II only in the presence of maltose. Such an interaction was not found with MCP I (cf. Fig. 1). In a similar approach, Richarme [1982a] studied the binding of the purified maltose receptor to membrane vesicles of *E. coli*. He found that the binding was dependent on the presence of maltose in the medium and on the presence of

MCP II in the membrane; membrane vesicles from mutants defective in the *tar* (but not *tsr*) gene product did not bind the maltose receptor even in the presence of maltose. Another finding was that imposition of membrane potential, positive outside, across the vesicles membrane by a valinomycin-induced potassium efflux significantly increased the binding of the receptor to the vesicles [Richarme, 1982a]. This requirement of membrane potential for binding is, almost always, naturally maintained in vivo by the proton-motive force [Padan et al., 1976].

Interestingly, but not necessarily correlated, the inverse relationship between binding and membrane potential has also been found: Binding of an attractant to the receptor causes a transient increase in the membrane potential of intact *E. coli* cells [see Eisenbach, 1982, 1983, for summaries of previous reports and for resolving apparently conflicting data]. By using different probes and techniques, it was shown that the measured change is a true increase in membrane potential rather than a change in the surface charge of the membrane [Eisenbach et al., 1984]. This increase in membrane potential, or hyperpolarization, was found to occur in response to each of the nine different attractants tested [Eisenbach, 1982]. The hyperpolarization was thoroughly investigated for the attractant D-galactose and its nonmetabolizable analog D-fucose. It was found to be correlated with chemotaxis to galactose rather than with transport of galactose or its metabolism [Eisenbach et al., 1983a] and possibly to be the result of an efflux of the organic cation decarboxylated *S*-adenosyl-methionine (M. Eisenbach, unpublished data). The significance of this hyperpolarization or cation efflux is still a mystery. It is puzzling that the hyperpolarization depends only on binding of a substrate to the receptor [Eisenbach et al., 1983a] and not on the binding of the receptor to the MCP, as *trg* mutants do become hyperpolarized by galactose or fucose (M. Eisenbach, unpublished data). Currently there is no obvious explanation for this puzzle.

How can sensory transduction in the periplasm, as described above, occur in view of the low mobility of the receptors within the periplasm? Calculations of Brass et al. [1986], based on the number of protein molecules in the periplasm and on the dimensions of the periplasmic space, have revealed that there may be little or no aqueous space in the periplasm. Brass et al. [1986] therefore suggested that the periplasm may contain semiordered chains of associated binding protein molecules and that substrate molecules may move along these chains of receptor molecules toward the cytoplasmic membrane (three to four protein molecules are sufficient to fill in the distance between the outer and cytoplasmic membranes). Evidence for such association has been already reported [Rasched et al., 1976; Richarme, 1982b; Mowbray and Petsko, 1983]. However, the idea of receptor chains is not obligatory. It appears that even if the diffusion of ligand is buffered, the ligand will cross the periplasm and reach the receptor near the cytoplasmic membrane in a relatively short time.

In either case, when the signal eventually reaches the membrane, the complex galactose–receptor may either interact with the appropriate MCP, Trg (MCP III) in this case, or interact with the membrane components of the transport system, MglA [Harayama et al., 1983; Muller et al., 1985], depending on the location of the receptor.

IV. SENSORY TRANSDUCTION ACROSS THE CYTOPLASMIC MEMBRANE

The versatility of systems that transduce the sensory signal across the cytoplasmic membrane may imply a diversity of transduction mechanisms. I shall therefore deal initially with each system separately.

A. Sensory Transduction by Methyl-Accepting Chemotaxis Protein (MCP)

The MCP serves three functions in bacterial chemotaxis: It binds the ligand (either the attractant or the attractant–receptor complex; see Table I), it sends an excitatory signal into the cytoplasm, and it is involved in adaptation to attractants or repellents by being methylated or demethylated, respectively (see section V.B.). Sequencing of the genes that code for the MCPs allowed the determination of the regions that are responsible for these functions. Each MCP molecule contains two stretches of hydrophobic residues, one near the N terminus and the other further down the sequence at a distance equivalent to 40% of the polypeptide length [Boyd et al., 1983; Krikos et al., 1983; Russo and Koshland, 1983; Bollinger et al., 1984]. Assuming that these stretches are the transmembrane segments of the protein, Krikos et al. [1983] and independently Russo and Koshland [1983] suggested a model for the MCPs (Fig. 4), according to which the domain between these two segments is on the periplasmic side of the membrane (residues 33–190 of Tsr), and the domain between the second hydrophobic stretch and the C terminus (residues 216–end) is on the cytoplasmic side of the membrane. The periplasmic segment is considered to be the ligand-binding domain of the MCP. This domain is the segment with the largest divergence among the four known MCPs (only 26% homology), which fits well with the requirement for specificity of the binding sites. In line with this model are 1) studies with chimeric MCPs exhibiting ligand specificities [Krikos et al., 1985], 2) the finding that a proteolytic fragment of the Tar protein from residues 1 to 259 retains the aspartate-binding function [Mowbray et al., 1985], and 3) the discovery that all MCP mutants with defects in chemotaxis to specific attractants have single amino acid substitutions in this segment only [Park and Hazelbauer, 1986a; Lee et al., 1988; Wolff and Parkinson, 1988]. The cytoplasmic portion of the MCP contains the methylation sites and the binding sites for the enzymes methyltransferase and methylesterase (see section V.B.1.). The stretches that contain the pre-

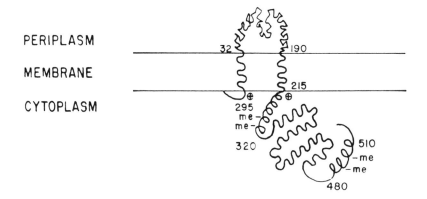

Fig. 4.   A model for MCP. Me, Sites of methylation. See text for details. [Reproduced from Krikos et al., 1983, with permission of the publisher.]

sumed binding sites are highly conserved (91–100% identity among the four MCPs), as would be expected for stretches on different proteins that interact with a common enzyme. This part of the model is supported by 1) site-directed mutagenesis affecting specific residues in the cytoplasmic portion of the MCP [Terwilliger et al., 1986b; Nowlin et al., 1988], 2) amplification of a mutational change of a single amino acid in this portion [Park and Hazelbauer, 1986b], 3) studies of proteolytic fragments of this region [Mowbray et al., 1985; Nowlin et al., 1987], 4) studies with hybrid MCPs [Slocum et al., 1987], and 5) the phenotypic behavior and the molecular activities retained in bacteria containing a truncated *tar* gene, encoding only the C-terminal subdomain of the MCP [Oosawa et al., 1988b]. This portion of the MCP should be responsible for signaling to the subsequent components of the chemotaxis machinery. And indeed, nearly all MCP mutations with defects in signaling were located in the cytoplasmic portion of the MCP [Mutoh et al., 1986; Kaplan and Simon, 1988; Ames and Parkinson, 1988].

In a very elegant study involving site-directed cross-linking, Milligan and Koshland [1988] have shown that MCP II is a dimer. This conclusion probably holds also for other MCPs. What are the possible ways by which an MCP dimer can transduce from its periplasmic to its cytoplasmic face the information that a ligand is bound there? By analogy to other systems, several modes may be possible in principle: 1) opening of an ion channel, as in the acetylcholine receptor [Changeux and Revah, 1987]; 2) association of monomers (or dissociation of dimers), as suggested for the insulin receptor [Heffetz and Zick, 1986] and the epidermal growth factor (EGF) receptor [Yarden and Schlessinger, 1987]; 3) major conformational change of the protein or vertical displacement of the protein within the membrane [Borochov and Shinitzky, 1976]. What is known about these modes of function?

1. Specific ion channels have not been found in *E. coli* or in any other small bacterium. The only channels found in *E. coli* were of two types: pressure-activated ion channels [Martinac et al., 1987] that most likely reside in the outer membrane, not in the cytoplasmic membrane [Saimi et al., 1988] and therefore cannot participate in signal transduction across the cytoplasmic membrane; and voltage-activated channels having no selective permeability [Saimi et al., 1988]. Also the latter channels appear to be irrelevant for chemotaxis, because they open more frequently upon membrane depolarization [Saimi et al., 1988], whereas such depolarization or any other consistent change in membrane potential does not occur in *E. coli* in response to attractants or to repellents (other than those that lower intracellular pH) [Snyder et al., 1981], unless respiratory inhibitors are present [Eisenbach, 1982]. Furthermore, indirect studies of whether ion channels play a role in chemotaxis yielded negative results. Thus, if ion channels were involved in sensory transduction, systematic variations of the ionic composition of the medium in which the bacteria are suspended should have affected chemotaxis [Jaffe, 1979]. This was not the case: Neither elimination of specific ions from the suspending medium [Adler, 1973] nor addition of specific ions to perturb passive efflux through ion channels [Eisenbach et al., 1985] affected the chemotaxis process.

2. Milligan and Koshland [1988] have shown that the signaling is not by a change in the aggregation state of the MCP. MCP II was found to retain its dimeric state even after the addition of saturating concentrations of its ligand, the attractant aspartate. On the contrary, the observed effect of aspartate was stabilization of the dimer: It prevented the rapid exchange between the subunits of the MCP.

3. Unlike the first two possibilities, conformational changes of the MCP do appear to play a major role in signaling. Overproduction of the C-terminal half of MCP II of wild-type *E. coli* and of two *tar* mutants, one locked in "smooth swimming signal" and the other in "tumbling signal," revealed major differences in the oligomeric sizes, the susceptibility to degradation, and the ion-exchange behavior of the three fragments, indicative of different conformations for each of the signaling modes [Kaplan and Simon, 1988]. In a different approach, Falke and Koshland [1987] constructed seven different mutants by site-directed mutagenesis, each containing a new cysteine residue at a different position in the primary structure of MCP II. They measured the rate of crosslinking two solubilized monomers of MCP II into a dimer via disulfide bonds between the cysteine residues and found that addition of aspartate had a large effect on the rate of formation of the disulfide bonds. This again indicates that binding of ligand, in this case the attractant aspartate, brings about

major changes in the conformation of the protein. It remains to be seen whether these conformational changes, stimulated at the periplasmic side of the membrane and expressed throughout the protein molecule, are sufficient to transmit the sensory signal to the next target or whether vertical displacement of the protein within the membrane also occurs as a result of the conformational changes.

B. Sensory Transduction by the Phosphotransferase System

The phosphoenolpyruvate-dependent carbohydrate:phosphotransferase system (PTS) enzymes II are membrane proteins that transport certain hexoses, hexosamines, polyhydric alcohols, and disaccharides [Postma and Lengeler, 1985]. They were identified as the chemoreceptors for these sugars by Adler and Epstein [1974]. Twelve such systems are known. The mechanism of transport is summarized in Figure 5. The following is a description of the main steps [Kaback, 1968; Kundig and Roseman, 1971a,b; Pecher et al., 1983]. Enzyme II is activated by phosphorylation, carried out by two cytoplasmic protein kinases, enzyme I and histidine-containing protein (HPr), with phosphoenolpyruvate as the phosphate donor. In the case of the D-glucose and a plasmid-

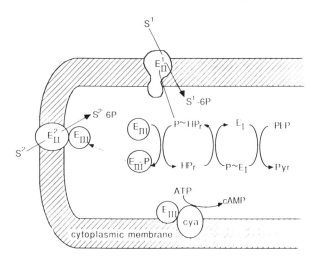

Fig. 5.   A model for the mechanism of sugar transport by the PTS system. See text for details. S^1 and E_{II}^1 are the sugars and enzymes II, respectively, involved in the transport of N-acetylglucosamine, trehalose, mannose, galacticol, fructose, glucitol, mannitol, β-glucosides, L-sorbose, dihydroxyacetone, and lactose. S^2 and E_{II}^2 are involved in the transport of glucose and sucrose [Postma and Lengeler, 1985]. E_I, E_{II}, and E_{III} represent enzymes I, II, and III, respectively; S, sugar; HPr, histidine-containing protein; PEP, phosphoenolpyruvate, Pyr, pyruvate; cya, adenylate cyclase. Based on Pecher et al. [1983], Postma and Lengeler [1985], and on personal communication with J. Lengeler.

encoded sucrose transport system, a third kinase, enzyme III, is required for the phosphorylation. The carbohydrate binds to the phosphorylated enzyme II and then is translocated across the membrane. At the same time the carbohydrate is phosphorylated by the enzyme. Enzyme II is rephosphorylated by the cytoplasmic proteins as before, and a new cycle of transport starts. As shown in Figure 5, there are two classes of enzyme II: enzyme III–dependent enzyme, e.g., enzymes II of glucose and sucrose; and enzyme III–independent enzyme, e.g., enzymes II of manitol and N-acetylglucosamine [Postma and Lengeler, 1985]. During the transport of the carbohydrate, a phosphate group is transferred from phosphate–HPr to enzyme III, in the first class, or to the enzyme III-like domain at the C terminus of enzyme II, in the second class. In a second step, the phosphate group is transferred from enzyme III to enzyme II or from the enzyme III-like domain to the enzyme II domain. In each case a histidine–phosphate is involved. In the presence of a substrate, the phosphate group is transferred from the phosphorylhistidine to form substrate- 6-phosphate [Ebner and Lengeler, 1988; Saier et al., 1988; Vogler and Lengeler, 1988]. Like MCP, enzyme II contains hydrophobic (probably membrane-spanning) domains, a substrate-binding site toward the periplasm, and a hydrophilic domain in the cytoplasm [Ebner and Lengeler, 1988; J. Lengeler, personal communication].

The signal transduction system of the PTS across the cytoplasmic membrane is independent of the MCP transduction system. This was shown by studying deletion mutants having no MCPs and no CheR and CheB proteins. Even though these mutants could not respond chemotactically to MCP-recognized stimuli, they did respond to PTS sugars [Niwano and Taylor, 1982; Pecher et al., 1983; J. Lengeler, personal communication]. The functions of enzyme II as a transporter and as a sensory transducer are tightly linked, probably unified. The evidence for this statement can be summarized as follows.

1. All enzyme II–negative mutants for a single carbohydrate that have been isolated were invariably defective in both chemotaxis and transport/phosphorylation [Lengeler et al., 1981]. Several thousand mutants in 10 different systems (D-mannitol, D-glucitol, galactitol, D-glucose, D-mannose, N-acetyl-D-glucosamine, D-fructose, β-glucopyranosides, cellobiose, and D-sorbose) have been tested (J. Lengeler, personal communication). Despite intensive searches, no mutant has been found having an enzyme II–catalyzed transport without chemotactic activity or showing a positive chemotaxis while lacking transport activity [Lengeler, 1975; Lengeler et al., 1981].

2. Substrate specificity and affinity are similar in the transport/phosphorylation and chemotaxis processes [Lengeler et al., 1981].

3. Enzyme II mutants with altered affinity for the substrate have altered K_m values for transport, phosphorylation, and chemotaxis [Lengeler et al., 1981].

A major functional difference between enzyme II and MCP is that in the former it is probably the phosphorylation/dephosphorylation of enzyme II/ enzyme III, not the binding of a substrate, that triggers the chemotactic signal [Lengeler et al., 1981]. This conclusion is based on the observations that no metabolism of the attractant is needed beyond phosphorylation to elicit chemotactic response [Adler and Epstein, 1974; Lengeler et al., 1981], on the one hand, and that binding of the sugar attractant to enzyme II is not always sufficient to bring about chemotaxis (e.g., *pts* mutants cannot respond chemotactically to PTS sugars in spite of the presence of enzyme II in their membrane [Lengeler et al., 1981]), on the other hand. The signal is not the phosphorylated attractant, as is evident from the observation that nonmetabolizable analogs of sugar attractants are chemotactically active, whereas phosphorylated sugars, e.g., glucose-6-phosphate or fructose-6- phosphate, are not active. Thus, in the case of the PTS, it appears that the chemotactic signal originates at the cytoplasmic side of the membrane; the attractant, not the signal, crosses the membrane. A somewhat similar phenomenon was recently found in *Rhod. sphaeroides,* in which uptake [Ingham and Armitage, 1987] and metabolism [Poole and Armitage, 1989] of the attractant are required in order to elicit a chemotactic response.

C. Sensory Transduction via Other Membrane Components

Other membrane components that recognize chemotactic stimuli are the system(s) specific for oxygen and the system that senses changes in proton-motive force. Oxygen is, for the time being, the only substance known to be either an attractant or a repellent for *E. coli* and *S. typhimurium,* depending on its concentration [Shioi et al., 1987]. When the concentration of dissolved oxygen is equal to or lower than the concentration in equilibrium with air (≤ 0.25 mM), oxygen is an attractant. When the concentration is higher (e.g., when a bacterial suspension is exposed to atmosphere of pure oxygen), oxygen acts as a repellent. The difference between the opposing sensitivities is more than three orders of magnitude: the half-maximal attractant response is at 0.7 μM dissolved oxygen, whereas that of the repellent response is at 1 mM [Shioi et al., 1987]. Based on the different affinities for oxygen, Shioi et al. [1987] concluded that there are distinct receptors for oxygen, one for attraction and one for repulsion.

The receptors for attractant oxygen were identified as cytochromes *o* [Laszlo et al., 1984] and *d* [Shioi et al., 1988]. However, these cytochromes are not receptors in the usual sense of the word, because strict binding of oxygen to them does not bring about a chemotactic response. It is the metabolism of oxygen or the effect of oxygen on the redox potential of a signaling component [Glagolev and Sherman, 1983] or on the proton-motive force of the cell that initiates the response.

It is possible that the attraction to oxygen is a particular case of a more general one, a protometer, i.e., a hypothetical device that senses changes in proton-motive force [Glagolev, 1980; Taylor, 1983]. It should be noted, however, that there is no direct proof for the existence of such a device. It is also worth mentioning that an increase in the proton-motive force is not the only change in $\Delta\bar{\mu}_H +$ that causes smooth swimming. A change to the other extreme, i.e., a reduction in the proton-motive force, also causes smooth swimming [Khan and Macnab, 1980a], albeit not an attractant response: There is no adaptation to low proton-motive force; Che⁻ mutants are affected too [Khan and Macnab, 1980a]; and uncouplers, which reduce the proton-motive force, are repellents, not attractants [Ordal and Goldman, 1975; Shioi et al., 1988]. The reader is referred to Taylor (this volume) for an elaboration of oxygen taxis and proton-motive force-sensing.

The receptor for oxygen that brings about a repellent response has not been identified. This is not surprising in view of the fact that any specific receptor for repellents in the usual sense of the word, i.e., a receptor that initiates a repellent behavior in response to binding of the repellent, has not been identified.

D. Repellent Sensing

Discussing signal transduction via the membrane that leads to a repellent response is not simple because of the lack of knowledge on repellent receptors. As discussed above, such receptors have not been identified, excluding perhaps the sensors for acidification and for weak organic acids, such as formate, acetate, benzoate, and salicylate, which act by lowering the internal pH of the cell [Repaske and Adler, 1981; Kihara and Macnab, 1981].

For both the acidification and the organic acids the sensor was identified as MCP I [Slonczewski et al., 1982; Krikos et al., 1985]. In the case of a change in the external pH, a site in the periplasmic domain of MCP I responds to the pH change [Krikos et al., 1985]. The result is possibly a major conformational change that can be read by the cytoplasmic components of the chemotaxis machinery, as in the case of the attractants serine and aspartate (see section IV.A.). In the case of weak organic acids, the signal is transduced by passive diffusion of the nonionized form of the acid across the membrane. The acid is ionized within the cell, the intracellular pH is lowered, and the change in pH is detected by MCP I. Thus, even for the case of external acidification or weak organic acids, MCP I is not a receptor in the usual or narrow sense of the word. These are pH-sensitive sites, not attractant-binding sites, that bring about the presumed conformational changes of MCP I. In the broader sense of the word, however, these sites may be considered as proton (or hydroxyl)-binding sites. By constructing mutants with chimeric MCPs, Kirkos et al. [1985] found that such sites reside on both the periplasmic and cytoplasmic domains of MCP I. MCP II has analogous sites, but these are attractant sites: A decrease in pH (internally or externally) causes an attractant response. The MCP I response is dominant. Therefore, when both MCPs are functional, the observed response is that of a repellent. In a mutant in which MCP I is missing or not functional, the MCP II–mediated attractant response is observed.

What about sensory transduction in the case of other repellents? A definitive answer to this question cannot be given. I shall try, however, to consider possible modes of signaling in view of the available data. A variety of different substances are included in this group of repellents: amino acids such as leucine and valine, indole and its derivatives, alcohols such as isopropanol, ions such as Co^{2+} and Ni^{2+}, and others [Tsang et al., 1973; Tso and Adler, 1974]. A common denominator for all these repellents is not obvious.

On the basis of competition experiments and additivity experiments, both Tsang et al. [1973] and Tso and Adler [1974] concluded that repellent receptors should exist. This conclusion was further supported by the isolation of mutants defective in their response to L-leucine but not to indole [Tso and Adler, 1974]. (Both repellents are detected by MCP I [Table I].) However, because no receptor for the above-mentioned repellents has been identified, we should consider the repellent receptors as putative ones. The lack of positive identification of repellent receptors should not be considered as evidence against their existence. The repellent concentrations required to elicit a chemotactic response are in the millimolar range or even higher. Thus, if repellent receptors exist, their affinity for the ligands (= repellents) is low. Receptors with low affinity for their ligands are difficult to identify. A similar situation exists in the olfactory system, where a large repertoire of odorants can be detected, albeit with a very low affinity. For this reason the issue of whether there are receptors in the olfactory system is still controversial [Lancet and Pace, 1987]. In a different system, in at least one case in which the existence of receptors is unquestionable, the affinity of the yet-unidentified receptors to their ligands is very low. These are the taste receptors and especially the sugar receptors. The concentration of sugar needed to elicit a half-maximal response is in a range as high as 0.5 M(!) [Jakinovich, 1981; Teeter and Brand, 1987]. The chemotactic signal triggered by most of the known repellents is mediated by a specific MCP [Springer et al., 1977]. (An exception is the group of aliphatic alcohols and polyalcohols, the signal to which is mediated by any MCP [Oosawa and Imae, 1983, 1984; Eisenbach et al., 1990a].) Therefore, if indeed there are receptors in the bacterial cell for most of the repellents, these receptors should be either periplasmic or the MCPs themselves (cf. Fig. 2). Ravid and Eisenbach [1984a] and Eisenbach et al. [1990a] found that spheroplasts lacking periplasm retain their responsiveness to repellents but lose their responsiveness to maltose, the receptor for which is periplasmic. In view of these findings, the probability of periplasmic receptors for repellents appears to be low. Therefore the most likely possibility in this category is that the MCPs are also receptors for repellents, albeit with a low affinity. In such a case the sensory signal is presumably transduced across the membrane by major conformational changes of the MCP, as was concluded for the case of attractants (see section IV.A.). Perhaps we have here a unique combination of a versatile receptor with a large variety of low-affinity ligands. The MCP appears to combine the versatility of cytochrome P-450 (which exhibits nonselectivity and high versatility [Black, 1987]) with the low affinity of the sugar receptors of the taste system.

A different possibility that has been raised is that there are no receptors for repellents and the repellents have a nonspecific effect on one or more of the membrane properties [Seymour and Doetsch, 1973; Ordal and Goldman, 1976], e.g., the membrane fluidity [Macnab, 1985]. The high concentrations of repellents needed to elicit a chemotactic response and the lack of stereospecificity of the repellent response (e.g., the potency of D- and L-leucine or D- and L-phenylalanine as repellents is comparable [Tso and Adler, 1974]) are in line with this possibility. A change in the membrane fluidity may, e.g., cause a vertical displacement of the MCP and thus transduce the signal across the membrane or it may affect the turnover of the protein activity. As a matter of fact, many of the substances classified as unsaturated fatty acids, short aliphatic alcohols, hydrophobic amino acids, and aromatic compounds in the extensive repellent screening of Tso and Adler [1974] for *E. coli* may induce a disorder in the lipid domain expressed as an increase in the membrane fluidity [Shinitzky, 1984; Yuli et al.,1982; M. Shinitzki, personal communication], the more effective substances being more potent repellents. However, two main lines of evidence argue against the possibility that the classic repellents work by fluidizing the membrane: 1) Direct measurements of the changes in membrane fluidity of *E. coli* in response to repellent stimulation do not reveal a consistent value that elicits a behavioral response [Eisenbach et al., 1990a], and 2) there is no effect of the membrane fluidity on the tumbling frequency of nonstimulated cells [Miller and Koshland, 1977]. Another general membrane property that could, in principle, mediate a repellent response is the membrane potential, but, again, consistent changes in the potential in response to repellents have not been found [Snyder et al., 1981]. It thus appears that the possibility that repellents have nonspecific effects on a membrane property is not likely.

It was recently found that some repellents may cause an additional response at the level of the flagellar motor. One of the effects of repellents is an increase in the frequency of pauses. A high repellent concentration may bring the motor to a complete stop. Removal of the repellent restores the rotation [Lapidus et al., 1988]. This complete stop occurs also in energized, cytoplasm-free flagellated envelopes of *S. typhimurium* [Eisenbach et al., 1990b]. Because the envelopes lack the chemotaxis machinery [Eisenbach and Adler, 1981; Ravid and Eisenbach, 1984a], it may be concluded that under certain conditions some repellents may affect the motor directly. Alternatively, under these conditions the repellents may be sensed by the cytoplasmic membrane and the information transduced at the membrane level directly to the motor. In view of the findings described in the preceding paragraph, the likelihood of this alternative is low.

E. Conclusion

Based on the survey in this section, it seems that there are versatile mechanisms for transducing the signal across the membrane: major conformational changes, as in the case of MCP-mediated recognition of attractants and repellents; active transport of the attractant across the membrane, as in the case of PTS; stimulant diffusion through the membrane followed by MCP modulation from the inside, as in the case of weak organic acids and bases; and general modulation of a membrane property such as the proton-motive force.

V. SIGNAL TRANSDUCTION WITHIN THE CYTOPLASM

The points of origin of sensory signaling within the cytoplasm are from the MCPs, the PTS, and the other membrane receptors. The final target is the switch at the base of the flagellar motor. I shall first deal with the excitatory signal from a single point of origin. Then the available data will be examined to determine whether they indicate one common excitatory signal from all the points of origin or separate signals. A separate discussion will be devoted to the adaptation signal and to the question of whether both the excitation and adaptation processes are triggered by a common signal or whether the adaptation process is triggered by a feedback mechanism and follows the excitation. In view of the distinct differences between large and small bacterial species with respect to excitatory signaling, each of these species will be dealt with separately.

A. Excitation in Small Bacterial Species

In principle, the excitatory signal between the points of origin at the membrane and the membrane-associated switch could be a change in the membrane potential, a change in the concentration of a specific ion within the cytoplasm, or chemical reactions of diffusible substances in the cytoplasm. Cytoskeleton-like interactions will not be considered here because, to the best of my knowledge, no solid or confirmed data have been published to show the existence of cytoskeleton filaments in the bacterial cell.

Historically, changes in the membrane potential and changes in the concentrations of specific ions were the first signaling candidates to be investigated, presumably because of the analogy to sensory transduction in the nervous system. As discussed in section III above, changes in membrane potential, stimulated by attractants, were indeed found. Additional support for electrical signaling was the finding that an externally applied, electromagnetically induced electric field inhibits the chemotaxis process by 70% and at the same time enhances the motility of the cells [Eisenbach et al., 1983b]. However, both the inhibitory effect of the electric field and the attractant-stimulated changes in the membrane potential could well be indirect. Two subsequent lines of evidence argued against the involvement of membrane potential in signaling. 1) *E. coli* cells were found to be excitable, adaptable, and fully chemotactic under conditions of clamped membrane potential, i.e., conditions under which signaling by fluctuations in the membrane potential is impossible [Margolin and Eisenbach, 1984]. Similar but less extensive observations were reported also for *Streptococcus* [Manson et al., 1977] and *B. subtilis* [Margolin and Eisenbach, 1984]. 2) Segall et al. [1985] produced long filamentous cells of *E. coli* and showed that only flagella near the stimulation site responded to an attractant, added by iontophoretic pulse. This indicated that the range of the excitatory signal (only a few micrometers) is shorter than the range calculated for a change in the membrane potential. As a matter of fact, this evidence argues against any long-range mode of signaling, and, indeed, surface charge changes were also eliminated as a factor in chemotactic signaling [Eisenbach et al., 1985]. It therefore seems justified to conclude with a high degree of confidence that the excitatory signal is not electrical in nature.

The same experiments with filamentous cells of *E. coli* were used to eliminate signaling by diffusion of ions in the cytoplasm. Segall et al. [1985] calculated that simple release and binding of a small molecule or an ion is improbable, because this requires a diffusion coefficient several hundred times smaller than the actual measured coefficients in cytoplasm-like media. This negative conclusion came on a background of nonconclusive evidence for some kind of involvement of ions, predominantly Ca^{2+}, in the chemotaxis machinery [see, e.g., Ordal, 1977, but also section I in Ordal, 1985]. A reasonable statement about the state of the art with regard to ions in chemotaxis is that changes in the concentration of a specific ion are not the excitatory signal [see Eisenbach et al., 1985, for summary of data on Ca^{2+} as well as on other ions and intracellular pH]. All the supportive phenomena that have been observed could be explained on the basis of indirect effects on enzymes within the cell. For example, in a recent study Matsushita et al. [1988] demonstrated partial inhibition of chemotaxis by Ca^{2+} channel blockers, as measured by swarm and capillary assays. However, rings were formed in the swarm assays, and accumulation was observed in the capillary even with the most potent blockers. It therefore seems to me that, unlike the conclusion of Matsushita et al., Ca^{2+} is not likely to play a major role in bacterial chemotaxis in general, and in the excitation process in particular. The involvement of H^+, K^+, Na^+, NH_4^+, and Mg^{2+} fluxes in the chemotaxis machinery was eliminated by direct measurements [Eisenbach et al., 1985]. The possibility of indirect participation of Ca^{2+} in the signaling mechanism still calls for further experimentation. The success of Gangola and Rosen [1987] to measure the intracellular concentration of Ca^{2+} in E. coli cells opens perhaps the way for a direct determination of the involvement of Ca^{2+} in the signaling process.

One of the most important conclusions from the study of the range of signaling in filamentous cells is that the excitatory signal is inactivated as it moves away from its point of origin [Segall et al., 1985]. This is in favor of the possibility that the excitatory signal is a combination of chemical reactions among diffusible substances within the cytoplasm. Recent data, summarized below in a semichronological order, support this notion.

The "natural" rotation of the bacterial motor is counterclockwise. At least part of the chemotaxis machinery is needed for clockwise rotation. This has been shown by both genetic and in vitro approaches. Flagella of mutants, that lack large parts of the cytoplasmic chemotaxis machinery because of deletions of che genes, always rotate counterclockwise [Parkinson and Houts, 1982; Wolfe et al.,1987; Eisenbach et al., 1990b]. Accordingly, cytoplasm-free cell envelopes [Eisenbach and Adler, 1981], isolated from wild-type bacteria by relatively short penicillin treatment and subsequent osmotic lysis (Fig. 6), rotate their flagella exclusively counterclockwise [Eisenbach and Adler, 1981; Ravid and Eisenbach, 1984a]. The counterclockwise bias of the envelopes is due to the loss of cytoplasm. This was proven by preparing envelopes from clockwise mutants (Fig. 7) and showing that envelopes prepared from mutants whose defective, clockwise-causing gene product was cytoplasmic, acquired a counterclockwise bias, just like wild-type envelopes, whereas mutants whose defective gene product was associated with the membrane retained their clockwise bias (Table IV; see Fig. 7 for a more detailed explanation) [Ravid and Eisenbach, 1984a; see Eisenbach and Matsumura, 1988, for review]. Neither mutants with the cytoplasmic che genes deleted [Parkinson and Houts, 1982] nor wild-type envelopes [Ravid and Eisenbach, 1984a] respond to chemotactic stimuli.

The next stage was the identification of the cytoplasmic constituent that causes clockwise rotation, followed by the identification of the constituents that participate in regulating the direction of rotation and in transducing the excitatory signal. Searching for a protein candidate rather than low-molecular-weight candidates was a logical first step, because the nonresponsive, counterclockwise-biased intact che mutants presumably contained close to normal levels of low-molecular-weight substances. Six of the che gene products are cytoplasmic proteins (Table III). Two of them, the CheY and CheZ pro-

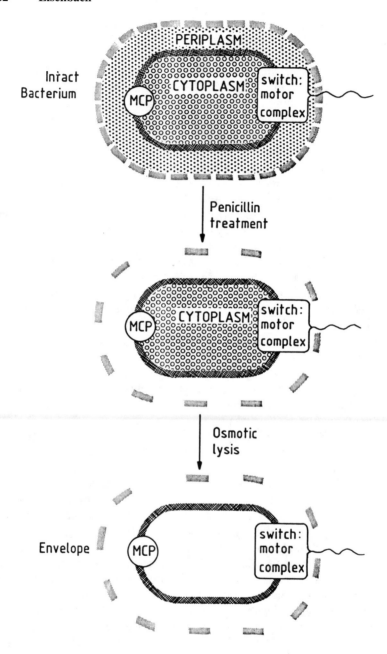

Fig. 6. The main steps in the preparation of cell envelopes. The scheme is not drawn to scale. [Reproduced from Eisenbach et al., 1985, with permission of the publisher.]

INTACT CELL   CELL ENVELOPE

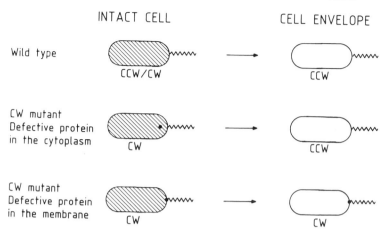

Fig. 7. The rationale of experiments aimed at determining whether the cytoplasm release is the cause of the counterclockwise bias of tethered envelopes. The scheme demonstrates that envelopes, prepared from mutants whose defective gene product is in the cytoplasm, should be similar to those prepared from the wild-type parent and have therefore counterclockwise (CCW) bias (the defective gene product presumably being released with the rest of the cytoplasm). Envelopes prepared from mutants whose defective gene product resides in the cytoplasmic membrane should contain the defective gene product and might retain the clockwise (CW) bias [Ravid and Eisenbach, 1984a].

teins, have been shown by genetic reversion analysis (second-site suppression analysis) to interact with the switch [Parkinson et al., 1983; Yamaguchi et al., 1986] and thus became primary candidates to be tested. Mutation in the *cheZ* gene leads to clockwise bias [Parkinson, 1978, 1981], indicating that its gene product may be involved in counterclockwise rotation. Using the same logic, the CheY protein may be involved in clockwise rotation, because *cheY* mutants

TABLE IV. Flagellar Rotation in Behavioral Mutants and Their Derived Cell Envelopes*

Strain	Relevant phenotype	Location of gene product	Cell proportion in	
			Intact bacteria	Cell envelopes
ST1	Wild type		20% CCW, 80% CCW-cw†	100% CCW
ST171	CheA,B‡	Cytoplasm	17% CW-ccw, 83% CW	100% CCW
ST450	CheB	Cytoplasm	16% CW-ccw, 84% CW	100% CCW
ST120	CheC	Membrane	100% CW	100% CW
MY1	CheV	Membrane	84% vibrating, 16% CW	86% CCW, 14% CW

*Reproduced from Eisenbach and Matsumura [1988], with permission of the publisher.
†CCW-cw, counterclockwise rotation with occasional, brief periods of clockwise rotation; CW-ccw, clockwise rotation with occasional, brief periods of counterclockwise rotation.
‡Strain ST171 [Aswad and Koshland, 1975b] was considered to be a *cheZ* mutant, until Kutsukake and Iino [1985] showed it to be a *cheAcheB* double mutant.

rotate exclusively counterclockwise [Parkinson, 1978, 1981]. These data made the CheY protein the preferred candidate for being tested as the primary cytoplasmic constituent that causes clockwise rotation [Parkinson, 1981; Lengeler, 1982; Ravid and Eisenbach, 1984a; Segall et al., 1985].

Two approaches have been used for testing CheY. In one approach a plasmid containing the *cheY* gene and a regulatable promoter was constructed, introduced into wild-type and mutant strains, and used to express the *cheY* gene at different levels [Clegg and Koshland, 1984; Wolfe et al., 1987]. Overproduction of CheY caused clockwise bias in both the wild-type and the mutant strains lacking all other cytoplasmic *che* gene products. The ability of CheY to cause clockwise rotation in a strain that lacks any other cytoplasmic *che* gene products indicated that CheY causes clockwise rotation by interaction with the switch. This approach could not, however, distinguish between a direct interaction of CheY with the switch and an indirect interaction, e.g., via some small molecule [Clegg and Koshland, 1984]. The other approach, carried out in parallel, involved insertion of purified CheY into cytoplasm-free envelopes. The CheY protein was overexpressed and purified [Matsumura et al., 1984]. Wild-type envelopes containing purified CheY were prepared by inclusion of the protein in the lysis medium during the preparation of the envelopes (Fig. 6) [Ravid et al., 1986]. As a result, some of the tethered envelopes rotated exclusively clockwise (Fig. 8). The fraction of envelopes that did so increased

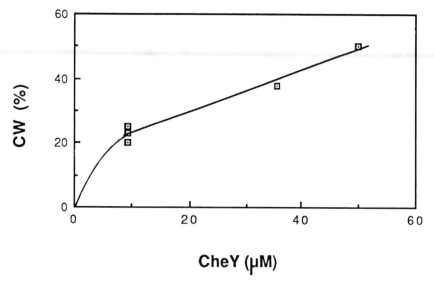

Fig. 8.   The fraction of clockwise (CW)-rotating envelopes as a function of the presumed internal concentration of CheY. The rotation was driven by DL-lactate.

with the concentration of CheY. When the internal concentration of purified CheY was 40–45 μM (around 44,000 molecules per cell), about one-half of the envelopes rotated clockwise [Eisenbach and Matsumura, 1988]. Because of the absence of any of the original cytoplasmic constituents in the envelopes, including small molecules, it was concluded that the interaction between CheY and the switch is direct.

On the basis of the above observations it is possible to conclude that repellents cause the MCP to transmit a clockwise signal to the flagellar motor, i.e., to trigger a cascade of events that eventually leads to direct interaction of CheY with the switch and to clockwise rotation. What about a counterclockwise signal? Because in the absence of a clockwise signal the motor rotates counterclockwise, one could argue that there is no need for a counterclockwise signal. However, to respond quickly to attractants, the bacteria must have means to deactivate or destroy the clockwise signal. Indeed, recent studies of Ames and Parkinson [1988] with MCP mutants locked in counterclockwise rotation indicated that the MCP can actively signal the motor to rotate counterclockwise. (Destruction of a clockwise signal is also considered here as an active counterclockwise signal.) Thus, while a Δtsr mutant alternates between both directions of flagellar rotation, there are mutants with point mutations in *tsr* that rotate in only one direction, either clockwise or counterclockwise, indicative of active clockwise and counterclockwise signaling. Furthermore, this active signaling is independent of the presence of other MCPs, because a strain deleted of all MCPs that alternates between both directions of rotation because of overproduction of CheY can be made to rotate predominantly counterclockwise or clockwise by introducing a second plasmid with an appropriately biased *tsr* signaling defect (P. Ames and J.S. Parkinson, personal communication).

The estimated number of switch molecules per bacterial cell is in the order of 100 or less [Ravid et al., 1986; R.M. Macnab, personal communication]. Why was there a need of about 400-fold larger number of CheY molecules to make one-half of the envelopes rotate clockwise? The same question applies also to intact bacteria, where the concentration of monomeric CheY in the cytoplasm is estimated to be about 20 μM [A. Stock et al., 1985] or in the order of 20,000 molecules per cell. One possibility is that the CheY protein is sequestered by being bound, e.g., to the MCPs, but thus far no evidence for an interaction between CheY and the MCPs has been obtained from second-site suppression analyses. Furthermore, CheY is homologous to the N terminus of CheB (see below), and as such one could argue that CheY is likely to interact with the MCP just as CheB does. However, because a proteolytic fragment of CheB that does not contain the CheY-homologous domain has even higher esterase activity (see section V.B.1.) than that of intact CheB [Simms et al., 1985], the MCP-binding site in CheB is probably not in the CheY-homologous domain. In other words, CheY apparently does not contain this

MCP-binding site. Another possibility, perhaps more likely, is that only a small fraction of the CheY molecules within the envelopes were active. Possibly related observations in the envelopes are that all the so-called active batches of CheY lost their activity with time and that the majority of the preparations were nonactive from the start [Eisenbach and Matsumura, 1988]. Apparently other substances are required to confer activity to CheY. These may be other Che proteins or low-molecular-weight substances in the cytoplasm.

1. Proteins. Among the cytoplasmic *che* gene products, the CheA, CheW, and CheZ proteins are considered to be involved in the excitation process. This is based on studies of the behavior of *che* mutants [Parkinson, 1981] and on overproduction of the Che proteins in bacteria deleted for genes that code for other cytoplasmic *che* gene products and MCPs [Kuo and Koshland, 1987; Wolfe et al., 1987]. What is the current knowledge about these three proteins?

a. CheZ. CheZ is a hydrophilic and very acidic protein [A. Stock and Stock, 1987]. It appears to be a homopolymer, constituted from at least 20 monomeric subunits [see Stock, 1988, for a review of CheZ]. Based on second-site suppression analysis it was concluded that CheZ interacts with the flagellar switch [Parkinson and Parker, 1979; Parkinson et al., 1983]. Because CheZ counteracts the action of CheY [Kuo and Koshland, 1987], one of the suggestions raised with regard to the role of CheZ was that it is a counterclockwise signal [e.g., Lengeler, 1982; Kuo and Koshland, 1987], in analogy to CheY, which was found to be a clockwise signal (see above). However, CheZ-free envelopes rotate counterclockwise [Ravid and Eisenbach, 1984a], and intact *cheZ* mutants respond to attractants with counterclockwise rotation [Parkinson, 1981; Wolfe et al., 1987; Eisenbach et al., 1990b]. It is therefore more reasonable to assume that CheZ terminates the interaction of CheY with the switch rather than being a signal itself [Ravid et al., 1986]. Evidence that apparently supports this suggestion was supplied by Wolfe et al. [1987], who found that intracellular production of CheZ increased the counterclockwise bias only when the cell also contained CheY and that cells containing CheA, CheW, CheY, and the MCPs did respond to attractants and repellents even though CheZ was absent. In spite of not being a counterclockwise signal, CheZ presumably does participate in the excitation process, because the response delay time of *cheZ* mutants is abnormally long [Segall et al., 1982; Block et al., 1982]. (The response delay time is the period of time lapsed between the addition of a stimulant and the response of the flagella. It therefore stands for the excitation time.)

b. CheA and CheW. In vitro studies indicate that CheA and CheW form a complex [P.I. Matsumura, personal communication; McNally et al., 1985] with a stoichiometry of two CheW monomers per CheA dimer ($K_d \sim 17 \mu M$) [Gegner and Dahlquist, 1991[1]]. It appears that both of them participate in the trans-

---

[1]This information was added after the completion of the manuscript.

mission of the signal rather than in controlling the direction of flagellar rotation, because signal transduction in mutant cells that lack CheA and CheW is not functional; nevertheless, the direction of rotation in such a mutant is still modulatable by CheY and CheZ [Clegg and Koshland, 1984; Wolfe et al., 1987]. CheA and CheW together are required for the transduction of the signal; production of both of them (in addition to CheY) is required for the purpose in a strain lacking all other *che* gene products [Conley et al., 1989]. Although initially CheA was considered to be a trimer or tetramer [Hess et al., 1987; Stock et al., 1988a] and CheW to be a homodimer [Stock et al., 1987a], recent data suggest that CheA is a dimer and CheW is a monomer [Gegner and Dahlquist, 1991].[2] Based on a consensus sequence, CheW may have a nucleotide-binding site [Stock et al., 1987a] but none has thus far been demonstrated. Unlike CheA (see below), little is known of the molecular function of CheW. These proteins are further discussed in section V.A.2.c.

2. Low-molecular-weight substances. Low-molecular-weight substances, examined for their involvement in signal transduction, are primarily *S*-adenosylmethionine (AdoMet), cGMP or cAMP, and ATP. The evidence accumulated in the literature for the possible involvement of these and other substances in the excitation process is summarized below.

a. AdoMet. Armstrong [1972a,b] and Aswad and Koshland [1975a] found that AdoMet is essential for chemotaxis. AdoMet was then found to be the precursor for MCP [Springer and Koshland, 1977] and CheZ [Stock et al., 1987b] methylation. MCP methylation is not involved in the excitation process of *E. coli* and *S. typhimurium,* but it may be involved in that of *B. subtilis.* Only in this species changes in the methylation levels of the MCPs occurred within less than 5 sec, much before adaptation is observed [Thoelke et al., 1988]. The role of this methylation in *B. subtilis* is, however, still obscure. Similarly, no role has been assigned to the methylation of CheZ [Silverman and Simon, 1977a], which is unaffected by chemotactic stimuli and is independent of any other component of the chemotaxis system [Stock et al., 1987b; Stock, 1988]. It does not seem that AdoMet may have any other role in chemotaxis besides these methylations [Borczuk et al., 1987] and being the precursor of decarboxylated AdoMet (dSAM) (see below).

b. cGMP and related compounds. Several reports proposed the possible involvement of cGMP [Black et al., 1980; Omirbekova et al., 1985] and cAMP or the corresponding cyclases [Black et al., 1983] in chemotaxis. However, subsequent studies called these propositions into question [Taylor et al., 1985; Tribhuwan et al., 1986; Vogler and Lengeler, 1987]. A reproducible experimental result obtained in several laboratories was that addition of a high concentration of cGMP (about 30 mM) caused a prolonged smooth swimming

[2]See footnote 1.

(about 30 min) [Black et al., 1980]. Although there was no attraction to cGMP-containing capillaries [Black et al., 1980], it is still possible that cGMP or a related compound is an attractant for *E. coli*. One way to discriminate between cGMP being an attractant or a regulator of chemotaxis is to carry out temporal assays for cGMP with specific MCP mutants to determine whether only one specific MCP senses the cGMP (as would be anticipated in the case of an attractant) or whether all the MCPs sense it (as would be expected in the case of a chemotactic regulator). Recent temporal assays carried out by K. Lewis (personal communication) indeed showed that a smooth swimming response is absent in mutants with deleted *tsr* or with point mutation in this gene but present in any other MCP mutants. It therefore seems reasonable to conclude that cGMP (or cAMP, guanylate cyclase, or adenylate cyclase) is not directly involved in transducing the chemotactic signal but rather is an attractant for *E. coli*. This conclusion appears to be justified in view of the extremely low number of cGMP molecules in a bacterial cell, e.g., less than one to three molecules per *E. coli* cell [Vogler and Lengeler, 1987].

   c. ATP and phosphorylation. ATP seems to be the only low-molecular-weight substance for which there is consistent strong evidence for being directly involved in the chemotaxis machinery. The involvement is beyond the ATP requirement for AdoMet synthesis. Bacteria depleted of ATP fail to tumble [Aswad and Koshland, 1975a; Springer et al., 1975; Galloway and Taylor, 1980; Khan and Macnab, 1980a; Kondoh, 1980; Arai, 1981; Shioi et al., 1982; Taylor et al., 1985], and the rotation of their flagella is counterclockwise biased. The minimal ATP level needed for tumbling is about 0.2 mM [Shioi et al., 1982]. The need of clockwise rotation for ATP is in the cytoplasm; envelopes prepared from a clockwise-biased switch mutant that is sensitive to ATP depletion rotated their flagella clockwise in spite of being devoid of ATP [Ravid and Eisenbach, 1984a; Eisenbach and Matsumura, 1988]. Based on these observations, it was logical to look for phosphorylation of Che proteins within the cell. Several laboratories have looked for such phosphorylation in vivo but were unable to detect any. A breakthrough was made when Hess et al. [1987], followed by Wylie et al. [1988] succeeded in isolating and purifying CheA and found that it is autophosphorylated in vitro by ATP.

   The *cheA* gene encodes two polypeptides, long and short, the long one having additional amino acids in the N-terminal domain [Smith and Parkinson, 1980]. Because the phosphorylation site is His 48 [Hess et al., 1988b], only the long polypeptide is phosphorylated [Hess et al., 1987]. Phosphorylated CheA can rapidly phosphorylate CheY in vitro (Fig. 9) [Hess et al., 1988c; Wylie et al., 1988]. This phosphotransferase activity of CheA is fully retained in the N-terminal domain of the protein. By using ATP analogs, Wong et al. [1988] found an ATP-binding site on CheY in addition to the site found by Hess et al. [1987]. Only pure CheY could be labeled by the analogs; no label-

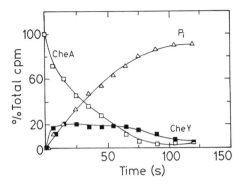

Fig. 9.   Phosphorylation of CheY by CheA and its dephosphorylation. The counts on the ordinate are ^{32}P counts obtained from radiolabeled bands of an autoradiogram of the time courses of CheY- and CheB-mediated dephosphorylation of CheA. [Reproduced from Hess et al., 1988c, with permission of the publisher.]

ing or phosphorylation of CheY was found in a cell extract. The pure CheY, however, was neither autophosphorylated nor adenylated by ATP [Wong et al., 1988]. Based on this finding, Smith et al. [1988] suggested that there are two ATP-binding sites in the chemotaxis pathway of CheY. By EPR measurements of a spin-labeled analog of ATP and by NMR measurements of ATP and AMP, Kar et al. [1988, 1991] concluded that the binding of ATP to CheY is via the phosphate groups and that the adenosine plays little or no role in the binding. This conclusion is in line with the observation of Stock et al. [1987a] that the CheY sequence (as well as that of CheA) does not contain discernible nucleotide-binding fingerprints. Because the CheY protein as a whole is homologous to the N-terminal portion of the CheB protein [A. Stock et al., 1985], it was not surprising to find out that also CheB, like CheY, was phosphorylated in vitro by CheA [Hess et al., 1988c]. Although the rate of CheA dephosphorylation by CheY was comparable with the dephosphorylation rate by CheB, the degree of phosphorylation of CheY was one order of magnitude higher than that of CheB: one to two phosphate groups per one CheY molecule and 0.1 to 0.2 groups per one CheB molecule [Hess et al., 1988c]. On the basis of the amino acid residues that are completely conserved between all proteins belonging to the group of response regulators (see end of section V.A.3.), Stock et al. [1988b, 1989[3]] have suggested that aspartyl groups are the sites of phosphorylation (residues 13 and 57 in the case of CheY). Subsequent studies of Sanders et al. [1989] and Bourret et al. [1990] con-

[3]See footnote 1.

firmed that Asp-57 of CheY is the phosphorylation site and that Asp-13 has an important role in the activity of the protein.[4]

Unlike phosphorylated CheA, which is very stable, phosphorylated CheY is quickly and spontaneously dephosphorylated in vitro [Hess et al., 1988c; Wylie et al., 1988]. Both the phosphorylation and dephosphorylation processes of CheY are enhanced by other proteins. Thus CheW enhances (in rate and extent) the phosphorylation of CheY in vitro [Borkovich et al., 1989], whereas CheZ enhances its dephosphorylation [Hess et al., 1988c]. The effect of CheW is much more pronounced in the presence of MCP. CheZ enhances the dephosphorylation without becoming phosphorylated itself. When both CheW and CheZ are present, CheZ dominates, i.e., the phosphorylation of CheY by CheA is slower than in the absence of these proteins [Borkovich et al., 1989]. CheZ is also able to dephosphorylate CheA (but not CheB), albeit at a very slow rate. Being so slow in comparison with the dephosphorylation effect of CheY on CheA or CheZ on CheY [Hess et al., 1987, 1988c], this CheZ-dependent dephosphorylation of CheA is presumably secondary and has no significant role in vivo. The observations that the excitory signal is unstable [Segall et al., 1985], that CheY interacts with the switch (see above), and that CheZ enhances the dephosphorylation of CheY, taken together with the suggestion that CheZ terminates the interaction of CheY with the switch, argue for CheY–phosphate being a signal for clockwise rotation. The supporting evidence in favor of this proposition can be summarized as follows. 1) Production of CheY by a plasmid within a MCP-less mutant that also lacks all the cytoplasmic *che* gene products caused clockwise rotation that was dependent on the presence of ATP internally [Smith et al., 1988]; 2) site-specific mutagenesis that changed the phosphorylation site, His 48, to 13 different amino acids caused total loss of the chemotactic activity of the mutants [Hess et al., 1988b]; and 3) defective CheA proteins were isolated from *cheA* mutants and tested for phosphorylation activity in vitro [Oosawa et al., 1988a]. The large majority of the proteins were found to be defective in at least one aspect of phosphorylation: They either had abnormal levels or rates of autophosphorylation or were unable to phosphorylate CheY and/or CheB. Mutations with similar phenotypes were found to be grouped together in the same region of the *cheA* gene. Mutations with different phenotypes were found to be in different locations in the gene. Based on the classification of the phenotypes and the location of the mutations, Oosawa et al. [1988a] concluded that there are three functional domains in CheA: one domain (the N terminus) for the interaction with CheY and CheB, one domain for regulating the phosphorylation and the stability of the protein, and one domain (the C terminus) for receiving input signals regulating CheA activity.

---

[4]See footnote 1.

In a very elegant study, Borkovich et al. [1989] looked for the minimal system needed for affecting CheY phosphorylation by MCP in vitro. This system involves, in addition to MCP II–containing membrane vesicles and CheY, the proteins CheA and CheW. Thus the phosphorylation of CheA and CheY in the presence of CheW was much enhanced by the presence of MCP. Addition of aspartate (an attractant for MCP II) to this mixture caused a drastic inhibition of CheY phosphorylation. Hence the modulation of CheY phosphorylation involves CheA and CheW. Another illuminating observation of Borkovich et al. [1989] was that the MCP-mediated enhancement of the rate of CheA autophosphorylation was dependent on the presence of CheY, indicative of the existence of a complex between CheA and CheY.

If indeed phosphorylated CheY is the active form of the protein, as the above observations suggest, an intriguing question that comes up is how could CheY bring about clockwise rotation in a mutant that lacks CheA and the other cytoplasmic Che proteins [Clegg and Koshland, 1984; Kuo and Koshland, 1987; Wolfe et al., 1987; Smith et al., 1988] or in wild-type, cytoplasm-free cell envelopes [Ravid et al., 1986]? The question is even more intriguing in view of the finding that CheY is not autophosphorylated in vitro. The data available to date cannot supply an answer to this question. Possible explanations, all without any supporting evidence, are as follows.

1. Nonphosphorylated CheY may also be active, i.e., it may also interact with the switch and bring about clockwise rotation, but its affinity to the switch may be much lower than that of CheY–phosphate [Hess et al., 1988c]. Thus overproduction of CheY in intact bacteria or inclusion of high CheY concentrations in envelopes may compensate for the low affinity or activity of nonphosphorylated CheY.

2. Assuming the existence of ''cross-talk'' among sensory transduction systems [Ronson et al., 1987], it is possible that a small fraction of the CheY molecules in the cells becomes phosphorylated by homologous systems. The CheY–phosphate thus produced may be sufficient to cause clockwise rotation [Hess et al., 1988c]. A cross-talk between proteins involved in nitrogen assimilation (Ntr) and chemotaxis was indeed demonstrated recently: CheY could be phosphorylated by NR_{II} (NtrB), and the latter could even suppress the smooth swimming phenotype of a *cheA* mutant [Ninfa et al., 1988]. How can cross-talk be responsible for CheY phosphorylation in the case of CheY-containing envelopes, which apparently do not contain sufficient residual ATP in the cell? (Assuming at least 10^4 dilution of the original internal cell content during the lysis of the cells to form envelopes, the average ATP content in the envelopes should be less than 0.5 μM.) Furthermore, inclusion of a high ATP concentration together with CheY in the envelopes was not sufficient to activate

apparent nonactive CheY (M. Eisenbach, unpublished data). Perhaps membrane-bound, autophosphorylated kinases (e.g., EnvZ, PhoR, and CpxA [Igo and Silhavy, 1988; Stock et al., 1988b; Bourret et al., 1989]) can transfer their phosphate groups to the inserted CheY in the absence of their original substrate proteins. This possibility can be put to the test by comparing the activity of CheY in wild- type envelopes with that of CheY in envelopes of mutants lacking membrane-bound kinases.

3. It is possible that some preparations of envelopes contained remnants of CheA and ATP, sufficient to make the inserted CheY active. This may explain also the large variability in the activity of different CheY batches. However, the reservations just raised with regard to the very large (at least 10^4) dilution of the cytoplasmic content holds also here. It is possible, perhaps, that there are variations in the degree of cytoplasm release from one envelope to another. Though variations are likely, they should be rather small because each envelope studied is first examined for lack of endogenous energy source, indicative of lack of cytoplasm [Ravid and Eisenbach, 1984a,b]. Therefore the remnants of CheA and ATP in the envelopes are probably at very low concentrations, much below substrate quantities. Thus it seems that this explanation may hold only if extremely low concentrations of CheY−phosphate are sufficient to cause clockwise rotation in envelopes.

4. An explanation analogous to the one in 3 above, but for intact bacteria, is that the strains used in the experiments with CheY overproduction carried the deletion Δ(cheA−cheZ)2209, which causes the formation of two CheA::CheZ fusion proteins [Kuo and Koshland, 1987; Wolfe et al., 1988]. One of these proteins still contains the long polypeptide of CheA, which may be sufficient for CheY phosphorylation [Hess et al.,1988b].

In principle, any of the above explanations or a combination thereof may hold. Further experiments are required to determine which, if any, of the explanations is correct.

One direct way to test the hypothesis that phosphorylated CheY is the clockwise signal is to include CheY together with CheA and ATP in flagellated envelopes and to look for restoration of clockwise rotation in comparison to the same but CheA-free envelopes. Such studies are in progress (R. Barak and M. Eisenbach, unpublished data). Until there is direct evidence for the role of CheY−phosphate, one may not conclude that the phosphorylation of CheY is the whole picture. The overall mechanism of the transduction of the excitatory signal within the cytoplasm is probably more complicated.

d. Acetyladenylate. Another low-molecular-weight substance that may be required for the activity of CheY is acetyladenylate. Wolfe et al. [1988] found that acetate, but not the more potent repellent benzoate, enhanced clockwise rotation in strains having normal levels of CheY but lacking other cytoplasmic Che proteins and MCPs. The effect was not observed in the absence of CheY. By using metabolic inhibitors and mutants deficient in acetate metabolism and by modifying the growth conditions, Wolfe and colleagues showed that acetyladenylate is the substance needed, together with CheY, for generating clockwise rotation and for normal chemotaxis. It is not clear at this stage whether the activation of CheY by acetyladenylate is correlated with the hypothesized activation of CheY by CheA-mediated phosphorylation and, if it is, how. Because CheY phosphorylation by CheA was observed in the absence of acetyladenylate [Borkovich et al., 1989], it seems reasonable to assume that acetyladenylate is somehow involved in the interaction of CheY–phosphate with the switch rather than in the phosphorylation itself. This involvement should be in trace amounts, to comply with the observation that CheY causes clockwise rotation in cytoplasm-free envelopes [Ravid et al., 1986]. Other possibilities are that acetyladenylate acts on the switch rather than on CheY or that its action is to counteract the function of CheZ and thus to avoid dephosphorylation of CheY or its removal from the switch. Again, experiments with cell envelopes containing CheY, acetyladenylate, and perhaps also other *che* gene products may clarify the picture. Because it is reasonable to assume that the metabolic state of bacteria may affect the chemotaxis process directly and because acetyladenylate is related (via acetyl-CoA) to the citric acid (Krebs) cycle, it is possible that the effect of acetyladenylate on the apparent activity of CheY is the link between the metabolic state of the bacteria and the chemotaxis process.

3. Model. To suggest a model for the transduction of the excitatory signal in the cytoplasm, let us summarize the observations discussed above that have been made about the excitation process.

i. The direction of flagellar rotation in the absence of cytoplasmic Che proteins is exclusively counterclockwise.

ii. A mutant deleted of the *cheA, cheW,* or *cheY* gene is always counterclockwise biased. An unstimulated mutant deleted of the *cheZ* gene is always clockwise biased.

iii. The MCP can trigger clockwise and counterclockwise signals. The counterclockwise signal may be one that actively terminates the clockwise signal.

iv. The excitatory signal is quickly deactivated in vivo.

v. CheY interacts with the flagellar switch both in vivo and in vitro and causes clockwise rotation.

vi. Tethered, cytoplasm-free cell envelopes can rotate only in one direction, either counterclockwise (wild-type envelopes) or clockwise (envelopes from switch mutants or CheY-containing envelopes from wild type). They seldom reverse.

vii. Acetyladenylate might be required in vivo intracellularly for expressing the activity of CheY.

viii. There is an ATP requirement for clockwise rotation. The requirement is at the level of the cytoplasm.

ix. CheA is autophosphorylated in vitro by ATP.

x. Phosphorylated CheA phosphorylates CheY in vitro and, to a lesser degree, CheB.

xi. Many *cheA* mutants have a phosphorylation-related defect.

xii. CheY-phosphate is unstable and quickly releases inorganic phosphate in vitro.

xiii. CheZ acts on the interaction of CheY with the switch in vivo and terminates it. CheZ has no effect in the absence of CheY.

xiv. CheZ enhances the dephosphorylation of CheY in vitro.

xv. CheW and MCP together enhance the CheA-mediated phosphorylation of CheY in vitro.

xvi. The effect of CheZ on CheY (observation xiv) is dominant over the effect of CheW on CheY (observation xv).

xvii. CheY interacts with CheA in vitro in stoichiometric, not catalytic, ratios.

xviii. CheA and CheW are required for transduction of the signal from MCP in vivo.

xix. MCP-mediated enhancement of the rate of CheA phosphorylation is dependent on the presence of CheY.

xx. CheA and CheW form a complex in vitro.

xxi. Based on a consensus sequence, CheW appears to have a nucleotide-binding site.

Because no experimental data are available with regard to the function of CheW and the data for the functions of other Che proteins are, at best, incomplete, every model suggested at this stage will be deficient and merely a speculation. Nevertheless, such a model warrants publication because—to quote a proverb attributed to Picasso—"a model is a lie that helps you see the truth," and it may serve as a working hypothesis for future experiments. A speculative model for repellent-stimulated excitation process, in which I try to comply with most of the observations above, is proposed below. In addition to the listed observations, the model is based on two ideas that were discussed above, for which the evidence is indirect and incomplete: a) Only CheY–phosphate

Fig. 10.   Schematic model for excitatory signal transduction triggered by repellents. The drawing is for a single stimulatory event. Under continuous stimulation, the MCP conformation in panels D–H should be clockwise (MCP^{cw}), and the cycle shown in Figure 12 should function. See text for details.

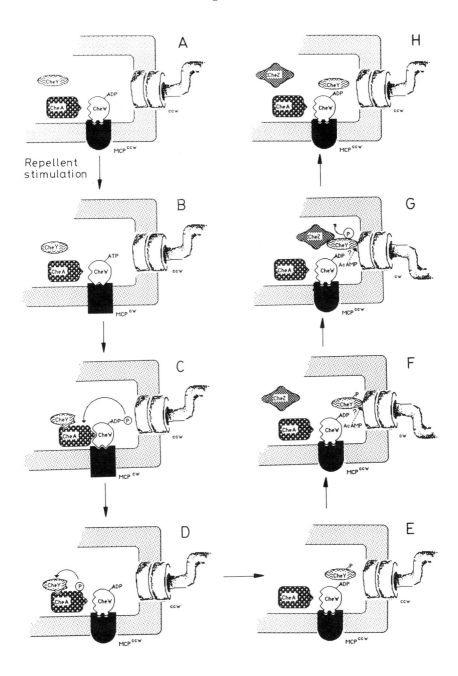

can interact with the switch and bring about clockwise rotation, and b) MCP can be in distinct clockwise and counterclockwise conformations (MCP^{cw} and MCP^{ccw}, respectively). The model is schematically drawn in Figure 10 for repellent stimulation, and it consists of the following stages and steps.

1. Repellent stimulation (either repellent addition or attractant removal) shifts the conformation of MCP from the counterclockwise (Fig. 10A) to the clockwise (Fig. 10B) conformation. (Based on observation iii and idea b.)

2. CheW, reminiscent of G proteins in eukaryotic systems [Dunlap et al., 1987; Gilman, 1987], binds either ATP or ADP. MCP^{cw} has high affinity for CheW(ATP), whereas MCP^{ccw} has high affinity for CheW(ADP). Thus the change from MCP^{ccw} to MCP^{cw} in response to repellent stimulation results in a conformational change of CheW that facilitates exchange of ATP for ADP and, at the same time, increases the affinity of CheW for CheA (Fig. 10B). (Based on observations viii, xviii, xx, xxi, and idea b. The basis for the proposed direct interaction between the MCP and CheW is the recent finding of Liu and Parkinson [personal communication] that there is allele-specific suppression between *tsr* and *cheW* mutations. Furthermore, the existence of MCP–CheW and CheW–CheA complexes is indicated by the observation of Parkinson [personal communication] that overexpression of CheW has a very inhibitory effect on chemotaxis in wild-type cells, inhibition that can be removed by expressing either MCP or CheA at high levels. This suggests that these three proteins are in mutual interaction. There is no information in the literature for the number of CheW molecules per cell; therefore the stoichiometry between MCP [at least 3,500 MCP molecules per cell; Clarke and Koshland, 1979; Hazelbauer and Harayama, 1983] and CheW is unknown.)

3. CheW(ATP) binds CheA, which in turn binds CheY. As a result of CheY binding, the phosphorylation of CheA is enhanced (Fig. 10C). (Based on observations xv and xvii–xx. The complex between CheA and CheY is proposed on the basis of observation xix [Borkovich et al., 1989]. The requirement of CheW to be bound to the MCP while phosphorylating CheA provides the reason for the observation that a mutant deleted for all the MCPs can rotate its flagella counterclockwise only. This requirement, however, is not absolute, because CheW in the absence of MCP [but in the presence of CheA] can augment clockwise rotation. Yet MCP^{cw} can further enhance the clockwise bias provided that CheW is present [Liu and Parkinson, personal communication].)

4. As a consequence of CheA phosphorylation, the complex CheA–CheY is detached from CheW and CheY is phosphorylated by CheA (Fig. 10D). (Observations x and xi.)

5. CheY–phosphate, just formed, is detached from CheA (Fig. 10E), interacts with the switch, and causes it to change into the clockwise conformation (Fig. 10F). (Observations i, ii, and v and idea a.)

6. As long as CheY–phosphate is bound to the switch, the switch is in the clockwise conformation. Only when CheY is dephosphorylated by CheZ (Fig. 10G) can it detach from the switch and the latter can relax to the energetically favored counterclockwise conformation (Fig. 10H). (Observations i, ii, iv, vi, xii–xiv and xvi and idea a. See Khan and Macnab [1980a] and Eisenbach et al. [1990b] for discussions about the energy levels of the switch. It is assumed here that spontaneous dephosphorylation of CheY [Hess et al., 1988c; Wylie et al., 1988] can occur only when the protein is free; when it is bound to the switch [Fig. 10F], CheZ is needed for the task. This assumption, however, is not obligatory for the model.)

Figure 10 was drawn for a single event of stimulation. It should be noted that as long as the repellent stimulation persists, the clockwise conformation of MCP will prevail (unlike Fig. 10D). MCP^{cw} can return to MCP^{ccw} only when the repellent stimulation ceases (as in Fig. 10) or adaptation commences (see section V.B.1.). If these conditions are not fulfilled, another cycle, starting with step 2, can operate in parallel to steps 4–6.

In the case of attractant stimulation, the mechanism of excitation appears to be different than just the reverse mechanism, because neither CheW nor CheZ are obligatory for counterclockwise signaling [Stewart et al., 1988; Liu and Parkinson, personal communication]. It is possible that counterclockwise signaling involves CheA binding to MCP^{ccw} with a resultant inhibition of CheA phosphorylation, thus accounting for observation iii, i.e., that the counterclockwise signal is active. Furthermore, CheW(ADP) perhaps stabilizes the counterclockwise conformation of MCP, as indicated by the finding of Liu and Parkinson (personal communication) that excessive levels of CheW within the cell cause counterclockwise rotation. It is also possible that the activity of CheZ is regulatable, thus that attractant stimulation either activates CheZ or makes it available. P. Matsumura (personal communication) recently found evidence for a complex between the short polypeptide of CheA and CheZ. Matsumura precipitated either of these proteins by specific antibodies and then probed with antibodies against the other protein. On the basis of this finding it is possible to postulate that CheA regulates the activity or the availability of CheZ as well.

What is the case under unstimulated conditions? What does determine the conformation of the switch then? Because the flagella reverse stochastically and there is no reversal synchrony among flagellar motors on a given cell in the absence of a stimulus [Macnab and Han, 1983; Ishihara et al., 1983], the effect on the switch should be local. It is not likely that the MCP fluctuates between clockwise and counterclockwise conformations and thus affects the switch. If this were the case, all the flagella on a given cell should have reversed synchronously. Thus the switch either fluctuates between its clockwise and counterclockwise conformations without any stimulation, spending more time in the counterclockwise conformation because of being energetically favored [Khan and Macnab, 1980a; Eisenbach et al., 1990b], or responds to occasional encounters with CheY–phosphate. The former alternative of uncontrolled switching is not likely, because in such a case the phenotypic behavior of a CheA$^-$, CheW$^-$, or CheY$^-$ mutant should have been the same as that of the wild type. This is not the case. Furthermore, low levels of CheY–phosphate are maintained even in the presence of CheZ [Borkovich et al., 1989].

A legitimate question that may result from the model is why is there a need for a mediator (CheW) between CheA and the MCP. In principle, if CheA could interact directly with the MCP, the excitation should have been as efficient as in the current model. Two types of answers may be given here, one factual and the other argumentative. Factually, CheW enhances the CheA-mediated phosphorylation. This is so even in vitro [Borkovich et al., 1989]. But what is the logic behind such an arrangement? 1) It may provide initial amplification. The gain of the processing system for a positive signal (attractant stimulation) in *E. coli* is very high [Berg, 1988]. Although the gain may be lower in processing a negative signal [Koshland et al., 1988], any model for signal transduction should contain a step or steps of amplification. According to the model, one molecule of repellent can stimulate several cycles of CheW(ADP)–CheW(ATP) exchange, during which time several CheY–phosphate molecules are formed [cf. steps b–e in Fig. 12, below). Thus one molecule of CheW can activate, in principle, many CheA and CheY molecules. (There appears to be a large excess of nonactive CheY molecules in the cell; Table III.) 2) Such an arrangement fits the central role of CheA in regulating the signal transduction process. CheW presumably fullfils in the excitation process a role similar to the one that CheB fullfils in the adaptation process (see section V.B.1.). In other words, this design allows CheA to sense the MCP conformation via CheW and, at the same time, to affect this conformation via CheB. As shown in Figure 11, such an arrangement together with the interaction of CheA with CheY indeed confers CheA a central regulatory role.

The model can provide immediate explanations for all the phenotypes observed in chemotaxis mutants. 1) CheA$^-$ and CheY$^-$ mutants are counterclockwise biased because of being unable to make CheY–phosphate. 2) An unstimulated CheZ$^-$ mutant is clockwise biased because of being unable to dephosphorylate CheY. The response delay time of this mutant for attractants is abnormally long [Segall et al., 1982; Block et al., 1982] because the level of CheY–phosphate in the cell may be abnormally high and its life time is prolonged in the absence of functional CheZ. Note that the response-delay time for attractants depends, according to the model, on the rate of CheY dephosphorylation. 3) CheW$^-$ mutants as well as mutants deleted of all their MCPs rotate only counterclockwise because of being unable to make CheY–

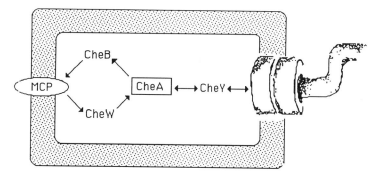

Fig. 11. A simplified scheme for emphasizing the central role of CheA in regulating signal transduction in bacterial chemotaxis.

phosphate. The phosphorylation of CheY by free CheA is much slower than the CheW-mediated phosphorylation and cannot compete with the rapid dephosphorylation of CheY by CheZ [Borkovich et al., 1989]. 4) *chew chez* double mutants rotate clockwise (J.S. Parkinson, personal communication). Here, again, the fast phosphorylation pathway of CheY cannot occur because of the absence of CheW, but this time CheY can be slowly phosphorylated by CheA because the phosphatase (CheZ) is absent.

One point that has not been considered yet is the function of acetyladenylate in the excitation process (observation vii). In the absence of any experimental results to indicate the mode of function of acetyladenylate, the possibilities discussed above (see section V.A.2.d.) may all be valid and they all fit the model.

It was shown in section IV that there are several independent systems that transduce the sensory signal across the membrane. Do the signals from all these systems converge in the cytoplasm to one common pathway of signal transduction, or do the pathways remain separated? The little information that has been published indicates convergence. It appears that all the systems require the cytoplasmic transduction system that involves CheA, CheW, CheY, and CheZ. Thus, an *E. coli* mutant lacking the MCPs, CheA, and CheW is unable to respond to oxygen or to the PTS sugars fructose or mannose [Taylor et al., 1988]. A CheAWYZ$^+$ strain responds to these stimuli. How these systems integrate with the major transduction system is still obscure. For the PTS it is possible, e.g., that, enzyme II, like MCP, also binds CheW and thus triggers the chain of events discussed above. Another possibility is that one or more of the phosphate-intermediates in the cytoplasm (Fig. 5) functions like CheW or even CheA. For example, it is quite conceivable that enzyme III functions like CheW. The involvement of CheA or CheW alone in PTS chemotaxis has not been examined yet. To distinguish between these possibilities, *cheA* and *cheW* mutants should be tested for their chemotactic responsiveness to PTS sugars. Recent complementation assays indicate that the phosphorylation state of HPr is sensed by the chemotaxis system [Lengeler and Vogler, 1989]. It is possible, for instance, that HPr phosphorylates CheY or CheA. Another interesting possibility raised by J. Lengeler (personal communication) is that the phosphoryl-chemotaxis protein (PCP) of the PTS system dephosphorylates CheY just like CheZ does. (PCP is a putative protein that was postulated to react to changes in the phosphorylation/dephosphorylation equilibrium of HPr/enzyme I [Lengler, 1982].) This may explain the somewhat-intriguing observation of Taylor et al. [1988] that CheZ is not obligatory for chemotaxis to a PTS sugar (but is obligatory for chemotaxis to oxygen).

Nucleotide sequence analysis of pairs of genes, whose products are involved in mutual regulation in bacteria, indicated that it is possible to divide the proteins into two groups: sensors that identify specific stimuli (not chemotactic) in the environment and regulators that control the expression of specific genes in response to the stimuli [Ronson et al., 1987]. The sensors have about 200 amino acid residues in the C terminus that are conserved. The regulators have a conserved region of about 120 residues in the N terminus. Based on this observation, Kofoid and Parkinson [1988] examined additional bacterial proteins involved in other signaling systems, including the chemotaxis system, for the presence of the consensus domain of the sensor (''transmitter'') and that of the regulator (''receiver''). And indeed they found that the MCPs as well as enzymes II of the PTS had a transmitter consensus sequence, whereas CheB and CheY had the receiver sequence. CheW (J.S. Parkinson, personal communication) and CheZ [Kofoid and Parkinson, 1988] had partial receiver sequences. Interestingly, CheA had both the receiver and transmitter sequences: three domains (of which two are partial, one at each end of the molecule) with receiver sequence and one domain with transmitter sequence. The suggested model (Figs. 10, 11) is in line with these findings of Kofoid and Parkinson, which emphasize the central role of CheA in regulating signal transduction [see also Parkinson, 1988].

There is no doubt that a major breakthrough in the understanding of excitatory signaling in small bacterial species has been made in recent years. It is conceivable that the near future will further clarify the picture and will provide the missing segments of the puzzle.

B. Adaptation

The adaptation process is an obligatory part of every behavioral system. For being able to detect small changes in the concentration of a stimulant, the bacteria must have a means of adjusting to constant levels of the stimulant. Today at least two systems of adaptation are known in small bacteria, but only one of them has been sufficiently investigated to supply the molecular basis for its mechanism. Each of these systems will be dealt with separately.

1. MCP-dependent adaptation. The MCP-dependent adaptation was the first system to be discovered and intensively investigated. The main actor in this system is the MCP. The secondary actors—but not the least important— are the methyltransferase (CheR) and the methylesterase (CheB). The story began when it was found that L-methionine is essential for chemotaxis: methionine-depleted cells lost their ability to tumble and became generally nonchemotactic [Adler and Dahl, 1967; Aswad and Koshland, 1974; Springer et al., 1975]. The need for a continuous supply of methionine was for AdoMet [Armstrong, 1972a,b; Aswad and Koshland, 1975a]. The fact that AdoMet is a methyl donor initiated a search for methylation reactions involved in chemotaxis. Soon after, Kort et al. [1975] identified attractant-stimulated methylation of membrane proteins and named them MCPs. The kinetics of the attractant-stimulated methylation of MCP was comparable to the kinetics of the behavioral adaptation of the bacteria to the attractant, and, vice versa, the rate of the repellent-stimulated demethylation was comparable to that of the adaptation to the repellent. It was therefore assumed that the methylation system is responsible for the adaptation [Goy et al., 1977; Springer et al., 1979]. Strong supportive evidence for this assumption came from the findings that a *cheR* mutant [Goy et al., 1978; Parkinson and Revello, 1978], in which the MCP cannot be methylated because of a defective methyltransferase, and a *cheB* mutant [Yonekawa et al., 1983], in which the MCP cannot be methylated because of a defective methylesterase, were severely impaired in adaptation.

What is currently known about the main actors in this adaptation system? I shall restrict myself to information that appears to be relevant to signal transduction. Other details can be found in the excellent review of Stewart and Dahlquist [1987] and in other reviews.

a. MCP. Much has been said about the MCPs in section IV.A., so only the aspects related to methylation and adaptation will be discussed here. In general, methylation of proteins is found either as *N*-methylation of basic amino acids, lysine or histidine, or as carboxymethylation of acidic residues, aspartate or glutamate. The common carboxymethylation in eukaryotes is of the aspartate residue [Clarke, 1985; van Waarde, 1987]. This is not the case in prokaryotes, where the methylation of MCP occurs only on glutamate residues [Kleene et al., 1977; Van der Werf and Koshland, 1977]. There are four to five methylation sites per molecule of MCP, of which two are glutamine residues converted to glutamate by CheB-catalyzed deamidation [Kehry et al., 1983; Terwilliger and Koshland, 1984; Nowlin et al., 1987, 1988]. Interestingly, no single methylation site is absolutely required for the function of the MCP, but loss of even a single methylatable residue prolongs the time required for adaptation [Nowlin et al., 1988]. This observation, taken together with the well-known phenomenon that methylation of MCP increases the clockwise bias of flagellar rotation whereas demethylation increases the counterclockwise bias, indicates that the MCP is modulatable to various extents by the methylation reaction and that these modulations are efficiently translated to signals affecting the flagellar switch. The level of MCP methylation is determined by the relative rates of its methylation and demethylation by the *cheR* and *cheB* gene products.

b. CheR. Like most other *che* gene products (Table III), pure CheR is a monomer [Simms et al., 1987b]. There are only about 200 CheR molecules per wild-type *S. typhimurium* cell. Most of them are bound to the MCP [Simms et al., 1987b], in accordance with the finding of Ridgway et al. [1977] that CheR is located in both the cytoplasm and the cytoplasmic membrane. The affinity of CheR to the MCP is in the range of $K_d = 1$ μM (Stock et al., 1984], about one order of magnitude higher than to AdoMet, the other substrate of CheR [Simms et al., 1987b]. No other proteins besides the MCPs were found to be methylated by CheR [Springer and Koshland, 1977; Clarke et al., 1980]. The only other reaction in which CheR was found to participate in vivo is the synthesis of *S*-methylglutathione in *E. coli,* a substance that does not appear to have any role in chemotaxis [Terwilliger et al., 1986a]. Indirect evidence for an interaction of CheR with CheY was supplied by DeFranco et al. [1979], who studied the functional homology of chemotaxis genes in *E. coli* and *S. typhimurium.* They found that both CheR and CheY from *E. coli* must be supplied to an *S. typhimurium* mutant lacking either of these proteins. Unlike most other Che proteins that are interspecies specific, this interaction between CheR and CheY is species specific. The CheR protein is a very slow enzyme (10 [mol methyl] · [mol enzyme]$^{-1}$ · min^{-1} at 30°C), so slow that it takes about 6 sec to accomplish a single methylation event [Simms et al., 1987b; Stock and Simms, 1987]. This sluggishness fits well the observed kinetics of the adaptation process. The methylation rate of MCP by CheR is not constant for each glutamate residue. For example, two sites on MCP II are readily methylated, and the other two sites are methylated 10–30-fold slower [Terwilliger et al., 1986c]. The relatively slow rate of the methylation, on the one hand, and the observation that *cheR* mutants are excitable and have normal excitation latencies [Block et al., 1982], on the other hand, strongly support the idea, mentioned above, that CheR and the methylation reaction are involved only in the adaptation process. The activity of CheR in vitro is enhanced by attractants and reduced by repellents [Kleene et al., 1979].

c. CheB. Like CheR, CheB is also found during subcellular fractionation to be located in both the cytoplasm and the cytoplasmic membrane [Ridgway et al., 1977], in spite of being a soluble cytoplasmic protein [Snyder et al., 1984; Simms et al., 1985]. CheB is a thiol enzyme [Snyder et al., 1984]. It contains two cysteine residues, of which one is crucial for the activity of the enzyme and is adjacent to a putative nucleotide-binding fold [Simms et al.,

1987a]. There is a remarkable sequence homology between the entire length of the CheY protein and the N terminus domain of CheB [A. Stock et al., 1985], which fits well with the phosphorylatability of both CheB and CheY by CheA (see section V.A.2.). CheB has two functions in chemotaxis: It demethylates the γ-glutamyl methyl esters of the MCP, forming methanol and γ-glutamyl carboxylate as products [Stock and Koshland, 1978; Toews and Adler, 1979); and it catalyzes the deamidation reaction discussed above, in which two glutamines on each MCP are transformed to methylatable glutamates. The deamidation reaction is irreversible. The methylesterase activity is specific for MCP [Snyder et al., 1984] and is fully maintained in the C-terminal half of CheB [Simms et al., 1985; Stewart and Dahlquist, 1988]. This activity in vitro is 5–10-fold higher when CheB is phosphorylated [Hess et al., 1988a; Stock et al., 1988b]. The function of the N-terminal region in vivo appears to be regulation of the activity of the protein [Stewart and Dahlquist, 1988]. This was not observed in vitro [Borczuk et al., 1986]. Like CheR, CheB is also not involved in the excitation but only in the adaptation process [Block et al., 1982; Yonekawa et al., 1983]. Its activity is affected by stimuli, albeit differently than CheR: attractants inhibit the demethylation activity, and repellents enhance it [Toews et al., 1979; Kehry et al., 1984]. This response of CheB to chemotactic stimuli requires the presence of CheA [Springer and Zanolari, 1984; Stewart and Dahlquist, 1988]. The response to repellents requires also CheW [Stewart and Dahlquist, 1988]. As in the case of CheR and CheY, there is circumstantial evidence for functional interaction between CheB and CheZ [DeFranco et al., 1979].

Based on the observations summarized above, it is apparent that methylation of MCP is the basis of adaptation of *E. coli* or *S. typhimurium* to attractants, whereas demethylation is the basis of adaptation to repulsive stimuli. Hazelbauer et al. [1989] have nicely established that methylation is crucial for MCP-dependent chemotaxis. They substituted alanyl residues for the methyl-accepting sites on MCP III, thus knocking out completely the methylatability of the protein without altering significantly its structure and stability. A mutant carrying this substituted MCP III and lacking other MCPs was normally excitable by ribose, an MCP III attractant, but it was not adaptable.

Of great interest is the recent observation of cross-talk among different MCPs. Hazelbauer et al. [1989] constructed a mutant carrying the substituted alanine-for-glutamate MCP III and normal MCPs I, II, and IV. They found that the chemotaxis defect caused by the lack of methyl-accepting sites on MCP III could be suppressed by the presence of the other MCPs, indicating that adaptation can commence by methylation of an MCP other than the one that was excited. Accordingly, Sanders and Koshland [1988] found that stimulation of MCP II by aspartate resulted in methylation of MCP I. Thus, while the excitation process is strictly MCP specific, the adaptation process is not. This finding endorses the idea discussed in section V.A. that the clockwise and counterclockwise signals transmitted by the MCPs are two active signals. The finding also suggests that methylation of MCP does not simply restore its prestimulus conformation, i.e., adaptation does not necessarily mean resetting the whole system to the starting point. The same conclusion emerges from studies of the mutual effects of two attractants interacting with the same MCP. MCP II has distinct binding sites for its ligand attractants maltose (being in complex with the maltose-binding protein) and aspartate [Mowbray and Koshland, 1987; Wolff and Parkinson, 1988]. Although saturating concentrations of either aspartate or maltose do not block the chemotactic response to the other attractant, thus confirming the distinct site for each attractant, the magnitude of the response is reduced [Wolff and Parkinson, 1988]. This reduced response implies not only that conformational changes at one site affect the signaling efficiency at the other site, but also that the adaptation process does not simply reverse the attractant-stimulated conformational change of the MCP [Wolff and Parkinson, 1988].

Are the MCPs, CheR, CheB, and AdoMet the only actors in the MCP- dependent adaptation? Probably not. Based on studies with ATP-depleted cells of *S. typhimurium*, Smith et al. [1988] have shown that there is no need in ATP for methylation (other than for the synthesis of AdoMet). However, as discussed above, the CheB protein is phosphorylated by CheA, and this phosphorylation enhances its activity and hence lowers the methylation level of MCP. Thus the methylation–demethylation process itself may not need ATP, but the signal for adaptation seems to involve ATP. Other actors may be the CheA and CheW proteins, because the aspartate-induced methylation of MCP I (but not of MCP II) requires the presence of these proteins [Sanders and Koshland, 1988] and because CheW overproduction causes a significant increase in the level of MCP methylation [Stewart et al., 1988]. Obviously, a clear distinction is made here between the methylation or the actual adaptation processes, on the one hand, and the signal for adaptation, on the other hand.

What is the signal for adaptation? Does stimulation of MCP trigger both the excitation and adaptation processes simultaneously or is there a kind of feedback mechanism for adaptation? Measurements carried out by Berg and Tedesco [1975] and endorsed by Kehry et al. [1985] apparently negate the former possibility, i.e., that the excitation and adaptation processes commence in parallel. In these measurements it was demonstrated that it is possible to adjust the magnitude of a positive stimulus (an attractant) through one MCP so as to balance exactly a negative stimulus (a repellent) through another MCP so that no behavioral response is observed. The adaptation time of a positive stimulus is longer than that of an equivalent negative stimulus, e.g., cells will adapt to addition of an attractant after a longer period of time than to the removal of the attractant. Therefore, if both the excitation and adaptation processes commenced simultaneously, the expected behavior of a mixture of positive and negative stimuli would be a transient negative response, i.e., a fast shift to clockwise bias and a gradual return to the unstimulated behavior. This has not been observed [cf. Stewart and Dahlquist, 1987]. Thus it appears that the signal for methylation and adaptation is triggered only subsequent to the initiation of the excitation process. This idea of a feedback mechanism is further supported by the findings (discussed above) that the demethylation activity is regulated by CheA [Springer and Zanolari, 1984] and also requires CheW [Stewart et al., 1988], that CheA phosphorylates CheB in vitro [Hess et al., 1988c] and increases its activity [Hess et al., 1988a; Stock et al., 1988b], and that methylation of MCP I, stimulated by an attractant for MCP II, requires CheA and CheW [Sanders and Koshland, 1988].

How does this feedback mechanism of MCP-dependent adaptation integrate within the general mechanism of signal transduction? Let us summarize the experimental observations that should be now incorporated into the model of signaling.

1. Methylation of MCP adapts the cell to attractants. This methylation is catalyzed by the methyltransferase CheR.

2. Demethylation of MCP adapts the cell to repulsive stimuli. The process is catalyzed by the methylesterase CheB.

3. Methylation of MCP increases the clockwise bias of flagellar rotation. Demethylation increases the counterclockwise bias.

4. The methylation process, assayed in vitro, is enhanced by attractants and inhibited by repellents. The demethylation process is enhanced by repellents and inhibited by attractants.

5. CheA is involved in the modulation of CheB activity by attractants, and both CheA and CheW are involved in its modulation by repellents.

6. Adaptation does not reset the conformation of the MCP to the prestimulus conformation.

7. Stimulation of one MCP can lead to methylation of another MCP with consequent adaptation. This cross-talk requires both CheA and CheW.

8. CheR and CheY may interact with each other and so may CheB and CheZ.

9. The turnover of CheR is very low and so is the number of CheR molecules per cell.

10. The degree of CheB phosphorylation in vitro by CheA is one order of magnitude lower than that of CheY.

11. Phosphorylation of CheB increases its esterase activity.

Considering these observations, the model may be expanded to include the adaptation process as follows. On the basis of observation 6, nine major conformational degrees of MCP should be considered: nonstimulated, attractant-stimulated, and repellent-stimulated conformations (designated as MCP, Att-MCP, and Rep-MCP, respectively), and in each of them the MCP may be highly methylated, or it may have medium or low levels of methylation (MCP_H, MCP_M, and MCP_L, respectively). Some of these conformations are clockwise conformations (MCP^{cw}), i.e., they transmit a clockwise signal, and the others are counterclockwise conformations (MCP^{ccw}). As long as the repellent stimulation persists, the cycle described for the excitation process (steps 1–5 on p. 176) can continue, subjected to the limitation of step 6 (p. 177). Under these conditions, the MCP conformation in Figure 10D–G should be $Rep\text{-}MCP_M^{cw}$, i.e., a repulsive stimulus (either repellent addition or attractant removal) causes the following reaction:

$$MCP_M^{ccw/cw} \xrightarrow{\text{repellent}} Rep\text{-}MCP_M^{cw}$$

Adaptation to repellents is caused by CheB-dependent demethylation of MCP. As a result of demethylation, the MCP conformation is changed to the counterclockwise conformation and CheY–phosphate is no longer formed. This is probably the reason for observation 3, that demethylation increases the counterclockwise bias.

How is the demethylation process regulated according to the model? As discussed in section V.A.3. and as suggested by observation 8, CheB and CheZ may form a complex in the cytoplasm. Because of the analogy of the N-domain of CheB to the entire length of CheY, it is reasonable to assume that CheB can form a complex with CheA similar to the CheA–CheY complex, though with a smaller prevalence and lower affinity. Thus interaction of CheB–CheZ with CheA may result in formation of CheA–CheB, during which CheA phosphorylates CheB and activates it to demethylate the MCP. CheZ is now free to dephosphorylate CheY–phosphate and thus to terminate the clockwise rotation. In this manner both the switch and MCP conformations are simultaneously modulated by CheZ and CheB, respectively.

According to the model, the sequence of events (for both the excitation and adaptation processes) that follow a repellent stimulation may be written as in Figure 12. As long as the repellent stimulation persists and adaptation is not yet effective, a cycle consisting of steps b–e can operate many times and produce much CheY–phosphate. Step f completes the excitation process. Some CheZ is always present and therefore the cycle b–e should continuously operate to produce sufficient amounts of CheY(P) and to compete with the CheZ-catalyzed dephosphorylation of CheY (step g). During adaptation, however, significant amounts of CheZ are produced in step h. Steps h–j are involved in the adaptation of the MCP, and step g in the adaptation of the switch.

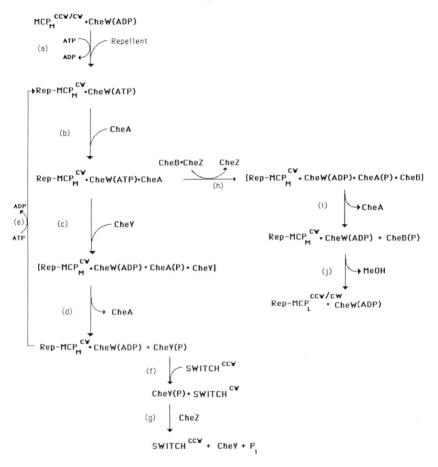

Fig. 12.   Sequence of excitation and adaptation events that follow a repellent stimulation.

In analogy, the sequence of events that follow an attractant stimulation may be described as follows:

k. $MCP_M^{ccw/cw}$–CheW(ADP) + attractant → Att-MCP_M^{ccw}–CheW(ADP).

To account for observation 5, CheZ may become available or active and CheB inactive by:

l. CheB–CheZ + CheA → CheB–CheA + CheZ.

Whatever the mechanism is for CheZ activation, the switch acquires or remains in the counterclockwise conformation according to step g in Figure 12 or according to any of the mechanisms discussed on p. 177, and the adaptation affects the MCP according to step m:

CheR

m. Att-MCP$_M^{ccw}$–CheW(ADP) + AdoMet $\rightarrow$
    Att-MCP$_H^{ccw/cw}$–CheW(ADP) + S-adenosylhomocysteine.

Now CheY(P) can be regenerated by a cycle similar to that in steps b–e in Figure 12.

How, according to the model, is the adaptation in response to a large-step stimulation so much slower than the excitation? For the case of attractant stimulation, the presumed cause of the difference is the sluggishness of CheR and the low number of CheR molecules per cell (observation 9). For the case of repellent stimulation, the proposed cause of the difference is the low degree of CheB phosphorylatability (observation 10).

All the observations but one were taken into account in the adaptation model. The observation that was not considered is the inhibition of the methylation reaction by repellents. This can be done by assuming that CheR is active (CheR*) only when it is in a complex with CheY (observation 8) and that the two forms are in equilibrium:

n. CheR*–CheY $\rightleftharpoons$ CheR + CheY.

The dissociation constant of CheR*–CheY is presumably very low. Excitation by repellents temporarily consumes CheY (eq. c in Fig. 12), shifting the equilibrium in eq. n to dissociation of the complex and resulting in a temporary decrease in CheR activity. As the adaptation proceeds, free CheY is formed (eq. g) and the equilibrium in eq. n is shifted back to association, thus restoring activity to CheR. The extremely small number of CheR molecules per cell enables regulation of CheR activity by CheY without perturbing other processes. Thus, during CheR activation, the formation of the complex CheR*–CheY has no significant effect on the concentration of CheY that is available to other functions of CheY. This is because of the small number of CheR molecules per cell [Simms et al., 1987b], on the one hand, and the relatively large number of CheY molecules per cell [Ravid et al., 1986], on the other hand. It would be of great interest to put to test the validity of eq. n as follows: 1) Examine whether addition of purified CheY to in vitro assays of CheR activity will increase the turnover of CheR, as the equation predicts. Thus the very low activity of purified CheR found in vitro by Simms et al.

[1987b] may be the consequence of CheY absence in those in vitro assays. On the other hand, in the cell-free extract used by Kleene et al. [1979] in their assays for examining the effects of attractants and repellents on the methylation activity in vitro, CheY was presumably present. 2) Examine whether the level of MCP methylation in a *cheY* mutant is as low as in a *cheR* mutant, as the equation predicts.

It is interesting to note that, according to the model, addition of a repellent to unstimulated bacteria is not completely equivalent to removal of an attractant from a suspension of adapted bacteria. Although both cases are considered as repellent stimulation, the initial conformation of the MCP is different in each case, $MCP_M^{ccw/cw}$ and $Att-MCP_L^{ccw/cw}$, respectively. The different conformations may be the cause of the difference in the behavioral responses to stimulus addition and removal observed, for example, in *che* mutants [Eisenbach et al., 1990b].

Although this review is devoted primarily to *E. coli* and *S. typhimurium,* the adaptation in *B. subtilis* is remarkably different, and the comparison between these species deserves special attention. Similarities between the adaptation machineries of *E. coli* and *B. subtilis* include: structural resemblance of the MCPs [Nowlin et al., 1985]; similar sites of methylation [Burger-Cassler and Ordal, 1982]; functional homologies between *E. coli's* CheR and CheB and *B. subtilis's* methyltransferase and methylesterase, respectively [Burgess-Cassler and Ordal, 1982; Nettleton and Ordal, 1989]; and attractant-stimulated crosstalk between MCPs [Bedale et al., 1988; Sanders and Koshland, 1988]. In spite of these similarities, the methylation and demethylation processes appear to fulfill in *B. subtilis* the opposite roles that they do in *E. coli:* Adaptation to attractants was found to be correlated with demethylation, whereas MCP methylation is apparently correlated with the excitation process [Goldman and Ordal, 1981; Goldman et al., 1982; Thoelke et al., 1988]. Accordingly, attractants inhibit methylation and stimulate demethylation of MCP in vitro [Goldman and Ordal, 1984]. Repellents have no effect on MCP methylation in vivo (M. Thoelke, W. Bedale, and G. Ordal, unpublished observations cited in Thoelke et al. [1987]). Another difference is that in *B. subtilis* there appears to exist an intermediate methyl acceptor, to which methyl groups are transferred from the MCPs. It was suggested by Tholke et al. [1987] that demethylation of this intermediate is the function that affords adaptation to attractants and formation of methanol. More studies are required for proposing a model for the excitation and adaptation processes in *B. subtilis* and for relating them to the corresponding mechanisms in *E. coli* and *S. typhimurium.*

2. MCP-independent adaptation. This type of adaptation covers two classes of stimuli: those that work by MCP-dependent excitation and those that work by MCP-independent excitation. Each of these classes will be dealt with separately.

The issue of MCP-independent adaptation (sometimes called methylation-independent adaptation) to MCP-mediated stimuli was controversial for a number of years. Recent careful studies appear, however, to remove at least some of the controversy. Chemotactic responses to MCP-mediated attractants or repellents were observed in the absence of CheR and/or CheB [J. Stock et al., 1981, 1985a,b; Block et al., 1982]. The responses were observed in swarm plates, capillary assays, and with tethered cells. The responses, however, were not complete and were only to small or moderate concentrations of stimulants. In light of these observations, J. Stock and Stock [1987] proposed that MCP methylation does not provide the main adaptation mechanism but rather provides a back-up mechanism. They suggested that MCP deamidation could be a way for adaptation. On the other hand, Hazelbauer et al. [1989] have demonstrated that MCP III is unable to mediate net chemotactic response in the absence of methylation. Weis and Koshland [1988] found no chemotactic response (i.e., no migration) to the attractant aspartate in a CheR$^-$CheB$^-$ mutant by the light-scattering technique of Dahlquist et al. [1972] unless excessive concentrations of aspartate were used. Under similar conditions but in tethering experiments, the mutant did respond and adapt. By careful studies of various mutants and using both the tethering and light-scattering techniques, Weis and Koshland [1988] were able to eliminate the possibilities that the MCP-independent adaptation was the result of 1) leakiness of the mutants used, 2) response to gradients of MCP-independent stimuli formed during the experiment (e.g., an oxygen gradient), or 3) cross-talk with another MCP-independent system. They showed that the methylation system is required for adaptation, but that CheR$^-$CheB$^-$ mutants can respond to steep gradients of stimuli though with an efficiency that is far below wild-type cells. The mechanism of this MCP-independent adaptation is not known. To examine what components of the chemotaxis machinery are involved in this adaptation, mutants having excitable but nonadaptable MCPs and lacking one or more of the Che proteins should be studied in temporal assays or tethering experiments.

Niwano and Taylor [1982] found that an *E. coli* mutant lacking MCPs I–III adapts to PTS sugars or oxygen stimulation. In retrospect, the finding that adaptation to these stimuli is MCP independent, is not surprising. It is quite reasonable that the entity that is involved in excitation is the one on which adaptation should act, thus restoring its ability to sense further changes in the stimulant concentration. In other words, if MCP is not involved in the excitation process, there is no apparent reason for being involved in the adaptation process. The mechanism of this MCP-independent adaptation is not known. As discussed in section V.A.3., enzyme II may have a function similar to that of MCP in excitation. If this is so, enzyme II is a likely candidate to be involved in the adaptation process to PTS sugars. As a matter of fact, rephosphorylation of any of the components involved in the excitation (Fig. 5) may initiate the adaptation process. Further studies are required to reveal the mechanism of adaptation to PTS sugars. (See Taylor, this volume, for a discussion of the adaptation process to oxygen.)

C. Signal Transduction in Large Bacterial Species

In large bacterial species (longer than 20 μm), a signaling system of the type discussed in section V.A. is not suitable, because it is a short-range signal [Segall et al., 1985]. Furthermore, even if the signal were not inactivated during traveling along this large distance, the delay response time would be longer than 4 sec for a 20 μm-long bacterium [Lee and Fitzsimons, 1976]. Because the delay response time in such species is very short, e.g., less than 20 msec in *Spirillum volutans* [Krieg et al., 1967], a signal based on diffusion is improbable. The signal should be electrical in nature [Berg, 1975; Snyder et al., 1981]. Direct electrophysiological measurements in large bacterial species have not been reported, but there is circumstantial evidence to support the idea of electrical signaling. Neurotoxins that block the activity of ion channels were found to inhibit the motility of *Rhodospirillum rubrum* and *Thiospirillum jenense* [Faust and Doetsch, 1971] and the chemotactic activity of *Spirochaeta aurantia* [Goulbourne and Greenberg, 1983b]. The act of reversing polarity, or of breaking or closing the electrical circuit, caused *Spirill. volutans* in an electric field instantly to reverse [Caraway and Krieg, 1972]. This observation is at best suggestive, because electric field was found to be effective also in *E. coli* [Eisenbach et al., 1983b], in which signaling is not electrical in nature. Perhaps the most convincing evidence was obtained in *Spiroch. aurantia,* in which a voltage clamp was found to inhibit chemotaxis [Goulbourne and Greenberg, 1983a], unlike in *E. coli* and *B. subtilis* [Margolin and Eisenbach, 1984]. It should be pointed out that although electrical signaling was suggested also for gliding cyanobacteria [Murvanidze and Glagolev, 1982], direct electrical measurements with vibrating electrodes did not reveal extracellular electrical currents [Jaffe and Walsby, 1985].

Although the mode of signaling appears to be known in large bacterial species, nothing is known of the identity of the transmitter and the receiver in them. These species may contain MCPs analogous to those of *E. coli, S. typhimurium,* or *B. subtilis* [Nowlin et al.,1985], but their involvement in signaling is at best speculative. The situation is similar with regard to adaptation. Attractant-stimulated carboxymethylation was found in *Spiroch. aurantia* [Kathariou and Greenberg, 1983], but the mechanism of adaptation and the role of methylation in this mechanism are totally unknown. Ironically, the electrical nature of the excitatory signal in large bacterial species had been known many years before anything was learned about the nature of the excitation signal in small bacterial species. Nowadays, the wheel has turned. Very little progress has been made in large species, probably because their genetic systems are less tractable. Much progress has been made in small bacteria because of the availability of genetic and molecular biology approaches that could be combined with other biochemical and physiological approaches.

VI. SIGNAL TRANSDUCTION IN OTHER TAXES

Bacteria are known to perform other types of taxis, in addition to chemotaxis, depending on the species and their habitat. Taxes that have been reported are thermotaxis, phototaxis, magnetotaxis, osmotaxis, and galvanotaxis. Recently also rheotaxis was identified in gliding mycoplasma [Rosengarten et al., 1988], i.e., gliding of cells upstream in a moving fluid, but nothing is known on the mechanism of this phenomenon. The most recently discovered phenomena in *E. coli* are the last ones in the list, osmotaxis and galvanotaxis. I shall deal with them first.

Li et al. [1988] found by using the chemical-in-plug method that most chemicals at concentrations as high as 1 OsM repel *E. coli* cells. Even substances that are attractants at lower concentrations, e.g., D-galactose, D-ribose, D-glucose, and D-mannose (cf. Table I), were found to be repulsive at concentrations of 1 M and above. This was not the case with the most potent attractants, L-serine, L-aspartate, and maltose, which were attractive at any concentration. In temporal assays, lower osmolarities than 1 OsM were sufficient to freeze the swimming of the bacteria for 1–2 min followed by incessant tumbling for up to hours [Li et al., 1988]. In analogy to repellents, which cause an attractant response (smooth swimming) upon their removal from the medium, it is interesting to know whether a change from high to normal osmolarity causes an attractant response. This has not been determined. However, the finding that *E. coli* are attracted to optimal osmolarities [Adler et al., 1988] is suggestive that this should indeed be the case. It appears that the chemotaxis machinery is involved in osmotaxis: Che⁻ mutants as well as mutants lacking MCPs I and II fail to carry out osmotaxis in the chemical-in-plug assay. It seems, however, that a large step increase in osmolarity may affect the flagellar motor directly, because even chemotaxis mutants, including switch mutants, respond in temporal assays to such an increase by tumbling that, surprisingly, results from counterclockwise rotation [Adler et al., 1988]. The sensing mechanism of either of these phenomena is not known.

Galvanotaxis in *E. coli* and *S. typhimurium* was discovered by Adler and Shi [1988] (see references cited there for earlier work in other bacterial species). Wild-type *E. coli* migrates toward the anode, whereas wild-type *S. typhimurium* migrates toward the cathode. Alignment of nonmotile bacteria in an electric field indicated that bacteria have a fixed dipole [Adler and Shi, 1988]. It is thus possible that galvanotaxis is composed of passive alignment and active swimming. Accordingly, tumbly bacteria show poor galvanotaxis, and none of the known gene products for chemotaxis is necessary for this type of taxis [Adler and Shi, 1988].

Similarly, magnetotaxis does not appear to have an active mechanism. Magnetosomes, composed of magnetite (Fe_3O_4) and located intracellularly, orient the cells in the geomagnetic field and thus direct them to swim along the lines of the magnetic field [see Blakemore, 1982, for a review]. A separate signaling system for magnetotaxis is therefore highly unlikely.

Although thermotaxis and especially phototaxis have been extensively investigated during the last decade, most of the research was at the level of the receptors and less, if any, at the level of signal transduction. From the little that is known, it appears that both the phototaxis and thermotaxis systems share the transduction system of the chemotaxis machinery. The difference between these systems seems to be at the receptor level rather than in the signal transduction. Recently, Spudich et al. [1988] and Alam et al. [1989] presented data that suggest the involvement of MCP-like membrane proteins in phototaxis of *H. halobium*. Phototaxis will not be dealt with here, and the reader is referred to Bogomolni and Spudich in this volume. *E. coli* has two thermoreceptors, MCPs I and II [Maeda and Imae, 1979; Mizuno and Imae, 1984; Imae, 1985]. MCP I mutants, defective in chemotaxis to serine, exhibit normal thermotaxis, indicating that there are distinct sites for serine binding and for thermosensing [Lee et al., 1988]. Adaptation to chemoattractants alter the thermosensing ability of the MCPs: MCP I, when adapted to L-serine, loses its ability to detect thermal stimuli; MCP II, when adapted to L-aspartate, generates an inverted sensory signal in response to thermal stimuli. It was suggested that the MCPs transduce the thermosensed signal across the membrane by conformational changes, and these changes are affected by the methylation levels of the MCPs [Mizuno and Imae, 1984; Imae, 1985]. Because the MCPs respond to alcohols that change the membrane fluidity [Eisenbach et al., 1990a] and the membrane fluidity is temperature dependent, it would be of interest to examine whether changing the fluidity of the membrane by rigidifying or fluidizing substances affects the thermoresponse of the bacteria. The transduction of the signal from the MCPs to the switch appears to be the same mechanism as in chemotaxis, because *cheA, cheW,* and *cheY* mutants do not respond to thermal stimuli [Imae, 1985].

Figure 13 shows the three major segments of the chemotaxis machinery: the membrane MCP, the cytoplasmic Che proteins, and the membrane switch–motor complex. The MCP is apparently a unique sensory transduction protein, having specific sensitivities to attractants, repellents, temperature changes, pH changes, and osmolarity changes. Some of the other stimuli do not use the MCPs but use other receptors that transduce the sensory signal to the chemotaxis machinery. Other extreme conditions may affect the motor directly.

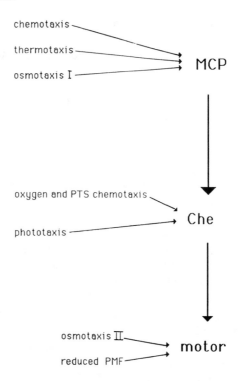

Fig. 13. A simplified scheme showing the involvement of the chemotaxis machinery in other taxes.

To conclude, the more that is known about the signal transduction in chemotaxis of bacteria, the more similarities to eukaryotic sensory systems (described elsewhere in this volume) emerge. It will not be a surprise if the molecular principles of signal transduction turn out to be universal, as is the case with genetics and metabolism.

ACKNOWLEDGMENTS

I thank H.C. Berg, G.L. Hazelbauer, J. Lengeler, K. Lewis, M. Manson, P. Matsumura, G. Ordal, J.S. Parkinson, and A. Wolfe for communicating manuscripts and experimental results before publication. J. Lengeler and J.S Parkinson are acknowledged for helpful discussions. H.C. Berg, K. Lewis, and J.S. Parkinson provided helpful comments and criticism. Work in my laboratory was supported by research grants from the U.S. National Institutes of Health (NIAID) and from the Minerva Foundation, Munich, Federal Republic of Germany.

VII. NOTE ADDED IN PROOF

Within the period of time between the date of the completion of this review and the date of its publication, several new observations, which support the model shown in Figures 10 and 12and discussed on pp. 173–180 and 185–189, were published. For example, the existence of ternary complexes involving CheA, CheW, and MCP was indicated by the studies of both Borkovich and Simon [Cell (1990) 63:1339–1348] and Gegner and Dahlquist [Proc Natl Acad Sci USA (1991) 88:750–754].

VIII. REFERENCES

Adler J (1965) Chemotaxis in *Escherichia coli*. Cold Spring Harbor Symp Quant Biol 30:289–292.

Adler J (1973) A method for measuring chemotaxis and use of the method to determine optimum conditions for chemotaxis by *Escherichia coli*. J Gen Microbiol 74:77–91.

Adler J (1978) Chemotaxis in bacteria. Harvey Lect 72:195–230.

Adler J (1985) The behavior of organisms. In Eisenbach M, Balaban M (eds): Sensing and Response in Microorganisms. Amsterdam: Elsevier, pp 9–13.

Adler J (1987) How motile bacteria are attracted and repelled by chemicals: An approach to neurobiology. Biol Chem Hoppe-Seyler 368:163–173.

Adler J, Dahl MM (1967) A method for measuring the motility of bacteria and for comparing random and non-random motility. J Gen Microbiol 46:161–173.

Adler J, Epstein W (1974) Phosphotransferase-system enzymes as chemoreceptors for certain sugars in *Escherichia coli* chemotaxis. Proc Natl Acad Sci USA 71:2895–2899.

Adler J, Hazelbauer GL, Dahl MM (1973) Chemotaxis towards sugars in *Escherichia coli*. J Bacteriol 115:824–847.

Adler J, Li C, Boileau AJ, Qi Y, Kung C (1988) Osmotaxis in *Escherichia coli*. Cold Spring Harbor Symp Quant Biol 53:19–22.

Adler J, Shi W (1988) Galvanotaxis in bacteria. Cold Spring Harbor Symp Quant Biol 53:23–25.

Alam M, Lebert M, Oesterhelt D, Hazelbauer GL (1989) Methyl-accepting taxis proteins in *Halobacterium halobium*. EMBO J 8:631–639.

Alam M, Oesterhelt D (1984) Morphology, function and isolation of halobacterial flagella. J Mol Biol 176:459–475.

Ames P, Parkinson JS (1988) Transmembrane signaling by bacterial chemoreceptors: *E. coli* transducers with locked signal output. Cell 55:817–826.

Anderson RA (1975) Formation of the bacterial flagellar bundle. In Wu TYT, Brokaw CJ, Brennen C (eds): Swimming and Flying in Nature. New York: Plenum, pp 45–56.

Arai T (1981) Effect of arsenate on chemotactic behavior of *Escherichia coli*. J Bacteriol 145:803–807.

Armitage JP, Keighley P, Evans MCW (1979) Chemotaxis in photosynthetic bacteria. FEMS Microbiol Lett 6:99–102.

Armitage JP, Macnab RM (1987) Unidirectional, intermittent rotation of the flagellum of *Rhodobacter sphaeroides*. J Bacteriol 169:514–518.

Armstrong JB (1972a) Chemotaxis and methionine metabolism in *Escherichia coli*. Can J Microbiol 18:591–596.

Armstrong JB (1972b) An *S*-adenosylmethionine requirement for chemotaxis in *Escherichia coli*. Can J Microbiol 18:1695–1701.

Aswad D, Koshland DE Jr (1974) Role of methionine in bacterial chemotaxis. J Bacteriol 118:640–645.

Aswad DW, Koshland DE Jr (1975a) Evidence for an *S*-adenosylmethionine requirement in the chemotactic behavior of *Salmonella typhimurium*. J Mol Biol 97:207–223.

Aswad D, Koshland DE Jr (1975b) Isolation, characterization and complementation of *Salmonella typhimurium* chemotaxis mutants. J Mol Biol 97:225–235.

Bedale WA, Nettleton DO, Sopata CS, Thoelke MS, Ordal GW (1988) Evidence for methyl group transfer between the methyl-accepting chemotaxis proteins in *Bacillus subtilis*. J Bacteriol 170:223–227.

Berg HC (1975) Chemotaxis in bacteria. Annu Rev Biophys Bioeng 4:119–136.

Berg HC (1988) A physicist look at bacterial chemotaxis. Cold Spring Harbor Symp Quant Biol 53:1–9.

Berg HC, Anderson RA (1973) Bacteria swim by rotating their flagellar filaments. Nature 245:380–382.

Berg HC, Brown DA (1972) Chemotaxis in *Escherichia coli* analysed by three-dimensional tracking. Nature 239:500–504.

Berg HC, Manson MD, Conley MP (1982) Dynamics and energetics of flagellar rotation in bacteria. Soc Exp Biol Symp 35:1–31.

Berg HC, Tedesco PM (1975) Transient response to chemotactic stimuli in *Escherichia coli*. Proc Natl Acad Sci USA 72:3235–3239.

Black RA, Hobson AC, Adler J (1980) Involvement of cyclic GMP in intracellular signaling in the chemotactic response of *Escherichia coli*. Proc Natl Acad Sci USA 77:3879–3883.

Black RA, Hobson AC, Adler J (1983) Adenylate cyclase is required for chemotaxis to phosphotransferase system sugars by *Escherichia coli*. J Bacteriol 153:1187–1195.

Black SD (1987) P-450 cytochromes: Structure and function. Adv Enzymol 60:35–87.

Blakemore RP (1982) Magnetotactic bacteria. Annu Rev Microbiol 36:217–238.

Block SM, Segall JE, Berg HC (1982) Impulse responses in bacterial chemotaxis. Cell 31:215–226.

Bollinger J, Park C, Harayama S, Hazelbauer GL (1984) Structure of the Trg protein: Homologies with and differences from other sensory transducers of *Escherichia coli*. Proc Natl Acad Sci USA 81:3287–3291.

Boos W, Gordon AS, Hall RE, Price HD (1972) Transport properties of the galactose-binding protein of *Escherichia coli:* Substrate-induced conformational change. J Biol Chem 247:917–924.

Borczuk A, Staub A, Stock J (1986) Demethylation of bacterial chemoreceptors is inhibited by attractant stimuli in the complete absence of the regulatory domain of the demethylating enzyme. Biochem Biophys Res Commun 141:918–923.

Borczuk A, Stock A, Stock J (1987) *S*-adenosylmethionine may not be essential for signal transduction during bacterial chemotaxis. J Bacteriol 169:3295–3300.

Borkovich KA, Kaplan N, Hess JF, Simon MI (1989) Transmembrane signal transduction in bacterial chemotaxis involves ligand-dependent activation of phosphate group transfer. Proc Natl Acad Sci USA 86:1208–1212.

Borochov H, Shinitzky M (1976) Vertical displacement of membrane proteins mediated by changes in microviscosity. Proc Natl Acad Sci USA 73:4526–4530.

Bourret RB, Hess JF, Borkovich KA, Pakula AA, Simon MI (1989) Protein phosphorylation in chemotaxis and two-component regulatory systems of bacteria. J Biol Chem 264:7085–7088.

Bourret RB, Hess JF, Simon MI (1990) Conserved aspartate residues and phosphorylation in signal transduction by the chemotaxis protein CheY. Proc Natl Acad Sci USA 87:41–45.

Boyd A, Kendall K, Simon MI (1983) Structure of the serine chemoreceptor in *Escherichia coli*. Nature 301:623–626.

Brass JM, Higgins CF, Foley M, Rugman PA, Birmingham J, Garland PB (1986) Lateral diffusion of proteins in the periplasm of *Escherichia coli*. J Bacteriol 165:787–794.

Burgess-Cassler A, Ordal GW (1982) Functional homology of *Bacillus subtilis* methyltransferase II and *Escherichia coli* cheR protein. J Biol Chem 257:12835–12838.

Caraway BH, Krieg NR (1972) Uncoordination and recoordination in *Spirillum volutans*. Can J Microbiol 18:1749–1759.

Changeux J-P, Revah F (1987) The acetylcholine receptor molecule: Allosteric sites and the ion channel. Trends Neurosci 10:245–250.

Clarke S (1985) Protein carboxyl methyltransferases: Two distinct classes of enzymes. Annu Rev Biochem 54:479–506.

Clarke S, Koshland DE, Jr (1979) Membrane receptors for aspartate and serine in bacterial chemotaxis. J Biol Chem 254:9695–9702.

Clarke S, Sparrow K, Panasenko S, Koshland DE Jr (1980) In vitro methylation of bacterial chemotaxis proteins: Characterization of protein methyltransferase activity in crude extracts of *Salmonella typhimurium*. J Supramol Struct 13:315–328.

Clegg DO, Koshland DE Jr (1984) The role of a signaling protein in bacterial sensing: Behavioral effects of increased gene expression. Proc Natl Acad Sci USA 81:5056–5060.

Conley MP, Wolfe AJ, Blair DF, Berg HC (1989) Both CheA and CheW are required for reconstitution of chemotactic signaling in *Escherichia coli*. J Bacteriol 171:5190–5193.

Dahlquist FW, Lovely P, Koshland DE Jr (1972) Quantitative analysis of bacterial migration in chemotaxis. Nature [New Biol] 236:120–123.

DeFranco AL, Koshland DE Jr (1981) Molecular cloning of chemotaxis genes and overproduction of gene products in the bacterial sensing system. J Bacteriol 147:390–400.

DeFranco AL, Parkinson JS, Koshland DE, Jr (1979) Functional homology of chemotaxis genes in *Escherichia coli* and *Salmonella typhimurium*. J Bacteriol 139:107–114.

DePamphilis ML, Adler J (1971) Attachment of flagellar basal bodies to the cell envelope: Specific attachment to the outer, lipopolysaccharide membrane and the cytoplasmic membrane. J Bacteriol 105:396–407.

Dunlap K, Holz GG, Rane SG (1987) G proteins as regulators of ion channel function. Trends Neurosci 10:241–244.

Ebner R, Lengeler JW (1988) DNA sequence of the gene *scrA* encoding the sucrose transport protein EnzymeII[Scr] of the phosphotransferase system from enteric bacteria: Homology of the EnzymeII[Scr] and EnzymeII[Bgl] proteins. Mol Microbiol 2:9–17.

Eisenbach M (1982) Changes in membrane potential of *Escherichia coli* in response to temporal gradients of chemicals. Biochemistry 21:6818–6825.

Eisenbach M (1983) Changes in membrane potential of *Escherichia coli* stimulated by galactose. In Oplatka A, Balaban M (eds): Biological Structures and Coupled Flows. New York: Academic Press, pp 349–352.

Eisenbach M (1990) Functions of the flagellar modes of rotation in bacterial motility and chemotaxis. Mol Microbiol 4:161–167.

Eisenbach M, Adler J (1981) Bacterial cell envelopes with functional flagella. J Biol Chem 256:8807–8814.

Eisenbach M, Constantinou C, Aloni H, Shinitzky M (1990a) Repellents for *Escherichia coli* operate neither by changing membrane fluidity nor being sensed by periplasmic receptors during chemotaxis. J Bacteriol 172:5218–5224.

Eisenbach M, Margolin Y, Ciobotariu A, Rottenberg H (1984) Distinction between changes in membrane potential and surface charge upon chemotactic stimulation of *Escherichia coli*. Biophys J 45:463–467.

Eisenbach M, Margolin Y, Ravid S (1985) Excitatory signaling in bacterial chemotaxis. In Eisenbach M, Balaban M (eds): Sensing and Response in Microorganisms. Amsterdam: Elsevier, pp 43–61.

Eisenbach M, Matsumura P (1988) In vitro approach to bacterial chemotaxis. Botan Acta 101:105–110.

Eisenbach M, Raz T, Ciobotariu A (1983a) A process related to membrane potential involved in bacterial chemotaxis to galactose. Biochemistry 22:3293–3298.

Eisenbach M, Wolf A, Welch M, Caplan SR, Lapidus IR, Macnab RM, Aloni H, Asher O (1990b) Pausing, switching and speed fluctuation of the bacterial flagellar motor and their relation to motility and chemotaxis. J Mol Biol 211:551–563.

Eisenbach M, Zimmerman JE, Ciobotariu A, Fischler H, Korenstein R (1983b) Electric field effects on bacterial motility and chemotaxis. Bioelectrochem Bioenerg 10:499–510.

Engelmann W (1882) Bot Ztg 40:419–426.

Falke JJ, Koshland DE, Jr (1987) Global flexibility in a sensory receptor: A site-directed cross-linking approach. Science 237:1596–1600.

Faust MA, Doetsch RN (1971) Effect of drugs that alter excitable membranes on the motility of *Rhodospirillum rubrum* and *Thiospirillum jenense*. Can J Microbiol 17:191–196.

Galloway RJ, Taylor BL (1980) Histidine starvation and adenosine 5'-triphosphate depletion in chemotaxis of *Salmonella typhimurium*. J Bacteriol 144:1068–1075.

Gangola P, Rosen BP (1987) Maintenance of intracellular calcium in *Escherichia coli*. J Biol Chem 262:12570–12574.

Gegner JA, Dahlquist FW (1991) Signal transduction in bacteria: CheW forms a reversible complex with the protein kinase CheA. Proc Natl Acad Sci USA 88:750–754.

Gilman AG (1987) G proteins: Transducers of receptor-generated signals. Annu Rev Biochem 56:615–649.

Glagolev AN (1980) Reception of the energy level in bacterial taxis. J Theor Biol 82:171–185.

Glagolev AN, Sherman MY (1983) The glucose phosphotransferase system is involved in *Escherichia coli* oxygen taxis. FEMS Microbiol Lett 17:147–150.

Glagolev AN, Skulachev VP (1978) The proton pump is a molecular engine of motile bacteria. Nature 272:280–282.

Goldman DJ, Ordal GW (1981) Sensory adaptation and deadaptation by *Bacillus subtilis*. J Bacteriol 147:267–270.

Goldman DJ, Ordal GW (1984) In vitro methylation and demethylation of methyl-accepting chemotaxis proteins in *Bacillus subtilis*. Biochemistry 23:2600–2606.

Goldman DJ, Worobec SW, Siegel RB, Hecker RV, Ordal GW (1982) Chemotaxis in *Bacillus subtilis:* Effects of attractants on the level of methylation and methyl-accepting chemotaxis proteins and the role of demethylation in the adaptation process. Biochemistry 21:915–920.

Gotz R, Schmitt R (1987) *Rhizobium meliloti* swims by unidirectional, intermittent rotation of right-handed flagellar helices. J Bacteriol 169:3146–3150.

Goulbourne EA, Jr, Greenberg EP (1983a) A voltage clamp inhibits chemotaxis of *Spirochaeta aurantia*. J Bacteriol 153:916–920.

Goulbourne EA, Jr, Greenberg EP (1983b) Inhibition of *Spirochaeta aurantia* chemotaxis by neurotoxins. J Bacteriol 155:1443–1445.

Goy MF, Springer MS, Adler J (1977) Sensory transduction in *Escherichia coli:* Role of a protein methylation reaction in sensory adaptation. Proc Natl Acad Sci USA 74:4964–4968.

Goy MF, Springer MS, Adler J (1978) Failure of sensory adaptation in bacterial mutants that are defective in a protein methylation reaction. Cell 15:1231–1240.

Harayama S, Bollinger J, Iino T, Hazelbauer GL (1983) Characterization of the *mgl* operon of *Escherichia coli* by transposon mutagenesis and molecular cloning. J Bacteriol 153:408–415.

Harwood CS, Rivelli M, Ornston LN (1984) Aromatic acids are chemoattractants for *Pseudomonas putida*. J Bacteriol 160:622–628.

Hazelbauer GL, Harayama S (1979) Mutants in transmission of chemotactic signals from two independent receptors of *E. coli*. Cell 16:617–625.

Hazelbauer GL, Harayama S (1983) Sensory transduction in bacterial chemotaxis. Int Rev Cytol 81:33–70.

Hazelbauer GL, Harayama S, Engstrom P (1982) Special features of chemotaxis towards maltose. Ann Microbiol 133A:191–194.

Hazelbauer GL, Park C, Nowlin DM (1989) Adaptational "crosstalk" and the crucial role of methylation in chemotactic migration by *Escherichia coli*. Proc Natl Acad Sci USA 86:1448–1452.

Hedblom ML, Adler J (1980) Genetic and biochemical properties of *Escherichia coli* mutants with defects in serine chemotaxis. J Bacteriol 144:1048–1060.

Hedblom ML, Adler J (1983) Chemotactic response of *Escherichia coli* to chemically synthesized amino acids. J Bacteriol 155:1463–1466.

Heffetz D, Zick Y (1986) Receptor aggregation is necessary for activation of the soluble insulin receptor kinase. J Biol Chem 261:889–894.

Hess JF, Bourret RB, Oosawa K, Matsumura P, Simon MI (1988a) Protein phosphorylation and bacterial chemotaxis. Cold Spring Harbor Symp Quant Biol 53:41–48.

Hess JF, Bourret RB, Simon MI (1988b) Histidine phosphorylation and phosphoryl group transfer in bacterial chemotaxis. Nature 336:139–143.

Hess JF, Oosawa K, Kaplan N, Simon MI (1988c) Phosphorylation of three proteins in the signaling pathway of bacterial chemotaxis. Cell 53:79–87.

Hess JF, Oosawa K, Matsumura P, Simon MI (1987) Protein phosphorylation is involved in bacterial chemotaxis. Proc Natl Acad Sci USA 84:7609–7613.

Hildebrand E, Dencher N (1975) Two photosystems controlling behavioral responses of *Halobacterium halobium*. Nature 257:46–48.

Hirota N, Kitada M, Imae Y (1981) Flagellar motors of alkalophilic *Bacillus* are powered by an electrochemical potential gradient of Na^+. FEBS Lett 132:278–280.

Hobot JA, Carlemalm E, Villiger W, Kellenberger E (1984) Periplasmic gel: New concept resulting from reinvestigation of bacterial cell envelope ultrastructure by new methods. J Bacteriol 160:143–152.

Igo MM, Silhavy TJ (1988) EnvZ, a transmembrane environment sensor of *Escherichia coli* K-12, is phosphorylated in vitro. J Bacteriol 170:5971–5973.

Iino T (1985) Structure and assembly of flagella. In Nanninga N (ed): Molecular Cytology of *Escherichia coli*. London: Academic Press, pp 9–37.

Iino T, Komeda Y, Kutsukake K, Macnab RM, Matsumura P, Parkinson JS, Simon MI, Yamaguchi S (1988) New unified nomenclature for the flagellar genes of *Escherichia coli* and *Salmonella typhimurium*. Microbiol Rev 52:533–535.

Imae Y (1985) Molecular mechanism of thermosensing in bacteria. In Eisenbach M, Balaban M (eds): Sensing and Response in Microorganisms. Amsterdam: Elsevier, pp 73–81.

Imae Y, Oosawa K, Mizuno T, Kihara M, Macnab RM (1987) Phenol: A complex chemoeffecter in bacterial chemotaxis. J Bacteriol 169:371–379.

Ingham CJ, Armitage JP (1987) Involvement of transport in *Rhodobacter sphaeroides* chemotaxis. J Bacteriol 169:5801–5807.

Ishihara A, Segall JE, Block SM, Berg HC (1983) Coordination of flagella on filamentous cells of *Escherichia coli*. J Bacteriol 155:228–237.

Jaffe LF (1979) Control development by ionic currents. In Cone RA, Dowling JE (eds): Membrane Transduction Mechanisms. New York: Raven Press, pp 199–231.

Jaffe LF, Walsby AE (1985) An investigation of extracellular electrical currents around cyanobacterial filaments. Biol Bull 168:476–481.

Jakinovich W, Jr (1981) Comparative study of sweet taste specificity. In Cagan RH, Kare MR (eds): Biochemistry of Taste and Olfaction. New York: Academic Press, pp 117–138.

Kaback HR (1968) The role of phosphoenolpyruvate–phosphotransferase system in the transport of sugars by isolated membrane preparations of *Escherichia coli*. J Biol Chem 243:3711–3724.

Kaplan N, Simon MI (1988) Purification and characterization of the wild-type and mutant carboxy-terminal domain of *Escherichia coli* Tar chemoreceptor. J Bacteriol 170:5134–5140.

Kar L, de Croos PZ, Johnson ME, Matsumura P (1991) Binding of phosphate containing compounds to CheY protein: Specificity and affinity. (Submitted).

Kar L, Lee Y, Matsumura P, Johnson M (1988) Interaction of spin-labeled analog of adenosine triphosphate with the chemotaxis protein, CheY, abstracted. Biophys J 53:74a.

Kathariou S, Greenberg EP (1983) Chemoattractants elicit methylation of specific polypeptides in *Spirochaeta aurantia*. J Bacteriol 156:95–100.

Kehry MR, Bond MW, Hunkapiller MW, Dahlquist FW (1983) Enzymatic deamidation of methyl-accepting chemotaxis proteins in *Escherichia coli* catalyzed by the *cheB* gene product. Proc Natl Acad Sci USA 80:3599–3603.

Kehry MR, Doak TG, Dahlquist FW (1984) Stimulus-induced changes in methylesterase activity during chemotaxis in *Escherichia coli*. J Biol Chem 259:11828–11835.

Kehry MR, Doak TG, Dahlquist FW (1985) Sensory adaptation in bacterial chemotaxis: Regulation of demethylation. J Bacteriol 163:983–990.

Khan S, Macnab RM (1980a) The steady-state counterclockwise/clockwise ratio of bacterial flagellar motors is regulated by proton-motive force. J Mol Biol 138:563–597.

Khan S, Macnab RM (1980b) Proton chemical potential, proton electrical potential and bacterial motility. J Mol Biol 138:599–614.

Kihara M, Macnab RM (1981) Cytoplasmic pH mediates pH taxis and weak-acid repellent taxis of bacteria. J Bacteriol 145:1209–1221.

Kleene SJ, Hobson AC, Adler J (1979) Attractants and repellents influence methylation and demethylation of methyl-accepting chemotaxis proteins in an extract of *Escherichia coli*. Proc Natl Acad Sci USA 76:6309–6313.

Kleene SJ, Toews ML, Adler J (1977) Isolation of glutamic acid methyl ester from an *Escherichia coli* membrane protein involved in chemotaxis. J Biol Chem 252:3214–3218.

Kofoid EC, Parkinson JS (1988) Transmitter and receiver modules in bacterial signaling proteins. Proc Natl Acad Sci USA 85:4981–4985.

Koiwai O, Hayashi H (1979) Studies on bacterial chemotaxis: IV. Interaction of maltose receptor with a membrane-bound chemosensing component. J Biochem 86:27–34.

Kondoh H (1980) Tumbling chemotaxis mutants of *Escherichia coli:* Possible gene-dependent effect of methionine starvation. J Bacteriol 142:527–534.

Kondoh H, Ball CB, Adler J (1979) Identification of a methyl-accepting chemotaxis protein for the ribose and galactose chemoreceptors of *Escherichia coli*. Proc Natl Acad Sci USA 76:260–264.

Kort EN, Goy MF, Larsen SH, Adler J (1975) Methylation of a membrane protein involved in bacterial chemotaxis. Proc Natl Acad Sci USA 72:3939–3943.

Koshland DE, Jr (1980) Bacterial Chemotaxis as a Model Behavioral System. New York: Raven Press.

Koshland DE, Jr, Sanders DA, Weis RM (1988) Roles of methylation and phosphorylation in the bacterial sensing system. Cold Spring Harbor Symp Quant Biol 53:11–17.

Kossmann M, Wolff C, Manson MD (1988) Maltose chemoreceptor of *Escherichia coli:* Interaction of maltose-binding protein and the Tar signal transducer. J Bacteriol 170:4516–4521.

Krieg NR, Tomelty JP, Wells JS, Jr (1967) Inhibition of flagellar coordination in *Spirillum volutans*. J Bacteriol 94:1431–1436.

Krikos A, Conley MP, Boyd A, Berg HC, Simon MI (1985) Chimeric chemosensory transducers of *Escherichia coli*. Proc Natl Acad Sci USA 82:1326–1330.

Krikos A, Mutoh N, Boyd A, Simon MI (1983) Sensory transducers of *E. coli* are composed of discrete structural and functional domains. Cell 33:615–622.

Kundig W, Roseman S (1971a) Sugar transport: I. Isolation of a phosphotransferase system from *Escherichia coli*. J Biol Chem 246:1393–1406.

Kundig W, Roseman S (1971b) Sugar transport: II. Characterization of constitutive membrane-bound enzymes II of the *Escherichia coli* phosphotransferase system. J Biol Chem 246:1407–1418.

Kuo SC, Koshland DE, Jr (1987) Roles of *cheY* and *cheZ* gene products in controlling flagellar rotation in bacterial chemotaxis of *Escherichia coli*. J Bacteriol 169:1307–1314.

Kutsukake K, Iino T (1985) Refined genetic analysis of the region II *che* mutants in *Salmonella typhimurium*. Mol Gen Genet 199:406–409.

Lancet D, Pace U (1987) The molecular basis of odor recognition. Trends Biochem Sci 12:63–66.

Lapidus IR, Welch M, Eisenbach M (1988) Pausing of flagellar rotation is a component of bacterial motility and chemotaxis. J Bacteriol 170:3627–3632.

Larsen SH, Adler J, Gargus JJ, Hogg RW (1974a) Chemomechanical coupling without ATP: The source of energy for motility and chemotaxis in bacteria. Proc Natl Acad Sci USA 71:1239–1243.

Larsen SH, Reader RW, Kort EN, Tso W-W, Adler J (1974b) Change in direction of flagellar rotation is the basis of the chemotactic response in *Escherichia coli*. Nature 249:74–77.

Laszlo DJ, Fandrich BL, Sivaram A, Chance B, Taylor BL (1984) Cytochrome *o* as a terminal oxidase and receptor for aerotaxis in *Salmonella typhimurium*. J Bacteriol 159:663–667.

Lederberg J (1956) Linear inheritance in transductional clones. Genetics 41:845–871.

Lee AG, Fitzsimons JTR (1976) Motility in normal and filamentous forms of *Rhodospirillum rubrum*. J Gen Microbiol 93:346–354.

Lee L, Mizuno T, Imae Y (1988) Thermosensing properties of *Escherichia coli tsr* mutants defective in serine chemoreception. J Bacteriol 170:4769–4774.

Lengeler J (1975) Mutations affecting transport of the hexitols D-mannitol, D-glucitol, and galactitol in *Escherichia coli* K-12: Isolation and mapping. J Bacteriol 124:26–38.

Lengeler JW (1982) The biochemistry of chemoreception, signal-transduction and adaptation in bacterial chemotaxis. In Marme D, Marre E, Hertel R (eds): Plasmalemma and Tonoplast: Their Functions in the Plant Cell. Amsterdam: Elsevier, pp 337–344.

Lengeler J, Auburger A-M, Mayer R, Pecher A (1981) The phosphoenolpyruvate-dependent carbohydate: Phosphotransferase system enzymes II as chemoreceptors in chemotaxis of *Escherichia coli* K12. Mol Gen Genet 183:163–170.

Lengeler JW, Vogler AP (1989) Molecular mechanisms of bacterial chemotaxis towards PTS-carbohydrates. FEMS Microbiol Rev 63:81–92.

Li C, Boileau AJ, Kung C, Adler J (1988) Osmotaxis in *Escherichia coli*. Proc Natl Acad Sci USA 85:9451–9455.

Macnab RM (1977) Bacterial flagella rotating in bundles: A study in helical geometry. Proc Natl Acad Sci USA 74:221–225.

Macnab RM (1985) Biochemistry of sensory transduction in bacteria. In Colombetti G, Lenci F, Song P-S (eds): Sensory Perception and Transduction in Aneural Organisms. New York: Plenum Press, pp 31–46.

Macnab RM (1987a) Molecular architecture and assembly: Flagella. In Ingraham J, Low KB, Magasanik B, Schaechter M, Umbarger HE, Neidhardt FC (eds): *Escherichia coli* and *Salmonella typhimurium*: Cellular and Molecular Biology, Washington, DC: ASM Publications, pp 70–83.

Macnab RM (1987b) Motility and chemotaxis. In Ingraham J, Low KB, Magasanik B, Schaechter M, Umbarger HE, Neidhardt FC (eds): *Escherichia coli* and *Salmonella typhimurium*: Cellular and Molecular Biology. Washington, DC: ASM Publications, pp 732–759.

Macnab RM, Aizawa S-I (1984) Bacterial motility and the bacterial flagellar motor. Annu Rev Biophys Bioeng 13:51–83.

Macnab RM, DeRosier DJ (1988) Bacterial flagellar structure and function. Can J Microbiol 34:442–451.

Macnab RM, Han DP (1983) Asynchronous switching of flagellar motors on a single bacterial cell. Cell 32:109–117.

Macnab RM, Koshland DE, Jr (1972) The gradient-sensing mechanism in bacterial chemotaxis. Proc Natl Acad Sci USA 69:2509–2512.

Macnab RM, Ornston MK (1977) Normal-to-curly flagellar transitions and their role in bacterial tumbling: Stabilization of an alternative quaternary structure by mechanical force. J Mol Biol 112:1–30.

Maeda K, Imae Y (1979) Thermosensory transduction in *Escherichia coli:* Inhibition of the thermoresponse by L-serine. Proc Natl Acad Sci USA 76:91–95.

Manson MD, Blank V, Brade G, Higgins CF (1986) Peptide chemotaxis in *E. coli* involves the Tap signal transducer and the dipeptide permease. Nature 321:253–256.

Manson MD, Boos W, Bassford PJ, Jr, Rasmussen BA (1985) Dependence of maltose transport and chemotaxis on the amount of maltose-binding protein. J Biol Chem 260:9727–9733.

Manson MD, Tedesco PM, Berg HC (1980) Energetics of flagellar rotation in bacteria. J Mol Biol 138:541–561.

Manson MD, Tedesco P, Berg HC, Harold FM, van der Drift C (1977) A protonmotive force drives bacterial flagella. Proc Natl Acad Sci USA 74:3060–3064.

Margolin Y, Eisenbach M (1984) Voltage-clamp effects on bacterial chemotaxis. J Bacteriol 159:605–610 [Errata: 161 (1985) 823.]

Martinac B, Buechner M, Delcour AH, Adler J, Kung C (1987) Pressure-sensitive ion channel in *Escherichia coli*. Proc Natl Acad Sci USA 84:2297–2301.

Matsumura P, Rydel JJ, Linzmeier R, Vacante D (1984) Overexpression and sequence of the *Escherichia coli cheY* gene and biochemical activities of the CheY protein. J Bacteriol 160:36–41.

Matsushita T, Hirata H, Kusaka I (1988) Calcium channel blockers inhibit bacterial chemotaxis. FEBS Lett 236:437–440.

Matsuura S, Shioi J-I, Imae Y (1977) Motility in *Bacillus subtilis* driven by an artificial protonmotive force. FEBS Lett 82:187–190.

McNally D, Vacante D, Matsumura P (1985) Overexpression and partial purification of the *cheA* and *cheW* gene products, abstracted. Fed Proc 44:1768.

Mesibov R, Adler J (1972) Chemotaxis towards amino acids in *Escherichia coli*. J Bacteriol 112:315–326.

Metzner P (1931) Bewegung der Pflanzen, in Handworterbuch der Naturwissenschaften 2. Aufl., Jena.

Miller JB, Koshland DE, Jr (1977) Membrane fluidity and chemotaxis: Effects of temperature and membrane lipid composition on the swimming behavior of *Salmonella typhimurium* and *Escherichia coli*. J Mol Biol 111:183–201.

Milligan DL, Koshland DE, Jr (1988) Site-directed cross-linking: Establishing the dimeric structure of the aspartate receptor of bacterial chemotaxis. J Biol Chem 263:6268–6275.

Mizuno T, Imae Y (1984) Conditional inversion of the thermoresponse in *Escherichia coli*. J Bacteriol 159:360–367.

Mowbray SL, Foster DL, Koshland DE, Jr (1985) Proteolytic fragments identified with domains of the aspartate chemoreceptor. J Biol Chem 260:11711–11718.

Mowbray SL, Koshland DE, Jr (1987) Additive and independent responses in a single receptor: Aspartate and maltose stimuli on the Tar protein. Cell 50:171–180.

Mowbray SL, Petsko GA (1983) The X-ray structure of the periplasmic galactose binding protein from *Salmonella typhimurium* at 3.0-Å resolution. J Biol Chem 258:7991–7997.

Muller N, Heine H-G, Boos W (1985) Characterization of the *Salmonella typhimurium mgl* operon and its gene products. J Bacteriol 163:37–45.

Murvanidze GV, Glagolev AN (1982) Electrical nature of the taxis signal in Cyanobacteria. J Bacteriol 150:239–244.

Mutoh N, Oosawa K, Simon MI (1986) Characterization of *Escherichia coli* chemotaxis receptor mutants with null phenotypes. J Bacteriol 167:992–998.

Mutoh N, Simon MI (1986) Nucleotide sequence corresponding to five chemotaxis genes in *Escherichia coli*. J Bacteriol 165:161–166.

Nettleton DO, Ordal GW (1989) Functional homology of chemotactic methylesterases from *Bacillus subtilis* and *Escherichia coli*. J Bacteriol 171:120–123.

Ninfa AJ, Ninfa EG, Lupas AN, Stock A, Magasanik B, Stock J (1988) Crosstalk between bacterial chemotaxis signal transduction proteins and regulators of transcription of the Ntr regulon: Evidence that nitrogen assimilation and chemotaxis are controlled by a common phosphotransfer mechanism. Proc Natl Acad Sci USA 85:5492–5496.

Niwano M, Taylor BL (1982) Novel sensory adaptation mechanism in bacterial chemotaxis to oxygen and phosphotransferase substrates. Proc Natl Acad Sci USA 79:11–15.

Nowlin DM, Bollinger J, Hazelbauer GL (1987) Sites of covalent modification in Trg, a sensory transducer of *Escherichia coli*. J Biol Chem 262:6039–6045.

Nowlin DM, Bollinger J, Hazelbauer GL (1988) Site-directed mutations altering methyl-accepting residues of a sensory transducer protein. Proteins Struct Funct Genet 3:102–112.

Nowlin DM, Nettleton DO, Ordal GW, Hazelbauer GL (1985) Chemotactic transducer proteins of *Escherichia coli* exhibit homology with methyl-accepting proteins from distantly related bacteria. J Bacteriol 163:262–266.

Omirbekova NG, Gabai VL, Sherman MY, Vorobyeva NV, Glagolev AN (1985) Involvement of Ca^{2+} and cGMP in bacterial taxis. FEMS Microbiol Lett 28:259–263.

Oosawa K, Hess JF, Simon MI (1988a) Mutants defective in bacterial chemotaxis show modified protein phosphorylation. Cell 53:89–96.

Oosawa K, Imae Y (1983) Glycerol and ethylene glycol: Members of a new class of repellents of *Escherichia coli* chemotaxis. J Bacteriol 154:104–112.

Oosawa K, Imae Y (1984) Demethylation of methyl-accepting chemotaxis proteins in *Escherichia coli* induced by the repellents glycerol and ethylene glycol. J Bacteriol 157:576–581.

Oosawa K, Mutoh N, Simon MI (1988b) Cloning of the C-terminal cytoplasmic fragment of the Tar protein and effects of the fragment on chemotaxis of *Escherichia coli*. J Bacteriol 170:2521–2526.

Ordal GW (1977) Calcium ion regulates chemotactic behavior in bacteria. Nature 270:66–67.

Ordal GW (1985) Bacterial chemotaxis: Biochemistry of behavior in a single cell. CRC Crit Rev Microbiol 12:95–130.

Ordal GW, Gibson KJ (1977) Chemotaxis toward amino acids by *Bacillus subtilis*. J Bacteriol 129:151–155.

Ordal GW, Goldman DJ (1975) Chemotaxis away from uncouplers of oxidative phosphorylation in *Bacillus subtilis*. Science 189:802–805.

Ordal GW, Goldman DJ (1976) Chemotactic repellents of *Bacillus subtilis*. J Mol Biol 100: 103–108.

Ordal GW, Nettleton DO (1985) Chemotaxis in *Bacillus subtilis*. In Dubnau D (ed): The Molecular Biology of the Bacilli. New York: Academic Press, pp 53–72.

Padan E, Zilberstein D, Rottenberg H (1976) The proton electrochemical gradient in *Escherichia coli* cells. Eur J Biochem 63:533–541.

Park C, Hazelbauer GL (1986a) Mutations specifically affecting ligand interaction of the Trg chemosensory transducer. J Bacteriol 167:101–109.

Park C, Hazelbauer GL (1986b) Mutation plus amplification of a transducer gene disrupts general chemotactic behavior in *Escherichia coli*. J Bacteriol 168:1378–1383.

Parkinson JS (1976) *cheA*, *cheB*, and *cheC* genes of *Escherichia coli* and their role in chemotaxis. J Bacteriol 126:758–770.

Parkinson JS (1978) Complementation analysis and deletion mapping of *Escherichia coli* mutants defective in chemotaxis. J Bacteriol 135:45–53.

Parkinson JS (1981) Genetics of bacterial chemotaxis. Soc Gen Microbiol Symp 31:265–290.

Parkinson JS (1988) Protein phosphorylation in bacterial chemotaxis. Cell 53:1–2.

Parkinson JS, Hazelbauer GL (1983) Bacterial chemotaxis: Molecular genetics of sensory transduction and chemotactic gene expression. In Gene Function in Prokaryotes. Cold Spring Harbor, New York: Cold Spring Harbor Laboratory, pp 293–318.

Parkinson JS, Houts SE (1982) Isolation and behavior of *Escherichia coli* deletion mutants lacking chemotaxis functions. J Bacteriol 151:106–113.

Parkinson JS, Parker SR (1979) Interaction of the *cheC* and *cheZ* gene products is required for chemotactic behavior in *Escherichia coli*. Proc Natl Acad Sci USA 76:2390–2394.

Parkinson JS, Parker SR, Talbert PB, Houts SE (1983) Interactions between chemotaxis genes and flagellar genes in *Escherichia coli*. J Bacteriol 155:265–274.

Parkinson JS, Revello PT (1978) Sensory adaptation mutants of *Escherichia coli*. Cell 15:1221–1230.

Pecher A, Renner I, Lengeler JW (1983) The phosphoenolpyruvate-dependent carbohydrate: Phosphotransferase system enzymes II, a new class of chemosensors in bacterial chemotaxis. In Sund H, Veeger C (eds): Mobility and Recognition in Cell Biology. Berlin: Walter de Gruyter & Co., pp 517–531.

Pfeffer W (1881–1885) Lokomotorische Richtungsbewegung durch chemische Reize. Unters Botan Inst Tubingen 1:363–482.

Pfeffer W (1888) Ueber chemotaktische Bewegungen von Bakterien, Flagellaten und Volvocineen. Unters Botan Inst Tubingen 2:582–661.

Poole PS, Armitage J (1989) Role of metabolism in the chemotactic response of *Rhodobacter sphaeroides* to ammonia. J Bacteriol 171:2900–2902.

Postma PW, Lengeler JW (1985) Phosphoenolpyruvate:carbohydrate phosphotransferase system of bacteria. Microbiol Rev 49:232–269.

Rasched I, Shuman H, Boos W (1976) The dimer of the *Escherichia coli* galactose-binding protein. Eur J Biochem 69:545–550.

Ravid S, Eisenbach M (1984a) Direction of flagellar rotation in bacterial cell envelopes. J Bacteriol 158:222–230. [Errata: 159 (1984) 433.]

Ravid S, Eisenbach M (1984b) Minimal requirements for rotation of bacterial flagella. J Bacteriol 158:1208–1210.

Ravid S, Matsumura P, Eisenbach M (1986) Restoration of flagellar clockwise rotation in bacterial envelopes by insertion of the chemotaxis protein CheY. Proc Natl Acad Sci USA 83:7157–7161.

Repaske DR, Adler J (1981) Change in intracellular pH of *Escherichia coli* mediates the chemotactic response to certain attractants and repellents. J Bacteriol 145:1196–1208.

Richarme G (1982a) Interaction of the maltose-binding protein with membrane vesicles of *Escherichia coli*. J Bacteriol 149:662–667.

Richarme G (1982b) Associative properties of the *Escherichia coli* galactose binding protein and maltose binding protein. Biochem Biophys Res Commun 105:476–481.

Ridgway HF, Silverman M, Simon MI (1977) Localization of proteins controlling motility and chemotaxis in *Escherichia coli*. J Bacteriol 132:657–665.

Ronson CW, Nixon BT, Ausubel FM (1987) Conserved domains in bacterial regulatory proteins that respond to environmental stimuli. Cell 49:579–581.

Rosengarten R, Klein-Struckmeier A, Kirchhoff H (1988) Rheotactic behavior of a gliding mycoplasma. J Bacteriol 170:989–990.

Russo AF, Koshland DE, Jr (1983) Separation of signal transduction and adaptation functions of the aspartate receptor in bacterial sensing. Science 220:1016–1020.

Saier MH, Jr, Yamada M, Erni B, Suda K, Lengeler J, Ebner R, Argos P, Rak B, Schnetz K,

Lee CA, Stewart GC, Breidt F, Jr, Waygood EB, Peri KG, Postma PW, Doolittle RF (1988) Sugar permeases of the bacterial phosphoenolpyruvate- dependent phosphotransferase system: Sequence comparisons. FASEB J 2:199–208.

Saimi Y, Martinac B, Gustin MC, Culbertson MR, Adler J, Kung C (1988) Ion channels in *Paramecium*, yeast and *Escherichia coli*. Trends Biochem Sci 13:304–309.

Sanders DA, Gillece-Castro BL, Stock AM, Burlingame AL, Koshland DE, Jr (1989) Identification of the site of phosphorylation of the chemotaxis response regulator protein, CheY. J Biol Chem 264:21770–21778.

Sanders DA, Koshland DE, Jr (1988) Receptor interactions through phosphorylation and methylation pathways in bacterial chemotaxis. Proc Natl Acad Sci USA 85:8425–8429.

Segall JE, Block SM, Berg HC (1986) Temporal comparisons in bacterial chemotaxis. Proc Natl Acad Sci USA 83:8987–8991.

Segall JE, Ishihara A, Berg HC (1985) Chemotactic signaling in filamentous cells of *Escherichia coli*. J Bacteriol 161:51–59.

Segall JE, Manson MD, Berg HC (1982) Signal processing times in bacterial chemotaxis. Nature 296:855–857.

Seymour FWK, Doetsch RN (1973) Chemotactic responses by motile bacteria. J Gen Microbiol 78:287–296.

Shinitzky M (1984) Membrane fluidity and cellular functions. In Shinitzky M (ed): Physiology of Membrane Fluidity, Vol 1. Boca Raton, FL: CRC Press, pp 1–51.

Shioi J, Dang CV, Taylor BL (1987) Oxygen as attractant and repellent in bacterial chemotaxis. J Bacteriol 169:3118–3123.

Shioi J-I, Galloway RJ, Niwano M, Chinnock RE, Taylor BL (1982) Requirement of ATP in bacterial chemotaxis. J Biol Chem 257:7969–7975.

Shioi J, Imae Y, Oosawa F (1978) Proton-motive force and motility of *Bacillus subtilis*. J Bacteriol 133:1083–1088.

Shioi J, Tribhuwan RC, Berg ST, Taylor BL (1988) Signal transduction in chemotaxis to oxygen in *Escherichia coli* and *Salmonella typhimurium*. J Bacteriol 170:5507–5511.

Silverman M, Simon M (1974) Flagellar rotation and the mechanism of bacterial motility. Nature 249:73–74.

Silverman M, Simon M (1977a) Chemotaxis in *Escherichia coli:* Methylation of *che* gene products. Proc Natl Acad Sci USA 74:3317–3321.

Silverman M, Simon M (1977b) Identification of polypeptides necessary for chemotaxis in *Escherichia coli*. J Bacteriol 130:1317–1325.

Simms SA, Cornman EW, Mottonen J, Stock J (1987a) Active site of the enzyme which demethylates receptors during bacterial chemotaxis. J Biol Chem 262:29–31.

Simms SA, Keane MG, Stock J (1985) Multiple forms of the CheB methylesterase in bacterial chemosensing. J Biol Chem 260:10161–10168.

Simms SA, Stock AM, Stock JB (1987b) Purification and characterization of the *S*-adenosylmethionine:glutamyl methyltransferase that modifies membrane chemoreceptor proteins in bacteria. J Biol Chem 262:8537–8543.

Simon MI, Krikos A, Mutoh N, Boyd A (1985) Sensory transduction in bacteria. Curr Top Membr Transp 23:3–16.

Slocum MK, Halden NF, Parkinson JS (1987) Hybrid *Escherichia coli* sensory transducer with altered stimulus detection and signaling properties. J Bacteriol 169:2938–2944.

Slonczewski JL, Macnab RM, Alger JR, Castle AM (1982) Effects of pH and repellent tactic stimuli on protein methylation levels in *Escherichia coli*. J Bacteriol 152:384–399.

Smith RA, Parkinson JS (1980) Overlapping genes at the *cheA* locus of *Escherichia coli*. Proc Natl Acad Sci USA 77:5370–5374.

Smith JM, Rowsell EH, Shioi J, Taylor BL (1988) Identification of a site of ATP requirement for signal processing in bacterial chemotaxis. J Bacteriol 170:2698–2704.

Snyder MA, Stock JB, Koshland DE, Jr (1981) Role of membrane potential and calcium in chemotactic sensing by bacteria. J Mol Biol 149:241–257.

Snyder MA, Stock JB, Koshland DE, Jr (1984) Carboxymethyl esterase of bacterial chemotaxis. Methods Enzymol 106:321–330.

Springer MS, Goy MF, Adler J (1977) Sensory transduction in *Escherichia coli:* Two complementary pathways of information processing that involve methylated proteins. Proc Natl Acad Sci USA 74:3312–3316.

Springer MS, Goy MF, Adler J (1979) Protein methylation in behavioral control mechanisms and in signal transduction. Nature 280:279–284.

Springer MS, Kort EN, Larsen SH, Ordal GW, Reader RW, Adler J (1975) Role of methionine in bacterial chemotaxis: Requirement for tumbling and involvement in information processing. Proc Natl Acad Sci USA 72:4640–4644.

Springer MS, Zanolari B (1984) Sensory transduction in *Escherichia coli:* Regulation of the demethylation rate by the CheA protein. Proc Natl Acad Sci USA 81:5061–5065.

Springer WR, Koshland DE, Jr (1977) Identification of a protein methyl-transferase as the *cheR* gene product in the bacterial sensing system. Proc Natl Acad Sci USA 74:533–537.

Spudich EN, Hasselbacher CA, Spudich JL (1988) Methyl-accepting protein associated with bacterial sensory rhodopsin I. J Bacteriol 170:4280–4285.

Spudich JL, Stoeckenius W (1979) Photosensory and chemosensory behavior of *Halobacterium halobium.* J Photobiochem Photobiophys 1:43–53.

Stewart RC, Dahlquist FW (1987) Molecular components of bacterial chemotaxis. Chem Rev 87:997–1025.

Stewart RC, Dahlquist FW (1988) N-terminal half of CheB is involved in methylesterase response to negative chemotactic stimuli in *Escherichia coli.* J Bacteriol 170:5728–5738.

Stewart RC, Russell CB, Roth AF, Dahlquist FW (1988) Interaction of CheB with chemotaxis signal transduction components in *Escherichia coli:* Modulation of the methylesterase activity and effects on cell swimming behavior. Cold Spring Harbor Symp Quant Biol 53:27–40.

Stock A (1988) *N*-methylmethionine at the amino terminus of a protein required for bacterial chemotaxis. In Zappia V, Galletti P, Porta R, Wold F (eds): Advances in Post-Translational Modifications of Proteins and Aging. New York: Plenum, pp 387–399.

Stock A, Chen T, Welch D, Stock J (1988a) CheA protein, a central regulator of bacterial chemotaxis, belongs to a family of proteins that control gene expression in response to changing environmental conditions. Proc Natl Acad Sci USA 85:1403–1407.

Stock A, Koshland DE, Jr, Stock J (1985) Homologies between *Salmonella typhimurium* CheY protein and proteins involved in the regulation of chemotaxis, membrane protein synthesis, and sporulation. Proc Natl Acad Sci USA 82:7989–7993.

Stock A, Mottonen J, Chen T, Stock J (1987a) Identification of a possible nucleotide binding site in CheW, a protein required for sensory transduction in bacterial chemotaxis. J Biol Chem 262:535–537.

Stock AM, Mottonen JM, Stock JB, Schutt CE (1989) Three-dimensional structure of CheY, the response regulator of bacterial chemotaxis. Nature 337:745–749.

Stock A, Schaeffer E, Koshland DE, Jr, Stock J (1987b) A second type of protein methylation reaction in bacterial chemotaxis. J Biol Chem 262:8011–8014.

Stock A, Stock JB (1987) Purification and characterization of the CheZ protein of bacterial chemotaxis. J Bacteriol 169:3301–3311.

Stock AM, Wylie DC, Mottonen JM, Lupas AN, Ninfa EG, Ninfa AJ, Schutt CE, Stock JB (1988b) Phosphoproteins involved in bacterial signal transduction. Cold Spring Harbor Symp Quant Biol 53:49–57.

Stock J, Borczuk A, Chiou F, Burchenal JEB (1985a) Compensatory mutations in receptor function: A reevaluation of the role of methylation in bacterial chemotaxis. Proc Natl Acad Sci USA 82:8364–8368.

Stock JB, Clarke S, Koshland DE, Jr (1984) The protein carboxymethyl-transferase involved in *Escherichia coli* and *Salmonella typhimurium* chemotaxis. Methods Enzymol 106:310–321.

Stock J, Kersulis G, Koshland DE, Jr (1985b) Neither methylating nor demethylating enzymes are required for bacterial chemotaxis. Cell 42:683–690.

Stock JB, Koshland DE, Jr (1978) A protein methylesterase involved in bacterial sensing. Proc Natl Acad Sci USA 75:3659–3663.

Stock JB, Koshland DE, Jr (1981) Changing reactivity of receptor carboxyl groups during bacterial sensing. J Biol Chem 256:10826–10833.

Stock JB, Maderis AM, Koshland DE, Jr (1981) Bacterial chemotaxis in the absence of receptor carboxymethylation. Cell 27:37–44.

Stock J, Simms S (1987) Methylation, demethylation, and deamidation at glutamate residues in membrane chemoreceptor proteins. In Zappia V, Galletti P, Porta R, Wold F (eds): Advances in Post-Translational Modifications of Proteins and Aging. New York: Plenum, pp 201–212.

Stock J, Stock A (1987) What is the role of receptor methylation in bacterial chemotaxis? Trends Biochem Sci 12:371–375.

Szmelcman S, Schwartz M, Silhavy TJ, Boos W (1976) Maltose transport in *Escherichia coli* K12: A comparison of transport kinetics in wild-type and λ-resistant mutants with the dissociation constants of the maltose-binding protein as measured by fluorescence quenching. Eur J Biochem 65:13–19.

Taylor BL (1983) Role of proton motive force in sensory transduction in bacteria. Annu Rev Microbiol 37:551–573.

Taylor BL, Johnson MS, Smith JM (1988) Signaling pathways in bacterial chemotaxis. Botan Acta 101:101–104.

Taylor BL, Tribhuwan RC, Rowsell EH, Smith JM, Shioi J (1985) Role of ATP and cyclic nucleotides in bacterial chemotaxis. In Eisenbach M, Balaban M (eds): Sensing and Response in Microorganisms. Amsterdam: Elsevier, pp 63–71.

Teeter JH, Brand JG (1987) Peripheral mechanisms of gustation: Physiology and biochemistry. In Finger TE, Silver WL (eds): Neurobiology of Taste and Smell. New York: John Wiley & Sons, pp 299–329.

Terwilliger TC, Bollag GE, Sternberg DW, Jr, Koshland DE, Jr (1986a) *S*-methyl glutathione synthesis is catalyzed by the *cheR* methyltransferase in *Escherichia coli*. J Bacteriol 165:958–963.

Terwilliger TC, Koshland DE, Jr (1984) Sites of methyl esterification and deamination on the aspartate receptor involved in chemotaxis. J Biol Chem 259:7719–7725.

Terwilliger TC, Wang JY, Koshland DE, Jr (1986b) Surface structure recognized for covalent modification of the aspartate receptor in chemotaxis. Proc Natl Acad Sci USA 83:6707–6710.

Terwilliger TC, Wang JY, Koshland DE, Jr (1986c) Kinetics of receptor modification: the multiply methylated aspartate receptors involved in bacterial chemotaxis. J Biol Chem 261:10814–10820.

Thipayathasana P, Valentine RC (1974) The requirement for energy transducing ATPase for anaerobic motility in *Escherichia coli*. Biochim Biophys Acta 347:464–468.

Thoelke MS, Bedale WA, Nettleton DO, Ordal GW (1987) Evidence for an intermediate methylacceptor for chemotaxis in *Bacillus subtilis*. J Biol Chem 262:2811–2816.

Thoelke MS, Parker HM, Ordal EA, Ordal GW (1988) Rapid attractant-induced changes in methylation of methyl-accepting chemotaxis proteins in *Bacillus subtilis*. Biochemistry 27:8453–8457.

Toews ML, Adler J (1979) Methanol formation in vivo from methylated chemotaxis proteins in *Escherichia coli*. J Biol Chem 254:1761–1764.

Toews ML, Goy MF, Springer MS, Adler J (1979) Attractants and repellents control demethylation of methylated chemotaxis proteins in *Escherichia coli*. Proc Natl Acad Sci USA 76:5544–5548.

Tribhuwan RC, Johnson MS, Taylor B (1986) Evidence against direct involvement of cyclic GMP or cyclic AMP in bacterial chemotactic signaling. J Bacteriol 168:624–630.

Tsang N, Macnab RM, Koshland DE, Jr (1973) Common mechanism for repellents and attractants in bacterial chemotaxis. Science 181:60–63.

Tso W-W, Adler J (1974) Negative chemotaxis in *Escherichia coli*. J Bacteriol 118:560–576.

Van der Werf P, Koshland DE, Jr (1977) Identification of a γ-glutamyl methyl ester in bacterial membrane protein involved in chemotaxis. J Biol Chem 252:2793–2795.

van Waarde A (1987) What is the function of protein carboxyl methylation? Comp Biochem Physiol 86B:423–438.

Vogler AP, Lengeler JW (1987) Indirect role of adenylate cyclase and cyclic AMP in chemotaxis to phosphotransferase system carbohydrates in *Escherichia coli* K-12. J Bacteriol 169:593–599.

Vogler AP, Lengeler JW (1988) Complementation of a truncated membrane-bound EnzymeII[Nag] from *Klebsiella pneumoniae* with a soluble EnzymeIII in *Escherichia coli* K12. Mol Gen Genet 213:175–178.

Vyas NK, Vyas MN, Quiocho FA (1988) Sugar and signal-transducer binding sites of the *Escherichia coli* galactose chemoreceptor protein. Science 242:1290–1295.

Weis RM, Koshland DE, Jr (1988) Reversible receptor methylation is essential for normal chemotaxis of *Escherichia coli* in gradients of aspartic acid. Proc Natl Acad Sci USA 85:83–87.

Wolfe AJ, Conley MP, Berg HC (1988) Acetyladenylate plays a role in controlling the direction of flagellar rotation. Proc Natl Acad Sci USA 85:6711–6715.

Wolfe AJ, Conley MP, Kramer TJ, Berg HC (1987) Reconstitution of signaling in bacterial chemotaxis. J Bacteriol 169:1878–1885.

Wolff C, Parkinson JS (1988) Aspartate taxis mutants of the *Escherichia coli* Tar chemoreceptor. J Bacteriol 170:4509–4515.

Wong LS, Johnson MS, Taylor BL (1988) Evidence for ATP binding to the CheY protein in bacterial chemotaxis, abstracted. FASEB J 2:A574.

Wylie D, Stock A, Wong C-Y, Stock J (1988) Sensory transduction in bacterial chemotaxis involves phosphotransfer between Che proteins. Biochem Biophys Res Commun 151:891–896.

Yamaguchi S, Aizawa S-I, Kihara M, Isomura M, Jones CJ, Macnab RM (1986) Genetic evidence for a switching and energy-transducing complex in the flagellar motor of *Salmonella typhimurium*. J Bacteriol 168:1172–1179.

Yarden Y, Schlessinger J (1987) Epidermal growth factor induces rapid reversible aggregation of the purified epidermal growth factor receptor. Biochemistry 26:1443–1451.

Yonekawa H, Hayashi H, Parkinson JS (1983) Requirement of the *cheB* function for sensory adaptation in *Escherichia coli*. J Bacteriol 156:1228–1235.

Yuli I, Tomonaga A, Snyderman R (1982) Chemoattractant receptor functions in human polymorphonuclear leukocytes are divergently altered by membrane fluidizers. Proc Natl Acad Sci USA 79:5906–5910.

Zukin RS (1979) Evidence for a conformational change in the *Escherichia coli* maltose receptor by excited-state fluorescence life-time data. Biochemistry 18:2139–2145.

Zukin RS, Hartig PR, Koshland DE, Jr (1977a) Use of a distant receptor group as evidence for a conformational change in a sensory receptor. Proc Natl Acad Sci USA 74:1932–1936.

Zukin RS, Strange PG, Heavey LR, Koshland DE, Jr (1977b) Properties of the galactose binding protein of *Salmonella typhimurium* and *Escherichia coli*. Biochemistry 16:381–386.

Sensory Receptors and Signal Transduction: 209–231
© 1991 Wiley-Liss, Inc.

Genetic Analysis of G Protein-Coupled Receptors and Response in Yeast

Lorraine Marsh

Department of Cell Biology, Albert Einstein College of Medicine,
Bronx, New York 10461

I. INTRODUCTION

A. Communication Between Cells During Yeast Mating

Yeast G protein–coupled receptors function during mating. Haploid cells of *a*- and α-mating types produce and respond to mating factors, initiating the cell fusion process that culminates in the formation of diploid cells (Fig. 1). Cells of the α-mating type produce α-factor, a peptide of 13 amino acid residues [Duntze et al., 1970]. Cells of the **a**-mating type produce **a**-factor, an unrelated farnesylated and methylated peptide of 12 amino acid residues [Anderegg et al., 1988; Xue et al., 1989]. An inability either to make mating factors or to respond to them prevents cells from mating [MacKay and Manney, 1974; Hartwell, 1980; Kurjan, 1985; Michaelis and Herskowitz, 1988].

Treatment of an **a**- or α-strain of yeast with purified or synthetic mating factor of the opposite mating type leads to a set of responses, similar in each case, including arrest in the G1 phase of the cell cycle, morphological changes, and induction of gene products required for cell fusion (Fig. 2) [reviewed in Cross et al., 1988, and Marsh and Herskowitz, 1988b]. Because response to mating factors in each cell type is similar and much of the signalling pathway is identical in both cell types, I will use the phrase ''mating factor response'' to refer to both the response of **a**-cells to α-factor and α-cells to **a**-factor. The receptors for both **a**-factor and α-factor are integral membrane proteins. Response is coupled to activation of a heterotrimeric G protein. Mutations that affect one or more aspects of mating or mating factor response have been characterized. The genes affected by these mutations have been cloned by complementation. These genetic data combined with biochemical studies have led to a detailed understanding of production and response to mating factors. The genetics and molecular biology underlying cell specialization in yeast mating type determination has been recently reviewed [Herskowitz, 1989]. In this review, I focus on genetic analysis of signal response in yeast, with a special emphasis on signal transduction across the plasma membrane and the manner in which genetic and biochemical approaches complement one another.

B. Using Yeast Genetics to Study Signalling

The budding yeast *Saccharomyces cerevisiae* is especially suited for genetic studies of cellular processes, since it can grow as either a haploid or diploid.

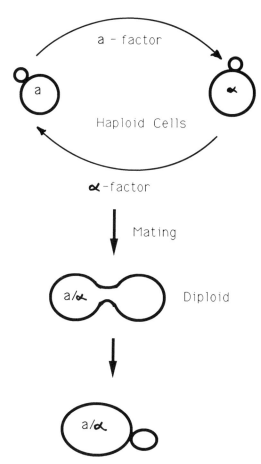

Fig. 1. Mating factors participate in a signalling pathway required for successful yeast cell fusion. Haploid cells of the **a**-mating type produce *a*-factor and respond to α-factor. Haploid cells of the α-mating type produce α-factor and respond to **a**-factor. The process of mating culminates in the formation of a diploid zygote with both **a** and α genetic material. Mutations in *STE* (STErile) genes block mating. Diploid progeny can replicate vegetatively as budding cells that resemble the haploids or undergo meiosis and sporulation to regenerate haploid cells.

In addition, molecular techniques including regulatable expression vectors and gene replacement techniques are relatively simple in this organism. The strength of genetics is its ability to identify genes based on their function in the living organism. Mutations in the genes encoding proteins involved in the signalling pathway lead to specific defects in signalling. However, the identification and cloning of these genes have not always been sufficient to define how the pro-

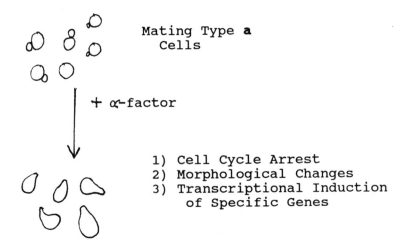

Mating Type **a**
Cells

+ α-factor

1) Cell Cycle Arrest
2) Morphological Changes
3) Transcriptional Induction
   of Specific Genes

Fig. 2. Cells of the a-mating type exposed to synthetic α-factor peptide exhibit specific responses. The α-factor receptor and other gene products of the signalling pathway are required for these responses.

tein works on a molecular level. Also, genetics cannot, per se, identify second messengers or other small molecules involved in intracellular signalling. It is not yet known if such molecules are involved in signalling in yeast. However, the genetic approach provides a complement to other more traditional ways of studying signalling.

Much of our knowledge of signalling pathways in mammalian systems comes from the biochemical study of in vitro systems that appear to mimic events that occur in the cell. Two limitations of such systems are 1) an in vitro system may function under some conditions in the absence of a component involved in vivo in the cell and 2) the target of a component of the signalling pathway may be difficult to identify (e.g., physiological kinase substrates). In theory, a genetic approach can identify every gene product involved in a cellular process. Once identified, these products can be further studied by both genetic and biochemical techniques.

A variety of increasingly sophisticated screens have been used to identify mutations affecting mating and/or response in yeast. The simplest screen involves the identification of mutants that cannot mate at wild-type levels [MacKay and Manney, 1974]. Other screens identify mutants with more specific defects, for example, resistance to the growth-inhibiting effects of α-factor [Hartwell, 1980]. Table I summarizes the genes whose products are known to be involved in signal transduction during response to mating factors. The specific functions of several yeast proteins involved in this process

TABLE I. Genes Involved in Signal Transduction During Mating in Yeast

Gene*	Function
STE2	α-Factor receptor
STE3	a-Factor receptor
GPA1	
(same as SCG1 and CDC70)	G_α-subunit
STE4	G_β-subunit
STE18	G_γ-subunit
SST2	May regulate G protein activity
STE5	?
FUS3	Kinase?
CDC36	?
CDC39	?
SRM1	?
STE7	Kinase?
STE11	Kinase?
STE12	Transcriptional activator of target genes

*Genes are ordered very roughly as they are thought to act: from the receptors to the target gene activator. For references, see text.

have been deduced by sequence homology with known gene products and/or by biochemical characterization.

II. THE α-FACTOR RECEPTOR

A. Identification of the α-Factor Receptor

1. **Genetic studies.** Receptor genes were identified, among other genes involved in signalling, in large-scale screens for genes whose products were required for yeast mating. Mutations in the *STE2* gene led to an inability to mate and an inability to respond to α-factor [MacKay and Manney, 1974; Hartwell, 1980]. Several lines of evidence suggested the possibility that *STE2* might encode a receptor gene. First mutations in *STE2* did not affect the ability of cells to produce mating factors. This result suggested that *STE2* was involved specifically in response to α-factor. Second, mutations in *STE2* blocked responsiveness in only one cell type. Cells of *a*-mating type were unresponsive to α-factor if they contained a mutation in *STE2*, but cells of α-mating type with a mutation in *STE2* still responded to *a*-factor. Most other mutations that specifically blocked cell responsiveness to mating factors acted in both mating types. The *STE2* gene was cloned from a genomic yeast library by complementation of the mating defect of strains with a mutation in *STE2* [Nakayama et al., 1985; Burkholder and Hartwell, 1985].

2. **Evidence that the *STE2* gene encodes a receptor.** Studies with radiolabeled α-factor showed that specific α-factor–binding sites could be detected on *a*-cells but not on α-cells [Jenness et al., 1983, 1986]. Evidence that *STE2*

might encode this receptor came from the observation that binding of α-factor was temperature sensitive in a strain with a temperature-sensitive mutation in *STE2* [Jenness et al., 1983]. Evidence that STE2 had direct physical interaction with α-factor came from the following experiment. *S. cerevisiae STE2* was replaced with an *STE2* homolog from the yeast *Saccharomyces kluyveri* (see below). *S. cerevisiae* strains expressing the *S. kluyveri STE2* responded better to *S. kluyveri* α-factor (which differs at 5 of 13 residues from *S. cerevisiae* α-factor [Egel-Mitani and Hansen, 1987]) than to *S. cerevisiae* α-factor [Marsh and Herskowitz, 1988a]. Thus *STE2* encodes the protein that physically interacts with α-factor, since it alone confers discrimination among α-factor–related peptides. α-Factor has also been crosslinked, albeit with low efficiency, to the *STE2* gene product [Blumer et al., 1988]. Expression of STE2 in *Xenopus* oocytes leads to α-factor–binding sites, but no coupling to cell responses is observed [Yu et al., 1989]. Indirect immunofluorescence of a *STE2–lacZ* fusion that retained receptor activity demonstrated that the receptor is localized to the cell surface [Marsh and Herskowitz, 1988b].

   3. α-Factor–binding studies. The α-factor receptor has not been purified, but considerable biochemical data have been derived by the study of α-factor binding to intact cells and isolated membranes. α-Factor binds to intact cells with an equilibrium dissociation constant of 6×10^{-9} [Jenness et al., 1986] to 2×10^{-8} [Raths et al., 1988]. Scatchard analysis is consistent with the genetic evidence that yeast have only one type of receptor for α-factor. There are roughly 10^4 binding sites per cell as determined by binding of ^{35}S- or ^{3}H-labeled α-factor or by binding competition studies [Jenness et al., 1986; Raths et al., 1988]. Binding sites can also be detected in isolated yeast membranes [Blumer et al., 1988; Blumer and Thorner, 1990]. The α-factor receptor appears to contain a single α-factor–binding site. There is no evidence of receptor or ligand cooperativity.

   The ligand affinity of many G protein–coupled receptors is increased by association of receptor and G protein. The yeast α-factor receptor behaves similarly. Affinity for α-factor is reduced in a yeast strain with a mutation in the G protein β-subunit gene *STE4* [Jenness et al., 1987]. Strains carrying a high-copy plasmid with the *STE2* gene express about 15-fold more α-factor–binding sites of about 10-fold lower affinity [Blumer et al., 1988]. Such strains exhibit normal sensitivity to α-factor. One possibility is that G protein is limiting in yeast so that excess receptors are unable to interact with G protein and therefore bind α-factor more weakly. Yeast membranes exposed to the nonhydrolyzable GTP analog GTP$_\gamma$S exhibit a ninefold lower affinity for α-factor than untreated membranes, suggesting that in yeast, as in mammalian cells, the high-affinity form of the receptor is associated with G protein with GDP bound [Blumer and Thorner, 1990].

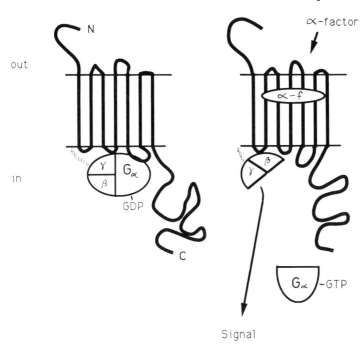

Fig. 3. A model for the molecular action of a yeast receptor. The α-factor receptor encoded by the *STE2* gene is an integral membrane protein thought to span the membrane seven times. Ligand binding may lead to GDP/GTP exchange on the G_α-subunit of a heterotrimeric G protein, freeing the $G_{\beta\gamma}$-subunits to transmit a signal to other protein(s). The G_γ- subunit may be tethered to the membrane via a farnesyl modification. The carboxyl-terminal intracellular domain of the receptor is the target of desensitization. Signal transduction via the *a*-factor receptor is probably similar.

C. Structure of the α-Factor Receptor

1. Primary structure. DNA sequencing of the *STE2* gene showed that it encoded a protein of 48 kD [Nakayama et al., 1985; Burkholder and Hartwell, 1985]. Further analysis revealed that the encoded protein had features of integral membrane proteins with seven hydrophobic, potential membrane-spanning domains (Fig. 3). Thus it resembles members of the large family of integral membrane receptors coupled to G proteins, including receptors as diverse as rhodopsin, the adrenergic receptors, and the *Dictyostelium* cAMP receptor [Dixon et al., 1986; Klein et al., 1988]. However, there is little sequence identity with these other receptors.

Additional insight into important conserved features has come from the comparison of *STE2* from *S. cerevisiae* (c-*STE2*) to an *STE2* homolog from the yeast *S. kluyveri* (k-*STE2*) [Marsh and Herskowitz, 1988a]. The encoded proteins of *S. cerevisiae* and *S. kluyveri* are of similar size: c-STE2 has 431 amino acid residues, and k-STE2 has 426. Overall the predicted amino acid sequences of the two receptor genes are 50% identical, but there is about 66% identity in the central core region that includes the seven hydrophobic segments presumed to span the membrane and their associated loops. Most strikingly, the hydrophobicity plots of the core regions of the two receptors are almost superimposable in this region (L. Marsh, unpublished observation), supporting the hypothesis that the presence of seven hydrophobic segments is a significant, not incidental, feature of these receptors. The single longest stretch of complete identity between c-STE2 and k-STE2 includes residues 231–245 in the predicted third intracellular loop, suggesting that this region plays some special role in receptor function. The equivalent region of the α- and β-adrenergic receptors has been shown to be responsible for coupling to G proteins [Kobilka et al., 1988]. The carboxyl-terminal region, which lies inside the cell (see below), is almost completely unconserved between c-STE2 and k-STE2, although in both proteins the region is highly hydrophilic with an abundance of Ser and Thr residues. Both c-STE2 and k-STE2 have potential sites for glycosylation in the amino-terminal region, but the specific sites are different. The α-factor receptor of *S. cerevisiae* has been shown to be *N*-glycosylated, probably at two or three sites [Blumer et al., 1988].

    2. Ligand-binding domains. Two types of ligand binding have been described for G protein–coupled receptors. Rhodopsin and the adrenergic receptors interact with their small ligands via receptor residues in the hydrophobic membrane-spanning domains [Findlay and Pappin, 1986; Dixon et al., 1987]. The lutropin–choriogonadotropin (LH-CG) receptor binds its 28–38 kD glycoprotein ligands via the external N terminus of the receptor [McFarland et al., 1989]. It is not known whether the activation of the LH-CG receptor requires interaction with hydrophobic residues in addition to the interaction with the N terminus.

    The ligand specificity differences of c-STE2 and k-STE2 have been exploited to begin to map α-factor–binding domains of the α-factor receptor (L. Marsh, in preparation). Both hybrid receptor and mutagenesis techniques have been used. Data from c-STE2/k-STE2 hybrids (all fully functional as receptors) define two regions (residues 45–168 and 250–303) that confer ligand specificity. These regions are mostly within the core of the protein that contains the seven hydrophobic, potential membrane-spanning domains and associated loop regions (roughly, residues 48–301). The two regions separated in the primary sequence may be in close proximity in the final folded structure of the receptor. Since these data suggest that the proposed extracellular N terminus of the receptor does not contribute to ligand specificity, it seems likely that the small peptide α-factor interacts with its receptor more as epinephrine interacts with the adrenergic receptors and less as the glycoprotein lutropin binds to the LH-CG receptor. Indeed, the domains responsible for ligand specificity of the adrenergic receptors [Kobilka et al., 1988] are positioned quite analogously to those that have been identified for the α-factor receptors. Point mutations that alter ligand specificity of the α-factor receptor (L. Marsh, in preparation) also fall into hydrophobic regions of the receptor homologous to those important for ligand specificity in the β-adrenergic receptor [Strader et al., 1987]. Detailed understanding of ligand binding and receptor activation await more complete structural studies of the α-factor and related receptors.

3. Desensitization domain. The large hydrophilic, carboxy-terminal domain of the α-factor receptor is not required for ligand binding or G protein activation. Although deletions or insertions in regions of the *STE2* gene encoding potential membrane-spanning domains totally abolished function, the entire carboxyl terminus up to the end of the seventh hydrophobic domain (residues 295–431) could be deleted without abolishing signalling [Reneke et al., 1988; Konopka et al., 1988; L. Marsh, unpublished data]. A *lacZ* fusion to *STE2* in this region produced a protein that retained the ability to signal and presumably retained the native α-factor receptor topology [Marsh and Herskowitz, 1988b]. The β-galactosidase moiety of this STE2–lacZ fusion lies inside the cell, since cell rupture was required to expose β-galactosidase activity (L. Marsh and I. Herskowitz, unpublished data). Therefore, the carboxyl terminus of the α-factor receptor is probably intracellular. The phosphorylation of this domain, described below, provides additional evidence that it lies inside the cell.

The carboxyl-terminal domain may play a role in receptor desensitization or inactivation. Cells expressing truncated but functional receptors were hypersensitive to α-factor. The extent of hypersensitivity confered by truncated receptors roughly corresponded to the extent of the truncation so that the smallest receptors confered the greatest hypersensitivity. Since there is a gradual transition from normal sensitivity to hypersensitivity with increasingly greater truncations, it seems unlikely that some specific structural motif within the carboxy-terminal domain is involved in regulating receptor activity. An attractive hypothesis is that the α-factor receptor desensitization is mediated by phosphorylation at multiple sites on the Ser- and Thr-rich carboxyl-terminal domain much as the adrenergic receptors [Bouvier et al., 1987] and the *Dictyostelium* cAMP receptor [Vaughan and Devreotes, 1988] are phosphorylated during down-regulation. STE2 is constitutively phosphorylated on carboxyl-terminal residues [Reneke et al., 1988]. Phosphorylation increases, though a modest twofold, on exposure to α-factor [Reneke et al., 1988].

Presumably some protein(s) involved in receptor desensitization interact with the C-terminal region of the receptor. Perhaps a kinase related to the β-adrenergic receptor kinase or rhodopsin kinase is involved [Bouvier et al., 1987]. If such a kinase exists, it has not yet been identified. A candidate kinase gene cloned by its ability at high gene-dosage to reduce sensitivity to α-factor apparently acts further downstream in the signalling pathway [Courchesne et al., 1989]. It is conceivable that desensitization involves more than a change in the extent of receptor phosphorylation.

D. Receptor Internalization

In several instances it appears that surface G protein–coupled receptors are internalized or sequestered in response to exposure to ligand. The β-adrenergic receptor is converted to an inaccessible form that migrates differently from surface forms on sucrose gradients [Waldo et al., 1983]. The *Dictyostelium* cAMP receptor aggregates and moves into vesicles after prolonged exposure to cAMP [Wang et al., 1988].

The α-factor receptor is internalized after exposure to α-factor [Jenness and Spatrick 1986; Chvatchko et al., 1986]. The receptor is the only protein in yeast currently known to be subject to specific endocytosis. Treating cells with α-factor leads to a rapid decrease in surface α-factor–binding sites over the course of about 30 min and then a reaccumulation of binding sites [Jenness and Spatrick, 1986]. *STE2* mRNA levels increase about three- to fourfold after exposure to α-factor [Hartig et al., 1986]. Expression of a *STE2–lacZ* fusion similarly rises about 2.5-fold [Marsh and Herskowitz, 1988b]. The reaccumulation of surface α-factor receptors apparently depends on this increased production of receptor. In strains unable to induce increased expression of *STE2* after exposure to α-factor, because of mutations in downstream components of the signalling pathway or treatment with cycloheximide, surface receptors are lost and do not reappear [Jenness and Spatrick, 1986]. Receptor internalization does not require G_α (*GPA1*) or G_β (*STE4*) [Blinder et al., 1989; Jenness and Spatrick, 1986]. Coated pits appear not to be required for receptor internalization, since clathrin heavy chain–defective *chc1*) cells still internalize α-factor [Payne et al., 1988].

Receptor internalization may play a role in receptor inactivation, but it does not appear to be the sole mechanism. Most of the carboxyl- terminal–truncated receptors previously described that confer hypersensitivity to α-factor internalize normally when exposed to α-factor, suggesting that internalization does not constitute the sole mechanism of receptor inactivation [Reneke et al., 1988; Konopka et al., 1988]. However, the mutant receptor with the largest truncation (*STE2*–trunc296) that confers the greatest hypersensitivity apparently fails to internalize in response to α-factor. Thus internalization may play some role in receptor inactivation. The data from truncated receptors are consistent with an internalization signal in the region defined by residues 296–313. Alternatively, the *STE2*–trunc296 mutation may affect internalization by some indirect effect on protein structure.

Radioactive α-factor is internalized [Jenness and Spatrick, 1986; Chvatchko et al., 1986], and the internalized α-factor is eventually degraded [Chvatchko et al., 1986]. Isogenic strains that do not express the α-factor receptor do not internalize α-factor, demonstrating that this process is receptor-mediated. A fluorescent α-factor analog with fluorescein attached to Lys-7 is also internalized in a receptor-dependent fashion (L. Marsh and F. Naider, in preparation). Fluorescence microscopy reveals that small internal vesicles are labeled in the first 5 min. Later, the vacuole (a lysozome equivalent in yeast) is labeled.

III. THE a-FACTOR RECEPTOR

A. Genetic Studies

The gene encoding the a-factor receptor (*STE3*) was originally identified in the same genetic screen that yielded *STE2* [MacKay and Manney, 1974]. Mutations in the *STE3* gene only block mating and mating factor response in cells of α-mating type. The *STE3* gene, like *STE2*, was cloned by complementation of the mating defect associated with mutations in the gene [Hagen et al., 1986; Nakayama et al., 1985].

B. Evidence That the *STE3* Gene Encodes the a-Factor Receptor

Although *STE3* almost undoubtably encodes the a-factor receptor, the evidence for this conclusion is less extensive than the evidence that *STE2* encodes the α-factor receptor. One important experiment suggests that STE3 binds a-factor. If an **a**-cell is engineered to express STE3 instead of the usual STE2, it then responds to a-factor instead of α-factor [Bender and Sprague, 1989]. Thus STE3 protein alone (or with some factor expressed in both cell types) interacts with a-factor. In addition, this intriguing experiment suggests that signalling components other than the receptors function in common in both cell types.

C. Structure of the a-Factor Receptor

The a-factor receptor gene (*STE3*) encodes a protein with a predicted M_r of 54 kD [Nakayama et al., 1985; Hagen et al., 1986]. Analysis of the primary structure of the encoded protein suggests that the a-factor receptor, like the α-factor receptor, is an integral membrane protein with seven membrane-spanning domains and a long hydrophilic carboxyl terminus. Interestingly, despite the potentially similar structure, the a-factor and α-factor receptors have no sequence identity on the amino acid level. Experiments with *STE3* fusions to invertase (*SUC2*) are consistent with the suggestion that STE3 shares the topology of other G protein–coupled receptors [Clark et al., 1988]. The invertase moiety is glycosylated when fused to a region predicted to form the third extracellular loop of the receptor but is not glycosylated when fused to carboxyl-terminal positions predicted to lie inside of the cell. The a-factor receptor itself contains five potential sites for N-glycosylation, but none are predicted to lie outside the cell, and in fact none are glycosylated in vivo [Clark et al., 1988].

No data are currently available on a-factor interaction with its receptor. It has been difficult to demonstrate specific binding of a-factor to α-cells, presumably because the extreme hydrophobicity of a-factor causes a high level of nonspecific binding. However, synthetic a-factor is active in inducing cellular responses at nanomolar concentrations, suggesting that the a-factor receptor has an affinity for its ligand in the same range as that of the α-factor receptor for α-factor [Xue et al., 1989]. Expression of *STE3* mRNA is increased three- to six-fold in α-cells in response to a-factor [Hagen and Sprague, 1984]. Experiments have not been performed to determine if the a-factor receptor is internalized. Ligand-mediated endocytosis of the a-factor receptor would not be surprising, given the functional similarities between the a-factor receptor and the α-factor receptor.

IV. YEAST G PROTEINS

A. Introduction

The a-factor and α-factor receptors appear to be coupled to a single heterotrimeric yeast G protein (guanine nucleotide–binding protein) present in both cell types. In the mammalian systems that have been studied, activation of receptor is associated with replacement of GDP with GTP on the α-subunit of G protein and separation of the G_α-subunit from the $G_{\beta\gamma}$-subunit [Stryer and Bourne, 1986]. A similar process may occur in yeast. However, in yeast, unlike some other well-studied systems it is the free $G_{\beta\gamma}$-subunit rather than the G_α-subunit that is responsible for activating signalling targets [Dietzel and Kurjan, 1987a; Whiteway et al., 1989; reviewed in Marsh and Herskowitz, 1987] (Fig. 3).

B. Yeast G_α-Subunits

1. Identification of G_α genes. The yeast gene encoding the G_α-subunit involved in mating factor response was discovered almost simultaneously by two very different approaches. These approaches epitomize the similarity of yeast signalling to mammalian systems and the power of yeast genetics to identify gene products based on their function. One group identified yeast genes that cross-hybridized to a rat $G_{\alpha i}$ DNA probe [Nakafuku et al., 1987, 1988], whereas the other used a genetic screen to detect genes capable of modulation of mating factor response [Dietzel and Kurjan, 1987a].

Genes encoding two G_α homologs were identified in yeast by their ability to cross-hybridize to a rat $G_{\alpha i}$ probe [Nakafuku et al., 1987, 1988]. One of these, *GPA1*, was subsequently shown to be involved in mating factor response [Miyajima et al., 1987]. The other (*GPA2*) may be coupled to some as yet undiscovered receptor involved in modulation of cAMP, but no phenotype is yet associated with disruption of the *GPA2* gene [Nakafuku et al., 1988]. For the purposes of this review, the term "G_α" will refer only to the product of the *GPA1* gene. A gene identical to *GPA1* (*SCG1*) was identified by its ability at high gene-dosage to reduce the hypersensitivity of a strain with a mutation in the *SST2* gene (see below) to α-factor [Dietzel and Kurjan, 1987a]. This second approach demonstrated that *SCG1* was involved in some fashion in response to mating factors. Subsequently it was recognized that the *CDC70* gene was also identical to *GPA1/SCG1* [Jahng et al., 1988]. A temperature-sensitive mutation in *CDC70* led, at the nonpermissive temperature, to cells arrested at a stage resembling that of cells exposed to mating factors.

2. Role of G_α. To determine the function of G_α in yeast cells, the gene for G_α (*GPA1/SCG1*) was deleted from the yeast chromosome. Haploid cells without G_α died or grew slowly [Miyajima et al., 1987; Dietzel and Kurjan, 1987a]. The arrested phenotype resembled that of cells exposed to mating factors. Using conditional alleles or *GPA1* under the regulatable control of a *GAL1* promoter, it was shown that elimination of G_α activity led to all of the responses characteristic of mating factor response, including induction of specific gene transcription of mating factor inducible products [Jahng et al., 1988; Matsumoto et al., 1988]. Elimination of G_α activity also partially overcame the mating defect of a receptorless strain. G_α thus formally inhibits response, and the binding of α-factor to receptor formally leads to G_α inactivation.

3. Structural analysis of yeast G_α. The yeast G_α-subunit encoded by *SCG1/GPA1* gene contains 472 amino acid residues and is 45% identical to rat $G_{\alpha i}$ [Dietzel and Kurjan, 1987a; Miyajima et al., 1987; Nakafuku et al. 1987]. Like mammalian G_α, the yeast protein is membrane associated, suggesting lipophilic modification [Blumer and Thorner, 1990]. The regions of strongest identity including the guanine nucleotide–binding consensus region and GTP hydrolysis region. Homology in other regions is also generally high, though the yeast protein has 110 extra amino acid residues (residues 126–235) not found in the mammalian G_α-subunits. The role, if any, of this extra domain is not known. The strong similarity to mammalian G protein and the evidence that it plays a role in mating factor signalling suggests that yeast G_α physically interacts with receptor as mammalian G_α-subunits interact with, for example, rhodopsin or β-adrenergic receptor. The ability of a GTP analog to affect the affinity of receptor for α-factor, described above, supports this conclusion [Blumer and Thorner, 1990]. Rat $G_{\alpha s}$ expressed in yeast complements the growth defect associated with a deficiency in yeast G_α but does not restore mating factor responsiveness [Dietzel and Kurjan, 1987a]. The effects of mammalian G_α expressed in yeast is dominant; that is, mammalian G_α interferes with the functioning of yeast G_α [Kang et al., 1990]. These results are consistent with the hypothesis that mammalian G_α can interact with yeast $G_{\beta\gamma}$ subunits but cannot be activated by yeast receptors.

A mutation in yeast G_α (*SCG1* Asn-388 to Lys-388) analogous to those thought to lead to constitutive activation of *ras* by destabilization of interaction with GDP confered a phenotype similar to that of inactivation of the G_α gene, that is, constitutive response [Kurjan, 1990]. Other mutations in the G_α gene were dominant and led to an inability to respond [Kurjan, 1990]. These results are consistent with the previously described model in which G_α with GDP bound serves to inhibit response.

C. Yeast $G_{\beta\gamma}$-subunits

1. Identification of the G_β and G_γ genes. The β- and γ- subunits of yeast G proteins are considered together, since they seem to function together as activators of responses to mating factors. Mutations in the genes that encode these proteins lead to similar phenotypes. Mammalian G protein β- and γ-subunits copurify as a tight complex [Stryer and Bourne, 1986].

The G_β-subunit in yeast is encoded by the *STE4* gene [Whiteway et al., 1989]. Mutations in this gene were first identified because they interfered with mating ability and confered resistance to α-factor [MacKay and Manney, 1974]. G_β is required for signalling. Strains that do not contain any G_β (because the *STE4* gene is deleted) cannot respond to mating factors. Special mutations in the *STE4* gene have been identified that lead to activation of mating factor responses in the absence of mating factors [Blinder and Jenness, 1989]. These special mutations may weaken G_α–G_β interactions while retaining the ability to activate downstream proteins.

The G_γ-subunit in yeast is encoded by the *STE18* gene [Whiteway et al., 1989]. A mutation in this gene was first identified by a screen involving a strain of yeast designed both to overproduce α-factor and to be hypersensitive to it. The original mutation confered a remarkable phenotype. Cells carrying this mutation were more sensitive to low levels of α-factor than to high levels [Whiteway et al., 1989]. The mutation in the *STE18* gene that confered this phenotype may block modification of the product (see below). Special mutations in the *STE4* gene that confered an identical phenotype were identified in the same screen. The exact mechanism by which certain mutations in *STE4* and *STE18* confer immunity to the effects of high mating factor concentrations without affecting response to lower levels of factors is unclear. However, the fact that only mutations in these two genes have been found to confer this phenotype suggests that *STE4* and *STE18* may share some common role in response. Deletion of the *STE18* gene, like deletion of *STE4*, leads to a complete inability to respond to mating factors at any concentration.

2. Role of $G_{\beta\gamma}$. The G_β and G_γ proteins are formally activators of response, since their absence blocks signaling. The G_α-subunit is formally an inhibitor of response, because its absence results in constitutive activation. An attractive possibility is that G_α in its GDP-bound state inhibits $G_{\beta\gamma}$ [Dietzel and Kurjan, 1987a; Blumer and Thorner, 1990]. Receptor activation may catalyze GDP–GTP exchange, leading to release of free G_α–GTP and free $G_{\beta\gamma}$. The free $G_{\beta\gamma}$ would then active the next step in response. Supporting this model is the observation that *STE4* or *STE18* deletion mutations block the constitutive response confered by mutations in the G_α-subunit gene [Whiteway et al., 1989; Blinder et al., 1989]. Though rat $G_{\alpha s}$ fails to transmit a signal from the α-factor receptor [Dietzel and Kurjan, 1987a], it does not block signalling from the temperature-activated alleles of STE4 described earlier [Blinder et al., 1989]. Thus signalling information moves along the following path: 1) receptor, 2) G_α, 3) $G_{\beta\gamma}$, and 4) cellular responses.

Though G_α–GTP is directly coupled to the activation of enzyme systems or ion channels in most of the best-studied mammalian systems [Stryer and Bourne, 1986], other instances of $G_{\beta\gamma}$-coupled responses have been reported [e.g., Jelsema and Axelrod, 1987]. Mechanistically, there would seem to be no reason why the major conformational changes that must accompany GDP/GTP exchange and G_α dissociation from $G_{\beta\gamma}$ might not be coupled to responses in either fashion.

3. G protein subunit stoichiometry. A predicted consequence of the model above is that a balanced G protein subunit ratio would be required to prevent either constitutive signaling or supression of signaling. These predictions are borne out in fact. Overexpression of G_α (SCG1) led to inhibition of mating and resistance to the growth inhibitory effects of α-factor [Kang et al., 1990; Cole et al., 1990]. Overexpression of G_β (STE4) alone or with G_γ (STE18) led to constitutive mating factor responses and partially overcame the mating defect of a receptorless strain [Whiteway et al., 1990; Cole et al., 1990]. It had been previously noted that *STE4* could be cloned from a low-copy but not a high-copy clone bank [MacKay, 1983] presumably because overexpression mimicked mating factor treatment and led to inhibition of cell division. STE18 overexpression alone has no effect, suggesting that it is normally present in excess, but a mutation in *STE18* blocked the effects of overexpression from *STE4*, confirming that both G_β- and G_γ-subunits are required for signaling. G_α overexpression suppresses the phenotype of G_β overexpression [Whiteway et al., 1990; Cole et al., 1990] presumably by restoring balanced expression of the subunits and converting free $G_{\beta\gamma}$-subunits back to $G_{\alpha\beta\gamma}$ heterotrimers.

4. Structural analysis of $G_{\beta\gamma}$. The *STE4* gene product is predicted to be a protein of 423 amino acid residues, 40% identical to mammalian G_β. *STE18* encodes a predicted product of 110 amino acid residues with weak but significant homology to transducin G_γ-subunit [Whiteway et al., 1989]. Though the *STE18* gene is only weakly similar to the sequenced mammalian G_γ-subunits, they share an important feature. STE18 and G_γ sequences end with a consensus amino acid sequence (Cys- Aliphatic-Aliphatic-Xaa) for farnesylation [Whiteway et al., 1989]. A farnesylated product is apparently required for mating factor response [Schafer et al., 1989]. Certain mutations of *RAM1* [Powers et al., 1986] (also known as *DPR1*), a gene required for farnesylation of *a*-factor and Ras proteins in yeast, also block the ability of yeast to respond to mating factors. This effect may be mediated by a specific failure to farnesylate STE18 protein [Matsumoto et al., 1988]. One might speculate that lipophilic modification of G_γ enhances membrane association and increases the effective concentration of $G_{\beta\gamma}$ near the receptor.

These observations support the idea that yeast G protein subunits function similarly to mammalian G protein. However, details of interaction with receptors and effectors will require further study.

D. A Potential Modulator of G Protein Activity

Some gene products appear not to participate directly in signalling but rather to modulate response. One of these, encoded by the *SST2* gene, may be involved in recovery from response, perhaps by facilitating G_α and $G_{\beta\gamma}$ reassociation. The SST2 protein is predicted to contain 698 amino acid residues and is not known to be homologous to other proteins [Dietzel and Kurjan, 1987b]. Mutations in the *SST2* gene make strains of either mating type hypersensitive to mating factor and prolong responses [Chan and Otte, 1982]. This hypersensitivity is additive with the hypersensitivity conferred by a truncated α-factor receptor, demonstrating that SST2-mediated desensitization proceeds via a different pathway [Konopka et al., 1988; Reneke et al., 1988], i.e., SST2 probably acts on a target other than the receptor. Overexpression of SST2 leads to decreased sensitivity to mating factors [Dietzel and Kurjan, 1987b].

The transcription of the SST2 product is highly induced after exposure to mating factors [Dietzel and Kurjan, 1987b]. The function of SST2 seems to be to turn off response (since too much SST2 reduces response and too little SST2 causes prolonged response). The target of SST2 may be the yeast G_α protein. The gene for yeast G_α was cloned, on the basis of its ability, at high gene-dosage, to reduce the hypersensitivity of an *SST2* mutant strain [Dietzel and Kurjan, 1987a]. An idea that awaits testing is that the function of the SST2 product is to stimulate the intrinsic GTPase activity of G_α as GAP protein stimulates Ras GTPase in mammalian cells and IRA proteins stimulate the GTPase of RAS1,2 in yeast [McCormick et al., 1988; Tanaka et al., 1990]. According to this highly speculative model, SST2 would facilitate G_α reassociation with $G_{\beta\gamma}$ and promote recovery from signalling. Perhaps SST2 analogs play roles in the modulation of receptor responses in other organisms.

V. OTHER SIGNALLING COMPONENTS

A. Intracellular Signal Transduction

A large number of other genes have been implicated in the signalling steps between the activation of G protein and the transcriptional control of target genes. However, the precise biochemical roles that these products play are not clear. Some may act indirectly. A defect in some of these genes (e.g., *STE5, STE7, STE11, STE12, FUS3*) leads to an inability to respond to mating factors [MacKay and Manney, 1974; Hartwell, 1980; Fields et al., 1988; Elion et al., 1990], whereas a defect in others (*CDC36, CDC39, CDC72, CDC73, SRM1*) [Reed et al., 1988; Clark and Sprague, 1989; Lopes et al., 1990] leads to constitutive response. The relationships between the different products and the parts that they play is complex and poorly understood. The role of some of these products in signalling may be indirect, e.g., some may be transcriptional regulators of products that in turn are directly involved in signalling. Epistasis analysis may help to determine the order in which these proteins act [Blinder et al., 1989; Nakayama et al., 1988]. It is not known whether second messengers are involved in signalling. The current understanding of interactions between these products has been reviewed [Marsh and Herskowitz, 1988b].

B. Transcriptional Activation by the STE12 Protein

The final target for transcriptional activation of genes by both mating factors is the DNA consensus sequence TGAAACA, active in either orientation upstream of target genes [Kronstad et al., 1987; Trueheart et al., 1987]. The transcriptional activator that binds to these target sequences is encoded by the *STE12* gene [Dolan et al., 1989; Errede and Ammerer, 1989]. The STE12 protein binds its target DNA sequence whether or not the cell has been stimulated, so it may be subject to some modification that activates its function [Dolan et al., 1989]. The *STE7* and *STE11* genes encode kinases that are candidates for the proteins involved in such a modification [Fields et al., 1988; Teague et al., 1986]. Transcriptional activation by both mating factors is mediated by *STE12*, underscoring the fact that the intracellular signalling pathway from the α-factor receptor and the *a*-factor receptor are identical.

VI. REGULATION OF RESPONSE

A. Cell-Type-Specific Responses

With the exception of receptors, the proteins required for response to both a-factor and α-factor are the same [Bender and Sprague, 1989]. However, the responses of **a**-cells and α-cells are not completely identical, though many proteins are induced in both cell types. A specific example illustrates this point. Agglutinins are synthesized in response to mating factors. Cells of the **a** type express only **a**-agglutinin [Watzele et al., 1988], and cells of the α type express only α-agglutinin [Lipke et al., 1989]. Both agglutinins require the transcriptional activator STE12 for expression. How is the expression of different gene products induced after activation of the same transcriptional activator? The answer seems to be that inducible genes may be under the control of several regulators. Thus the activation of STE12 alone creates only the *potential* that genes with its target DNA sequence will be expressed. Other regulators, especially those at the mating type locus, *MAT*, which controls mating type determination (**a** or α) for the cell [Strathern et al., 1981], also determine whether a given gene can be expressed in response to mating factors. In this example, the α-agglutinin gene *Agα1* contains upstream sites for transcriptional regulation by both mating factors, via *STE12*, and the mating type locus, via *MATα1* [Lipke et al., 1989]. Thus the mating type locus exerts control over cell responses in a parsimonious fashion: 1) Control is exerted over the type of receptor expressed, controlling which mating factor to which the cell will respond; and 2) control is exerted over the genes that are the targets of mating factor induction, controlling the nature of the response [Herskowitz, 1989; Marsh and Herskowitz, 1988b]. Thus the response is cell-type specific even though most of the signalling machinery is not cell-type specific.

B. Prevention of Signalling in Diploid Cells

Diploid yeast cells (or, more properly, **a**/α diploid cells, since heterozygosity at the mating type locus provides this regulation) do not respond to mating factors. This failure to respond makes good sense, since diploids are the product of a successful mating event and further mating would be deleterious. Triploid cells, for example, have segregation problems during meiosis that lead to high inviability of the resulting spores [Mortimer and Hawthorne, 1969]. In diploid cells the signalling pathway is inactivated at multiple steps. Receptors are not expressed, G protein subunits are not expressed, and STE12 is not expressed [reviewed in Marsh and Herskowitz, 1988b]. The dismantling of the response system is evident by the fact that a homozygous deletion of the G_α gene does not lead to constitutive response in *a*/α diploids [Dietzel and Kurjan, 1987a].

VII. SUMMARY

In reviewing the receptor/signal transduction system involved in mating factor response in yeast, the most striking feature is the extent of similarity to mammalian G protein–coupled receptors. Many of the characteristics of these systems are present: integral membrane receptors with seven potential membrane-spanning domains, receptor phosphorylation, and internalization; and heterotrimeric G protein apparently activated by guanine nucleotide exchange. Those aspects that are different serve to stretch our thinking about the fundamental features of this highly conserved signalling system. The ease with which genes can be manipulated in yeast should permit detailed structure–function studies of the underlying mechanisms of receptor and G protein activation and interaction.

The yeast system has several curiosities to be explored. The α-factor receptor and **a**-factor receptor have no apparent sequence identity with one another (or mammalian receptors), yet they appear to interact with the same G protein. Perhaps there are conserved features in the secondary structure of the receptors that are not apparent from the primary sequence. The SST2 product that modulates response is intriguing. One might ask whether analogous proteins modulate response in mammalian cells. Other novel yeast gene products whose functions are not yet known, other than that they play some role in response in yeast, may also have analogs in mammalian cells.

VIII. REFERENCES

Anderegg RJ, Betz R, Carr SA, Crabb JW, Duntze W (1988) Structure of *Saccharomyces cerevisiae* mating hormone *a*-factor. J Biol Chem 263:18236–18240.

Bender A, Sprague GF, Jr (1989) Pheromones and pheromone receptors are the primary determinants of mating specificity in the yeast *Saccharomyces cerevisiae*. Genetics 122:463–476.

Blinder D, Bouvier S, Jenness DD (1989) Constitutive mutants in the yeast pheromone response: Ordered function of the gene products. Cell 56:479–486.

Blinder D, Jenness DD (1989) Regulation of postreceptor signaling in the pheromone response pathway of *Saccharomyces cerevisiae*. Mol Cell Biol 9:3720–3726.

Blumer KJ, Reneke JE, Thorner J (1988) The STE2 gene product is the ligand-binding component of the α-factor receptor of *Saccharomyces cerevisiae*. J Biol Chem 263:10836–10842.

Blumer KJ, Thorner J (1990) β and τ subunits of a yeast guanine nucleotide–binding protein are not essential for membrane association of the α subunit but are required for receptor coupling. Proc Natl Acad Sci USA 87:4363–4367.

Bouvier M, Leeb-Lundberg LMF, Benovic JL, Caron MG, Lefkowitz RJ (1987) Regulation of adrenergic receptor function by phosphorylation. J Biol Chem 262:3106–3113.

Burkholder AC, Hartwell LH (1985) The yeast α-factor receptor: Structural properties deduced from the sequence of the *STE2* gene. Nucleic Acids Res 13:8463–8475.

Chan RK, Otte CA (1982) Isolation and genetic analysis of *Saccharomyces cerevisiae* mutants supersensitive to G1 arrest by *a*-factor and α-factor pheromones. Mol Cell Biol 2:11–20.

Chvatchko Y, Howald I, Riezman H (1986) Two yeast mutants defective in endocytosis are defective in pheromone response. Cell 46:355–364.

Clark KL, Davis NG, Wiest DK, Hwang-Shum J-J, Sprague GF, Jr (1988) Response of yeast α cells to a factor pheromone: Topology of the receptor and identification of a component of the response pathway. Cold Spring Harbor Symp Quant Biol 53:611–627.

Clark KL, Sprague GF (1989) Yeast pheromone response pathway: Characterization of a suppressor that restores mating to receptorless mutants. Mol Cell Biol 9:2682–2694.

Cole GM, Stone DE, Reed SI (1990) Stoichiometry of G protein subunits affects the *Saccharomyces cerevisiae* mating pheromone signal transduction pathway. Mol Cell Biol 10:510–517.

Courchesne WE, Kunisawa R, Thorner J (1989) A putative protein kinase overcomes pheromone-induced arrest of cell cycling in *S. cerevisiae*. Cell 58:1107–1119.

Cross F, Hartwell LH, Jackson C, Konopka JB (1988) Conjugation in *Saccharomyces cerevisiae*. Annu Rev Cell Biol 4:429–457.

Dietzel C, Kurjan J (1987a) The yeast *SCG1* gene: A G_α-like protein implicated in the *a*- and α-factor response pathway. Cell 50:1000–1010.

Dietzel C, Kurjan J (1987b) Pheromonal regulation and sequence of the *Saccharomyces cerevisiae* *SST2* gene: A model for desensitization to pheromone. Mol Cell Biol 7:4169–4177.

Dixon RA, Kobilka BK, Strader DJ, Benovic JL, Dohlman HG, Frielle T, Bolanowski MA, Bennett CD, Rands E, Diehl RE, Mumford RA, Slater EE, Sigal IS, Caron MG, Lefkowitz RJ, Strader CD (1986) Cloning of the gene and cDNA for mammalian β-adrenergic receptor and homology with rhodopsin. Nature 321:75–79.

Dixon RAF, Sigal IS, Rands E, Register RB, Candelore MR, Blake AD, Strader CD (1987) Ligand binding to the β-adrenergic receptor involves its rhodopsin-like core. Nature 326:73–77.

Dolan JW, Kirkman C, Fields S (1989) The yeast STE12 protein binds to the DNA sequence mediating pheromone induction. Proc Natl Acad Sci USA 86:5703–5707.

Duntze W, MacKay VL, Manney TR (1970) *Saccharomyces cerevisiae*: A diffusible sex factor. Science 168:1472–1474.

Egel-Mitani M, Hansen MT (1987) Nucleotide sequence of the gene encoding the *Saccharomyces kluyveri* α mating pheromone. Nucleic Acids Res 15:6303.

Elion EA, Grisafi PL, Fink GR (1990) *FUS3* encodes a cdc2$^+$/CDC28-related kinase required for the transition from mitosis into conjugation. Cell 60:649–664.

Errede B, Ammerer G (1989) STE12, a protein involved in cell-type-specific transcriptional and signal transduction in yeast, is part of protein–DNA complexes. Genes Dev 3:1349–1361.

Fields S, Chaleff DT, Sprague GF, Jr (1988) Yeast *STE7*, *STE11*, and *STE12* genes are required for expression of cell-type-specific genes. Mol Cell Biol 8:551–558.

Findlay JBC, Pappin DJC (1986) The opsin family of proteins. Biochem J 238:625–642.

Hagen DC, McCaffrey G, Sprague GF, Jr (1986) E evidence the yeast *STE3* gene encodes a receptor for the peptide pheromone *a* factor: Gene sequence and implications for the structure of the presumed receptor. Proc Natl Acad Sci USA 83:1418–1422.

Hagen DC, Sprague GF, Jr (1984) Induction of the yeast α-specific *STE3* gene by the peptide pheromone *a*-factor. J Mol Biol 178:835–852.

Hartig A, Holly J, Saari G, MacKay VL (1986) Multiple regulation of STE2, a mating-type-specific gene of *Saccharomyces cerevisiae*. Mol Cell Biol 6:2106–2114.

Hartwell LH (1980) Mutants of *Saccharomyces cerevisiae* unresponsive to cell division control by polypeptide mating hormone. J Cell Biol 85:811–822.

Herskowitz I (1989). A regulatory hierarchy for cell specialization in yeast. Nature 342:749–757.

Jahng K-Y, Ferguson J, Reed S (1988) Mutations in a gene encoding the α subunit of a *Saccharomyces cerevisiae* G protein indicate a role in mating pheromone signaling. Mol Cell Biol 8:2484–2493.

Jelsema CL, Axelrod J (1987) Stimulation of phospholipase A_2 activity in bovine rod outer segments by the B_γ subunits of transducin and its inhibition by the α subunit. Proc Natl Acad Sci USA 84:3623–3627.

Jenness DD, Burkholder AC, Hartwell LH (1983) Binding of α-factor pheromone to yeast *a* cells: Chemical and genetic evidence for an α-factor receptor. Cell 35:521–529.

Jenness DD, Burkholder AC, Hartwell LH (1986) Binding of α-factor pheromone to *Saccharomyces cerevisiae* *a* cells: Dissociation constant and number of binding sites. Mol Cell Biol 6:318–320.

Jenness DD, Goldman BS, Hartwell LH (1987) *Saccharomyces cerevisiae* mutants unresponsive to α-factor binding and extragenic suppression. Mol Cell Biol 7:1311–1319.

Jenness DD, Spatrick P (1986) Down regulation of the α-factor pheromone receptor in *S. cerevisiae*. Cell 46:345–353.

Kang Y-S, Kane J, Kurjan J, Stadel JM, Tipper DJ (1990) Effects of expression of mammalian

G_α and hybrid mammalian-yeast G_α proteins on the yeast pheromone response signal transduction pathway. Mol Cell Biol 10:2582–2590.

Klein PS, Sun TJ, Saxe CL, Kimmel AR, Johnson RL, Devreotes PN (1988) A chemoattractant receptor controls development in *Dictyostelium discoidum*. Science 241:1467–1472.

Kobilka BK, Kobilka TS, Daniel K, Regan JW, Caron MG, Lefkowitz RJ (1988) Chimeric $\alpha 2$-, $\beta 2$-adrenergic receptors: Delineation of domains involved in effector coupling and ligand binding specificity. Science 240:1310–1316.

Konopka JB, Jenness DD, Hartwell LH (1988) The C-terminus of the *Saccharomyces cerevisiae* α-pheromone receptor mediates an adaptive response to pheromone. Cell 54:609–618.

Kronstad JW, Holly JA, MacKay VL (1987) A yesat operator overlaps an upstream activation site. Cell 50:369–377.

Kurjan J (1985) α-Factor structural gene mutations in *Saccharomyces cerevisiae*: Effects on α-factor production and mating. Mol Cell Biol 5:778–796.

Kurjan J (1990) G proteins in yeast *Saccharomyces cerevisiae*. In Birnbaumer L, Iyengar I, (eds): G proteins. New York: Academic Press, pp 571–599.

Lipke PN, Wojciechowicz D, Kurjan J (1989) AGα1 is the structural gene for the *Saccharomyces cerevisiae* α-agglutinin, a cell surface glycoprotein involved in cell-cell interactions during mating. Mol Cell Biol 9:3155–3165.

Lopes MD, Ho J-Y, Reed SI (1990) Mutations in cell division cycle genes CDC36 and CDC39 activate the *Saccharomyces cerevisiae* mating pheromone response pathway. Mol Cell Biol 10:2966–2972.

MacKay VL (1983) Cloning of yeast *STE* genes in 2 μm vectors. Methods Enzymol 101:325–343.

MacKay VL, Manney TR (1974) Mutations affecting sexual conjugation and related processes in *Saccharomyces cerevisiae*. I. Isolation and phenotypic characterization of nonmating mutants. Genetics 76:255–271.

McCormick F, Adari H, Trahey M, Halenbeck R, Koths K, Martin GA, Crosier WJ, Watt K, Rubinfeld B, Wong G (1988) Interactions of ras p21 proteins with GTPase activating protein. Cold Spring Harbor Symp Quant Biol 53:849–854.

McFarland KC, Sprengle R, Phillips HS, Kohler M, Rosemblit N, Nikolics K, Segaloff DL, Seeburg PH (1989) Lutropin–choriogonatropin receptor: An unusual member of the G protein–coupled receptor family. Science 245:494–499.

Marsh L, Herskowitz I (1987) Conservation of a receptor/signal transduction system. Cell 50:995–996.

Marsh L, Herskowitz I (1988a) STE2 protein of *Saccharomyces kluyveri* is a member of the rhodopsin/β-adrenergic receptor family and is responsible for recognition of the peptide ligand α-factor. Proc Natl Acad Sci USA 85:3855–3859.

Marsh L, Herskowitz I (1988b) From membrane to nucleus: The pathway of signal transduction in yeast and its genetic control. Cold Spring Harbor Symp Quant Biol 53:557–565.

Matsumoto K, Nakafuku M, Nakayama N, Miyajima I, Kaibuchi K, Miyajima A, Brenner C, Arai K, Kaziro Y (1988) The role of G proteins in yeast signal transduction. Cold Spring Harbor Symp Quant Biol 53:567–575.

Michaelis S, Herskowitz I (1988) The *a*-factor pheromone of *Saccharomyces cerevisiae* is essential for mating. Mol Cell Biol 8:1309–1318.

Miyajima I, Nakafuku M, Nakayama N, Brenner C, Miyajima A, Kaibuchi K, Arai K, Kaziro Y, Matsumoto K (1987) GPA1, a haploid-specific essential gene, encodes a yeast homolog of mammalian G protein which may be involved in mating factor signal transduction. Cell 50:1011–1019.

Mortimer RK, Hawthorne DC (1969) Yeast genetics. In Rose AH, Harrison JS (eds): The Yeasts, Vol I. New York: Academic Press, p 386.

Nakayama N, Kaziro Y, Arai K-I, Matsumoto K (1988) Role of *STE* genes in the mating factor signaling pathway mediated by *GPA1* in *Saccharomyces cerevisiae*. Mol Cell Biol 8:3777–3783.

Nakayama N, Miyajima A, Arai K (1985) Nucleotide sequences of *STE2* and *STE3*, cell type-specific sterile genes from *Saccharomyces cerevisiae*. EMBO J 4:2643–2648.

Nakafuku M, Itoh H, Nakamura S, Kaziro Y (1987) Occurrence in *Saccharomyces cerevisiae* of a gene homologous to the cDNA coding for the α subunit of mammalian G protein. Proc Natl Acad Sci USA 84:2140–2144.

Nakafuku M, Obara T, Kaibuchi K,Miyajima I, Miyajima H, Itoh H, Nakamura S, Arai K, Matsumoto K, Kaziro Y (1988) Isolation of a second G protein homologous gene (GPA2) from *Saccharomyces cerevisiae* and studies on its possible functions. Proc Natl Acad Sci USA 85:1374–1378.

Payne GS, Baker D, Tuinen EV, Schekman R (1988) Protein transport to the vacuole and receptor-mediated endocytosis by clathrin heavy chain–deficient yeast. J Cell Biol 106:1453–1461.

Powers S, Michaelis S, Broek D, Santa Anna-A S, Field J, Herskowitz I, Wigler M (1986) RAM, a gene of yeast required for a functional modification of RAS proteins and for production of mating pheromone a-factor. Cell 47:413–422.

Raths SK, Naider F, Becker JM (1988) Peptide analogues compete with the binding of α-factor to its receptor in *Saccharomyces cerevisiae*. J Biol Chem 263:17333–17341.

Reed SI, Ferguson J, Jahng K-Y (1988) Isolation and characterization of two genes encoding yeast mating pheromone signalling elements: *CDC72* and *CDC73*. Cold Spring Harbor Symp Quant Biol 53:621–627.

Reneke JE, Blumer KJ, Courchesne WE, Thorner J (1988) The carboxyl-terminal segment of the yeast α-factor receptor is a regulatory domain. Cell 55:221–230.

Schafer WR, Kim R, Sterne R, Thorner J, Kim S-H, Rine J (1989) Genetic and pharmacological suppression of oncogenic mutations in *ras* genes of yeast and humans. Science 245:379–385.

Strader CD, Sigal IS, Register RB, Candelore MR, Rands E, Dixon RAF (1987) Identification of residues required for ligand binding to the β-adrenergic receptor. Proc Natl Acad Sci USA 84:4384–4388.

Strathern J, Hicks J, Herskowitz I (1981) Control of cell type in yeast by the mating type locus. J Mol Biol 147:357–372.

Stryer L, Bourne HR (1986) G proteins: A family of signal transducers. Annu Rev Cell Biol 2:391–419.

Tanaka K, Nakafuku M, Satoh T, Marshall MS, Gibbs JB, Matsumoto K, Kaziro Y, Tohe A (1990) *S. cerevisiae* genes *IRA1* and *IRA2* encode proteins that may be functionally equivalent to mammalian *ras* GTPase activating protein. Cell 60:803–807.

Teague MA, Chaleff DT, Errede B (1986) Nucleotide sequence of the yeast regulatory gene *STE7* predicts a protein homologous to protein kinases. Proc Natl Acad Sci USA 83:7371–7375.

Trueheart J, Boeke JD, Fink GR (1987) Two genes required for cell fusion during yeast conjugation: Evidence for a pheromone-induced surface protein. Mol Cell Biol 7:2316–2328.

Vaughan RA, Devreotes PN (1988) Ligand-induced phosphorylation of the cAMP receptor from *Dictyostelium discoideum*. J Biol Chem 263:14538–14543.

Waldo GL, Northup JK, Perkins JP, Harden TK (1983) Characterization of an altered membrane form of the β-adrenergic receptor produced during agonist-induced desensitization. J Biol Chem 258:13900–13908.

Wang M, Van Haastert PJ, Devreotes PN, Schaap P (1988) Localization of chemoattractant receptors on *Dictyostelium discoideum* cells during aggregation and down-regulation. Dev Biol 128:72–77.

Watzele M, Kils F, Tanner W (1988) Purification and characterization of the inducible *a* agglutinin of *Saccharomyces cerevisiae*. EMBO J 7:1483–1488.

Whiteway M, Hougan L, Dignard D, Thomas DY, Bell L, Saari GC, Grant FJ, O'Hara P, MacKay

VL (1989) The *STE4* and *STE18* genes of yeast encode potential β and τ subunits of the mating factor receptor-coupled G protein. Cell 56:467–477.

Whiteway M, Hougan L, Thomas DY (1990) Overexpression of the *STE4* gene leads to mating response in haploid *Saccharomyces cerevisiae*. Mol Cell Biol 10:217–222.

Xue CB, Caldwell GA, Becker JM, Naider F (1989) Total synthesis of the lipopeptide *a*-mating factor of *Saccharomyces cerevisiae*. Biochem Biophys Res Commun 162:253–257.

Yu L, Blumer KJ, Davidson N, Lester HA, Thorner J (1989) Functional expression of the yeast α-factor receptor in *Xenopus* oocytes. J Biol Chem 264:20847–20850.

Sensory Receptors and Signal Transduction: 233–255
© 1991 Wiley-Liss, Inc.

Archaebacterial Rhodopsins: Sensory and Energy Transducing Membrane Proteins

Roberto A. Bogomolni and John L. Spudich*

Department of Chemistry, University of California, Santa Cruz, California 95035
(R.A.B.); Department of Anatomy and Structural Biology and Department of
Physiology and Biophysics, Albert Einstein College of Medicine, Bronx,
New York 10461 (J.L.S.)

I. CELLULAR FUNCTION OF RETINAL PROTEINS IN BACTERIA

Membranes of the halophilic (salt-loving) archaebacteria of the genus *Halobacteria* contain a family of photochemically reactive chromoproteins that use retinal in their chromophore.[1] They resemble structurally the visual pigments (rhodopsins) of higher animals. The bacterial rhodopsins not only carry out photosensory reception, but also convert light energy into ionic electrochemical potential to drive metabolic processes. To date, eight bacterial rho-

*The present address of John L. Spudich is: Department of Microbiology and Molecular Genetics,
University of Texas Medical School, Houston, TX 77030.

[1]In this review, we consider the "chromophore" to consist of the retinylidene moiety as well as
protein residues and possible inorganic components that interact with it to generate the color
characteristic of the pigment.

dopsins have been described. Three distinct membrane functions are carried out by members of this group: light-driven proton ejection from the cell [Oesterhelt and Stoeckenius, 1973], light-driven chloride uptake [Schobert and Lanyi, 1982], and phototaxis reception [Bogomolni and Spudich, 1982].

Two phototaxis receptors, sensory rhodopsins I [Bogomolni and Spudich, 1982] and II [Takahashi et al., 1985] (sR-I and sR-II) have been found in *Halobacterium halobium* [for review, see Spudich and Bogomolni, 1988]. A pigment similar to sR-II has been detected in the haloalkalophilic species *Halobacterium pharaonis* [Bivin and Stoeckenius, 1986]. The sensory rhodopsins detect variations in light intensity and color in the organism's environment. This information is processed to modulate the individual cells' swimming behavior so that cell populations are attracted to or repelled from particular regions of illumination [Hildebrand and Dencher, 1975; Dencher and Hildebrand, 1979].

It has been shown that neither sR-I nor sR-II function as electrogenic ion pumps [Spudich and Spudich, 1982; Bogomolni and Spudich, 1982; Ehrlich et al., 1984; Spudich and Bogomolni, 1988] and that their subsequent phototaxis signals do not propagate as electrical impulses along the membrane [Oesterhelt and Marwan, 1987]. A possibility suggested is that sR-I transfers information via physical interaction of the activated photoreceptor to an intrinsic membrane transducing protein (a methyl-accepting protein of approximately 97,000 kD [Spudich et al., 1988, 1989].

The five remaining bacterial rhodopsins are electrogenic ion transporters rather than photosensory transducers. The first discovered and best characterized of the bacterial rhodopsin family is the light-driven proton pump bacteriorhodopsin (bR) in *H. halobium* [Oesterhelt and Stoeckenius, 1971]. Two additional bR-like proton pumps, archaerhodopsin I and II (aR-I and aR-II) have been reported in an Australian halobacterium [Mukohata et al., 1988a,b]. Inwardly directed chloride transport is carried out by halorhodopsin (hR) in *H. halobium* [Schobert and Lanyi, 1982], and an hR-like pigment has been characterized in the haloalkalophilic *H. pharaonis* [Bivin and Stoeckenius, 1986; Lanyi et al., 1990a].

Comprehensive reviews of specific bacterial rhodopsins [sR-I and sR-II, Spudich and Bogomolni, 1988; bR and hR, Stoeckenius and Bogomolni, 1982; Stoeckenius, 1985; Khorana, 1988; Oesterhelt and Tittor, 1989; Lanyi, 1990; Mathies et al., 1991] are available. This review focuses on recent progress on mechanistic aspects of their function and a comparative analysis of their molecular properties. It is becoming apparent that the members of this family, despite their varied functions, share a common structural design. It now seems profitable to seek in the available information insights into the design principles that confer energy and sensory transducing functions on these chromoproteins.

II. CELLULAR LOCALIZATION

All of the bacterial rhodopsins are found embedded in the cytoplasmic membranes of the cells. bR laterally aggregates into a two-dimensional hexagonal lattice (purple membrane) that can be separated from the remainder of the membrane [Oesterhelt and Stoeckenius, 1974]. Formation of lattice aggregates has not been demonstrated for other bacterial rhodopsins, but circular dichroism (CD) measurements in native membranes suggest that hR may exist as small oligomers [Sugiyama and Mukohata, 1984]. Similar measurements confirmed the CD results for hR and did not detect specific aggregation of sR-I in membranes compared under the same conditions [Hasselbacher et al., 1988]. Measurement of their rotational mobility provides additional information on the state of the pigments in the native membrane. bR is essentially immobile in the purple membrane lattice [summarized by Cherry, 1982], but will function as monomers even when not present in a lattice structure [Dencher and Heyn, 1978]. bR is fully functional and mobile in the absence of a lattice, polarization anisotropy measurements showing a rotational diffusion time in this condition of 150 μsec [Cherry et al., 1977b]. hR and sR-I both exhibit rotational motions in the 200–300 μsec range in their native membranes (R.A. Bogomolni, unpublished data). These times are consistent with small aggregates rather than free monomers [Cherry et al., 1977a,b].

III. MOLECULAR STRUCTURE

bR consists of a single polypeptide of 248 amino acid residues arranged in seven membrane-spanning α-helical segments (Fig. 1) [Khorana, 1988]. Retinal is covalently bound to the ϵ-amino group of Lys-216 in the carboxyl-terminal helix in a protonated Schiff base linkage [Bayley et al., 1981; Katre et al., 1981; Lemke and Oesterhelt, 1981]. Furthermore, the retinal interacts noncovalently with protein residues that form the retinal binding pocket [reviewed by Stoeckenius and Bogomolni, 1982]. A similar structure for hR (250 residues) can be inferred from its amino acid sequence, which exhibits homology with bR in the retinal linkage site and some additional sequence conservation [Blanck and Oesterhelt, 1987] (Fig. 1). Incorporation of radiolabeled retinal into the chromophoric pockets of sR-I and sR-II allowed identification of their apoproteins in denaturing gels as distinct bands at 25,000 and 23,000 M_r, respectively [Sundberg et al., 1985; E.N. Spudich et al., 1986]. Similar apparent molecular weights were obtained when sR-I and sR-II were selectively radiolabeled and separated under gel conditions that did not resolve the two bands [Scherrer et al., 1987b]. The sR-I chromoprotein has been purified [Schegk and Oesterhelt, 1988] and its gene cloned and sequenced [Blanck et al., 1989]. The sR-I protein sequence exhibits homology to bR especially in those residues associated with the bR retinal binding site (Fig. 1).

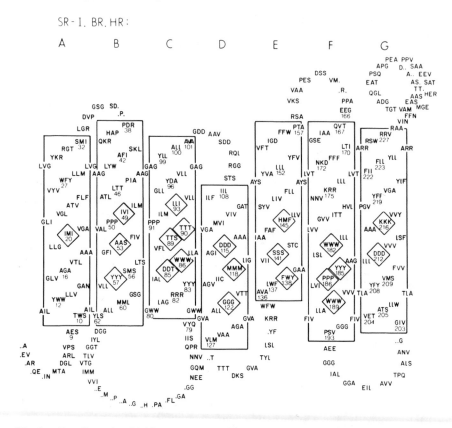

Fig. 1. Two-dimensional folding model of *H. halobium* retinylidene proteins sensory rhodopsin I (sR-I), bacteriorhodopsin (bR), and halorhodopsin (hR) (first, second, and third letters at each position, respectively). Numbers correspond to bR residues. Diamonds indicate residues placed in the retinal-binding pocket of bR on the basis of spectroscopic and diffraction data. A–G refer to the seven transmembrane α-helices. [Redrawn from Henderson et al., 1990.]

The three-dimensional structure of bR was originally determined at 7 Å resolution by pioneering use of low-dose electron microscopy and electron diffraction techniques [Unwin and Henderson, 1975]. The structure consisted of seven transmembrane rods roughly perpendicular to the membrane plane. The protein sequence could be arranged into seven amphiphobic membrane-spanning α-helical segments, but determining which of the 5,040 (7!) ways of assigning the sequence helices to the observed rods has required over a decade of diffraction analysis [Engelman et al., 1980; Engelman and Zaccai, 1980; Seiff et al., 1986; Trewhella et al., 1986; Henderson et al., 1990]. Khorana and coworkers have applied site-specific mutagenesis of a synthetic bR gene (*bop*) to identify protein residues interacting with retinal [Khorana, 1988]. In the procedure, the *bop* gene containing specific residue replacements are expressed in *Escherichia coli*, the mutant bR purified and reconstituted into lipid vesicles, and analyzed by molecular spectroscopy and other biophysical techniques [Hackett et al., 1987; Ahl et al., 1988; Braiman et al., 1988a,b; Marinetti et al., 1989; Otto et al., 1989; Rothschild et al., 1989; Altenbach et al., 1990]. Complementary information has been obtained from mutant *H. halobium* producing defective bR [Gerwert et al., 1989; Butt et al., 1989; Tittor et al., 1989]. These various approaches have culminated in the structure shown in Figure 1.

The retinal lies in a cleft formed by the transmembrane helices of bR [Heyn et al., 1988]. The Schiff base linkage is approximately midway across the membrane [King et al., 1979; Heyn et al., 1988] and the retinal polyene chain is inclined ~20° toward the extracellular surface of the membrane [Heyn et al., 1977; Bogomolni et al., 1978; Korenstein and Hess, 1978; Clark et al., 1980]. The β-ionone ring is therefore ~10 Å below the membrane surface [Leder et al., 1989]. The protonated Schiff base carries a positive charge that must be neutralized by anionic species, which may derive from several protein residues. The bonding, orientation, and additional interactions of retinal with the protein have been studied by spectroscopic techniques on native and mutant pigments, isotopically substituted pigments, and pigments containing retinal analogs. This information has been combined with recent structural studies with a resolution parallel to the membrane of 3.5 Å from electron cryomicroscopy and electron diffraction to generate an atomic resolution map of bR [Henderson et al., 1990]. Along the axis normal to the membrane only 10 Å resolution was achieved, and therefore ambiguities remain in the atomic coordinates along this axis. In addition, the positions and extents of the segments that link transmembrane α-helices and the position of the Schiff base linkage have not been precisely located.

hR and sR-I exhibit 32% and 26% identity with bR in their primary sequences, respectively [Blanck and Oesterhelt, 1987; Blanck et al., 1989]. Assigning these residues the same coordinates as those of bR reveals similarities as well as distinct differences in their structures [Henderson et al., 1990]. The hydrophobic retinal-binding pockets of all three proteins are essentially identical, consistent with earlier spectroscopic evidence [J.L. Spudich et al., 1986; Lanyi et al., 1988; Fodor et al., 1987, 1989].

The gene-derived sequences of *halobium* hR and *pharoanis* hR [Blanck and Oesterhelt, 1987; Lanyi et al., 1990a] are highly homologous, and the former is shown in Figure 1. Differences from bR are the larger number of arginine residues, most of which are concentrated on the protein surfaces, and the presence of only a single lysine in hR (the retinal-binding Lys-242). The residues of the retinal-binding site are conserved as well as the equivalents of Arg-82 and Arg-175 in bR (Arg-108 and Arg-200, respectively, in hR). A significant difference is that the Asp-85 and Asp-96, which function as proton relay groups in bR, are missing in hR.

Even though there is no direct access of water to the pocket interior, all three deduced structures contain a presumably water-filled crevice that penetrates several angstroms from the extracellular surface of the molecule to near the chromophore [Henderson et al., 1990]. Appropriately positioned groups could bridge the exchange of ions between the exterior milieu and the Schiff base environment. Isotope labeling and infrared difference spectroscopy implicated aspartic acids in this process [Engelhard et al., 1985]. In fact, in bR Asp-85 appears to relay the Schiff base proton to the exterior during the pumping cycle [Braiman, 1988; Stern et al., 1989; Butt et al., 1989; Otto et al., 1990]. This aspartate is conserved in sR-I, but whether it undergoes protonation changes during the photochemical reaction cycle is not determined. An additional aspartate (Asp-96) mediates reprotonation of the Schiff base from the cytoplasmic side of the membrane [Braiman et al., 1988a; Otto et al., 1989; Butt et al., 1989; Holz et al., 1989]. Asp-96 is not conserved in either hR or sR-I. Differences at this position and in other residues on the cytoplasmic side of the proteins may have profound implications in determining ion specificity and whether an ion is translocated across the protein. In bR Asp-96 is a component of a proton channel of ~2 Å in diameter from the cytoplasm to the Schiff base [Henderson et al., 1990]. In sR-I this channel appears to be blocked by hydrophobic residues. In hR, on the other hand, the channel is wider (~3 Å).

IV. LIGHT ABSORPTION AND COLOR REGULATION

The wavelengths of maximal absorption of bR and hR depend on whether the pigments have been preilluminated. Dark-adapted values are shifted 10 and 5 nm, respectively, to the blue of the light-adapted values. Absorption spectra of the light-adapted pigments is shown in Figure 2. The isomeric configuration of the retinylidene moiety in light-adapted bR and hR is all-*trans*. These forms are metastable and spontaneously decay in the dark (bR in hours and hR in days) into a mixture of 13-*cis* and all-*trans* isomers of the retinylidene moiety [Oesterhelt and Stoeckenius, 1971; Scherrer et al., 1987a; Kamo et al., 1985]. Forms containing all-*trans* retinal in the light-adapted or dark-adapted condition are functional in ion pumping, whereas the 13-*cis* forms are not. SR-I [Tsuda et al., 1985; Fodor et al., 1989] and sR-II (T. Takahashi, B. Yan, K. Nakanishi, and J.L. Spudich, unpublished data) contain all-*trans* retinal as the predominant (possibly exclusive) isomer, and light/dark adaptation as in bR and hR has not been observed. The absence of thermal isomerization of retinal in sR-I appears to be a fundamental difference from the ion pumps. All-*trans* retinal linked as an unprotonated Schiff base in model compounds absorbs near 380 nm. Protonation of the Schiff base nitrogen shifts the absorp-

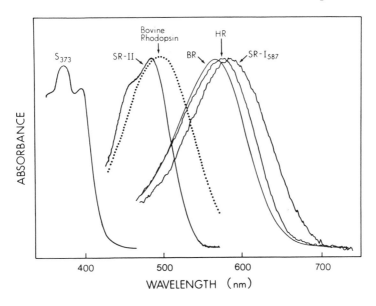

Fig. 2. Absorption spectra of *H. halobium* bR, hR, and sR-I in the native membrane [redrawn from Spudich and Bogomolni, 1983] and of the repellent form of sR-I, S_{373}, calculated from photostationary state absorption changes by the authors. [The spectra of sR-II and bovine rhodopsin are from Takahashi et al., 1990, and Koutalos et al., 1989, respectively.]

tion to ~445 nm. Noncovalent interactions in the binding pockets of the apoproteins cause the additional shifts ("opsin shifts" [Nakanishi et al., 1980]) to longer wavelengths shown by all of the known bacterial rhodopsins. Factors that have been suggested to contribute to the opsin shifts of retinylidene pigments are configurational changes of the retinal structure [Harbison et al., 1985; Lugtenburg et al., 1986; Baselt et al., 1989; Takahashi et al., 1990], interactions of the retinal with charged protein residues [Nakanishi et al., 1980; J.L. Spudich et al., 1986; Lanyi et al., 1988], and the strength of hydrogen bonding of the Schiff base proton [Fodor et al., 1989]. This field has been recently reviewed by Ottolenghi and Sheves [1989] and by Mathies et al. [1991].

Configurational contributions to the absorption spectrum arise from the isomeric configuration of the double-bond system (e.g., *cis* forms absorb at shorter wavelengths) or from torsional stress around C–C bonds that determines the degree of single- or double-bond character (bond order) and the degree of planarity of the system. The conjugated polyene extends into the b-ionone ring, which contributes one double bond to the system. In model compounds, as in free retinal, steric interactions prevent the ring from being coplanar with the chain. This deviation from planarity results in a higher energy transition and therefore blue-shifted absorption. The angle of the polyene chain to the ring is one parameter that is subject to modulation by the protein to determine its color as well as the vibronic features of its absorption spectrum [Takahashi et al., 1990, and references therein]. In bR, planarization of the ring has been shown by solid-state NMR and accounts for ~1,200 cm^{-1} of opsin shift [Harbison et al., 1985]. Optical spectroscopic evidence for ring/chain coplanarity based on retinal analog studies has been reported for sR-I [Fodor et al., 1989] and sR-II [Takahashi et al., 1990].

Two possible configurations for the ring double bond are *trans* or *cis* with respect to the nearest double bond in the polyene chain. In bR [Harbison et al., 1985; Smith et al., 1989] and in hR and sR-I [Fodor et al., 1987, 1989], the configuration is 6-s-*trans*. This structure differs from that of the visual pigment rhodopsin, which in the photolyzed all-*trans* form contains a 6-s-*cis* retinal.

Perturbations of tryptophan absorption and emission [Becher and Ebrey, 1977; Schreckenbach et al., 1977] associated with chromophore formation, perturbation in tryptophan spectra during the photocycle, transfer of excitation energy from retinal to tryptophan [Bogomolni et al., 1978; El-Sayed et al., 1981; Polland et al., 1986], and effects of tryptophan replacement in bR mutants [Khorana, 1988] indicate a strong coupling between the retinal and tryptophan residues of the bR protein. These observations are consistent with the participation of tryptophanes in the retinal-binding pocket (Fig. 1). The extent to which these interactions contribute to chromophore absorption and photochemical properties is not clear.

Electrostatic interactions have been proposed to be a factor in color regulation [Nakanishi et al., 1980] and have been shown to regulate color in model compounds [Baasov and Sheves, 1985]. From energetic considerations, charge neutralization must occur at the protonated Schiff base, and a priori additional interactions could occur along the chain or ring portion of the retinal. The presence of a charge pair near the ring has been inferred from ^{13}C-NMR data from isotopically substituted bR analogs [Harbison et al., 1985]. Another approach based on analysis of spectral properties of a series of retinal analog pigments led to models for the electrostatic environment of bR [J.L. Spudich et al., 1986; Lugtenburg et al., 1986], sR-I (J.L. Spudich et al., 1986], and hR [Lanyi et al., 1988]. The independently derived models for each of the three pigments are closely similar, consisting of a negative charge acting as counterion to the Schiff base proton and also a charge pair (or dipole) near the ring consistent with the NMR data [Harbison et al., 1985]. Replacement by site-directed mutagenesis of aspartate residues, some of which were primary candidates for the negatively charged counterion, had less effect on chromophore color than expected if single residues provided the Schiff base proton counterion and the negative charge of the ring charge pair [Khorana, 1988]. This could indicate that the NMR and retinal analog results require reinterpretation. On the other hand, compensatory movements of other charged residues are expected to occur in the mutant bR to avoid an uncompensated charge and to reestablish a salt bridge in the hydrophobic protein interior. For each of these three pigments, it has been shown that the hydrogen bond strength of the Schiff base proton is progressively less in the order bR, hR, sR-I, and this factor has been suggested to be responsible for their differences in absorption maxima [Fodor et al., 1989].

V. PHOTOCHEMICAL REACTIONS AND MOLECULAR TRANSFORMATIONS

Following photoexcitation, retinylidene pigments exhibit only very weak fluorescence; decay from the excited state occurs mainly via radiationless transitions or by formation of metastable photochemical products, which store a substantial fraction of the photon energy [Birge, 1990]. The currently accepted quantum yield for this primary reaction is about 0.6–0.7 for bR and hR [Oesterhelt and Tittor, 1989]. These high-energy products return spontaneously to the original state via a series of thermal reactions each of which affects the chromophore absorption properties. The resulting color changes have been used to define spectral intermediates of this cyclic process, which occurs in the range of 7–15 msec for the ion pumps and 0.3–1.0 sec for the sensory pigments (Fig. 3). These transitions have been used as temporal markers to which other molecular events in the chromoprotein are referred. A priori additional molecular events in the protein do not have to result in chromophore spectral shifts or to occur in synchrony with them. However the experimental finding is that most processes (e.g., proton release and uptake by bR, intramolecular proton transfer reactions and other charge displacements, and other molecular rearrangements) show close correlation with the formation and decay of spectral intermediates.

Mechanistic knowledge has been provided mainly by spectroscopic techniques, e.g., vibrational spectroscopy, NMR, CD, fluorescence and UV/visible absorption spectroscopy, and laser flash photolysis [reviewed by Mathies et al., 1991]. In the case of bR, studies of electrical transients caused by charge displacements have provided an additional important biophysical approach [Trissl and Gärtner, 1987; Keszthelyi and Ormos, 1980; Drachev et al., 1986; Butt et al., 1989; Otto et al., 1990]. Despite some fundamental differences, there are common features to the molecular transformations of both the sensory signaling pigments and the ion pumps. We first discuss bR for which site-specifically mutated and other altered forms have greatly facilitated interpretation of the molecular processes underlying the photochemical reaction cycle.

SENSORY RHODOPSIN I

SENSORY RHODOPSIN II

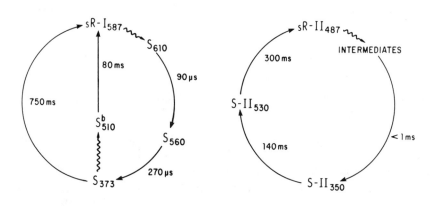

BACTERIORHODOPSIN

HALORHODOPSIN

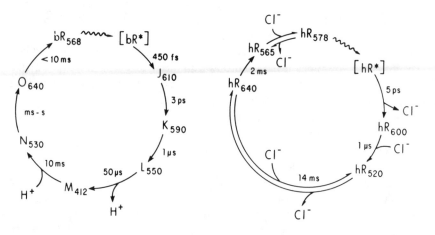

Fig. 3. Photochemical reaction cycles of *H. halobium* retinylidene proteins. Wavy arrows indicate light-driven reactions, other arrows indicate thermal reactions for which half-lives are shown, and subscripts denote absorption maxima of intermediate species. Only the photocycles associated with transport and phototaxis signaling functions are shown. sR-I data are from Bogomolni and Spudich [1987], sR-II data are from Tomioka et al. [1986], and bR and hR data are from Oesterhelt and Tittor [1989]; for the hR photocycle, see also Zimanyi and Lanyi [1989].

A. bR, a Light-Driven Proton Pump

Recent work has focused on the elucidation of the path of the proton during the bR pumping photocycle. Early proton relay models were proposed based on an icelike conduction pathway onto which an excess proton is injected, e.g., by the light-driven Schiff base deprotonation, and transported passively into the aqueous medium [Nagle and Morowitz, 1978; Rastogi and Zundel, 1981]. The current emerging view is that although static conduction paths may exist in portions of the overall path, the key vectorial proton transport steps occur by localized proton transfer reactions activated by small transient sequential rearrangements of charged protein side chains during the photocycle. The unidirectionality of proton transport is a consequence of temporal coordination of these movements. The groups that intervene in these key steps have been elucidated primarily by amino acid replacement by site-specific mutagenesis of the bR gene [Khorana, 1988] and altered bR in *H. halobium* proton pump mutants [Soppa and Oesterhelt, 1989].

The photochemical reaction cycle kinetics and intermediate states (Fig. 3) were intially identified by their absorption properties in the UV/visible range, which reflect chromophoric transitions [Lozier et al., 1975]. The first chemical process that has been detected following photoexcitation is isomerization of retinal around its C13–C14 double bond. *Trans* to *cis* isomerization occurs within 200 fsec, generating the earliest ground state intermediate, J [Mathies et al., 1988]. Chromophore and protein relaxations in the picosecond time scale generate an intermediate state, K (Fig. 3). The formation of K appears to involve a proton transfer reaction or change in hydrogen bonding in Tyr-185 [Dollinger et al., 1987; Braiman et al., 1988b; Lin and Mathies, 1989]. A species, K_L, with a slight shift in absorption to the blue appears in nanoseconds (at ambient temperature and neutral pH), presumably caused by further protein relaxations [Shichida et al., 1983].

The subsequent events and their relation to the proton pumping mechanism have been summarized in detail by Mathies et al. [1991]. K_L decays into L within 2 μsec. In the formation of L, protein residues enhance H-bonding to the Schiff base proton. As L decays into M, the Schiff base deprotonates and Asp-85 protonates, presumably serving as the immediate proton acceptor from the Schiff base. Proton release into the extracellular compartment is detected with some delay after appearance of the M intermediate. The chromophore of M contains therefore a 13-*cis* retinal attached via an unprotonated Schiff base linkage. Reprotonation of the Schiff base occurs in the transition of M to N. Three groups known to deprotonate in the later part of the photocycle are Asp-85, -96 and -212. Asp-85 has been implicated in the proton release path into the extracellular space, leaving the latter two aspartates as potential donors to the Schiff base.

To complete the cycle, proton uptake from the intracellular side must occur, and the reprotonated Schiff base chromophore must undergo a *cis* to *trans* isomerization about the retinylidene C13–C14 double bond. Reprotonation and isomerization take place sequentially during formation and decay of the last photocycle intermediates, N and O. One proton is released and one proton is taken up per each turn of the photocycle [Grzesiek and Dencher, 1986]. This pumping stoichiometry combined with the photoreaction quantum yield allows calculation of the energy conversion efficiency of bR, which is approximately 0.6 protons per photon absorbed. Protons are pumped in the intact cell against their resting electrochemical potential of about 200 mV (~10 Kcal/mole). The photons of lowest energy able to drive the pump (i.e., at the red edge of the absorption band) have an energy of about 40 Kcal/mole. Therefore, the efficiency of the pump may reach 25%.

Each proton transfer reaction with a component normal to the membrane plane is expected to generate a local electrical current. These charge displacements have been detected, their magnitudes interpreted in terms of distances of proton transfer, and, recently, this approach has been applied to a site-specifically mutated bR to correlate Asp-96–associated proton movement with reprotonation of the Schiff base during the decay of the M intermediate [Holz et al., 1989].

B. hR, a Light-Driven Chloride Pump

hR pumps chloride from the extracellular side to the cytoplasmic side of the membrane [Schobert and Lanyi, 1982]. The color, photochemical properties of hR and the capacity to transport are regulated by chloride and other anions [Ogurusu et al., 1982; Stoeckenius and Bogomolni, 1982; Schobert et al., 1983; Taylor et al., 1983; Schobert and Lanyi, 1986; Lanyi et al., 1990b]. Three anion binding sites have been distinguished. Sites I and III are relatively nonspecific. Site II is more specific for chloride than polyatomic anions (e.g., nitrate, thiocyanate) and is located on the extracellular side of the membrane. When site II is occupied by chloride the pigment is functional in chloride transport, its absorption maximum is 578 nm, and it exhibits a photocycle containing K, K_L, L, and O-like intermediates (Fig. 3). Site II is conserved in *halobium* hR and *pharaonis* hR, and the specificity of transported ions correlates with their binding affinities for site II. When both sites are unoccupied, hR absorbs maximally at 565 nm and exhibits a truncated photocycle. It is also inferred from spectroscopic and functional properties of hR that occupancy of site I only by an anion does not restores the full photocycle or transport. In contrast to that of bR, the hR photocycle has no detectable M-like intermediate and includes two steps that involve chloride-dependent equilibria [Zimanyi et al., 1989]. These latter steps could serve as the basis of a chloride transport mechanism if the chloride exchange processes take place at opposite sides of the membrane. The kinetics, stoichiometry, quantum yield, and sidedness of uptake and release are needed to link events in the photocycle with events in chloride transport.

Despite being a chloride pump and not having an M-like chromophoric state, hR shows striking similarities to bR in the chromophore conformations of its hR_{578}, hR_K, and hR_L intermediates [Smith et al., 1984; Polland et al., 1985; Fodor et al., 1987; Zimanyi et al., 1989]. However, even though hR_L does not undergo proton transfer from the Schiff base, intramolecular reactions characteristic of bR's M state occur in hR_L [Rothschild et al., 1988]. Although the locations and functional roles of anion binding sites I and III are still unclear, there is some suggestion from the sequence comparisons and anion binding and pumping specificities of *halobium* hR and *pharaonis* hR that these sites play a role in chloride release after its translocation [Lanyi et al., 1990a; Lanyi, 1990].

C. sR-I, a Color-Discriminating Phototaxis Receptor

The photochemical reactions of sR-I modulate reorientation behavior of swimming cells, controlling their direction of travel in light gradients. This molecule is unusual among known photoreceptors in that it exists in two spectrally distinct forms, each of which can be photoactivated to generate sensory signals [Bogomolni and Spudich, 1982; Spudich and Bogomolni, 1984]. Photoexcitation of the thermally stable species $sR-I_{587}$ (Fig. 3) suppresses directional reorientation (swimming reversals), thereby favoring cell migration into higher intensity regions of orange light. Therefore, $sR-I_{587}$ is an attractant photoreceptor. Another form of sR-I, a long-lived photointermediate (S_{373}; Fig. 3), is a repellent receptor. The thermal decay of S_{373} is slow, and constant orange background light absorbed by $sR-I_{587}$ generates a photostationary state in which the attractant and repellent forms of sR-I coexist. Photoexcitation of S_{373} induces swimming reversals and converts it back into $sR-I_{587}$. The activation of as few as one to two S_{373} molecules is sufficient to elicit a response [Spudich and Bogomolni, 1984]. The interconversion of the two receptor forms by light (photochromicity) and the opposite cellular signals associated with these photoreactions provide the cell with a simple yet highly effective color-discriminating capability with exquisite sensitivity.

The photochemical reaction cycle of sR-I is analogous to that of bR (Fig. 3). The first detected intermediate, S_{610}, forms in less than 10 nsec (M. Tsuda, personal communication) and decays in 80 μsec [Bogomolni and Spudich, 1982, 1987]. Similar red-shifted species occur as early intermediates in all retinylidene proteins (e.g., bathorhodopsin in bovine rhodopsin, K in bR). S_{610} decays to S_{560} with the slowest rate compared with analogous bathointermediates in other pigments. On the basis of their absorption spectra and close similarity to bR, one expects these three sR-I intermediates to contain 13-*cis* retinylidene chromophores, protonated in the first two and unprotonated in S_{373}. All-*trans* to 13-*cis* isomerization of retinal has been concluded to be required for formation of photochemical intermediates and phototaxis signaling by both sR-I and sR-II [Yan et al., 1990].

Because of the similarity of the sR-I photointermediates to those of bR, the alphabetic nomenclature developed for bR is conveniently used to describe the sR-I intermediates (i.e., S_{610}, S_{560}, and S_{373} are referred to as SR^K, SR^L, and SR^M, respectively). This is useful in light of the likely correspondence between molecular transformations in sR-I and bR. However, there are fundamental differences between the two chromoproteins, and therefore some processes that characterize bR intermediates may occur in sR-I at different states or not occur at all, considering that sR-I is not an ion pump.

An important difference between the photoactivation processes of sR-I and bR has become evident through incorporation of retinal analogs. Unlike the bR apoprotein (BOP), the sR-I apoprotein (SOP-I) does not form a retinylidene pigment with 13-*cis* retinal, as assessed by absorption measurements [Yan et al., in press], SDS-PAGE isolation of SOP-I after [^{3}H]-13-*cis* retinal addition and $CNBH_3^-$ reduction (E.N. Spudich, unpublished data), and by lack of pigment generation with 13-*cis* locked analog (J. Fukushima et al., in preparation). Unlike BOP [Gartner et al., 1988], SOP-I does not thermally isomerize all-*trans* 13-desmethyl retinal to 13-*cis*, and the corresponding analog sR-I pigment does not exhibit photochemical reactivity detectable at 1 msec resolution [Yan et al., in press]. This indicates that photoactivation of sR-I requires a specific steric interaction between the protein and the 13-methyl group of the retinal. This requirement differs from that of bR but resembles that of rhodopsin, in which steric interaction between the protein and the retinal 9-methyl group is crucial for photoactivation [Ganter et al., 1989].

Photoexcitation of sR-I does not cause proton fluxes or sustained hyperpolarization of the membranes of intact cells or vesicles [reviewed in Spudich and Bogomolni, 1988]. This rules out sR-I functioning as an electrogenic ion pump. One hypotheses for its function is based on the observation of several close behavioral and biochemical analogies with chemotaxis in eubacteria (e.g., *Escherichia coli*) [Spudich and Stoeckenius, 1980; Schimz, 1981; Bibikov et al., 1982]. In particular, proteins chemically similar to the intrinsic membrane methyl-accepting proteins that generate the signals modulating the flagellar motor in *E. coli* have been observed in *H. halobium* [Spudich et al., 1988; Alam et al., 1989], and one of these (an approximately 97 kD protein called methyl-accepting phototaxis protein-I [MPP-I] is lost simultaneously with the chromoprotein in three independently isolated sR-I signaling mutants [Spudich et al., 1988, 1989; E.N. Spudich, unpublished data]. Furthermore, a mutant that overproduces sR-I chromoprotein also overproduces MPP-I to a similar extent [Spudich et al., 1988]. There is evidence a distinct methyl-accepting protein exists for sR-II [Spudich et al., 1989]. The type of methylation of these *H. halobium* proteins (carboxylmethylesterification) is in eubacteria characteristic of the methyl-accepting signaling proteins of chemotaxis [Simon et al., 1985]. Furthermore, methylation/demethylation as assessed by changes in carboxylmethyl turnover rate is regulated by chemostimuli and photostimuli [Alam et al., 1989] and specifically by the attractant and repellent receptor forms of sR-I [Spudich et al., 1989]. Evidence indicating a diffusible signal in *H. halobium* phototaxis as in eubacterial chemotaxis strengthens this analogy [Marwan and Oesterhelt, 1987]. Our working model is that "activated" sR-I chromoprotein interacts with MPP-I, which relays the signal to the flagellar motor.

Results have been presented supporting the hypothesis that cyclic nucleotides, Ca^{2+}, and a G protein are also involved in the photosensory transduction chain in *H. halobium* [Schimz and Hildebrand, 1987; Schimz et al., 1989]. The analogy to the visual transduction system would have interesting physiological and evolutionary implications. Also, fumarate has been implicated as a component in the signaling pathway [Marwan et al., 1990].

In general, for a photocycling receptor any of its photointermediates could in principle initiate the signaling process via either of two classes of mechanisms. In the first class, the active intermediate acquires a conformation that allows it to interact with a component of the signaling system. The intermediate is the "activated" (or "signaling") receptor state. In this sense, meta-II, which interacts with the G protein transducin, is the signaling state of bovine rhodopsin [Bennett et al., 1982]. In the second class, a signal is generated during the transition between two intermediates of the photocycle. For example, the transition may be chemically coupled to a reaction that generates a signal. In this case the amount of signal produced will depend on the frequency of the transition, while in the former case the amount of signal will depend on the concentration of the signaling state.

Retinal analogs that increase the lifetime of S_{373} enhance the sensitivity of the cells to sR-I_{587}–mediated attractant stimuli [McCain et al., 1987; Yan and Spudich, in press]. Since these analogs decrease the frequency of photocycling (and thereby of all transitions in the photocycle), the result supports a mechanism in which S_{373} is the signaling state of the attractant receptor sR-I_{587}. A similar approach indicates that S-II_{530} and S-II_{350} are signaling states in the sR-II photocycle (B. Yan et al., in preparation).

D. sR-II, a Repellent Receptor for Blue-Green Light

sR-II is the only retinylidene pigment present in significant concentrations in exponential phase *H. halobium* cells [Tomioka et al., 1986b]. sR-II exhibits a pronounced shoulder in its absorption spectrum (Fig. 2), attributable to vibrational fine structure [Takahashi et al., 1990]. sR-II absorbs maximally near the energy peak of the solar spectrum at the earth surface and therefore provides a sensitive avoidance response to light when the cells have ample respiratory activity. Synthesis of bR, hR, and sR-I are induced by the decrease in oxygen tension as cells enter stationary phase and require light as an energy source [Oesterhelt and Stoeckenius, 1974].

Photoreaction cycle intermediates can be trapped at cryogenic temperatures and the sequence of thermal states obtained by stepwise warming of the sample. This technique was used to identify early intermediates in the sR-II photocycle [Imamoto et al., 1988]. At room temperature later intermediates have been resolved [Tomioka et al., 1986a; Wolff et al., 1986; Scherrer et al., 1987b] (Fig. 3). Like bR and sR-I, the sR-II photocycle exhibits intermediates with K-, L-, and M-like absorption. An O-like intermediate is also observed, as in bR.

Thus far only repellent responses have been detected in mutants containing sR-II and lacking sR-I. sR-II, like sR-I, is not an electrogenic ion pump. sR-I attractant and sR-II repellent signals add algebraically in their effect on swimming reversal frequency (J.L. Spudich, unpublished data), and simultaneous activation of the sR-I attractant form and sR-II mutually cancel in their effects on the methylation system [Spudich et al., 1989]. This modulation indicates the existence of an sR-II–related methyl-accepting protein that must be distinct from the sR-I methyl-accepting protein MPP-I because sR-II functions in its absence [Spudich et al., 1989]. An sR-II–associated methyl-accepting protein is yet to be identified.

VI. PERSPECTIVES

The elucidation of the pumping mechanisms is expected to continue rapidly because of the diversity of spectroscopic techniques rich in structural information applied to genetically engineered pigments. It is likely that structures of intermediate states will approach the resolution achieved for bR in the near future, that the structure of bR will be further refined to true atomic resolution, and that this arsenal of methods will be successfully extended to hR. These structures combined with the results from spectroscopy should generate firm models for the residues that form the intramolecular paths of ion transport. However, this will provide only a static picture. The dynamics of charge transport between these groups will require use of techniques that provide information on time-dependence and physical mechanisms of charge conductivity. For example, how does one account for the large charge displacement distance observed in the final step reprotonating the Schiff base (>10 Å)?

Reasoning by analogy with the molecular transformations in bR should guide studies of the photoactivation of the sensory receptors. However, the pumps function as individual polypeptides, whereas the sensory rhodopsins signal through additional components. Thus their signaling mechanisms cannot be elucidated by studies only of the purified chromoproteins in isolation. Efforts to apply spectroscopic methods in the intact native membrane system are beginning to be successful. This work will help to identify the minimum components for information transfer from the photoactivated chromoprotein. Functional reconstitution of these signaling components into lipid bilayers or detergent micelles will contribute toward resolving the molecular transformations that accomplish information transfer.

Sensory transduction in halobacteria has profitted from mutant isolation and analysis and now is being examined by molecular genetic approaches, which have played a central role in the related eubacterial chemotaxis system. Procedures for isolation of phototaxis mutants in halobacteria are available, and the molecular genetics of halobacteria is in a rapid phase of development. The tools for the expression of genetically modified chromoproteins and subsequent components are close at hand.

Transport and sensory transduction, previously regarded as being carried out by fundamentally different molecular machinery, are accomplished by the archaebacterial rhodopsins through subtle modifications of a common molecular design. With this system, nature has provide us with a wonderful opportunity to understand molecular mechanisms and the evolution of these two fundamental membrane protein functions.

VII. REFERENCES

Ahl PL, Stern LJ, During D, Mogi T, Khorana HG, Rothschild KJ (1988) Effects of amino acid substitutions in the F helix of bacteriorhodopsin. J Biol Chem 263:13594–13601.

Alam M, Lebert M, Oesterhelt D, Hazelbauer GL (1989) Methyl-accepting taxis proteins in *Halobacterium halobium*. EMBO J 8:631–639.

Altenbach C, Marti T, Khorana HG, Hubbell WL (1990) Transmembrane protein structure: Spin labeling of bacteriorhodopsin mutants. Science 248:1088–1092.

Baasov T, Sheves M (1985) Model compounds for the study of spectroscopic properties of visual pigments and bacteriorhodopsin. J Am Chem Soc 107:7524–7533.

Baselt DR, Fodor SPA, van der Steen R, Lugtenburg J, Bogomolni RA, Mathies RA (1989) Halorhodopsin and sensory rhodopsin contain a C_6C_7-s-*trans* retinal chromophore. Biophys J 55:193–196.

Bayley H, Huang K-S, Radhakrishnan R, RossAH, Takagaki Y, Khorana HG (1981) The site of attachment of retinal in bacteriorhodopsin. Proc Natl Acad Sci USA 78:2225–2229.

Becher B, Ebrey TG (1977) The quantum efficiency for the photochemical conversion of the purple membrane protein. Biophys J 17:185–191.

Bennett N, Michel-Villaz M, Kuhn H (1982) Light-induced interaction between rhodopsin and the GTP-binding protein. Metarhodopsin II is the major photoproduct involved. Eur J Biochem 127:97–103.

Bibikov SI, Baryshev VA, Glagolev AN (1982) The role of methylation in the taxis of *Halobacterium halobium* to light and chemo-effectors. FEBS Lett 146:255–258.

Birge RR (1990) Nature of the primary photochemical events in rhodopsin and bacteriorhodopsin. Biochim Biphys Acta 1016:293–327.

Bivin DB, Stoeckenius W (1986) Photoactive retinal pigments in haloalkaliphilic bacteria. J Gen Microbiol 132:2167–2177.

Blanck A, Oesterhelt D (1987) The halo-opsin gene. II. Sequence, primary structure of halorhodopsin and comparison with bacteriorhodopsin. EMBO J 6:265–273.

Blanck A, Oesterhelt D, Ferrando E, Schegk ES, Lottspeich F (1989) Primary structure of sensory rhodopsin I, a prokaryotic photoreceptor. EMBO J 8:3963–3971.

Bogomolni RA, Spudich JL (1982) Identification of a third rhodopsin-like pigment in phototactic *Halobacterium halobium*. Proc Natl Acad Sci USA 79:6250–6254.

Bogomolni RA, Spudich JL (1987) The photochemical reactions of bacterial sensory rhodopsin-I: Flash photolysis study in the one microsecond to eight second time window. Biophys J 52:1071–1075.

Bogomolni RA, Stubbs L, Lanyi JK (1978) Illumination dependent changes in the intrinsic fluorescence of bacteriorhodopsin. Biochemistry 17:1037–1041.

Braiman MS, Mogi T, Marti T, Stern LJ, Khorana HG, Rothschild KJ (1988a) Vibrational spectroscopy of bacteriorhodopsin mutants: Light-driven proton transport involves protonation changes of aspartic acid residues 85, 96 and 212. Biochemistry 27:8516–8520.

Braiman MS, Mogi T, Stern LJ, Hackett NR, Chao BH, Khorana HG, Rothschild KJ (1988b) Vibrational spectroscopy of bacteriorhodopsin mutants: I. Tyrosine-185 protonates and deprotonates during the photocycle. Proteins 3:219–229.

Butt HJ, Fendler K, Bamberg E, Tittor J, Oesterhelt D (1989) Aspartic acids 96 and 85 play a central role in the function of bacteriorhodopsin as a proton pump. EMBO J 8:1657–1663.

Cherry RJ (1982) Transient dichroism of bacteriorhodopsin. Methods Enzymol 88:248–254.

Cherry RJ, Heyn MP, Oesterhelt D (1977a) Rotational diffusion and excitation coupling of bacteriorhodopsin in the cell membrane of *Halobacterium halobium*. FEBS Lett 78:25–30.

Cherry RJ, Muller U, Schneider G (1977b) Rotational diffusion of bacteriorhodopsin in lipid membranes. FEBS Lett 80:465–469.

Clark NA, Rothschild KJ, Luippold DA, Simon BA (1980) Surface-induced lamellar orientation of multilayer membrane arrays: Theoretical analysis and a new method with application to purple membrane fragments. Biophys J 31:65–96.

Dencher NA, Heyn MP (1978) Formation and properties of bacteriorhodopsin monomers in the non-ionic detergents octyl-b-D-glucoside and Triton X-100. FEBS Lett 96:322–326.

Dencher NA, Hildebrand E (1979) Sensory transduction in *Halobacterium halobium*: Retinal protein pigment controls UV-induced behavioral response. Z Naturforsch 34:841–847.

Dollinger G, Eisenstein L, Lin S-L, Nakanishi K, Termini J (1987) The role of tyrosine in the proton pump of bacteriorhodopsin. In Ebrey TG, Frauenfelder H, Honig B, Nakanishi K (eds): Biophysical Studies of Retinal Proteins. Urbana, IL: University of Illinois Press, pp 120–125.

Drachev LA, Kaulen AD, Skulachev VP, Zorina VV (1986) Protonation of a novel intermediate P is involved in the M → bR step of the bacteriorhodopsin photocycle. FEBS Lett 209:316–320.

Ehrlich B, Schen C, Spudich JL (1984) Bacterial rhodopsins monitored with fluorescent dyes in vesicles and in vivo. J Membrane Biol 82:89–94.

El-Sayed MA, Karvaly B, Fukomoto JM (1981) Primary step in the bacteriorhodopsin photocycle: Photochemistry or excitation transfer? Proc Natl Acad Sci USA 78:7512–7516.

Engelhard M, Gerwert K, Hess B, Kreutz W, Siebert F (1985) Light-driven protonation changes of internal aspartic acids of bacteriorhodopsin: An investigation by static and time-resolved infrared difference spectroscopy using (4-13C) aspartic acid labelled purple membrane. Biochemistry 24:400–407.

Engelman DM, Henderson R, McLachlan AD, Wallace BA (1980) Path of the polypeptide in bacteriorhodopsin. Proc Natl Acad Sci, USA 77:2023–2027.

Engelman DM, Zaccai G (1980) Bacteriorhodopsin is an inside-out protein. Proc Natl Acad Sci USA 77:5894–5898.

Fodor SPA, Bogomolni RA, Mathies RA (1987) Structure of the retinal chromophore in the hRL intermediate of halorhodopsin from resonance Raman spectroscopy. Biochemistry 26:6775–6778.

Fodor SPA, Gebhard R, Lugtenburgh J, Bogomolni RA, Mathies RA (1989) Structure of the retinal chromophore in sensory rhodopsin I from resonance Raman spectroscopy. J Biol Chem 264:18280–18283.

Ganter UN, Schmid ED, Perez-Sala D, Rando RR, Siebert F (1989) Removal of the 9-methyl group of retinal inhibits signal transduction in the visual process: A Fourier transform infrared and biochemical investigation. Biochemistry 28:5954–5962.

Gärtner W, Oesterhelt D, Vogel J, Maurer R, Schneider S (1988) Photocycles of bacteriorhodopsins containing 13-alkyl-substituted retinals. Biochemistry 27:3497–3502.

Gerwert K, Hess B, Soppa J, Oesterhelt D (1989) Role of aspartate-96 in proton translocation by bacteriorhodopsin. Proc Natl Acad Sci USA 86:4943–4947.

Grzesiek S, Dencher NA (1986) Time-course and stoichiometry of light-induced proton release and uptake during the photocycle of bacteriorhodopsin. FEBS Lett 208:337–342.

Hackett NR, Stern LJ, Chao BH, Kronis KA, Khorana HG (1987) Structure–function studies on bacteriorhodopsin: V. Effects of amino acid substitutions in the putative helix F. J Biol Chem 262:9277–9284.

Harbison GS, Smith SO, Pardoen JA, Courtin JML, Lugtenburg J, Herzfeld J, Mathies RA, Griffin RG (1985) Solid state 13C-NMR detection of a perturbed 6-s *trans* chromophore in bacteriorhodopsin. Biochemistry 24:6955–6962.

Hasselbacher CA, Spudich JL, Dewey TG (1988) Circular dichroism of halorhodopsin: Comparison with bacteriorhodopsin and sensory rhodopsin I. Biochemistry 27:2540–2546.

Henderson R, Baldwin JM, Ceska TA, Zemlin F, Beckmann E, Downing KH (1990) Model for the structure of bacteriorhodopsin based on high-resolution electron cryo-microscopy. J Mol Biol 213:899–929.

Heyn MP, Cherry RJ, Muller U (1977) Transient and linear dichroism studies on bacteriorhodopsin: Determination of the orientation of the 568 nm all-*trans* retinal chromophore. J Mol Biol 117:607–620.

Heyn MP, Westerhausen J, Wallat I, Seiff F (1988) High sensitivity neutron diffraction of membranes: Location of the Schiff's base end of the chromophore of bacteriorhodopsin. Proc Natl Acad Sci USA 85:2146–2150.

Hildebrand E, Dencher N (1975) Two photosystems controlling behavioral responses of *Halobacterium halobium*. Nature 257:46–48.

Holz M, Drachev LA, Mogi T, Otto H, Kaulen AD, Heyn MP, Skulachev VP, Khorana HG (1989) Replacement to aspartic acid-96 by asparagine in bacteriorhodopsin slows both the decay of the M intermediate and the associated proton movement. Proc Natl Acad Sci USA 86:529–533.

Imamoto Y, Schichida Y, Yoshizawa T, Takahashi T, Tomioka H, Kamo N, Kobatake Y (1988) Low temperature spectrophotometric study on photoreaction cycle of phoborhodopsin. In Hara T (ed): Molecular Physiology of Retinal Proteins. Osaka, Japan: Yamada Science Foundation, pp 361–362.

Kamo N, Hazemoto N, Kobatake Y, Mukohata Y (1985) Light and dark adaptation of halorhodopsin. Arch Biochem Biophys 23:90–96.

Katre NV, Wolber PK, Stoeckenius W, Stroud RM (1981) Attachment site(s) of retinal in bacteriorhodopsin. Proc Natl Acad Sci USA 78:4068–4072.

Keszthelyi L, Ormos P (1980) Electrical signals associated with the photocycle of bacteriorhodopsin. FEBS Lett 109:189–193.

Khorana HG (1988) Bacteriorhodopsin, a membrane protein that uses light to translocate protons. J Biol Chem 263:7439–7442.

King GI, Stoeckenius W, Crespi HL, Schoenborn BP (1979) The location of retinal in the purple membrane profile by neutron diffraction. J Mol Biol 130:395–404.

Korenstein R, Hess B (1978) Immobilization of bacteriorhodopsin and orientation of its transition moment in purple membrane. FEBS Lett 89:15–20.

Koutalos Y, Ebrey TG, Tsuda M, Odashima K, Lien T, Park MH, Shimizu N, Derguini F, Nakanishi K, Gilson HR, Honig B (1989) Regeneration of bovine and octopus opsins in situ with natural and artificial retinals. Biochemistry 28:2732–2739.

Lanyi JK (1990) Halorhodopsin, a light-driven electrogenic chloride-transport system. Physiol Rev 70:319–330.

Lanyi JK, Duschl A, Hatfield GW, May K, Oesterhelt D (1990a) The primary structure of a halorhodopsin from *Natronobacterium pharaonis*: Structural, functional, and evolutionary implications for bacterial rhodopsins and halorhodopsins. J Biol Chem 265:1253–1260.

Lanyi JK, Duschl A, Vdaro G, Zimanyi L (1990b) Anion binding to the chloride pump, halorhodopsin, and its implications for the transport mechanism. FEBS Lett 265:1–6.

Lanyi JK, Zimanyi L, Nakanishi K, Derguini F, Okabe M, Honig B (1988) Chromophore/protein and chromophore/anion interactions in halorhodopsin. Biophys J 53:185–191.

Leder RO, Helgerson SL, Thomas DD (1989) The transverse location of the retinal chromophore in the purple membrane by diffusion-enhanced energy transfer. J Mol Biol 209:683–701.

Lemke HD, Oesterhelt D (1981) Lysine 216 is a binding site of the retinyl moiety in bacteriorhodopsin. FEBS Lett 128:255–260.

Lin SW, Mathies RA (1989) Orientation of the protonated retinal Schiff base group in bacteriorhodopsin from absorption linear dichroism. Biophys J 56:653–660.

Lozier RH, Bogomolni RA, Stoeckenius W (1975) Bacteriorhodopsin: A light-driven proton pump in *Halobacterium halobium*. Biophys J 15:955–962.

Lugtenburg J, Muradin-Szweykowska M, Heeremans CC, Pardoen JA, Harbison GS, Herzfeld J, Griffin RG, Smith SO, Mathies RA (1986) Mechanism for the opsin shift of retinal's absorption in bacteriorhodopsin. J Am Chem Soc 108:3104–3105.

Marinetti T, Subramaniam S, Mogi T, Marti T, Khorana HG (1989) Replacement of aspartic residues 85, 96, 115, or 212 affects the quantum yield and kinetics of proton release and uptake by bacteriorhodopsin. Proc Natl Acad Sci USA 86:529–533.

Marwan W, Oesterhelt D (1987) Signal formation in the halobacterial photophobic response mediated by a fourth retinal protein (P480). J Mol Biol 195:333–342.

Marwan W, Schafer W, Oesterhelt D (1990) Signal transduction in *Halobacterium* depends on fumarate. EMBO J 9:355–362.

Mathies RA, Brito Cruz CH, Pollard WT, Shank CV (1988) Direct observation of the femtosecond excited-state *cis/trans* isomerization in bacteriorhodopsin. Science 240:777–779.

Mathies RA, Lin SW, Ames JB, Pollard WT (1991) From femtoseconds to biology: Mechanism of bacteriorhodopsin's light-driven proton pump. Annu Rev Biophys Biophys Chem (in press).

McCain DA, Amici LA, Spudich JL (1987) Kinetically resolved states of the *Halobacterium halobium* flagellar motor switch and modulation of the switch by sensory rhodopsin I. J Bacteriol 169:4750–4758.

Mukohata Y, Sugiyama Y, Ihara K, Yoshida M (1988a) An Australian halobacterium contains a novel proton pump retinal protein: Archaerhodopsin. Biochem Biophys Res Commun 151:1339–1345.

Mukohata Y, Sugiyama Y, Ihara K, Yoshida M (1988b) An Australian halobacterium contains archaerhodopsin. In Hara T (ed): Molecular Physiology of Retinal Proteins. Osaka, Japan: Yamada Science Foundation, pp 125–130.

Nagle JF, Morowitz HJ (1978) Molecular mechanisms for proton transport in membranes. Proc Natl Acad Sci USA 75:298–302.

Nakanishi K, Balogh-Nair V, Arnaboldi M, Tsujimoto K, Honig B (1980) An external point-charge model for bacteriorhodopsin to account for its purple color. J Am Chem Soc 102:7945–7947.

Oesterhelt D, Marwan W (1987) Change of membrane potential is not a component of the photophobic transduction chain in *Halobacterium halobium*. J Bacteriol 169:3515–3520.

Oesterhelt D, Stoeckenius W (1971) Rhodopsin-like protein from the purple membrane of *Halobacterium halobium*. Nature [New Biol] 233:149–152.

Oesterhelt D, Stoeckenius W (1973) Functions of a new photoreceptor membrane. Proc Natl Acad Sci USA 70:2853–2857.

Oesterhelt D, Stoeckenius W (1974) Isolation of the cell membrane of *Halobacterium halobium* and its fractionation into red and purple membrane. Methods Enzymol 31:667–678.

Oesterhelt D, Tittor J (1989) Two pumps, one principle: Light-driven ion transport in halobacteria. Trends Biochem Sci 14:57–61.

Ogurusu T, Maeda A, Sasaki N, Yoshizawa T (1982) Effects of chloride on the absorption spectrum and photoreactions of halorhodopsin. Biochim Biophys Acta 682:446–451.

Otto H, Marti T, Holz M, Mogi T, Lindau M, Khorana HG, Heyn MP (1989) Aspartic acid-96 is the internal proton donor in the reprotonation of the Schiff base of bacteriorhodopsin. Proc Natl Acad Sci USA 86:9228–9232.

Otto H, Marti T, Holz M, Mogi T, Stern LJ, Engel F, Khorana HG, Heyn MP (1990) Substitution of amino acids Asp-85, Asp-212, and Arg-82 in bacteriorhodopsin affects the proton release phase of the pump and the pK of the Schiff base. Proc Natl Acad Sci USA 87:1018–1022.

Ottolenghi M, Sheves M (1989) Synthetic retinals as probes for the binding site and photoreactions in rhodopsins. J Membr Biol 112:193–212.

Polland H-J, Franz MA, Zinth W, Kaiser W, Hegemann P, Oesterhelt D (1985) Picosecond events in the photochemical cycle of the light-driven chloride-pump halorhodopsin. Biophys J 47:55–59.

Polland H-J, Franz MA, Zinth W, Kaiser W, Oesterhelt D (1986) Energy transfer from retinal to amino acids—A time-resolved study of the ultraviolet emission of bacteriorhodopsin. Biochim Biphys Acta 851:407–415.

Rastogi PP, Zundel G (1981) Proton translocation in hydrogen bonds with large proton polarizability formed between a Schiff base and phenols. Biochem Biophys Res Commun 99:804–812.

Rothschild KJ, Bousche O, Braiman MS, Hasselbacher CA, Spudich JL (1988) Fourier transform infrared study of the halorhodopsin chloride pump. Biochemistry 27:2420–2424.

Rothschild KJ, Braiman MS, Mogi T, Stern LJ, Khorana HG (1989) Conserved amino acids in F-helix of bacteriorhodopsin form part of a retinal binding pocket. FEBS Lett 250:448–452.

Schegk ES, Oesterhelt D (1988) Isolation of a prokaryotic photoreceptor: Sensory rhodopsin from halobacteria. EMBO J 7:2925–2933.

Scherrer P, Mathew MK, Sperling W, Stoeckenius W (1987a) Isomer ratio in dark-adapted bacteriorhodopsin. In Ebrey TG, Frauenfelder H, Honig B, Nakanishi K (eds): Biophysical Studies of Retinal Proteins. Urbana, IL: University of Illinois Press, pp 206–211.

Scherrer P, McGinnis K, Bogomolni RA (1987b) Biochemical and spectroscopic characterization of the blue-green photoreceptor in *Halobacterium halobium*. Proc Natl Acad Sci USA 84:402–406.

Schimz A (1981) Methylation of membrane proteins is involved in chemosensory and photosensory behavior of *Halobacterium halobium*. FEBS Letters 125:205–207.

Schimz A, Hildebrand E (1987) Effects of cGMP, calcium and reversible methylation on sensory signal processing in halobacteria. Biochim Biophys Acta 923:222–232.

Schimz A, Hinsch K-D, Hildebrand E (1989) Enzymatic and immunological detection of a G-protein in *Halobacterium halobium*. FEBS Lett 249:59–61.

Schobert B, Lanyi JK (1982) Halorhodopsin is a light driven chloride pump. J Biol Chem 257:10306–10313.

Schobert B, Lanyi JK (1986) Electrostatic interaction between anions bound to site I and the retinal Schiff base of halorhodopsin. Biochemistry 25:4163–4167.

Schobert B, Lanyi J, Cragoe EJ, Jr (1983) Evidence for a halide-binding site in halorhodopsin. J Biol Chem 258:15158–15164.

Schreckenbach T, Walckhoff B, Oesterhelt D (1977) Studies on the retinal–protein interaction in bacteriorhodopsin. Eur J Biochem 76:499–511.

Seiff F, Westerhausen J, Wallat I, Heyn MP (1986) Location of the cyclohexene ring of the chromophore of bacteriorhodopsin by neutron diffraction with selectively deuterated retinal. Proc Natl Acad Sci USA 83:7746–7750.

Shichida Y, Matuoka S, Hidaka Y, Yoshizawa T (1983) Absorption spectra of intermediates of bacteriorhodopsin measured by laser photolysis at room temperatures. Biochim Biophys Acta 723:240–246.

Simon MI, Krikos A, Mutoh N, Boyd A (1985) Sensory transduction in bacteria. Curr Top Membr Transp 23:3–16.

Smith SO, de Groot HJM, Gebhard R, Courtin JML, Lugtenburg J, Herzfeld J, Griffin RG (1989) Structure and protein environment of the retinal chromophore in light- and dark-adapted bacteriorhodopsin studied by solid-state NMR. Biochemistry 28:8897–8904.

Smith SO, Marvin MJ, Bogomolni RA, Mathies RA (1984) Structure of the retinal chromophore in the hR578 form of halorhodopsin. J Biol Chem 259:12326–12329.

Spudich EN, Hasselbacher CA, Spudich JL (1988) A methyl-accepting protein associated with bacterial sensory rhodopsin I. J Bacteriol 170:4280–4285.

Spudich EN, Spudich JL (1982) Control of transmembrane ion fluxes to select halorhodopsin-deficient and other energy-transduction mutants of *Halobacterium halobium*. Proc Natl Acad Sci USA 79:4308–4312.

Spudich EN, Sundberg SA, Manor D, Spudich JL (1986) Properties of a second sensory receptor protein in *Halobacterium halobium* phototaxis. Proteins 1:239–246.

Spudich EN, Takahashi T, Spudich JL (1989) Sensory rhodopsins I and II modulate a methylation/demethylation system in *Halobacterium halobium* phototaxis. Proc Natl Acad Sci USA 20:7746–7750.

Spudich JL, Bogomolni RA (1983) Spectroscopic discrimination of the three rhodopsinlike pigments in *Halobacterium halobium* membranes. Biophys J 43:243–246.

Spudich JL, Bogomolni RA (1984) Mechanism of colour discrimination by a bacterial sensory rhodopsin. Nature 312:509–513.

Spudich JL, Bogomolni RA (1988) Sensory rhodopsins of halobacteria. Annu Rev Biophys Biophys Chem 17:193–215.

Spudich JL, McCain DA, Nakanishi K, Okabe M, Shimizu N, Rodman H, Honig B, Bogomolni RA (1986) Chromophore/protein interaction in bacterial sensory rhodopsin and bacteriorhodopsin. Biophys J 49:479–483.

Spudich JL, Stoeckenius W (1980) Protein modification reactions in halobacterium photosensing. W Abstr Fed Proc FASEB 39:1972.

Stoeckenius W (1985) The rhodopsin-like pigments of halobacteria: Light energy and signal transducers in an archaebacterium. Trends Biochem Sci 10:483–489.

Stoeckenius W, Bogomolni RA (1982) Bacteriorhodopsin and related pigments of halobacteria. Annu Rev Biochem 52:587–615.

Sugiyama Y, Mukohata Y (1984) Isolation and characterization of halorhodopsin from *Halobacterium halobium*. J Biochem (Tokyo) 96:413–420.

Sundberg SA, Bogomolni RA, Spudich JL (1985) Selection and properties of phototaxis-deficient mutants of *Halobacterium halobium*. J Bacteriol 164:282–287.

Takahashi T, Tomioka H, Kamo N, Kobatake Y (1985) A photosystem other than PS370 also mediates the negative phototaxis of *Halobacterium halobium*. FEMS Microbiol Lett 28:161–164.

Takahashi T, Yan B, Mazur P, Derguini F, Nakanishi K, Spudich JL (1990) Color regulation in the archaebacterial phototaxis receptor phoborhodopsin (sensory rhodopsin II). Biochemistry 29:8467–8474.

Taylor ME, Bogomolni RA, Weber HJ (1983) Purification of photochemically active halorhodopsin. Proc Natl Acad Sci USA 80:6172–6176.

Tittor J, Soell C, Oesterhelt D, Butt H, Bamberg E (1989) A defective proton pump, point-mutated bacteriorhodopsin Asp→Asn is fully reactivated by azide. EMBO J 8:3477–3482.

Tomioka H, Takahashi T, Kamo N, Kobatake Y (1986a) Flash spectrophotometric identification of a fourth rhodopsin-like pigment in *Halobacterium halobium*. Biochem Biophys Res Commun 139:389–395.

Tomioka H, Takahashi T, Kamo N, Kobatake Y (1986b) Action spectrum of the photoattractant response of *Halobacterium halobium* in early logarithmic growth phase and the role of sensory rhodopsin. Biochim Biophys Acta 884:578–84.

Trewhella J, Popot J-L, Zaccai G, Engelman DM (1986) Localization of two chymotryptic fragments in the structure of renatured bacteriorhodopsin by neutron diffraction. EMBO J 5:3045–3049.

Trissl HW, Gärtner W (1987) Rapid charge separation and bathochromic absorption shift of flash-excited bacteriorhodopsins containing 13-*cis* or all-*trans* forms of substituted retinals. Biochemistry 26:751–758.

Tsuda M, Nelson B, Chang C-H, Govindjee R, Ebrey TG (1985) Characterization of the chromophore of the third rhodopsin-like pigment of *Halobacterium halobium* and its photoproduct. Biophys J 47:721–724.

Unwin PNT, Henderson R (1975) Molecular structure determination by electron microscopy of unstained crystalline specimens. J Mol Biol 94:425–440.

Wolff EK, Bogomolni RA, Scherrer P, Hess B, Stoeckenius W (1986) Color discrimination in halobacteria: Spectroscopic characterization of a second sensory receptor covering the blue-green region of the spectrum. Proc Natl Acad Sci USA 83:7272–7276.

Yan B, Nakanishi K, Spudich JL (1991) Activation of archaebacterial sensory rhodopsin-I: Evidence for a steric trigger. Proc Natl Acad Sci USA (in press).

Yan B, Spudich JL (1991) Evidence the repellent receptor form of sensory rhodopsin-I is an attractant signaling state. Photochem Photobiol (in press).

Yan B, Takahashi T, Johnson R, Derguini F, Nakanishi K, Spudich JL (1990) All- *trans*/13-*cis* isomerization of retinal is required for phototaxis signaling by sensory rhodopsins in *Halobacterium halobium*. Biophys J 57:807–814.

Zimanyi L, Keszthelyi L, Lanyi JK (1989) Transient spectroscopy of bacterial rhodopsins with an optical multichannel analyzer. 1. Comparison of the photocycles of bacteriorhodopsin and halorhodopsin. Biochemistry 28:5165–5172.

Zimanyi L, Lanyi JK (1989) Transient spectroscopy of bacterial rhodopsins with an optical multichannel analyzer. 2. Effects of anions on the halorhodopsin photocycle. Biochemistry 28:5172–5178.

Index